Regulating Regional Power Systems

Edited by **Clinton J. Andrews**

QUORUM BOOKS
Westport, Connecticut • London

Library of Congress Cataloging-in-Publication Data

Regulating regional power systems / edited by Clinton J. Andrews.
        p.   cm.
    Includes bibliographical references and index.
    ISBN 0–89930–943–7 (alk. paper)
      1. Electric utilities—Government policy—United States.
  I. Andrews, Clinton J.
  HD9685.U5R435   1995
  333.73′92′0973—dc20   94–21702

British Library Cataloguing in Publication Data is available.

Library of Congress Catalog Card Number: 94–21702
ISBN: 0–89930–943–7

First published in 1995

Quorum Books, 88 Post Road West, Westport, CT 06881
An imprint of Greenwood Publishing Group, Inc.

Printed in the United States of America

∞™

The paper used in this book complies with the
Permanent Paper Standard issued by the National
Information Standards Organization (Z39.48–1984).

10 9 8 7 6 5 4 3 2 1

Contents

Illustrations

TABLES

Preface and Acknowledgments

My original intention in launching this project was to bring together regional modelers. Those of us who plan and analyze regional infrastructure encounter challenges due to the multiplicity of stakeholders, decision makers, and institutions that influence these systems. Yet analysis without context is uninteresting, and as I developed the project, its focus shifted toward the lively policy debate which intruded in exciting ways on our modeling efforts. Planners live with half an ear cocked to events in the disciplines of economics, engineering, law, and politics—and what I heard was fascinating. The electric power sector was restructuring along lines suggested by economists, and encountering difficulties well known to students of politics. Engineers were fighting rear guard actions to keep the lights on, while lawyers debated appropriate rationales for slicing the pie. There were many polemics and few efforts at synthesis. No one knew to what extent they could generalize the experience of their home region. The crucial question of how to redesign the regulatory system was all but ignored.

During the summer of 1993, I invited fifty key figures in academia, government, industry, and non-governmental organizations to meet and sort things out. They struggled mightily at a two-day symposium on electricity and federalism, which we hosted in the Woodrow Wilson School of Public and International Affairs at Princeton University. The papers commissioned for that meeting have evolved into this book; they reflect the mood at the symposium, which was contentious. The debate over regulatory reform is advancing, but it is nowhere near over.

Special thanks for financial support of this project are given to Public Service Electric and Gas, and General Public Utilities, the two largest New Jersey electric utilities. Warm gratitude for additional financial support is expressed toward the Japanese contributors to Princeton's new program in science, technology, and public policy: Kansai Electric Power Company, Chubu Electric Power Company, and Tokyo Electric Power Company. Invaluable help in organizing the symposium and book was provided by Christopher Mackie-Lewis, Henry Bienen, Michael Danielson, Samantha Kanaga, Saher Alam, Patricia Trinity, Shirley Canty, and Cynthia Andrews. All of the authors owe an intellectual debt to the more active of the symposium participants, many of whom doubled as reviewers: Robert Arnold, Frans Berkhout, Murty Bhavaraju, Bernard Black, Martin Boughman, Frank Cassidy, Jameson Doig, Gerald Garvey, Andrew Haughwout, Ned Helme, Robert Hirsh, Andrew Krantz, James Laity, Leon Lowery, Colin Loxley, Kenji Matsuo, Francis Murray Jr., Robin Roy, Edward Salmon, Roger Schwarz, Robert Socolow, and Frank von Hippel. I close with a personal note of thanks to Ellen Cotter for sharing the bumps and jolts of this ride with me.

One disclaimer: the opinions expressed in this publication are those of the authors and do not represent official positions of the organizations for which they work. Read and join the debate.

Clinton J. Andrews

PART I

TOPICAL PERSPECTIVES

1

Introduction: Electricity Meets Federalism

Clinton J. Andrews

When Thomas Edison built the Pearl Street power station in New York a century ago, his isolated generator served only a few dozen nearby customers. Now, interconnected systems serve millions and spill over state boundaries. With the dramatic growth of these systems, their government oversight has also expanded, including first local, then state, and ultimately federal regulators. The various jurisdictions have struggled to divide up responsibilities for monopoly regulation of the electric power industry. Two centuries after James Madison and his colleagues built a federal system of government for the United States, a fierce debate centers on two highly charged words —electricity and federalism.

Regional, multi-state power systems now have robust networks over which to transmit electricity. This permits the formation of competitive markets for electricity, while enterprises which generate, transmit, and distribute electricity de-integrate. Scholars from a variety of disciplines have scrutinized restructuring options for the electric power industry.[1] Their lessons are now being applied in policies encouraging transmission access, power market experiments, bidding regimes, and independent power production. As yet, however, they have not thoroughly examined the needed adjustments to the regulatory framework, especially those issues involving intergovernmental relations and tradeoffs among economic, environmental, and reliability goals for the industry.[2] One key to understanding these issues is the regional context of electric power systems.

Five show stoppers have paralyzed many utility policy debates:

- public versus private ownership of utilities,
- planning versus market-based decision making,
- state versus federal regulation,
- economic versus social regulatory emphasis, and
- commodity energy versus end-use service provision.

   None are trivial; each issue arises from differences in our core beliefs about the nature of government and industry—and each region of the United States views these concerns differently. Discussions of regulatory reform must confront these issues in order to overcome the barriers which stand in the way of real progress.

   Intelligent regulatory reform is important to many actors. Industry decision makers want clear new rules of the game in order to plan actively for the future. Governmental decision makers want both information and a political consensus to help them resolve tough tradeoffs. Consumers want the benefits of economic efficiency—adequate service at the lowest possible cost. Environmentalists want to minimize social costs. Given so many cooks, it is not surprising how odd the broth tastes. In 1983, Joskow and Schmalensee wrote that "the industry, consumers, and independent analysts all agree that the current system is not working well. They disagree, however, on precisely what the problems are and on the appropriate solutions."

   If it were possible at this time, I would have chosen to preempt another decade of disagreement by synthesizing a coherent direction for regulatory reform. The contributing authors are all motivated by a sense that significant reforms must accompany the restructuring of the industry; they believe that reform is feasible given recent legislation.[3] Unfortunately, however, the paralyzing issues of previous years must first be resolved. As a critical next step, this book focuses the debate by anchoring the discussion with a carefully selected set of case studies representing a range of regional decision-making contexts.

   The remainder of this chapter introduces regional issues, the current allocation of regulatory responsibilities, the debate over change, reform in a federal system, options for regulatory changes, modes of cooperation among actors, and the analytical basis for decision making. It then introduces different regional electric power systems to show how the debate is playing out on the ground.

REGIONAL CONTEXT

   Pursuit of scale economies in both supply and demand has resulted in a North American electric power system which operates on a regional, often multi-state basis. A regional system today may be organized in a variety of ways. The American Electric Power Company is an example of an integrated holding company spanning multiple jurisdictions. In New England, one finds a cooperative power-pooling arrangement which includes dozens of utilities in six states. Today, systems organized on a regional basis account for a majority of the kilowatthours sold in the United States.[4]

Slightly less than a century ago, Samuel Insull launched the "grow and build" business strategy that culminated in today's regional-scale industry structure (Hirsh, 1989, pp. 15-25). It exploited increasing returns to scale on the demand side, taking advantage of the diversity of large-scale demand to smooth out the system load factor and increase capacity utilization, thus reducing unit costs. Equally important, Insull's strategy exploited increasing returns to scale on the supply side by employing large turbines in lieu of small reciprocating engines, further reducing the cost of electricity. Growth involved expanding both the per capita consumption of electricity and the size of the interconnected service area.

Interconnecting systems allowed more cost-effective achievement of reliability targets; they spread the cost of meeting contingencies (backing up the loss of the largest unit) over a larger customer base. Lower unit costs also encouraged increasing consumption of this price-elastic product. The growth cycle continued, and when combined with monopoly franchises, ensured profitability and access to financing. Supply-side scale economies were not exhausted until the 1960s, when generators achieved a size of several hundred megawatts (Lee et al., 1990, pp. 94–100). Demand-side economies that exploit load diversity or reduce transactions costs, for example, have yet to be exhausted. Systems have been interconnected to exploit these economies, and some systems developed a regional operating approach as early as 1930. This became the normal mode of operation long before 1968, when the regional councils of the North American Electric Reliability Council (NERC) were formalized.[5]

In addition to their financial and reliability benefits, electric power systems organized at the regional level also acquire from their territories a regional identity. This may be based on similar fuel sources, demand characteristics, economic conditions, and environmental problems. Regulators in producer states logically seek to maximize the use of coal in Kentucky and hydro-power in Washington, for example. Resource-poor consumer states such as Massachusetts were early adopters of nuclear power and, more recently, they have encouraged major utility investments in energy efficiency. Load growth in sunbelt states has followed a different path than in rustbelt states, while air conditioning has differentially affected load shapes across regions. Likewise, pollution problems, such as the high levels of ground-level ozone afflicting northeastern states, have prompted calls for regional solutions. In short, physical and technical realities have made regions important.

Regional perspectives play important roles in two types of decisions: public policymaking, and utility operations and planning. In the operating and planning arenas, utilities may have to satisfy multiple regulators while cooperating at arm's length with potential competitors. The policy arena must face the traditional federalist question—Which level of government should do what?—as state regulators joust with each other and the Federal Energy Regulatory Commission (FERC) for jurisdiction over large, multi-state utility systems.

THE CURRENT ALLOCATION OF REGULATORY RESPONSIBILITIES

Although utility regulation started at the state and local levels, the growth in interstate electricity sales led in 1935 to federal preemption of responsibility for regulating interstate transmission and wholesale transactions by the Federal Power Commission and its successor agency, the FERC.[6] That same year saw the Securities and Exchange Commission gain responsibility for policing the structure, finances, and operations of many utilities.[7] The FERC was given additional responsibilities in 1978 to encourage cogeneration and small power producers, although implementation was performed by the states.[8] In 1992, the FERC was directed to spur the creation of a competitive wholesale market in electricity and to ensure generators access to transmission.[9]

The states have the primary role in economic regulation of the electric power sector and are responsible for retail rate setting and associated issues such as prudency reviews for utility investments, as well as market entry. Conflicts between state and federal jurisdictions arise when state retail rate setting determinations conflict with the wholesale rate decisions handed down by the FERC, although federal preeminence is well established (Jones, 1987). The increasingly regional character of electric power systems has led to increased jurisdictional conflict.[10]

To maintain system reliability, the industry voluntarily polices itself. This self-regulation effort, which relies on peer pressure and inter-firm cooperation, is motivated by both a desire to avoid governmental involvement in utility operations, and the existence of an explicit obligation to serve which accompanies the monopoly franchise.

Periodically, reformers threaten to bring the government back in as a formal standard-setter.[11]

Social regulation also has had significant effects on the electric power sector. At the federal level, the Environmental Protection Agency (EPA) has played a major regulatory role since 1970 by setting ambient air quality standards as well as highly prescriptive technology standards for emissions controls at electric power plants.[12] Recent legislation[13] has assigned tradable sulfur dioxide emissions allowances to utilities and the job of refereeing this market to the EPA. The EPA also approves state implementation plans for meeting a variety of federal environmental standards. The states have retained responsibility for implementing environmental regulations, and, in the spirit of "permissive" federalism, they may exceed minimum federal standards. The Nuclear Regulatory Commission has sole jurisdiction over the design, operating, and safety standards for the nation's nuclear power plants.

States have authority over siting decisions, which have become a key determinant of utility investment choices. The regional character of electric power systems periodically prompts recommendations that federal preemption is needed to ensure that right-of-ways are available to develop regionally optimal transmission networks, although voluntary coordination appears to have worked well to date (OTA, 1989, pp. 201–216).

Making tradeoffs among economic and social regulatory objectives is a key responsibility of government, yet it is an especially difficult task. Even with legislative direction, it typically requires levels of inter-agency coordination that are improbable in a federal system the size of the United States. When successful, legislation acknowledges multiple objectives, for example, specifying "reasonably available" control technology to meet environmental objectives at low economic cost.[14] Yet often legislation is purposefully vague, and regulations are written to reflect the interests of prevailing interest-group coalitions (Anton, 1989, pp. 181–204).

One historic solution has been to devolve much of this coordination to the state level to ensure that tradeoffs reflect local concerns and constraints. Reliability tradeoffs have been devolved to the industry level. Proponents of "competitive federalism" applaud this diversity and claim that it is crucial for preserving individual rights, freedom of choice, and innovative thinking (Wildavsky, 1990, pp. 55–57). However, egalitarians argue that such diversity hurts those states with fewer resources to defend the local public interest against either the national interest or the private interests of the regulated industries (e.g., Danielson et al., 1977, pp. 13–16).

A problem with resolving economic-social tradeoffs locally is that, when applied piecemeal to portions of regional electric power systems, spillovers may occur (Burtraw and Portney, 1991). For example, environmental constraints imposed in one state could affect electricity prices in neighboring states. If remedies based on regional coordination fail, then federal preemption becomes likely.

Voluntary coordination by firms and/or state governments, regional regulation, and increased federal responsibility are among the alternative decision-making mechanisms that have been proposed over time to accommodate the industry's regional character.[15] Many utilities in continental North America have grouped themselves into:

- control areas that are centrally operated,
- power pools that are centrally dispatched and cooperatively planned, and
- NERC regions that are voluntarily coordinated.

The FERC is encouraging the creation of a set of regional transmission groups to discuss economic issues. The U.S. Department of Energy and the Environmental Protection Agency have regional offices, and some state regulators are cooperating with their regional neighbors. Table 1.1 shows a range of possible coordination mechanisms.

THE DEBATE OVER CHANGE

Legislation is only the most recent driver of industry restructuring. Contributor Charles Stalon suggests that the focus on competition in the Energy Policy Act of 1992 merely crystallized common working hypotheses about the industry:

- that economies of scale in generation can be as efficiently exploited by competitive wholesale markets as by vertically integrated monopolies;
- that such markets depend on adequate transmission access;
- that prospective generators must be freed of some constraints imposed by the 1935 Public Utilities Holding Company Act (PUHCA) in order to flourish;
- that transmission networks will continue to function as regulated natural monopolies, but with an interstate scope; and
- that retail wheeling should only slowly be phased in so as to protect the assets of existing distribution companies.

Table 1.1
Range of Regulatory Coordination Options

	Independent State Action	Episodic Regional Club	Sequential Regional Club	Coordinated Regional Club	Consolidated Regional Club	Federal Preemption
Participation	voluntary	voluntary	voluntary	voluntary	mandatory	mandatory
Enforcement	self	self	self	self	institutional	federal
Forum	multi issue	single issue	single issue	multi issue	multi issue	multi issue
Governance	full state autonomy	much state autonomy	less state autonomy	little state autonomy	full regional authority	full federal authority
Resources	state only	few pooled	more pooled	many pooled	pooled only	federal only
Start-up	easy	fairly easy	less easy	difficult	very difficult	easy
Example	State Public Utility Commission rulemaking	One-time meeting on power purchase contract	Standing committee on cost allocation	Resolutions of New England Governors Conference	Northwest Power Planning Council decisions	FERC rulemaking

Adapted from Jones et al., (1992).

Stalon asserts that the technological imperatives moving industry regulation from the municipal to the state to the federal level are still continuing, and therefore, an increase in federal preemption of certain (drastically redefined) regulatory responsibilities is inevitable.

Contributors David Wooley and Alfred Cavallo take exception to this vision in their chapter. They caution against taking competition too far, to the point of allowing retail wheeling. They suggest that "competition alone is not a substitute for good long-range planning," and that retail wheeling will amount to little more than a "money grab by one customer sector [industrials]." Wooley and Cavallo point out that state-level regulatory innovations are making oversight "more open to the public, more environmentally sound, and more competitive in generation costs." They provide a spirited defense of continued state regulatory authority in most current functional areas, stating that "the current division of authority between state and federal governments is working."

Thus is the debate joined. Reformers push in divergent directions, but there are points of potential convergence. Systematic thinking about the options may help uncover areas of commonality.

CHANGE IN A FEDERAL SYSTEM

Regulators today well understand why issues of state-federal relations were able to provoke the last century's civil war. American federalism is nominally a dual system of government, with separate state and national bodies responsible for different governmental functions.[16] Although federal preeminence has been established in many policy areas, the sources of political power are distinctly local. Contributor Michael Danielson warns that "even under the most favorable conditions, federalism is difficult. Dividing power between center and periphery is always complex, frequently unstable, and often impossible." Yet he perceives the difficulties to be worth the benefits. The benefits of dispersed authority are to limit governmental power, bring government closer to the people, and sustain distinctive civic cultures.

The current allocation of U.S. regulatory responsibilities is very much an accumulation of incremental reactions by government to technical and economic imperatives. As such, it has an ad hoc character that leads many to believe we could do better if we took time to redesign the system from first principles. Contributors Kenneth Gordon and Christopher Mackie-Lewis identify three factors in the fiscal federalism literature to guide the allocation of regulatory responsibilities between the central and decentralized jurisdictions:

- centralize to prevent spillovers,
- decentralize to provide choice to mobile consumers, and
- assign responsibility to that level which can most accurately ascertain production and consumption preferences (easier when homogeneity exists within the jurisdiction).

They then identify three other factors worth considering:

- comparative access to relevant information,
- desirability of diversity and experimentation, and
- potential for regulatory capture.

Gordon and Mackie-Lewis suggest that for many regulatory areas, these factors on balance indicate a need for greater centralization of regulatory authority, in line with the Stalon proposal. However, they stress the need to reallocate regulatory responsibilities on a function-specific rather than monolithic basis. Given the existence of both market and government failures, they favor private provision of quasi-public goods like electricity as the lesser of two evils but stress the importance of careful regulatory oversight during the deregulation process.

In thinking about regulatory reform in a federal system, it is clear that there are political determinants, such as access to power and resources, the relative concentration of benefits and costs, and coalitions able to appropriate the benefits of change (Anton, 1989, pp. 30–38). Yet there are also likely to be economic determinants that indicate for each regulatory task which level of government has the best match of costs and benefits and the fewest spillovers (Oates, 1972, pp. 3–20). Ideally, this rethinking will acknowledge rather than be dictated by political pragmatism; it will focus on a broadly defined objective of economic efficiency and build in opportunities for innovation and diversity.

ALTERNATIVE REGULATORY APPROACHES

Three paradigms dominate discussions of regulatory alternatives —traditional, planning based, and market based. Their differences are polemical as well as real, ensuring heated discussion of their relative merits. Contributor Kenneth Rose suggests that current regulations typically blend elements of these approaches, indicating that some degree of complementarity exists behind the ideological conflict. For example, Massachusetts uses the results of integrated resource planning to specify the contents of utilities' competitive bidding packages for resource acquisition. Yet the appropriate role of the planning function is clearly entering flux as the electric power sector becomes more competitive. Reforms such as retail wheeling have the potential to eliminate any role for inter-firm and public planning. Lacking national consensus, state-level diversity in regulating distribution companies will continue, whereas federal actions may standardize transmission and generation regulation.

Regional regulation has been frequently proposed as a solution to the mismatch of electric power sector operations and regulatory jurisdictions.[17] Yet, as shown in Table 1.1, there is a range of options. Full-blown regional regulatory bodies are probably not appropriate for many tasks, and they are difficult to implement. Contributors Richard O'Neill and Charles Whitmore outline a more refined proposal: Make generation competitive; leave distribution in state hands, but switch to a "yardstick" regulatory approach; assign transmission regulation to the federal level using a "club regulation" approach; and realign federal-state-market jurisdictions. They would focus federal attention on Regional Transmission Groups that recognize "the partly competitive, partly cooperative nature of the transmission grid and the role of states as key players." Existing regional clubs, discussed in the regional case studies, provide insights into the efficacy of this approach. Club regulation has generated much general interest, although proposals differ on implementational details.[18]

MODES OF COOPERATION

The complex, fractionated system of regulation that has evolved under American federalism will most likely maintain such characteristics after regulatory reform. Thus, cooperation among actors will be crucial to keep the system working. Not only is there a shared responsibility for keeping the lights on, but also for developing a common vision of the future, fairly allocating risks and rewards, spurring continued investment and innovation, and pursuing economic efficiency. Cooperation has a number of dimensions: intergovernmental, public-private, and between firms. Both economic and social regulators have important cooperative challenges.

Contributor Kevin Kelly argues that specific types of cooperation are needed to realize the economic benefits of regional electric power markets. He outlines a spectrum of options including no change, state-state cooperation, federal-state joint boards, federal preemption, and industry self-regulation. He then proposes a number of possible options: that "no new cooperative mechanism may be needed for treating allowance trading issues, federal preemption may be appropriate for determining if market conditions allow wholesale price deregulation, state-to-state joint regulation might work best for regional integrated resource planning (IRP), industry self-regulation could be used for regional grid planning, and a federal-state joint board could be used for multi-state transmission line siting decisions."

Environmental regulators of several jurisdictions may have joint responsibility for a regional airshed. Contributors Praveen Amar, Michael Bradley, and Donna Boysen share their recent experience in developing a cooperative regional approach to controlling nitrogen oxides emissions. Environmental regulators from eight states are finding that issues of sovereignty limit the feasible level of cooperation on bottom-up regulatory initiatives.

Contributor Michehl Gent describes the industry self-regulation performed by NERC, which for a quarter of a century has defined "rules of the road" for reliable electric power system operations, and ensured that companies sharing the grid maintain adequate technical performance. Gent expects the organization will adapt to the changing regulatory environment and continue to support self-regulation of grid reliability without significant government oversight.

An increasingly competitive industry structure has the potential to affect the traditionally cooperative relationships within regional power pools. Skeptics suggest that continued reliance on a "Chinese regulatory model" (peer pressure and self-confession) may be inadequate. What may be needed is a switch from cooperative to contractual relationships among competitors, or the imposition of regulatory standards of operation (OTA, 1989). Yet it is worth noting, by way of analogy, that many believe the clubby Chinese transition to market-based decision making has gone more smoothly (from the producers' point of view) than the wide-open Russian reforms.

THE ANALYTICAL BASIS FOR DECISIONS

The high financial stakes and long planning horizons of the electric power sector have encouraged the development of a strong analytical basis for investment and regulatory decisions. Bottom-up[19] and top-down[20] modeling approaches have evolved, and both have offered relevant insights and have gained vocal proponents and detractors. Resolving regional issues depends in part on rethinking the use of such tools and rationalizing the flow of information among policy actors.

Contributor Benjamin Hobbs discusses the relative merits of top-down and bottom-up approaches to informing policy decisions. He suggests that "questions concerning the impact of state or local regulations on particular resource acquisition and system operation decisions [including environmental assessments] are best analyzed by [bottom-up] models that include detailed descriptions of options and operating constraints." Top-down, econometric models have the advantage of being more comprehensive than engineering-economic models, but often lack the detail necessary to evaluate policy options. The best models, according to Hobbs, combine features of top-down and bottom-up analysis to provide both comprehensiveness and policy detail in a transparent, simple-to-use manner. Creating such models requires cooperation among analysts in industry, academia, and multiple levels of government. Contributor Mary Hutzler reports that the federal government is building such a model (the National Energy Modeling System) for use by her department and others and that a wide-ranging, credibility-building process has indeed been required.

Yet good information is not accessible to all interested parties. Only a few policy actors have access to the necessary data and are capable of performing credible analysis; others must rely on more simplistic approaches. Broad participation in the debate on industrial restructuring and regulatory redesign is hindered by lack of access to adequate data and models.

THE EXTENT OF REGIONAL DIFFERENCES

Case studies of different regional electric power systems enrich the topical discussions of the initial chapters with empirical evidence and regional detail. To provide a balanced presentation, each case has an accompanying comment. The remainder of this introductory chapter shows the extent of regional differences, defines the regional context, and briefly introduces each case.

In different regions, the electric power sector has evolved along very different paths. Overall, the nation's 267 private investor-owned electric utilities provide 78 percent of total generation and 76 percent of energy sales; the 2,011 publicly owned utilities (municipalities and state agencies) represent 9 percent and 14 percent, respectively; the ten federal systems account for 8 percent and 2 percent, respectively; and the 953 cooperatives have 4 percent of generation and 7 percent of sales.[21]

The mix of private and public utilities differs dramatically by region, so that in the Northeast (New York and New England), for example, about 82 percent of net generation is supplied by private companies, 18 percent by public enterprises, and none by federal or cooperative enterprises. By contrast, in the West only 52 percent of electricity is privately generated, 21 percent comes from public

Figure 1.1
Typology of Decision Contexts

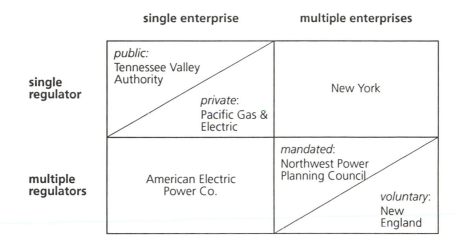

enterprises, 24 percent from federal agencies, and 4 percent from cooperatives (OTA, 1989, p. 161). Regions also differ in the sizes of enterprises and political jurisdictions, and the relative match between the resources of regulators and regulatees.

By comparing different systems[22] one may address a common set of questions from distinct experience bases. Key issues case studies can help illuminate include:

- the degree to which engineering, economic, and regulatory imperatives converge at the system-wide or regional level;

- the extent to which regional similarities or differences exist; and

- the relative efficacy of alternative analytical and procedural approaches for policy development.

Case studies may be located within the typological matrix shown in Figure 1.1. The rationale for this typology is that the structure of decision making for the system in question affects its performance and its adaptability to change. Regions with different degrees of dispersion in decision-making authority, and different matches between regulatory authority and enterprise structure, reveal different lessons. These existing regional clubs provide insights into the efficacy of alternative regulatory regimes. A brief discussion of each regional case follows. See the map in Figure 1.2 for their locations.

Figure 1.2
Regions Featured as Case Studies (bold) and NERC Regions (*italic*)

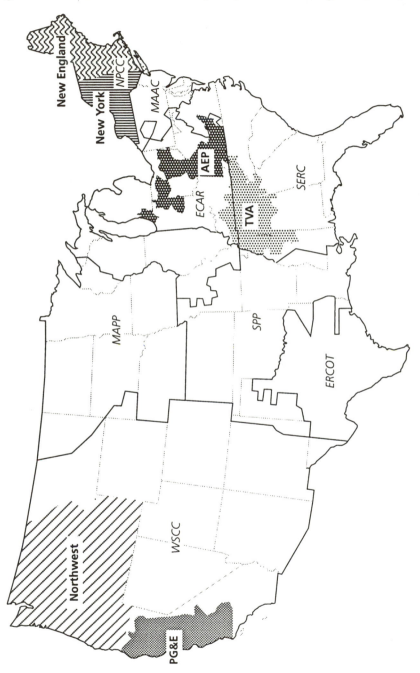

Northwest Power Planning Council

The most formal experiment with a regional club has taken place in the northwestern United States, where a decade ago Congress permitted the creation of an interstate compact, the Northwest Power Planning Council (NPPC). The Northwest already had a significant federal presence in the form of the Bonneville Power Administration (BPA), which marketed about 40 percent of the electricity sold in the region. According to contributor Richard Watson, the goal was to treat the region as if it were "one big utility," and develop a rational, long-term planning process through which the governors of the affected states—Idaho, Montana, Oregon, and Washington—could guide the investments of the BPA, and indirectly the utilities in the region.

The NPPC was successful in legitimizing conservation as a resource and in freeing the region from the "grow-and-build" mindset of the pre-1973 generation of utility planners. Yet as resource development started occurring without the involvement of the BPA, the role of the NPPC has been reduced to one of providing a common vision to guide decentralized investments. Watson expects this new role to remain viable under a more market-oriented environment, because the region will still need a vehicle for seeking consensus on the least societal cost investment path.

More problematic for the future of the NPPC is that this politically appointed regional body is poorly equipped to handle—and current law discourages—needed pricing reforms. This hydro-power-dominated region has large disparities between prices and marginal costs; rate structures frozen in place by the BPA connection include significant cross-subsidies and distorted price signals, according to commenter Kenneth Costello. Reforms may need to be driven from the top down by Congress and the federal courts, or from the bottom up by consumers; they are unlikely to come from this regional body.

New England

The dozens of utilities in New England coordinate their operations in a power pool that stretches across six small states. Contributor Stephen Connors reports that both utilities and regulators have had to work closely together to achieve the economic benefits of large-scale system operation in this region. Over time they have been relatively successful: the New England Power Pool (NEPOOL) is a tight power pool that performs not only an operating but also a planning function. New England state regulators likewise have hammered out a variety of inter-jurisdictional agreements to resolve fairness issues standing in the way of net economic gains.

Yet the New England region is changing. It is experiencing utility consolidation, such as the acquisition of Public Service of New Hampshire by Northeast Utilities. There has also been a steady erosion of state jurisdictional authority to the FERC. Connors' pessimism regarding the prospects for continued cooperation contrasts with commenter Barry Solomon's optimism; Solomon believes that the transition toward some modest level of competition need not be disruptive. Both authors foresee a continued role for cooperative regional planning to support a common vision of restructuring and reform. Especially critical will be improved coordination among regulators.

American Electric Power Company

American Electric Power (AEP) is one of the largest holding companies in the nation, with subsidiaries in seven states, significant FERC oversight, and its own control area. Contributor Raymond Maliszewski shows that AEP has achieved economies of integrated operation and planning by consolidating the ownership of a large system. Commenter Jerry Wissman indicates that the seven states with jurisdiction over portions of the AEP system have had only modest success at cooperation; they have often resorted to litigation to settle disputes.

For example, in 1984 AEP developed an agreement among its member companies providing a basis for allocating the costs and benefits of transmission investments. Each of the various state regulatory agencies viewed the agreement as a zero-sum game in which they were determined not to be the loser. Negotiations became deadlocked, and eventually the FERC had to rule on the appropriate allocation of transmission investment responsibilities. There was a clear difficulty in achieving consensus in a multi-jurisdictional environment with obvious winners and losers. The states are attempting to improve their handling of other regional issues and have developed a regional coordinating committee to deal with implications of the Clean Air Act Amendments of 1990.

New York: State and Power Pool

New York's electrical system and political boundaries are nearly identical, although it maintains interties with neighboring systems. Its many utilities coordinate their operations through a tight power pool that remains largely within state boundaries, meaning that their activities are regulated chiefly by one state government. Thus, in New York, regulatory decision-making power is relatively concentrated. Contributors Balet and Guinn indicate that significant efforts are undertaken to forge a common vision of the state's energy future through the vehicle of a periodic planning process. Commenter Richard Schuler demonstrates that federalism issues enter the New York agenda in key areas including international electricity trade with Canada, compensating for loop flows through the Midwest, and in reaping benefits from a competitive market for generation, given aged and expensive indigenous generating capacity.

Pacific Gas and Electric Company

Pacific Gas and Electric (PG&E) is a large enough utility that it has its own major control area, yet it operates primarily within the boundaries of one large state. Thus, both industry and regulatory decision-making authorities are quite concentrated.

Although large single-state companies are less affected by federalist issues than those crossing state lines, they are certainly affected by federal legislation and preemptions. Contributors Jackalyne Pfannenstiel, Steven Kline, and Kathleen Treleven report that such legislative shifts, beginning with the Public Utility Regulatory Policies Act (PURPA) and the Natural Gas Policy Act, have profoundly changed their company. It has already begun its process of vertical de-integration, and its regulated enterprise does not expect to build any more power plants. Commenter Lyna Wiggins is skeptical that spinning off generation will resolve problems, because regardless of who owns the capacity, they will still have trouble siting it. She perceives a continued need for planning to manage the spatial and equity aspects of decisions. Common ground may exist in relying on the market mechanism to help establish the optimal uses of existing generation sites.

Tennessee Valley Authority

The extent of regional differences becomes especially apparent in the discussion of the Tennessee Valley Authority (TVA) provided by contributor Mary Sharpe Hayes. This enterprise is the closest thing to a nationalized electricity producer that exists in the United States, and its electric power system serves portions of seven states, yet as a federal authority it is not responsible to state regulators. Although this self-regulated enterprise enjoys substantial autonomy of decision making, it also must live within important political constraints, having "stakeholders, not stockholders." Created by Congress in 1933 as part of Roosevelt's New Deal, its mandate is quite broad.

Commenter Allan Pulsipher suggests that the TVA board's lack of external accountability is a serious problem which has led over time to wasteful investments in unneeded nuclear capacity, among other ills. He proposes an opening up of decision making at the agency to ensure that the benefits of restructuring in the rest of the industry penetrate the TVA organization.

European Community

This case is not part of the taxonomy of U. S. decision contexts. Yet as Europe struggles to redefine the European Community's electric power policy, it is encountering a set of jurisdictional issues remarkably similar to those in the United States. There may opportunities for Europeans to learn from the U. S. experience, and vice versa.

American federalism is unusual in its uneasy, yet healthy balance between federal supremacy and state autonomy. The unique durability of this system of federalism is made clear by contributor Francis McGowan, who indicates that the European Community and its member states have not achieved the sort of dynamic equilibrium found in the United States. Instead, the sovereign states have only grudgingly given up even minor powers to the community government. Economic self-interest, and a view of electric utilities as instruments of social policy, have hindered transborder electricity trade and prevented meaningful coordination or planning.

Commenter Richard Tabors points out the great blessing that, even as national cultural differences are accentuated during the fierce negotiations surrounding the European Union, there is a similarity of objectives within the electric power industry. The cultural similarities among industry actors exceed those between each industry and its national government—operators will cooperate to keep the system up at nearly any cost. This blessing likely applies as well to the U.S. context, if it is not destroyed during the process of reform.

There is great regional diversity along key dimensions—ownership, decision process, jurisdiction, focus, and business definition. No reforms currently contemplated will remove all of these differences, and many actors prefer this diversity. Reformers will need to campaign on multiple fronts and expect haphazard victories.

THE REST OF THIS BOOK

In the rest of Part 1, leading experts discuss key aspects of regulatory reform in the electric power sector. Topics include the rationales for change, ways of thinking about change in a federal system, options for regulatory reform, the need for cooperation among actors, and the analytical basis for decisions.

Part 2 of this book contains case studies which show the extent of regional diversity in the U. S. electric power sector. These cases also illustrate how the topical themes discussed in Part 1 may play out, given the messy reality of actual regional systems. A concluding chapter pulls together from the contributed chapters two sets of conclusions:

- widely accepted premises and

- hotly disputed hypotheses about regulatory reform.

Together, these contributions provide a clear snapshot of today's situation and a tantalizing look into the cloudy crystal ball of the future. The snapshot shows that regulation in a federal system is a complex business, with many players, multiple objectives, and profound constraints. Given the messiness of the current situation, a clouded crystal ball is less troubling. There is a great deal of careful and creative thinking under way regarding the problems of reforming the regulation of regional systems. I hope that this volume advances the debate towards a set of reforms encouraging efficiency, stability, and fairness.

NOTES

1. Key contributions include Joskow and Schmalensee (1983) (economics), Hirsh (1989) (history) and OTA (1989) (technology).

2. An exception is Jones et al. (1992).

3. Landmarks include the Public Utilities Regulatory Policies Act of 1978, the Clean Air Act Amendments of 1990, and the Energy Policy Act of 1992.

4. Tight multi-state power pools, interstate utilities, multi-state holding companies (exempt and otherwise), and federal authorities moving power across state lines accounted for some 62 percent of electricity sales in 1990. Based on data in U. S. Department of Energy, *Financial Statistics* (1992).

5. According to PJM Management Committee (1992).

6. Federal Power Act of 1935, 16 U. S. C. 791a.

7. Public Utility Holding Company Act of 1935, 15 U. S. C. 79.

8. Public Utility Regulatory Policies Act of 1978, P. L. 95-615.

9. Energy Policy Act of 1992, P. L. 102-486.

10. Recent well-known cases include *Mississippi Power & Light v. Mississippi ex rel. Moore,* 108 S. Ct. 2428 (1988), and the proposed merger of Northeast Utilities and Public Service of New Hampshire (FERC Docket No. EC90-10-000).

11. An extensive analysis of the (lack of) need for government involvement may be found in U.S. Department of Energy (1981) pp. 95–97.

12. Clean Air Act Amendment of 1970, 42 U. S. C. 74.

13. Clean Air Act Amendments of 1990, P. L. 101–549.

14. See Title I of the Clean Air Act Amendments of 1990, P. L. 101-549.

15. See Jones et al. (1992). See also the legislative history of the Pacific Northwest Power Planning and Conservation Act, P. L. 96-501, and Congressional hearings on the National Governors' Association regional planning proposals, H. R. 5766, Serial No. 98-173, 1984.

16. A range of activities have seen total preemption by the federal government. The states have been "stripped of their powers to engage in economic regulation of airline, bus, and trucking companies, establish a compulsory retirement age for [some] employees, or regulate bankruptcies," as well as being required to enact statutes implementing inspection standards, equal employment opportunities, fair labor standards, health and safety standards, and voting rights. Other activities, such as environmental protection and utility regulation, have experienced only partial preemption, in which states assume responsibilities delegated by the national government. The feedback mechanisms allowing preemption relief are highly imperfect, because Congress may be slow to amend laws on the basis of adverse signals from the states (Zimmerman, 1993).

Yet federal preemption is not inevitable. There is a legitimate "diversity of subnational cultures and place-based interests," and states remain important proving grounds for subsequent national policies (Krane, 1993). This has certainly been true in the electric power sector, where local resource bases and institutional structures have created a great diversity in system characteristics among different regions of the country. Likewise, many of the national innovations in electricity regulation have originated in the states. However, there are many indications that electricity regulation is due for a "rethinking" of regulatory functions among actors at different levels of government, as Alice Rivlin (1992) more generally advocates.

17. For example, see testimony by R. Cavanagh in hearings for H. R. 5766, Serial No. 98-173, 1984.

18. For an interesting alternative to the O'Neill and Whitmore proposal, see Smith (1993) who espouses a doctrine of "divisable rights, indivisable facilities." All of these proposals need to deal with common costs. O'Neill and Whitmore note that most proposals sweep them under the rug. Clubs can have cooperative and competitive aspects, such as when country clubs, for example, routinely hold competitive club championships in which the rules of the competition are prescribed by the cooperative aspect of the club.

19. There is a strong tradition of engineering-economic modeling for optimizing electric power system operations and planning. These are useful for informing many types of business and policy decisions, especially those in which technical detail is important. Developed for use by individual utilities, these models are also routinely applied at the state and regional levels. They

typically suffer from unrealistic representations of the larger economy outside the electric power sector and an inability to model strategic actions in a competitive marketplace.

20. The comprehensive perspective of economic modeling is valuable for understanding policy variables and the relationships among various actors in the economy. Such models are often employed for studying national energy policy issues and have been adapted for use on state and regional economies, which are much more open systems. They are typically better at modeling macro policy options than detailed technology-related options and may not be able to address issues of social regulation. Their value also depends on the degree to which their assumptions, modeling relationships, and results have been accepted by policy actors. Linkages between the national-scale models and state or regional efforts rarely exist.

21. Source is U. S. Department of Energy. *Electric Power Annual 1990* (1992).

22. Systems are defined here as (usually) centrally dispatched control areas in which operating economies are achieved. According to Joskow and Schmalensee (1983) the minimum size for achieving such economies is about 10,000 MW.

REFERENCES

Anton, T. *American Federalism & Public Policy*. New York: Random House, 1989.

Burtraw, D., and P. Portney. "Environmental Policy in the United States." In D. Helm, editor. *Economic Policy Towards the Environment*. Oxford: Blackwell, 1991, pp. 289–317.

Cavanagh, R. Testimony. *Hearings on H. R. 5766*, Serial No. 98-173, U.S. Congress, 1984.

Danielson, M., A. Hershet, and J. Bayne. *One Nation, So Many Governments*. Lexington, MA: Lexington Books, 1977.

Hirsh, R. *Technology and Transformation in the American Electric Utility Industry*. Cambridge: Cambridge University Press, 1989.

Jones, D., R. Burns, F. Darr, M. Eifert, R. Graniere, R. Lock, and R. Poling. "Regional regulation of public utilities: opportunities and obstacles." Report no. NRRI 92-19. Columbus, OH: National Regulatory Research Institute, December 1992.

Jones, R. "Regulation of interstate electric power: FERC versus the states." *Natural Resources and the Environment*. 3 (Spring 1987).

Joskow, P., and R. Schmalensee. *Markets for Power*. Cambridge, MA: MIT Press, 1983.

Kincaid, J. "Constitutional federalism: labor's role in displacing places to benefit persons." *PS: Political Science & Politics*. 26 (June 1993): 172-177.

Krane, D. "American federalism, state governments, and public policy: weaving together loose theoretical threads." *PS: Political Science & Politics.* 26 (June 1993): 186-189.

Lee, T., B. Ball, and R. Tabors. *Energy Aftermath.* Boston: Harvard Business School Press. 1990.

Oates, W. *Fiscal Federalism.* New York: Harcourt Brace Jovanovich, 1972.

Ostrum, V. *The Political Theory of a Compound Republic.* 2nd edition. Lincoln, NE: Univ. of Nebraska Press, 1987.

PJM Management Committee. "The Pennsylvania-New Jersey-Maryland Interconnection." Informational brochure. Valley Forge, PA: PJM, 1992.

Rivlin, A. *Reviving the American Dream: The Economy, the States, and the Federal Government.* Washington, DC: Brookings, 1992.

Shannon, J., and J. Kee. "The rise of competitive federalism." *Public Budgeting and Finance.* 9 (Winter 1989): 5-20.

Smith, V. L. "Can Electric Power—A 'Natural Monopoly'—Be Deregulated?" in Hans H. Landsberg. ed. *Making National Energy Policy.* Washington, DC: Resources for the Future, 1993, pp. 131-151.

U.S. Congress. *Clean Air Act Amendment of 1970.* 42 U. S. C. 74

U.S. Congress. *Clean Air Act Amendments of 1990.* P. L. 101-549.

U.S. Congress. Congressional hearings on the National Governors' Association regional planning proposals, H. R. 5766, Serial No. 98-173, 1984.

U.S. Congress. *Electric Power Wheeling and Dealing.* OTA-E-409. Washington, DC: U. S. Congress, Office of Technology Assessment (OTA), 1989.

U.S. Congress. *Energy Policy Act of 1992.* P. L. 102-486.

U.S. Congress. *Federal Power Act of 1935.* 16 U. S. C. 791a.

U.S. Congress. *Pacific Northwest Power Planning and Conservation Act.* Legislative history. P. L. 96-501.

U.S. Congress. *Public Utility Holding Company Act of 1935.* 15 U. S. C. 79.

U.S. Congress. *Public Utility Regulatory Policies Act of 1978.* P. L. 95-615.

U.S. Department of Energy. *Electric Power Annual 1990.* DOE/EIA-0348(90). Washington, DC: U. S. Department of Energy, Energy Information Administration, 1992.

U.S. Department of Energy. *Financial Statistics of Selected Electric Utilities 1990.* [Investor- and Publicly-owned], DOE/EIA-0437(90)/1&2. Washington, DC: U. S. Department of Energy, Energy Information Administration, 1992.

U.S. Department of Energy. *The National Electric Reliability Study: Final Report.* DOE/EP-0004. Washington, DC: U.S. Department of Energy, Office of Emergency Operations, April 1981.

U.S. Federal Energy Regulatory Commission. "Proposed merger of Northeast Utilities and Public Service of New Hampshire." FERC Docket No. EC90-10-000 (1990).

U.S. Supreme Court. *Mississippi Power & Light v. Mississippi ex rel. Moore*, 108 S. Ct. 2428 (1988).

Wildavsky, A. "A double security: federalism as competition." *Cato Journal.* 10 (Spring/Summer 1990): 39-58.

Zimmerman, J. "Congressional regulation of subnational governments." *PS: Political Science & Politics.* 26 (June 1993):177-180.

2

Increasing Competition in the Electric Power Industry

Charles G. Stalon

Piecemeal regulation is a hallmark of the American political system.[1] The electric utility industry, with its many regulators, illustrates that tendency well.[2] At the federal level the industry's principal regulators are the Federal Energy Regulatory Commission (FERC), the Department of Energy (DOE), the Securities Exchange Commission (SEC), the Rural Electrification Administration (REA), and the Environmental Protection Agency (EPA). At the state level, its principal regulators are public utility commissions (PUCs), state and/or regional energy planning agencies, siting agencies, state EPAs, and municipalities. Government regulators, however, are not the only regulators of importance: The industry regulates itself in important dimensions through the North American Electric Reliability Council (NERC) and its nine regional reliability councils.

North America's interconnected generating firms and transmission-owning utilities (TOUs) create four synchronously operated, alternating current transmission networks: the Eastern Interconnection, the Texas Interconnection, the Western Interconnection, and the Hydro Quebec System. The NERC and its reliability councils have as their principal task the creation of "rules of the road" that ensure reliable and efficient operation of these interconnected networks. NERC committees and the committees of the regional councils provide utilities with forums through which they coordinate operations and planning.[3]

This regulatory system is partly a reflection of federalism but mostly it is a reflection of processes wherein both federal and state legislators repeatedly attempted to meet changing technologies and problems of organizational stress with minimal disruption to then-existing regulatory and industry structures. Consequently, the current regulatory system is far from the one that would result if a policy designer applied fundamental economic and political principles on a clean slate.[4] An industry leader says, "Although it is premature to term the vertically integrated utility a relic, it is time to acknowledge that both the vertically integrated utility and the regulatory structure that grew up with it are products of another era" (Codey, 1993).

RATIONALES FOR REFORM

Deficiencies in the system have called for changes for decades.[5] Many of these changes appear minor in the abstract, but to participants aware of precarious balances in the division of labor among regulators and of the importance of state-based political power of utilities, they appear radical. Pressures to change the system, however, proved strong enough to induce the Congress to initiate reforms with the Energy Policy Act of 1992 (EPAct). EPAct confirmed the congressional view stressed in the Public Utility Regulatory Policies Act of 1978 (PURPA) that the electric industry is an interstate industry subject to federal control in almost all dimensions of its regulated activities.

The two-year congressional debate that culminated in the enactment of EPAct crystallized five working hypotheses about the U.S. electric industry:

- First, economies of scale in generation can be as efficiently exploited by competitive wholesale power markets as they can by vertically integrated monopolies.

- Second, competitive, efficient wholesale power markets require that all generators be provided efficient access to transmission services, and this, in turn, requires that the FERC be authorized to order TOUs to provide such services.

- Third, competitive, efficient wholesale power markets require that the talents and financial strengths of IOUs and NUGs be freed of many of the constraints of the 1935 Public Utility Holding Company Act (PUHCA) so that such talents and strengths can be deployed into the non-utility-generating sector (and abroad) as opportunities arise.

- Fourth, electric transmission networks are natural monopolies functioning in interstate and international commerce, and as natural monopolies they will be regulated for the foreseeable future.

- Fifth, in order to slow the pace of transition and protect
  IOUs, GOUs, COUs, and regulatory agencies from the full
  force of competition for several more years, end-users, in
  states so requiring, are constrained to purchase power
  from "their" existing distribution companies. Consequently, the FERC is prohibited from ordering transmission services for a generator to sell directly to an end-user,
  and distribution companies retain their monopoly over
  power sales for a while.[6]

In short, EPAct laid the legal groundwork for competitive wholesale power markets.[7] Informed observers, however, see industrial end-
users gaining rights to buy power from the generator of their choice in
a few years. It appears plausible, therefore, to assert that regulators
should adopt the hypothesis that the current transition is destined to
produce bulk power markets.[8] One of the principal tasks of regulators,
therefore, is to ensure that such markets are competitive and efficient.
The modal estimate for the development of widespread retail wheeling, at least for large end-users, varies from state to state but seems to
focus on a time somewhat less than five years away.

The paradox of U.S. regulatory policy is that the industry's regulatory structure doesn't match either the congressional assertion of
the federal interest or the anticipated structure of the industry. EPAct
took important steps to create a legal environment that will allow,
even encourage, dramatic restructuring of the industry but took only
modest steps toward a more defensible system of regulation.

Leadership is needed to create an efficient industry structure and
a defensible division of labor among regulators. In the absence of a
congressional mandate, responsibility for leading the transition, to the
extent that can be done by federal agencies, falls on the DOE and the
FERC.[9]

WHAT INDUSTRY STRUCTURE WILL EPAct PRODUCE?

Although EPAct does not dictate the final structure of the industry or the timing of the transition, it does not leave regulators with
much discretion over either, although probably with much more discretion over timing than end results. The technology of the industry,
antitrust laws, and conflicting objectives of regulators, of which technology is the most important, will induce the industry to evolve into a
structure remarkably similar to that of the natural gas industry:
Namely, unregulated generators will sell power to state-regulated distribution companies (discos) over one or more federally regulated
transmission networks (transcos). Furthermore, these wholesale (and

bulk power) markets will not be only long-term contract markets. Short-term forward markets, approximating spot markets, will develop rapidly as NUGs look for customers for their unused capacity, and utilities look for alternatives to running expensive peaking units. Self-generators who have flexibility in their use of energy will seek in the ambiguity of language of EPAct to become peak period suppliers to utilities if the price is right.

Discos, for years to come, will own some generating capacity, and some may own generators indefinitely, but the efficiencies of competitive bulk power markets and the deficiencies of regulation will create irresistible pressures for discos to concentrate their attentions on (1) maintaining distribution systems, (2) buying power for their captive customers, and (3) as gas distribution companies and PUCs have always known, vigorously using federal forums to pressure federal regulators to preserve competition and create efficient transmission networks on which the industry depends.

Consequently, the principal problems for regulators created by EPAct are in managing the transition. In order to understand those problems, it is essential to review the current structure of regulation and the current structure of the industry.

THE ROOTS OF THE CURRENT REGULATORY SYSTEM

For obvious reasons, municipal governments were the first regulators of electric firms, but the political legitimacy of municipal regulation faded when electric utilities, exploiting the physics of alternating current, grew to serve more than one municipality (and rural customers between and around such municipalities) from common assets.[10] In the opening decades of the twentieth century, a coalition of reformers and industry leaders persuaded most states to complement municipal regulation of IOUs, with state regulation assuming the major role.[11]

Technological improvements that subverted the legitimacy of municipal regulation did not cease when state regulation began; they continued to expand the size of optimal areas of utility operation. Federal regulation, consequently, soon became a necessary complement to state regulation. In 1927 the U.S. Supreme Court held that state controls over interstate wholesale transactions violated the Commerce Clause of the U.S. Constitution.[12] PUCs, supported by utilities, persuaded the Congress to close this "regulatory gap" by enacting the Federal Power Act in 1935 (FPA), thereby imposing on the Federal Power Commission (FPC), predecessor of the FERC, a responsibility to regulate IOU interstate transactions.[13]

This effort to preserve the efficacy of state regulation was reinforced by PUHCA. PUHCA assigned to the SEC the responsibility to
dismantle some utility holding companies and to regulate the corporate and financial structures of those allowed to survive.[14] PUHCA
and the FPA were successful in restoring the effectiveness of PUCs for
decades, but transmission and generating technologies continued to
erode both the scope and legitimacy of such regulation.

The FPA imposed a division of labor between federal and state
regulators.[15] As this division (with exceptions mentioned shortly) still
defines powers and responsibilities of the FERC, it is worthwhile
reviewing its key provisions:

- The FPA imposed federal regulation on the "transmission
  of energy in interstate commerce and the sale of such
  energy at wholesale in interstate commerce."[16]

- It asserted that federal regulators "shall not have jurisdiction (with some minor exceptions) over facilities used for
  the generation of electric energy or over facilities used in
  local distribution or only for the transmission of electric
  energy in intrastate commerce, or over the facilities for the
  transmission of electric energy consumed wholly by the
  transmitter."[17]

- It granted to the FPC/FERC the power to create and
  enforce accounting standards for IOUs.

- It denied to the FPC/FERC any jurisdiction over GOUs
  and COUs.[18]

Consequently, and of particular relevance to current restructuring debates, the FERC, although it had plenary authority to price IOU
unbundled interstate transmission services, had only a very limited
ability to

- order the construction of transmission assets,[19]

- provide environmental approval or grant eminent domain
  for transmission lines to an IOU, or

- order the provision of transmission services.

Only the last deficiency was removed by EPAct; the others
remain.

PUCs and/or complementary state agencies, in contrast, have no
authority to price unbundled interstate transmission services and
have questionable authority to order an IOU to provide unbundled
interstate transmission services.[20] States do, however, have authority
to require construction of transmission lines and the power to site
such lines. They also have the power to deny an IOU the right to

construct transmission lines. In this age of NIMBY and NIMTOO,[21] this power threatens the efficiency of transmission networks, where it is often necessary to build lines in one state to benefit consumers in another.[22] The FERC's problem was described well by one group of authors. They noted,

> The two powers an economic regulator needs to be effective in controlling any monopoly industry are the power to set prices and the power to enforce an obligation to serve. These are the "twin scepters" of regulatory authority . . . [In the case of electric power transmission] the FERC holds one scepter and the state commissions hold the other. (Kelly et al., 1990, pp. 6, 7)

Expansions of Public Power

In the 1930s, while the federal government was moving to reverse the erosion of PUC regulatory powers over IOUs, it was also expanding the role of GOUs and COUs.[23] These programs included the encouragement of:

- watershed development, including electricity production;
- PMAs to market power from hydroelectric projects created by the Army Corps of Engineers and the Interior Department; and
- rural electric cooperatives.

Since economic regulation was (and is) widely seen as a method of holding prices down rather than as a method of gaining efficient prices, PUC-type regulation was not imposed on GOUs and COUs. The TVA was defined to be its own regulatory agency, and PMAs were executive branch agencies. Only the rural co-ops were regulated, but lightly so, by the REA of the U.S. Department of Agriculture.

Since the TVA, the PMAs, and the generation and transmission cooperatives created by rural co-ops built transmission lines for their own needs and interconnected those lines with IOU transmission lines, transmission networks became economic entities which no economic regulatory agency had authority to oversee. The networks grew incrementally as pairs of utilities interconnected for their mutual interests.

INTERCONNECTEDNESS AND FEDERAL REGULATION

Economies in generator use that motivated, at least in part, many of the horizontal mergers in the 1920s and 1930s continued to encourage such mergers after World War II. Complementing such mergers, and in many cases substituting for mergers when PUHCA or public opinion discouraged them, or public ownership rendered them impossible, were transmission line interconnections.[24] Not surprisingly, many of these interconnections connected IOUs and/or GOUs and/or COUs in different states.

As early as the 1950s the federal government acted to encourage interconnections and pooling. A large part of that encouragement was a threat to expand federal regulatory power if the industry failed to organize "voluntarily" to ensure "reliability." After the Great Northeast Blackout of 1965, federal pressure on the industry became intense. One result was the creation in 1968 of the North American Electric Reliability Council and its associated regional reliability councils.

These government sanctioned and protected, but "voluntary" joint ventures of utilities have become major components in the U.S. regulatory system. The operating rules and reliability standards created by these quasi-official agencies have become parameters for decision making in utilities, PUCs, the FERC, and other government regulators. Some of them must become parameters for NUGs as well.

In summary, by a sequence of actions in the 1950s, 1960s, and 1970s—each taken with an eye toward accommodating technological opportunities and minimizing disruptions to PUC regulation—the federal government expanded its influence over standards for operating transmission networks and the plants connected thereto. Its vehicle for accomplishing this objective was the self-interest of utilities. Since many PUCs supported the pursuit of greater utility cooperation, and the federal initiatives did not impinge directly on the core of PUC regulation—that is, determining prices, price structures, and rates of return—resistance was small.

Perhaps because there was such widespread support for actions improving "reliability," there was surprisingly little opposition when the Congress included language in PURPA that expanded FERC powers to set aside PUC rules and state laws that deter inter-utility cooperation.[25] Since this authority has not been exercised, it is not clear whether the FERC could reverse a decision by a PUC that denied an IOU the right to build a line intended to serve the interest of another utility but also will improve the reliability of service for the constructing utility. Utilities in this context include IPPs, QFs, and EWGs.

PURPA: DRAMATIC ASSERTION OF FEDERAL INTEREST

Two titles of PURPA, a six-title act, are of particular relevance to the current debate. Title I embodies the federal government's interest in retail rate design, an area of regulation previously considered to be wholly a state matter. It required state regulators to "consider" certain rate designs.[26] Title II reinvigorated the cogeneration sector of the electric industry by requiring utilities to buy power from "qualified" cogenerators and small power producers.[27] Furthermore, in PURPA, Congress attempted to create a partnership between the FERC and PUCs for implementing Section 210. The statute requires the FERC to certify QFs and establish rules under which QFs may sell power to and buy power from utilities. The statute also requires PUCs to implement the FERC rules. Section 210, thus, gives FERC authority over a discrete part of retail ratemaking and delegates a discrete part of federal wholesale authority to PUCs.

PURPA was a watershed. It conveyed the congressional view that the electric industry needed extensive federal regulation, extending even to retail rates and rate designs. It was no surprise, then, that EPAct required specific actions by PUCs.

PROBLEMS HIGHLIGHTED BY EPAct

The problem moved to the top of regulatory and industry agendas by EPAct can be described in three words: transmission, transmission, transmission. Building optimal networks and pricing network services is now the sine qua non of federal regulation of the electric industry. Success in this endeavor is crucial for efficiency of the industry and the success of state regulation. However, transmission networks are not currently owned by a single legal entity. If this form of ownership is permitted to continue, any "just and reasonable" earnings requirement must apply to separately owned segments of the network. Furthermore, for a transition period, which may be a long one, each utility with an obligation to serve at the retail level will insist on a right to add to its sub-network of transmission lines as it sees fit in order to satisfy its obligation.

Furthermore, for the first time in the history of the U.S. power industry, some builders of generating plants will be influenced in their plant location decisions by prices charged for transmission service. And, to a degree greater than in the past, the magnitude of power flows will be influenced by the location and amount of transmission capacity and by transmission prices.

While TOUs, the FERC, the DOE, and state regulators strategize to compromise their conflicting objectives, NUGs, selling and buying utilities, especially municipal utilities, are going to be changing the system. There are now many large, competent buyers and sellers who have legal rights to trade. Municipal utilities have been fighting for transmission rights for decades, many NUGs have been fighting for several years, and many utilities now prefer to buy power rather than build generating capacity. It surely will not take such parties long to develop new uses of the transmission networks. Furthermore, there clearly are substantial differences in generating cost in the system, and there are capacity shortages in some regions and capacity surpluses in others. The differences will generate many new trades, and that in turn will produce immediate and powerful pressures on the FERC to exploit its new powers. In a few years, the large industrial end-users will enter the market as powerful buyers, and their competitive pressures will change the system again.

Competitive power markets will not wait for regulators to find an elegant solution to their conflicts. The industry is moving too fast for that luxury.[28]

NOTES

1. Compare: "Our . . . control tradition has a basic weakness which derives from its history, and that is the belief in the efficacy of piecemeal supervision. . . . Our methods amount to an ad hoc structure, and function accordingly" (Hughes, 1977, p. 239).

2. "Utilities" herein includes investor-owned utilities (IOUs), government-owned utilities (GOUs), and customer-owned utilities (COUs). GOUs include municipal utilities, federal power marketing agencies (PMAs), the Tennessee Valley Authority (TVA), and state power agencies. COUs include rural electric cooperatives and generation and transmission cooperatives. PURPA (Public Utility Regulatory Policies Act) qualifying facilities (QFs), independent power producers (IPPs), and exempt wholesale generators (EWGs) are electric utilities under Federal Power Act definitions, but conventional language excludes them from the term. That convention is adopted here. Consequently, "utility" herein means a seller of electric energy who has a legal obligation to sell over and above a contract with the buyer. Non-utility generators (NUGs) include QFs, IPPs, EWGs, and industrial self-generators. When the distinction between NUGs on one hand and utilities with non-contract obligations on the other is to be stressed, the term "franchised utility" is used for the latter.

3. It is worth noting that some NERC committees are international in that the Eastern and Western Interconnections extend into Canada and the Western one also extends into Mexico.

4. Compare: "Whereas, Electric utility transmission, interconnection and wheeling policies are based upon an outdated federal regulatory system which has resulted in an irrational jurisdictional allocation of authority under which the states exercise jurisdiction over the siting and cost recovery of transmission facilities, while the Federal Energy Regulatory Commission

(FERC) claims exclusive jurisdiction over transmission pricing, and terms and conditions" (Resolution of the National Association of Regulatory Utility Commissioners [NARUC] adopted on July 24, 1991). See also Brown (1989a, 1989b).

5.   For example, in 1983, the National Governors Association (NGA), in recognition of the need to better regulate IOUs that are multi-state in character, called for a movement toward regional regulation of IOUs. In 1991, the NARUC revived this call. In 1986, the NGA recommended that states, by the creation of interstate compacts, cooperate to build transmission lines. In 1991, the DOE issued its *National Energy Strategy*, which called "for reconsidering the current division of regulatory authority over electric utilities between Federal and State agencies, in order to define more clearly their respective authorities and to minimize inconsistencies."

6.   EPAct seems to present new opportunities to industrial self-generators. They appear to be able to sell surplus power in the wholesale market. At the very least, this increases their bargaining power vis-a-vis their "native" utility and their "native" PUC.

7.   The terminology of power markets is evolving. In this chapter, wholesale power markets are markets in which NUGs can sell power only to utilities, and utility generators can sell only to other utilities and to end-users within their franchised or otherwise designated territories. The term "bulk power markets" is used to describe markets in which NUGs can sell power to some end-users, for example, to industrial end-users, and utilities can sell to end-users, at least large ones, in another utility's territory.

8.   Compare: (1) "The distinction between retail and wholesale access will soon blur" (James R. Leva, Chairman, President and CEO, General Public Utilities); (2) "I am convinced that retail wheeling will be a near-term reality because of the role that energy costs play in our industrial customers' ability to be competitive in international markets" (D. D. Hock, Chairman, President and CEO, Public Service Co. of Colorado); and (3) "Most industry observers sense that there is a strong and increasing demand for retail wheeling" (Stanley Bright, President, Chairman, and CEO, Iowa-Illinois Gas and Electric Co. "1993 Electric Executives' Forum," *Public Utilities Fortnightly*, June 1, 1993).

9.   Regulators could be helped immensely by constructive leadership from the DOE. It was for such reasons that the agency was created in the 1970s. The agency is not seriously hampered by the procedural constraints which hamper regulators, that is, by ex parte and sunshine rules. Consequently, the DOE can hold meetings, sponsor conferences, fund research, provide forums for negotiation, and otherwise exercise customary tools of leadership.

10. These technological changes also induced horizontal mergers of IOUs and the purchase of municipal utilities by IOUs in attempts to exploit economies of scale, which single municipal utilities, especially small ones, could not exploit. The swords forged in those battles have not all been turned into plowshares.

11. Municipal governments, in most states, continue to regulate

municipally owned utilities in almost all dimensions of their activities and to regulate IOUs in activities directly affecting municipally owned property.

12. *Public Utility Commission v. Attleboro Steam & Electric Co.*, 273 U.S. 83 (1927).

13. In 1977, the FPC was abolished and the FERC was created and formally made part of the U.S. Department of Energy.

14. PUHCA and the FPA failed to fill one important void in regulation. Interstate transmission networks were a vital and growing part of the system, but these laws gave no guidance as to how such networks were to be created and controlled, other than the implied responsibility of the FPC/FERC and the SEC to protect those multi-state holding companies accepted by the SEC from parochial pressures of states.

15. See Vince and Moot (1989) for a survey of principal legal debates in the last decade. See Stalon and Lock (1990) for an emphasis on the economic issues at stake in the federal-state jurisdictional conflicts of recent decades. Immediate past developments are narrated and analyzed in Vince and Moot (1990).

16. In FPA section 201(d), "a sale of electric energy at wholesale" is defined as "a sale of electric energy to any person for resale."

17. At its origin, the FPC/FERC gained authority to approve the construction of hydroelectric projects and to approve the construction of transmission lines needed to connect hydroelectric generators to a network. Similarly, the FERC's authority under PURPA to certify QFs has been interpreted to include authority to approve construction of transmission lines needed to connect QFs to a network.

18. Later legislation gave the FERC limited jurisdiction over prices charged by the Bonneville Power Administration.

19. Also, the FERC does not have authority to order the construction of generating or distribution assets. That deficiency, however, seems irrelevant to the restructuring debate.

20. Commissioner Ashley Brown of Ohio (1989a, 1989b) has argued persuasively that PUCs have ample powers to induce utilities subject to their jurisdictions to offer wheeling services. A point worthy of note is the lack of agreement of the significance of intrastate wheeling. Although a strong case can be made that, with the exception of the Electric Reliability Council of Texas region, there is no such phenomenon as intrastate wheeling within the contiguous forty-eight states, that view is not universal. The New York Public Service Commission (1990), for example, has expressed a counterview.

21. "Not in my back yard" and "not in my term of office."

22. A recent example of the destructive powers of parochialism is the failure of states to cooperate in building disposal sites for low-level nuclear waste. See the *New York Times*, Robert Reinhold, "States, Failing to Cooperate, Face a Nuclear Waste Crisis," December 28, 1992, p. A1. A second example is FERC/state conflicts over the relative priority of "native load" when the FERC orders transmission services. State regulators have usually taken the

position that "native load" customers of a utility ordered to provide transmission services must not lose by the transaction. In effect, the state regulators demand that every move be a Pareto move. Arguments that such a vigorous pursuit of "local fairness" would lower total welfare have generally fallen on deaf ears.

23. The diversity of the industry is described in OTA (1989). This study found 203 investor-owned utility operating companies in the industry in 1988. It also found 1,988 local, publicly owned systems, 994 rural electric cooperatives (including fifty-nine generation and transmission co-ops), fifty-nine public joint-action agencies, five federal power marketing agencies, the Tennessee Valley Authority, and several hundred NUGs, most of which are QFs. Actual control of the investor-owned segment of the industry is more centralized than the number 203 suggests because nearly one quarter of the investor-owned operating companies are subsidiaries of nine registered holding companies.

24. The industry creates much more value-added in the generation sector than in the transmission sector. In a stable economy, this fact would be of little regulatory consequence. There would be an optimal mix of the two types of assets, and creating that optimal mix would be the agreed-upon objective. On the other hand, in an economy as volatile as that of the United States, the difference in value-added is a fact with important regulatory consequences. In a world in which demands vary substantially with limited predictability, in a regulatory system in which the use of prices to ration capacity is not widely accepted, and in utilities in which there are high costs for failing to satisfy demands, an important element of economic efficiency is positive reserve margins for both generating capacity and transmission capacity. Both, however, are expensive, and to some extent they are substitutable for one another. In such a circumstance, it is logical to extensively substitute the cheaper input (transmission lines) for the more expensive input (generating plants).

25. Sec. 205 permits the FERC to "exempt electric utilities . . . from any provision of State law, or from any State rule or regulation, which prohibits or prevents the voluntary coordination of electric utilities."

26. EPAct, section 712, amended PURPA and extended the federal practice of regulating state regulators by requiring that each state evaluate four issues: potential for changes in the cost of capital of utilities that purchase power from EWGs, consequences of EWG capital structures, the desirability of pre-approval of long-term power purchases, and the necessity of evaluating supplier fuel supplies when purchasing power on long-term contracts. EPAct sections 111 and 115 also amended PURPA to require action by state regulators. See NRRI (1993).

27. The most recent FERC *Annual Qualifying Facilities Report* showed that 211 facilities applied for QF status in 1992, and between 1980 and September 30, 1992, 5,028 facilities were approved by the FERC. These facilities represent 107,200 MW of capacity (some of which has not yet been constructed). See *The Energy Daily,* February 10, 1993, p. 4.

28. For the pre-EPAct analysis and descriptions, this chapter relies somewhat on Stalon (2/91, 10/91, 10/93) and Stalon and Lock (1990).

REFERENCES

Bright, Stanley, D. D. Hock, and James R. Leva. "1993 Electric Executives' Forum." *Public Utilities Fortnightly* 131 (June 1, 1993): 19–63.

Brown, A. "State Power Over Transmission Access and Pricing: The Giant Will Not Sleep Forever." *Public Utilities Fortnightly* 124 (1989a): 21–33.

Brown, Ashley. "The Balkans Revisited: A Modest Plan for Transmission Reform." *The Electricity Journal* 2 (1989a).

Codey, Lawrence R. "1993 Electric Executives' Forum." *Public Utilities Fortnightly* 131 (June 1, 1993): 19-63.

Energy Daily, The. February 10, 1993, p.4.

Hughes, J. R. T. *The Governmental Habit*. New York: Basic Books, 1977.

Kelly, Kevin, Robert Burns, and Kenneth Rose. *An Evaluation of NARUC for the Key Issues Raised by The FERC Transmission Task Force Report*. Columbus, OH: National Regulatory Research Institute, January 1990.

National Association of Regulatory Utility Commissioners. Resolution of the National Association of Regulatory Utility Commissioners adopted on July 24, 1991 entitled "Resolution on Administrative and Legislative Reform of Electric Transmission Policy."

National Governors Association. *Moving Power: Flexibility for the Future*. Report of the Task Force on Electricity Transmission of the Committee on Energy and Environment, 1986.

National Governors Association. *Options for Structural Reform in Electric Regulation*. Report of the Task Force on Electricity Utility Regulation of the Committee on Energy and Environment, 1983.

National Regulatory Research Institute (NRRI). *A White Paper on the Energy Policy Act of 1992: An Overview for State Commissions on New PURPA Statutory Standards*. Columbus, OH: NRRI, April 1993.

New York Public Service Commission. "Proceeding on Motion of the Commission to Examine the Plans for Meeting Future Electricity Needs in New York State: Intrastate Wheeling." PSC Case 88-E-238. See in that case the "Report on Wheeling Cost," February 1990.

Reinhold, Robert. "States, Failing to Cooperate, Face a Nuclear Waste Crisis." *The New York Times*. December 28, 1992, p. A1.

Stalon, Charles G. "A Mostly Privately Owned System; The U.S. Power Regulatory System." Paper presented to the World Bank Conference in Mexico City, September 1991.

Stalon, Charles G. "Key Issues in the Electricity Industry Restructuring Debate." Testimony. U.S. House of Representatives, Subcommittee on Energy and Power of the Committee on Energy and Commerce, March 20, 1991.

Stalon, Charles G. "The FERC, Designated Driver and Head Herdsman for Restructuring the Electric Industry." *Electricity Journal*. June 1993.

Stalon, Charles G., and Reiner H. Lock. "State-Federal Relations in the Economic Regulation of Energy." *Yale Journal on Regulation* 7 (Summer 1990): 427–497.

U.S. Congress, Office of Technology Assessment (OTA). *Electric Power Wheeling and Dealing: Technological Considerations for Increasing Competition.* OTA-E-409. Washington, DC: OTA, May 1989.

U.S. Department of Energy. *National Energy Strategy: Powerful Ideas for America.* DOE/S-0082P. Washington, DC: Government Printing Office, February 1991.

U.S. Supreme Court. *Public Utility Commission v. Attleboro Steam & Electric Co.* 273 U.S. 83 (1927).

Vince, Clinton A., and John S. Moot. "Federal Preemption Versus State Utility Regulation in a Post-Mississippi Era." *Energy Law Journal* 1 (1989).

Vince, Clinton A., and John S. Moot. "Energy Federalism, Choice of Forum, and State Utility Regulation." *Administrative Law Review* 42 (1990): 323–392.

3

Real Planning, Sham Competition, and State Regulation

David R. Wooley and Alfred J. Cavallo

State regulation of electricity sales has a number of important benefits for the economy and the environment. Those benefits have not always been apparent, since serious defects in the traditional regulatory structure and utility planning in general have led to high costs, over-supply, inefficiency, and unnecessary pollution. The relatively recent advent of integrated resource planning, which takes advantage of demand-side management (DSM), public involvement, and increasingly sophisticated planning tools, means that the states are finally on the verge of implementing true least-cost planning systems that would avoid the mistakes of the past. Current pressures to overthrow state least-cost planning in favor of federal preemption or elimination of retail electric utility franchises (retail wheeling) arise not from inherent failures of regulation, but rather from a failure to regulate well.

It would be foolish to discard the benefits of intelligent resource planning just as it is beginning to bear fruit. To do so would eliminate important mechanisms to avoid local, regional, and global environmental damages from electric power production. The retail wheeling propositions would also create a series of severe inequities among customer groups and would tend to benefit only the short-term interests of one select group of electric customers. It would impose higher risks, particularly for large industrial and commercial customers. Retail wheeling is neither politically inevitable nor economically wise. It should be rejected in favor of regulatory forms which emphasize energy efficiency, equity among customer groups, environmental protection, and reduction of risk through long-range planning.

REGULATORY ADOLESCENCE AND MATURITY

Any examination of federal and state regulation of electric utilities must proceed from a clear understanding of where we stand in the evolution of regulatory forms. For example, New York is widely viewed as an innovator and as a state with considerable experience in least-cost planning. Although the former statement is true, the latter is a common, but mistaken, impression.

New York was one of the early states to undertake reforms that encourage and require utilities to use demand-side management as a serious resource. It also has required the use of competitive bidding for the acquisition of new resources, uses environmental externality values in selection of demand-side and generation resources, has established a comprehensive, accessible and acceptable state energy planning process, and has recognized the value of renewable energy investments.

However, all of this was accomplished only very recently. Full-scale DSM programs are less than three years old and have not yet begun to serve the efficiency needs of large industrial customers. The bidding process first emerged in the late 1980s, before the huge potential of DSM was accounted for in planning—an error that contributed significantly to the current over-capacity problem.

Moreover, energy policy reform in New York and in most states remains incomplete. New York utilities are pursuing only about half of the identified cost-effective DSM potential and frequently experience lost opportunities by failing to capture savings in the new construction market. Utilities artificially depress DSM investments by failing to fully account for all costs avoided by DSM[1] and have been slow to provide DSM services to important customer sectors, including large industries.

Utility integrated resource plans (IRPs) are currently, for the first time in New York, being exposed to public comment and Public Service Commission review. The review shows that many New York utility plans do poorly on the fundamentals. For example, in a period of over-capacity and in a state with an aging fleet of power plants, utility IRPs often fail to address plant retirement options.

It is only by comparison that New York looks advanced. Most other states are even further behind. Less than half of the states require integrated resource planning at all. Florida, a state facing massive load growth, is just now devising its first set of utility energy efficiency programs. Integrated resource planning and serious energy conservation are only just beginning in the lower Midwest, the South, and the Great Plains states.

As Professor Robert Socolow of Princeton recently stated, we are still low on the learning curve of true least-cost planning, but we are making rapid progress. The momentum toward better planning is strong. Energy conservation and renewable energy programs are gaining wider acceptance. The regulatory structures which created reliability problems, environmental damages, and cost explosions are being replaced by state regulation that is more open to the public, more environmentally sound, and more competitive.

From the perspective of federalism, this experience suggests that the current division of authority between the state and federal governments is working. The federal government is effectively encouraging states to adopt least-cost planning and to achieve greater reliance on energy efficiency and renewable energy resources. Its research and development activities, national appliance efficiency standards, federal procurement policies, and regional and global environmental mandates all provide needed direction, coordination, and incentives for state energy policy. Federal control over transmission access will lower generation costs by removing barriers to wholesale competition.

Beyond these functions, however, it would be a mistake to significantly increase federal control over electric power planning and operations. Circumstances affecting electric power supply and planning, environmental protection, and utility costs vary considerably from state to state. Federal agencies will never be well equipped to handle this diversity or to respond in real time to changes at the state level. States should retain authority over energy facility siting (including power plants and transmission lines), statewide energy planning, retail electricity markets, and utility planning. To disrupt this balance of power would endanger the chances of significant future gains in energy efficiency and environmental quality.

UNTAPPED BENEFITS OF LEAST-COST PLANNING

Even at this early stage, the benefits of least-cost planning are apparent. For example, in 1993 utility demand-side management programs in New York will displace the need for 355 MW of capacity, and avoid the need to generate 512 GWH from existing facilities.[2] By the year 2000, these programs will have produced almost 2,600 MW of cumulative summer capacity savings and 9,500 GWH of cumulative energy savings. The programs are highly cost effective and rigorously evaluated.[3]

The efficiency gains achieved to date represent real progress, but there remains a great deal more efficiency potential to be achieved. In New York, our estimates show that utilities are skipping cost-effective DSM opportunities that could achieve energy savings equal to the electricity consumed by a city of 700,000 people, would reduce air pollution by over 4 million tons, would diminish reliance on imported fuel, and produce 4,500 jobs.[4] These and other benefits can be achieved for costs that are less than would otherwise be spent on fuel, operations and maintenance, and other variable costs. From either a competitiveness or environmental perspective, these are benefits that the state can ill afford to miss. This conclusion is reinforced by a look at the industrial sector where a large and untapped efficiency potential exists. For the most part, utility programs have simply not offered energy efficiency programs that meet the needs of industrial customers, and here there is no good excuse for this failure.[5] If utility programs are properly targeted, the effect is to retain load and jobs in the service territory, increase the competitiveness of the industrial customer, lower variable generation expenses, reduce planning and fuel price escalation risks, reduce air pollution, and stabilize future rates by deferring the date when new capacity is needed.

State regulation and least-cost planning also create an opportunity to develop alternative energy resources which are not dependent on fossil fuels and are environmentally benign. One manifestation of this is a pending New York Public Service Commission (PSC) proceeding in which diverse parties are working out a plan to acquire 300 MW of renewable energy resources by the end of the decade. The commission has recognized that, even in a period of excess capacity, it is wise to build experience and capability with renewable energy as a hedge against uncertainty and risk associated with heavy reliance on fossil fuel.[6] Moreover, we are discovering that some renewables (e.g., wind,[7] biomass,[8] solar thermal power,[9] and "niche" or remote applications of photovoltaic systems[10])are cost effective today in many locations nationally.

This progress on energy efficiency and renewables would never have occurred without enlightened state regulation of retail electric sales; allowing individual states or regions to experiment with different policies has been an efficient way to test these in the market and select the best approach based on actual performance.[11]

Continuation of utility least-cost planning and state regulatory oversight is critical. Huge untapped DSM and renewable resources exist. Moreover, many states (including New York) will soon need to grapple with complex issues surrounding retirement of aging fossil and nuclear power plants and strains on transmission access and capacity. DSM and renewable energy resources provide the cushion needed for retirement of inefficient power plants with high fixed costs and help avoid the need for new transmission investments. They also reduce Clean Air Act compliance costs and the burden of any future regulation or taxation of greenhouse gas emissions. The problem of greenhouse gases is significant and poses important challenges for utilities and state governments.

The electric utilities are a major source of greenhouse gas (CO_2 and nitrogen oxides) emissions.[12] As such, they will be a central focus of federal greenhouse gas controls, which may come in the form of off-set requirements, taxes, or emission limitations. International agreements and domestic concern are propelling the United States toward some form of national CO_2 reduction program. Although the precise timing and form of such controls are still to be decided, the inevitable effect will be to increase the cost of reliance on fossil fuels. Thus, current emission rates of greenhouse gases are a source of increasing risk for utilities and their customers.[13] The risk can be mitigated if utilities and state governments continue to gain experience with energy efficiency and renewables and engage in intelligent resource planning. The needed utility research, development, and investments in efficiency and renewables will not happen in absence of long-range planning and state regulation of retail electric sales.

This is not to imply that there are no limits to effective regulation. The creation of a wholesale generation markets first in the Public Utility Regulatory Policies Act (PURPA) and in state competitive bidding initiatives, and later under the federal Energy Policy Act of 1992, promises an improvement over past regulatory forms. Competition also needs to be better integrated into existing regulatory mechanisms in regard to delivery of DSM services, Clean Air Act compliance, and other areas. However, competition alone is not a substitute for good long-range planning, and long-range, integrated resource planning does not occur in absence of effective regulation of retail electric sales markets. Competitive forces alone cannot engineer an efficient, environmentally safe and reliable electric supply.

DISADVANTAGES OF RETAIL WHEELING

Competition in the electric utility industry takes two forms, one real and the other phantom. Certainly utilities in some regions face competition in the form of large customers with opportunities to self-generate ("bypass"), shift production to other states, or close plants. They also face competition in wholesale power generation markets that will make it harder to sell power from high-cost units or resist power purchases that are less expensive than running their own plants. These are real and healthy forms of competition that should encourage utilities to lower costs, retire inefficient plants, offer better DSM services to vulnerable customers and make targeted use of rate discounts where truly needed to retain customers.

The competition phantom is known as retail wheeling. Retail wheeling would essentially mean ending utility franchise areas, allowing some customers to abandon local utilities so that they could buy power elsewhere, and forcing local utilities to transmit power to such customers. As currently proposed, it is not an increase in competition, but merely a money grab by one customer sector. Large customers who can take advantage of it will simply succeed in shifting a huge amount of costs onto small customers, as they swallow up available low-cost power. It is a phantom because it is not a real form of increased competition; its consequences are so unfair and risky that it is highly unlikely that any state legislature or commission would adopt it.

A retail wheeling market would operate on the assumption that short-term price signals are all that is necessary to ensure one single important result: the lowest possible short-term price of electricity. This assumption ignores many equally important or more important results such as long-term price stability, resource diversity, system reliability, safety and power quality, encouraging the use of energy efficient equipment, and pollution reduction (including CO_2 reduction).

Retail wheeling treats electricity as a commodity or an end in itself, rather than as a means to an end or a service. The commodity definition often leads to the problem of oversupply and load building (encouragement of higher consumption) on the part of the producer, and overuse and inefficient use on the part of the consumer. Electricity is, however, always purchased to produce a wide variety of services such as lighting, ventilation, or air conditioning; thus, obtaining electricity at the lowest short-term price is no guarantee that these services will be delivered for the lowest lifecycle cost.

Proponents concede that under a retail wheeling scheme, a utility could focus only on the immediate future and short-term prices. It could not afford to consider or invest in the long-term system benefits of DSM, nor could it help customers stabilize power costs through investments to meet the higher capital cost of energy efficient equipment, even if lifecycle savings were many times the initial price premium.[14] Such a utility also could not support long-term research and development programs, which are vital to the industry. Industrial, residential, and commercial customers in need of design assistance, technical advice, financing, or audit services regarding energy-efficient equipment would be left to fend for themselves.

Another powerful reason to reject retail wheeling is that it seeks a drastic reallocation of the nation's electric bill. Large industrial customers will benefit at the expense of residential and small-to-medium-sized commercial and industrial customers who have neither the time, expertise, nor load to attract and develop alternative electric supplies.

There is no logic to allowing one select set of customers to escape responsibility for legitimate supply costs incurred by utilities for their benefit. Once people realize that retail wheeling is merely a mechanism to enrich the few at the expense of the many, they will reject the concept.

Even for large customers, however, retail wheeling creates more risk than benefit. There is reason to believe that retail wheeling would create reliability-of-service problems, either from a shortage of resources or chaotic demands on the transmission and distribution system. Retail wheeling may also bring high costs, due to telemetering expenses, the need for higher reserve margin, and the imposition of greater uncertainty in supply and demand (EEI, 1992). Resource diversity, risk avoidance, economic development, and environmental factors which are accounted for in the least-cost planning requirements of many states would be irrelevant in a retail wheeling world. There is a significant risk that under retail wheeling large customers would watch relatively stable utility systems degenerate into a Balkanized tangle of weakened utilities and competing, financially shaky independent power producers. The probability that power quality and reliability will degrade is much higher in a system in which there is no long-term planning and where no entity has a long-term obligation to serve. These considerations should be foremost in minds of industrial customers who would suffer most from service interruptions and extreme price volatility.

The proponents of retail wheeling rarely deal with these problems. Arguments in support of retail wheeling tend to gloss over substance, and treat the elimination of utility franchise areas as an inevitable result of unstoppable market forces. There is usually no attempt to ask why public officials would decide to go down such a path even though it is clear that some action of a state commission, or more likely a state legislature, is needed to adopt retail wheeling. Although it may be theoretically possible to construct a retail wheeling system that fairly allocates costs and avoids a host of risks, it is likely that there would be no constituency for such a system. No one gets a windfall, and it would have few if any advantages over the currently developing regulatory forms. Moreover, it would require a new and potentially more complex form of regulatory oversight, would not achieve deregulation, nor would it result in greater competition than will be achieved through reform of wholesale markets.

The aura of inevitability about retail wheeling is as insubstantial as the pile of gold at the end of a rainbow. Even so, however, it is currently causing harm. Some utilities are beginning to cut DSM in the mistaken belief that retail competition is around the corner and that eliminating such programs will make them more competitive.

Such actions will only reduce rates in the very short term by infinitesimal amounts, at a time when even proponents do not expect retail wheeling to be adopted. In the longer term, such actions will increase fuel costs, advance the need date for expensive supply, and degrade the utilities' service relationship with their customers. Indeed, the elimination of conservation programs, the reduction of customer services, and the abandonment of long-range planning only serves to feed the retail wheeling frenzy, since a utility which abandons these functions will have fewer defenders.

Utilities and commissions need to begin to speak out about the negative aspects of retail wheeling. They need to firmly resist pressure to do away with efficiency programs, integrated resource planning, and other functions which serve the interests of customers, stockholders, and the public at large. It is time for utilities to defend the interests of their core constituency—the small- and medium-sized customers who will be hurt most by these proposals.

CONCLUSIONS

The debate over changes in utility regulation creates an important opportunity to inform the public and governments about the values of energy conservation and long-term, least-cost planning. It is a debate in which the well-documented public preference for clean power can be heard decisively. After savings and loan scandals, the American public does not view "regulation" as a boogie man, nor deregulation as a panacea. Environmental groups generally supported increased competition in wholesale electric power sales, but draw the line at retail wheeling, which they consider a sham variety of competition.

Retail wheeling can only promise short-term discounts for a select few, while imposing short- and long-term penalties on everyone else. This is simply an insufficient justification for eliminating state oversight and placing service reliability, regional and global environmental protection, energy security, industrial efficiency, and renewable energy development entirely at the mercy of a short-term commodity market.

NOTES

1.   Benefit/cost analyses for DSM programs in New York still do not adequately account for avoided transmission and distribution costs, Clean Air Act compliance costs, fuel price risk avoidance, comparative economic development values, and load and loss weighting of energy costs.

2. According to the New York Public Service Commission, March 18, 1993, p. 3.

3. In its order of March 18, 1993, the New York Public Service Commission stated: "The $530 million DSM investment proposed for these two years [1993, 1994] is estimated to provide lifetime energy, capacity and environmental benefits of $1.25 billion." The New York Commission found that DSM programs are justified even in a period of excess capacity because: "Cost effective DSM programs reduce the cost to New Yorkers of energy services, reduce a utility's long term total revenue requirement and thus reduce customers' overall bills, reduce reliance on imported fuels, and reduce environmental impacts."

4. See our comments before the New York Public Service Commission on September 14, 1992, p. 5 and Appendix A.

5. Evidence presented in the recent Niagara Mohawk rate case shows that large customers will do a limited amount of DSM on their own, usually confined to measures having a payback in lower electric bills of six months to two years. However, when an electric utility provides customer incentives (in the form of process efficiency audits, rebates, technical assistance, or financing) equal to or below its avoided cost, industrial customers will adopt a much wider range of efficiency measures. Several utilities have begun to target their DSM efforts to the industrial sector and report success in significantly reducing customers' electric power demand (by 30 percent in some cases) and in preventing industrial plant closure.

6. See New York Public Service Commission, October 14, 1992, pp. 1, 2.

7. In areas with good wind resources close to demand centers (California, Denmark, and other European countries), wind-generated electricity is fully competitive with electricity from new coal-fired power plants; the wind resources of the Great Plains are large enough to meet the demand for electricity in the entire United States. Wind-generated electricity now supplies about 1 percent of demand in California, and 3.5 percent in Denmark. See Cavallo et al. (1992) and Grubb and Meyer (1992).

8. The installed biomass generating capacity in the United States is 9 GW. In addition, it is also feasible to generate liquid or gaseous fuels (methanol and hydrogen) from biomass, which could satisfy a substantial portion of U.S. and world energy requirements (Johansson et al., 1992).

9. Solar thermal power plants based on parabolic trough concentrators provide 350 MW of electrical power at times of maximum demand in southern California (De Laquil et al., 1992).

10. Photovoltaic systems, although not yet cost effective for large-scale utility applications, are ideally suited for many off-grid locations where the distance to the nearest power line is more than one or two kilometers (Firor et al., 1992).

11. One example of this kind of creative state response was the implementation in California of the utility power purchase agreement known as the standard offer number 4 (SO4), which was critical to the establishment of the

utility scale wind and solar industry in that state. This addressed two major problems encountered by independent power producers: the lack of a long-term market and the inability to borrow money for longer than a ten-year term. The SO4 was a thirty-year contract; during the first ten years the price of electricity was set sufficiently high so that the installed capital cost of a facility could be paid off within that period. Thereafter, the price reverted to the avoided cost of electricity for the utility, which presumably could easily cover profits and operation and maintenance charges. Other examples include the DSM programs established in California, the Pacific Northwest, New England, and New York State.

12.   The CO_2 level in the atmosphere has increased by about 25 percent since the beginning of the industrial age, and in a business-as-usual scenario at projected levels of industrial activity, will double by the middle of the next century. Complex computer climate simulation models are used to predict the consequences of such an increase. Typical predictions (e.g., Manabe and Stouffer, 1993) include a gradual increase in surface temperature of about 3.5 °C, and a rise in mean sea levels of at least 1 m due only to the thermal expansion of the oceans (ice sheet melting would make the rise in sea levels much greater). More abrupt changes in the earth's climate due to increased CO_2 levels cannot yet be completely excluded (GRIP, 1993; Taylor et al., 1993). However, even the gradual changes predicted by the climate models would have major and perhaps catastrophic consequences for human and other populations.

13.   For a good exposition of environment-related investment risk see Cavanagh (1993).

14.   The classic example of this problem is the compact fluorescent light bulb, which will save a customer more than $50 over its 10,000-hour life and avoids a variety of utility system expenses (compared to incandescent bulbs), but which costs about $20, nearly fifty times as much as the equivalent incandescent bulb. Without utility rebates, consumers almost always buy incandescent bulbs.

REFERENCES

Cavallo, A. J., S. M. Hock, and D. R. Smith. "Wind Energy: Technology and Economics." In *Renewable Energy: Sources for Fuels and Electricity*, T. B. Johansson, H. Kelly, A. K. N. Reddy, and R. H. Williams, Washington, DC: Island Press, 1992. (Hereinafter cited as *Renewable Energy*.)

Cavanagh, R. "Utilities and CO_2 Emissions: Who Bears the Risks of Future Regulation?" *The Electricity Journal* (March 1993): 64–74.

De Laquil, P., D. Kearney, M. Geyer, and R. Diver. "Solar Thermal Electric Technology." In *Renewable Energy*.

Edison Electric Institute. "The Case Against Retail Wheeling, A response to Advocates of Retail Wheeling." Transmission Issues Monograph No.5. Washington, DC: EEI, July 1992.

Firor, K., R. Vigotti, and J. J. Iannucci. "Utility Field Experience With Photovoltaic Systems." In *Renewable Energy.*

Greenland Ice-core Project (GRIP) Members. "Climate Instability During the Last Interglacial Period Recorded in the GRIP Ice Core." *Nature* 364 (1993): 203–207.

Grubb, M. J,. and N. I. Meyer. "Wind Energy: Resources, Systems and Regional Strategies." In *Renewable Energy.*

Johansson, T. B., H. Kelly, A. K. N. Reddy, and R. H. Williams. "Renewable Fuels and Electricity for a Growing World Economy: Defining and Achieving the Potential." In *Renewable Energy.*

Manabe, S., and R. Stouffer. "Century Scale Effects of Increased Atmospheric CO_2 on the Ocean-Atmosphere System." *Nature* 364 (1993): 215–220.

New York Public Service Commission. "Comments of Public Interest Interveners on the 1993–1994 Annual and Long Range Demand Side Management and Integrated Resource Plans of the New York Electric Utilities." Filed in Case No. 28223 on September 14, 1992.

New York Public Service Commission. *Order Concerning 1993 and 1994 Demand Side Management Plans and HIECA Business Plans.* Case number 92-E-0621, et seq., issued and effective March 18, 1993.

New York Public Service Commission. *Proceeding on Motion of the Commission to Examine the Plans for Implementation of Renewable Resources as Part of Meeting Future Electricity Needs in New York State.* Order Instituting Proceeding, Case 92-E-0954, issued and effective October 14, 1992.

Taylor, K. C., C. U. Hammer, R. B. Alley, et al. "Electrical Conductivity Measurements from the GISP2 and GRIP Greenland Ice Cores." *Nature* 366 (1993): 549–552.

4

Thinking Politically about American Federalism

Michael N. Danielson

Even under the most favorable conditions, federalism is difficult. Dividing power between center and periphery is always complex, frequently unstable, and often impossible because of the unwillingness of the center to share power with the periphery. Underscoring these difficulties is the fact that most political systems are unitary. In these systems subunits are administrative subdivisions of the central government; they lack independent sources of authority. Provinces, departments, administrative regions, and local agencies depend on the central government for their legal authority and fiscal resources; their officials often are appointed by the national government, serving as agents of the center.

The United States is a rarity—a real federal system that separates and shares power between center and periphery in a dynamic equilibrium. Power is divided between the national government and the fifty state governments. States have independent sources of authority through their constitutions and a national constitution that reserves substantial powers to the states and the people in the Tenth Amendment. Each state is a substantially independent political system. States elect their own governors, legislators, and judges; state governments appoint their own officials. The national government cannot replace governors and other state officials, as can the center under India's version of federalism. States have their own revenue sources; states and their local subdivisions collect 44 percent of all the tax revenues in the United States. State and local governments do not depend on the central government for a substantial portion of their revenues; in 1990, only 18 percent of state and local revenues came from Washington.

Another critical benchmark of state autonomy is the fact that states determine their own policies. To be sure, federal assistance and standards, along with federal regulations and court rulings, influence almost every aspect of state policy. Nonetheless, considerable variations exist among states on all sorts of important policies, including the nature and incidence of taxes, the range and quality of services, and the coverage and size of benefits. Regulatory policies vary substantially from state to state, in terms of the extent of regulation, the regulatory mechanisms, the content of policies, and the effectiveness of enforcement.

American federalism is durable; the arrangement between nation and states forged in Philadelphia in 1787 has survived more than two centuries of tumultuous change in the nature of the economy, world, communications, politics, and government. Federalism succumbed neither to a civil war fought over the nature of the union, nor to the explosive growth of government in the twentieth century. As the century draws to a close, federalism is alive and well despite an endless litany of dire predictions about its imminent demise. Notwithstanding the enormous growth of the national government and the grave warning about the federal octopus, subnational government has been expanding more rapidly than the domestic activities of the national government. State and local expenditures more than doubled in the 1980s (from $432 billion in 1980 to $973 billion in 1990) while federal aid was increasing less than 50 percent (from $91 billion to $135 billion); during the same period, state and local governments added 15 percent more workers compared to a 7 percent rise in the federal work force.

The enduring strength of American federalism reflects strongly held political values in the United States. Dispersal of authority among levels of government is a critical element of the Madisonian concept of limited government that underlies the constitution. Federalism also embodies the concept of government close to the people, the Jeffersonian ideal of responsive grass roots government. And federalism recognizes that the American states are distinctive political systems. The colonies of Massachusetts, New York, and Virginia were not merely administrative subdivisions of the British realm, but were separate societies and polities with particular economic, social, and political interests. New states developed their own distinctive characteristics as the union expanded; and these differences were amplified by the fact that each new state had the same general powers, rights, and privileges as the original thirteen. Arizona, Colorado, Nevada, New Mexico, and Utah are separated by geometrical boundaries that cut through vast expanses of desert and mountain, yet each state is a distinctive polity with its own mix of policy preferences, taxes, expenditures, and regulatory activities.

Federalism also is sustained by the state and local electoral base of American polictics. Congress is rooted in state and local constituencies. National political parties in the United States are weak; they do not control or even significantly influence nominations for congressional seats; nor do they provide a substantial amount of the ever-larger campaign war chests that are needed to run for the Senate or House of Representatives. Congressional nominations are secured by winning state or district primaries. State legislatures determine who is eligible to vote in party primaries; they also redraw district boundaries for the House of Representatives following the decennial census. Senators and representatives must come from the state they represent; almost all representatives live in their district; and few members of Congress fail to maintain residences in their state or district or spend considerable amounts of time staying in touch with their constituency. The route to the presidency also runs through the states. Presidential nominations are sought through state primary elections, which provide opportunities to win delegates, to demonstrate to the nation and campaign contributors that a candidate is a winner, and to drive opponents out of the race for delegates and contributions.

The decentralized political base makes Washington, and especially Congress, sensitive to the interests of states and localities. Decentralized politics ensures that states and localities have shared in the growth of the national government. Most national domestic programs have been implemented through subnational governments. Through grants-in-aid, joint administration, and other forms of sharing, Congress and the White House have made state and local officials partners in the vast expansion of the responsibilities of the national government for education, energy, health, housing, pollution, transportation, and welfare.

By its nature, federalism is dynamic, and therefore potentially unstable. Relationships between the national government and the states are constantly being redefined by Congress, federal agencies, regulators, and the courts. Most important among the changes that have altered American federalism has been the steady expansion of national power. The federal government has grown in response to the increased interconnectedness of American society and its political economy. As the federal government grew, more and more interests organized for action at the national level, and most of these interests pressed Washington to do more. Groups also have been attracted by the economy of political effort in securing national action; getting new federal environmental or energy policies involves considerably less political investment and much higher prospects of success than seeking the same policy changes in each of fifty states.

Expansion of the national government also is a product of the natural inclination of federal officials to advance their interests by using the instrument at hand, the national government. Despite their state and local constituency base, members of Congress usually seek to use the resources of the government they can best influence, the national government, to respond to problems. The president's perspective is national and the presidency's prime means is the national government, regardless of fervent campaign speeches about the virtues of government close to the people. Federal agencies, like all organizations, seek more rather than less to do, bigger rather than smaller budgets, and expanding rather than contracting staffs. These natural tendencies have been amplified in the case of Congress by the growing importance in congressional elections of nationally based campaign funds raised by political action committees interested in having the federal government advance their interests.

Change has increased the connections and complexities in the American federal system. The basic pattern for the first century of the American republic was dual federalism. Washington and the states were largely separate spheres connected by relatively few intergovernmental ventures. After the Great Depression, fiscal federalism became the primary means of expanding the national government. Programs developed in Washington with national goals, standards, and money were implemented by states and their subdivisions. As the number of programs multiplied, relationships between Washington and the states became increasingly complex, with shared and overlapping responsibilities. Considerable variation evolved among policy arenas, with distinctive patterns shaped by history, crisis, and incremental change.

More recently, federalism has featured national rules without the shared resources that characterized the expansion of the federal system in the four decades following the election of 1932. Federal regulatory controls have expanded rapidly in recent years, in response to an ever-more interconnected economy and society, federal court rulings, expanding federal concerns for everything from endangered species to wetlands, and the effectiveness of organized interests in enlisting the power of the national government to make the work place safer, facilities more accessible to the handicapped, and the air cleaner. These multiplying federal mandates have been decried by governors, mayors, and other state and local officials, who insist that Washington has to put up resources or shut up.

Conflicts over federal mandates, over whether there should be national standards for air pollution or drinking water or reading skills —and if so, which governments (and therefore which sets of taxpayers) should bear the responsibility for meeting national standards—

underscore that federalism is a mixed blessing. Decentralization offers many benefits: multiple centers of power limit government; the decentralized American polity is responsive to subnational and place interests; the federal system encourages experimentation and innovation; and dispersed government broadens the recruitment of political elites and ensures that elite political socialization is not narrowly focused on the center. These benefits, however, have been realized at considerable cost, most of which are inherent in federalism. Because the states are distinctive, significant, albeit declining variations exist among states in educational achievement, income, welfare benefits, and a host of other indicators of life chances. Competition among states for economic development, federal aid, and national facilities grows ever more intense, yet adds relatively little net benefit to the economy or society as a whole. Federalism also appeals to those who seek something for nothing—states and localities who want federal money without strings, and Washington players that cannot resist the opportunity to exercise power without providing the resources to implement federal mandates.

Federalism is likely to continue to be dynamic, contentious, and very political. More federal rules and regulations are more likely than significant increases in national resources shared with state and local governments. These outcomes will continue to reflect the natural instincts and interests of federal officials and the influence of national groups and their money on members of Congress.

These developments will continue to exacerbate conflicts between the national government and the grass roots, and between the Washington interests and the state and local constituency base of Congress. These trends, however, do not alter the fundamental political reality of the necessity for members of Congress to win state or local primaries and elections. Nor do they reduce the influence that governors, mayors, and other state and local officials wield in national politics.

What are the lessons for energy policy that emerge from an overview of the political dynamics of the American federalism? One is that anyone contemplating redesign of an element of the federal system ignores politics at considerable peril. States cannot be dealt out of most equations, even when there is little in the way of a rational role for state government. The symbols of American federalism are powerful, and they are reinforced by the antipathy most citizens have toward Washington, big government, red tape, and all the other negative metaphors that cling to the national government like limpets. Governors, members of Congress, and others who defend the states will wax eloquently about government close to the people, grass roots government, and states' rights. They also will insist, probably successfully, that states' interests and differences be protected in any new intergovernmental arrangements for energy.

The political features of the American federal system have to be considered as an integral aspect of the problem. Successful policy changes have to pass muster politically. In short, find something useful for the states to do, and emphasize (if necessary, overemphasize) the importance of the state role in the proposed brave new world. Last but not least, do not worry too much about complexity; federalism works because of complexity by ada‚ :ing the general mechanism to the key players in and particular requirements of each policy arena.[1]

NOTE

1.   This chapter owes a considerable intellectual debt to Anton (1989), Elazar (1972), Grodzins (1966), Reagan (1972), and Riker (1964).

REFERENCES

Anton, Thomas J. *American Federalism and Public Policy*. New York: Random House, 1989.

Elazar, Daniel J. *American Federalism: A View from the South*. New York: Harper & Row, 1972.

Grodzins, Morton. *The American System*. Chicago: Rand McNally, 1966.

Reagan, Michael D. *The New Federalism*. New York: Oxford University Press, 1972.

Riker, William H. *Federalism: Origin, Operation, Significance*. Boston: Little, Brown, 1964.

5

A Basis for Allocating Regulatory Responsibilities

Kenneth Gordon and Christopher Mackie-Lewis

The regulation of electricity under our federal system is a complex, multi-level affair. The regulatory system has evolved into its current configuration as the result of perceived needs and problems during the last century, as markets and corporate structures responded to the growing needs of society. As with any evolutionary system, the state and Federal energy regulatory system has its share of redundancies and vestigial organs, most attributable to vagaries of the political process. At the national level alone, for example, two U.S. agencies—the Securities and Exchange Commission and the Federal Energy Regulatory Commission—share responsibility for various aspects of the electricity system. Although each holds a unique mandate and fulfills a valuable function, a more efficient system might assign regulatory responsibility in a more unitary fashion. Moreover, major portions of electricity regulation are reserved to the states. Retail rate setting, supply planning, and generation and transmission siting, for example, lie exclusively in the states' jurisdictions. As Danielson points out elsewhere in this volume, we should not expect optimal technical efficiency from a regulatory system under federalism, as political forces are deeply integrated into the decision process.

What can one say about the appropriate allocation of regulatory responsibilities among the various levels of the U.S. federal system?[1] The purpose of this chapter is to examine electricity regulation in the United States, with a particular emphasis on the allocation of regulatory responsibilities between the states and the Federal government. The chapter raises more questions than it offers explicit prescriptions. In large part, this is because there is no single correct answer that will prove valid for all states at all times and apply to all issues.

Any realistic discussion of this issue must take into account the inter-action of three relatively independent influences on the regulatory process: the goals of regulation, the underlying social and technical forces stimulating change and/or stress on the system, and the politi-cal-economic forces which contribute to the nature and direction of regulatory change. These influences and their interactive effects will differ across states, over time, and across issues. Each governmental body charged with providing for electricity regulation must therefore evaluate these influences situationally and use the insights from that evaluation to craft a solution unique to the specific problems it faces. An inevitable tension arises here, because the Federal government faces much greater diversity in its larger regulatory jurisdiction than does any single state. Federal regulators may find it difficult or impos-sible to adapt their own regulations to the many different situations they must address.

We begin by briefly reviewing the dynamics of our current system of electricity regulation, including both a treatment of the problem of identifying system goals and a look at some major stresses on the sys-tem. Following this review, we discuss the economic literature on fiscal federalism and the findings it generates which are relevant to electric-ity regulation. Next, we look at some of the less theoretical, more prag-matic constraints on the regulator's real-world decision processes. We conclude with a summary of the issues and implications of our analy-sis.

THE DYNAMICS OF ELECTRICITY REGULATION

Goals

The social goals of electricity regulation (and implicitly of electric-ity production) are much easier to lay out than to pin down. Electricity regulation poses dire challenges to a regulator. It is a large and critical infrastructure industry, composed of diverse competitive and monopo-listic parts, serving a host of highly differentiated customers and con-stituents across numerous jurisdictional boundaries. Consequently, it attempts to serve a very large number of undifferentiated and diffuse social, economic, and political goals. The end result is an inevitably politicized process, as governments attempt to prioritize among the various, often competing economic and social goals of the system in ways that meet the demands placed on them by their political constit-uents.

Even specifying the social goals can prove difficult. Most would agree that our electricity system should meet standards of economic efficiency, broadly conceived. But agreement on what constitutes efficiency can prove highly elusive. Some participants characterize environmental goals as integral to efficiency (the "externalities" argument), whereas others see such goals as desirable, but more appropriately addressed through other structures. Participants with formal training in economics and public policy may lean toward a more technical definition of efficiency: they might focus on the provision of service to narrowly targeted customers at highly differentiated rates, attempting to equate marginal (social) costs and benefits and to emphasize overall least-cost production. Others emphasize social equity and the protection of politically disadvantaged consumers. Both planners and free marketers want electricity used where it is most socially "desirable," but cannot always agree on how that is to be achieved.

We do not attempt to resolve these disputes here. Indeed, no simple, unique, or universal solution is possible. Instead, let us simply note that under any configuration of goals, certain parties are winners and others are losers. Therefore, the choice of goal is almost always implicitly equivalent to the selection of winners and losers. We cannot expect those affected to stand idly by while regulators introduce technical "fixes" of the regulatory process (such as reallocation of authority among federal levels), if such fixes change their status as winners, nor can we expect current losers to refrain from attempting to influence the change process in ways that allow them to win. This is the reason why regulation is a political act and why any discussion of regulation, especially a discussion of structural changes to the system, must account for explicitly political as well as technical aspects of the regulatory process and its outcomes. It therefore becomes essential that regulators understand not only who will be winners and losers under any proposed change, but also what capabilities these winners and losers possess for political action to modify the proposal.

Stresses on the System

Both the state and the national regulatory systems are responses to the presumed "natural monopoly" aspects of electricity production. Until fairly recently, regulation has been rationalized by the traditional objectives of classical monopoly regulation: ensuring sufficient revenues and profits by deterring the entry of other providers so that firms can continue to produce electricity, while attempting to protect the consumer from potential exploitation by state-defended monopolies (in economics jargon, preventing the "appropriation of consumer surplus," or "minimizing rents"). More recently, we have come to understand that monopoly profits also can be appropriated by other interests, such as environmentalists, conservation promoters, advocates for low-income customers, economic development interests, and so on. Nevertheless, an emphasis on goals of economic efficiency has remained a relative constant. In addition, the last two decades have witnessed sea-changes in the methods perceived as appropriate to regulatory practice, and these changes are rapidly transforming the electricity regulation system. The changes are on two tracks.

In the first, we are moving away from an emphasis on monopoly regulation, and taking the first steps toward deregulation of the generation portion of the industry. Transmission and retail distribution, however, still seem to be natural monopolies. In generation, we are moving toward an emphasis on market forces as the arbiters of social welfare. Here, traditional economic-regulatory concerns, such as rate of return, will become increasingly irrelevant in many states; they will be supplanted by concerns with the design of proper incentive structures, marginal-cost pricing systems, the development of markets for tradable emissions permits, and the like.

The second track in electricity planning involves an increased level of planning within the retail franchised utility. This is almost entirely a result of state policies. To the extent that this process results in better optimization and lower costs, it is entirely consistent with a more broadly competitive market in electricity. But where regulatory planning attempts to incorporate social goals of environmental improvement and redistribution into the mix of utility goals, the stage is set for serious conflict. So far, the two policy tracks being laid in electricity have moved forward fairly independently. They cannot continue to do so indefinitely, however, and the time when the tracks will cross is fast approaching.

Each of these changes in theory, perspective, and eventually practice introduces an element of stress, as incremental changes in discrete portions of the regulatory system introduce tensions within and among regulatory regimes. If we believed that at some point the transition to the market-competitive "new theory" of regulation would be complete, this might not be a cause for great concern. However, the large residual monopoly component in the electricity transmission and distribution system ensures that regulators will not throw out their old industrial organization handbooks any time soon.

These internal struggles are by no means the only sources of stress on the regulatory system; there are also problems from without. Throughout the history of electricity regulation, economic concerns have competed with a number of other, external political issues. Energy policy has important national security components, for example, and also has significant implications for environmental and other social-welfare concerns. Thus, increasing domestic demands that non-economic goals and constraints be factored into regulatory decisions combine with international concerns and potential threats to our energy supply to create a complex maze of strategic, tactical, political, and economic interactions at both the state and national levels.

Given that the "perfect world" of regulation is out of our reach, what can we hope to achieve with the limited understanding and resources that are realistically at our disposal? In terms of goals and stresses, perhaps the principal focus of regulatory efforts should be on identifying and reconciling competing goals for the regulatory system. Since no system can meet every goal, it becomes essential to determine which goals can be met and which of these feasible goals is viewed as most important by the principal constituents of the regulatory process. Here, the political system plays a vital role by aggregating the interests and preferences of a wide range of stakeholders. By providing a framework within which competing values can be prioritized and large-scale disputes over values can be conducted, the political process can offer at least temporary resolutions to the disputes which must be resolved before the more technical process of regulation can function effectively.

THE ECONOMICS OF FEDERALISM: WHERE SHOULD REGULATORY RESPONSIBILITIES BE ALLOCATED?

The economic literature on "fiscal federalism" offers some important insights into the factors and forces that may prove particularly important to regulators as they begin the process of aggregating interests, evaluating priorities, and designing incentives to achieve their system goals. Although much of the work in fiscal federalism concerns issues only vaguely related to our present interests—the design of optimal local tax structures, for example—all work in the field is united by a concern with two major issues that are of great relevance to our topic: the provision of "public goods" via taxation and governmental production, and the elimination or reduction of externalities through the proper assignment of rights and responsibilities among levels of government.

More recently, these two concerns have been joined by two more, both offshoots of research on achieving efficiency in a federal system: the impact of mobility on the attainment of economic efficiency and the importance to outcome predictions of correct specification of the production and consumption functions in empirical and theoretical models of fiscal federalism. These four categories are somewhat artificial, as each of the topics depends on the others in complex ways, but the categorization provides a useful analytical distinction from which to draw policy recommendations. Next, we discuss those aspects of each category which most directly impact the electricity regulatory process, and suggest ways in which the understandings generated in this research may affect regulators' analyses of potential policies and practices.

Public Good Provision and the Role of Government

The role of government in the provision of public goods is arguably the most central question in the fiscal federalism literature. It has had an important impact on at least one major force currently affecting electricity production and regulation: it is one source underpinning the movement toward competitive production of electricity.

Early (pre-1970s) work in fiscal federalism usually proceeded from the assumption that public officials were neutral, technically rational servants of the public good, without any identifiable interests of their own in policy outcomes. The models that resulted from these assumptions produced some fairly cheerful conclusions about the efficiency of governmental provision of goods and services. But beginning in the early 1970s, economists have persuasively argued that public provision of public goods is at best a necessary evil, and that assumptions about the selflessness of public servants are largely indefensible. The tendency of governmental agents to act in their own interests as well as (or instead of) the interests of those they govern has been shown by Niskanen (1975), who concluded that one could explain a great deal about public expenditures simply by assuming that the principal goal of bureaucrats was to maximize their budgets, and by Brennan and Buchanan (1977) who developed the "Leviathan" model of a public sector, which would gradually grow to swallow the private sector completely unless constrained by carefully designed incentives, checks, and balances.[2]

From this perspective, the government retains a legitimate role in providing true public goods, that is, those goods whose characteristics prevent the private sector from producing them at optimal levels through market allocative processes. But the question of how to provide partial, quasi-, or questionable public goods becomes more problematic. Under the pre-1970s assumptions, one could hope for reasonably efficient production of any good assigned to governments for provision, and thus it was good policy to err in favor of providing a suspect or quasi-public good through the public sector, rather than risking inefficient provision by the private markets. Under the newer school of thought and in the cold light of experience, governments are viewed as consistently less-desirable providers of goods and services than are the private markets, and any goods that have some promise for production under market conditions are assumed to be better left to the private sector. Although the new theory was not single-handedly responsible for the move to deregulation in a range of industries in the 1970s and early 1980s, it unquestionably contributed to the broad support such movements enjoyed among economists.[3]

The logic applied to public goods also applies to natural monopolies which, because of their underlying economic dynamics and consequent unique relationship with the government, are subject to many of the same forces that characterize the provision of public goods like police or military services. Until recently, electricity was considered a natural monopoly due to the increasing returns to scale characteristic of electricity production during most of its history. Therefore, it was assigned to the government for detailed oversight via monopoly franchise and pricing regulation. Under the new view of electricity, only transmission and retail distribution systems retain claim to natural monopoly status, while electricity production becomes a potentially competitive industry. As a result, the new theory argues that electricity production should be moved to a fully market-based provision process.

In our view, the current perspective is here to stay. Despite some disenchantment with the outcomes of deregulation, informal opinion within the policy communities still strongly favors a deregulatory approach. The lessons learned by airline and telephone deregulators were not that deregulation does not work, but rather that it was not a panacea. Regulators did learn, however, that partial deregulation was both more difficult to accomplish and more problematic politically than they had anticipated. Their response has been a more careful consideration of the processes of deregulation and an increased sensitivity to the potential need for continued regulation of some subordinate aspects of a largely deregulated industry.

The contemporary approach by regulators in many recently deregulated fields focuses on the persistent non-competitive aspects of the target industry, with the goal of "leveling the playing field" for competition as quickly, and as equitably, as possible. Rather than simply declaring victory and going home, regulators have learned that they must supervise the transition to competition as carefully as they have supervised any of the other major changes that have occurred in their industry over its history. Such supervision typically involves two key elements:

- It focuses on those firms that begin the transition process with disproportionate resources and/or competitive advantages and attempts to permit real competition in order to prevent a situation in which regulated monopolies transform themselves directly into unregulated monopolies.

- It emphasizes incentive structures rather than command-control processes in order to stimulate a market-oriented, incentive-driven philosophy and culture among the firms making the transition.

The second element has the additional virtue of reducing direct regulatory intervention into the newly competitive firms and reducing the temptation of regulators to hold onto authority over such firms any longer than is required.

Allocation of Rights/Responsibilities among Levels of Government

Fiscal federalism offers a theoretically simple prescription for preventing inefficiency in a federal system: simply allocate rights and responsibilities such that all externalities are eliminated; then let the markets rule (Oates 1968 and 1977 are the classic treatises on this subject). In other words, if society must provide a good (like electricity) which produces an external cost (like air pollution), the efficient solution with respect to the externality is to produce the good within a jurisdiction sufficiently large that it encompasses all individuals who experience either the benefits and/or the (direct and indirect) costs of the good.[4] Thus, if air pollution from the Ohio valley causes acid rain in Canada, fiscal federalism argues that one should create a super-jurisdiction encompassing both areas and allocate to this jurisdiction the right and responsibility to set policies relevant to electricity production and air pollution.[5]

According to the theory, for optimal efficiency it is important that each relevant jurisdiction contain a homogeneous citizenry. Citizens must value electricity to roughly the same degree and be offended by acid rain to roughly the same extent, in order that the *collectively* optimal levels of production and pollution are as close as possible to each *individual's* preferred levels. If jurisdictions are highly heterogeneous (which is a persistent problem at the Federal level, as well as within larger states), no single policy is likely to come very close to the ideal preferences of most residents.

Thus, the theory tells us to expect a predictable tradeoff: decentralization produces both increased regulatory efficiency, as smaller jurisdictions allow closer matching of policies to resident preferences, and an increased likelihood of important externalities. In the context of the current debate over state versus Federal regulation of electricity, the optimal tradeoff is uncertain. The states are large enough to contain a great deal of heterogeneity and diversity of preferences among their citizenry. At the same time, they are typically far smaller geographically than the area of incidence of the costs and benefits which accrue from the electricity production and consumption that occurs within their boundaries. The Federal government, by contrast, clearly is large enough to capture most externalities (though the acid rain problem is evidence that such capture is still imperfect). In fact, it is arguably too large for efficient capture of many if not most externalities, which typically affect regions rather than the nation as a whole. Further, the already significant problems with heterogeneous populations at the state level are only magnified at the Federal level. Fiscal federal theory seems to imply that electricity regulation might be most efficiently situated at some jurisdictional level *between* Federal and state, in much the same way that special tax districts at the local level overlap traditional geographic boundaries to provide services such as water, sewer, and special education.

Throughout its history, much of the policy debate around electricity regulation has attempted to answer the question: Are the states capable of optimal regulatory efficiency for electricity? Historically, the answer has been *generally not*, and the Federal government has stepped in to address some of the tradeoffs outlined above. More recently, the Federal government has answered *yes*, and pushed regulatory responsibility onto the states.

But the fiscal federalism literature suggests that the core policy question may need to be restructured. According to fiscal federalism, neither state nor the Federal government is capable of optimal regulation. The states are too small for many of the critical tasks in electricity regulation, and the Federal government too large. But we face a political reality, as Danielson points out elsewhere in this volume, in which states are and will remain an assigned jurisdiction for certain aspects of electricity regulation no matter the technical merits of such assignment. Given the political and technical realities, a better question may be: What can be done to address the limitations of both state-level and Federal regulation in an environment characterized by regional spillover effects and increasing competition?

Other authors in this volume take up this question in more organizational detail; let us simply note here that, according to the insights of fiscal federalism, any efficient answer requires some significant degree of formal or informal supra-state, infra-national coordination and cooperation. According to the theory, when planning and implementing such cooperation, regulators should pay explicit attention to matching the coordinating groups with the geographic distribution of the *specific* costs and benefits under discussion. The theory also suggests that regulators should think flexibly about cooperation. Most cooperative models are broad-spectrum efforts in which a committee from a fixed group of states addresses (more or less as a group) all known externalities regardless of their specific geographical distributions. A more efficient approach might view such bodies as simply providing a forum for the subset of their member states affected by a specific externality to engage in bilateral/ multilateral negotiations as problems arise. In this form, such groups might incorporate non-members for the duration of a specific problem/ negotiation, and few problems would demand the attention of every member.[6]

Mobility and Electricity Regulation

Mobility works to control governmental malfeasance in a fiscal federal system by serving as a proxy for market competition (see Wildasin, 1987, for a review of the literature and a treatment of the major theoretical issues). If governments become too inefficient in the provision of their public goods or attempt to appropriate too much private wealth through taxation, they create incentives for citizens to "vote with their feet" and relocate to another, more efficient or less acquisitive jurisdiction. In market terms, they choose to "buy" their location from another jurisdictional "vendor." This forces each jurisdiction to take every other potentially competitive jurisdiction into account when setting policies. In idealized settings, the pressures of competition among jurisdictions can produce outcomes that are socially optimal in much the same way that perfect competition among firms provides optimal market-allocative efficiency (Tiebout, 1956). When assessing the impact of mobility on a federal issue such as electricity regulation, the essential questions are: How much do jurisdictions compete, and how mobile are citizens?

These are well-studied issues in recent years, with a broad consensus emerging on some key points. To date, the findings indicate both that mobility is surprisingly high, and even relatively low levels of mobility serve as an effective, though not perfect, constraint on opportunistic behavior by governments (see, e.g., Epple and Zelenitz, 1981). Mobility also constrains the ability of governments to pursue redistributive policies.[7] Citizens and firms can move away from jurisdictions that attempt to expropriate their wealth without providing commensurate services.[8] This leads to the pervasive conclusion in the literature that the lower levels of federal systems are not effective at redistribution (e.g., cross-subsidization). Only if the acquisition of the resources to be redistributed occurs at the highest level of the system, so that citizens cannot move away from the jurisdiction to escape expropriation unless they are willing to leave the country altogether, is redistribution a viable policy option.

The degree to which mobility can constrain government opportunism is itself constrained by the amount of competition among states. Here, the findings echo those of monopoly and oligopoly theory: if a jurisdiction is "the only game in town" it has near-absolute power to act as it chooses; if it faces a small number of competitors then it still has the potential to collude and exercise some oligopoly power; but if it faces a large number of similar competitors then competition will almost certainly force it to behave in an efficient or near-efficient fashion.[9]

In a new regulatory order characterized by state-level regulation combined with more open wholesale electric markets, state regulators may find their ability to impose command-control or incentive regulation severely impaired by the impacts of mobility on the firms they regulate. Cross-subsidization is as impossible in a free market for electricity as is redistribution through taxation in a competitive market of local jurisdictions. Furthermore, mobility may extend this impairment of regulatory flexibility into areas that market forces alone would not touch. One can envision major direct electric consumers, for example, cutting deals with state electricity regulatory bodies for favorable regulatory structures (e.g., pricing policies or freedom from demand-side management requirements) in return for plant siting or relocation decisions that bring jobs to the state, and reelection to the state's political leaders.[10] As evidence on "smokestack chasing" attests, the game tends to be economically disastrous for the states once it has begun, but it is nearly impossible for a state's political leadership to avoid playing (see, e.g., Osborne, 1988). Current market (monopoly) structures limit the most egregious forms of this behavior, but increasing competition will open a host of opportunities for enterprising electricity producers and consumers to incite interstate competition on regulatory policies.

The theoretical solution to this problem requires interstate cooperation on a level high enough that the firm inciting competition cannot move outside the collective jurisdiction and stay in business. Whether this is also a practical solution remains to be seen. Unlike more general, proactive cooperation, the smokestack-chasing scenario pits state against state in a zero-sum (some would say negative-sum) game. Further, it tends to activate powerful political constituencies who normally take no interest in electricity policy (e.g., state legislators not usually concerned with electricity regulation), and against whom the regulatory agency has few or no effective political defenses. It seems unlikely that informal interstate cooperation would be able to survive a highly charged version of this game, and even formal cooperative bodies with clearly delegated powers of regulation might find themselves undermined from within.

Thus, mobility offers at least two insights for regulators interested in shaping the future course of their agencies and activities. On a strategic level, it suggests that regulators should give careful consideration to questions concerning the nature and direction of competition among the various producers and consumers of electricity under their purview. Once such constituencies and "markets" are identified, regulators should weigh them explicitly in considering what levels of regulatory constraint are feasible and which types of regulatory processes are effective in attaining their system goals. Generally, the more "competitive" a market (i.e., the more mobile a constituency and/or the more nearby and similar the state's or firm's competitors), the less effective and desirable will be any form of regulation. If the state (or the firm) retains some monopoly or oligopoly power in a specific geographic area or market segment, then command-control regulation may function effectively (though regulators may wish for reasons of consistency to eliminate such regulation even where it remains technically feasible); otherwise, market-based incentive structures may be the only effective weapons at the regulator's disposal.

The Specification of Production and Consumption Functions

As already noted while discussing system goals, virtually everyone agrees that economic efficiency, broadly conceived, should underlie any responsible system of electricity regulation. But how can one be certain that one has, in fact, developed a model that will incorporate a broad enough conception of efficiency to serve the needs of regulators or the general public? The vast majority of theoretical models of fiscal federalism are traditional, highly abstracted simplifications designed more for mathematical tractability than for real-world applicability. For the purposes of understanding incremental changes in an equilibrium situation, such abstractions are both necessary and appropriate. But as some authors have pointed out (Oates, 1991), consumption functions which hold no place for clean air or water, or for recreation —or production functions that incorporate labor, capital, and land as inputs but do not address pollution as an output—omit factors so critical to the determination of a true, socially optimal production level that one cannot plausibly claim to have even approximated optimality in their absence.

In one sense, this concern is simply the argument, elaborated earlier in the chapter, that failure to address externalities leads to inefficiency. But where that argument focused on jurisdictional solutions to the dilemma, this version focuses on more technical solutions. Unfortunately, the word "solutions" may be too strong: it is not clear that any single solution to this problem exists either in theory or in practice.

Certainly, regulators can develop procedures to ensure that all known outputs and inputs are incorporated into the planning process, and they can structure incentives in electricity markets to encourage firms and consumers to take account of externalities in their individual economic decisions. Integrated resource planning is one obvious attempt to pursue at least the first part of this approach. But regulators and planners can only incorporate those inputs and outputs which are sanctioned by their authorizing legislatures and/or governors, and ultimately by the citizenry of their state. Since public acceptance of and mobilization around, for example, an environmental threat tends to lag significantly behind its recognition in the technical community, and since investor-owned, profit-motivated firms will naturally and rightly resist the imposition of additional taxes or restrictions as long and as vociferously as possible, it becomes patently unreasonable to expect a close approximation to efficiency from any politicized system of regulation.

At present the direction of bias in the real-world regulatory system is uncertain.[11] But as the regulatory system moves toward market-based incentive processes and away from the command-control structures that permit sunk cost recovery, the tendency toward underpricing may grow stronger. It can be counteracted only by aggressive efforts on the part of regulators to ensure that external costs are incorporated into the market structure (e.g., through tradable emissions permits), and there are no simple or easy rules to tell regulators when they have included all relevant external costs.

To reiterate an earlier point, when pricing departs from the social optimum (e.g., the choice to include/exclude certain disputed external costs in the social welfare calculation), regulators end up choosing winners and losers. Whether the winners will be those who incur the external costs (e.g., pollution sufferers after tradable emissions permits) or those who accrue the benefits (producers and consumers without permits) will be a political, not a technical decision. But technical merit is not irrelevant in a political contest, as the move toward deregulation itself testifies. If regulators and planners work to craft regulatory policies that both function within the market environment (e.g., tradable emissions permits) and accurately incorporate as full a range as possible of the external social costs and benefits, they will have done all they can toward producing a socially optimal outcome. The rest of the job will lie with the political will and wisdom of those who oversee them and the constituents they serve.

BEYOND FISCAL FEDERALISM

The preceding section attempted to identify insights to be gained from a fairly theoretical literature in economics. Although these insights are certainly valuable, we suggest that they are not sufficient to address all of the concerns regulators are likely to face in our changing environment. In the allocation of responsibilities to a specific governmental level, for example, the fiscal federalism literature emphasized the efficiency tradeoffs of allocating regulatory responsibilities to higher and lower levels of the Federal system. But astute policymakers and regulators will certainly want to consider a range of other issues as well, as they seek to establish the appropriate jurisdictional level for various aspects of electricity regulation. Let us suggest at least three reasons why a state (for example) might reach a conclusion about appropriate allocation that differs from the one predicted by fiscal federalism theory.

First, the state might observe a comparative advantage to one level over another in the gathering of information critical to the regulatory process. Fiscal federalism theory generally assumes that all actors possess perfect (usually costless) information on all aspects of the production and regulation process. In reality, of course, access to information differs systematically along a variety of dimensions. Much access ultimately depends on the government's legal powers of discovery and coercion, which suggests that state or national actors—or their formally delegated proxies—might have informational advantages over informal cooperative or coordinating bodies. But decisions about comparative information advantages should not be made from a short-term perspective: technical expertise and special knowledge tend to flow over time to the loci of power and authority. Thus, even a coordinating body, if delegated sufficient discovery powers, will most likely develop over time the expertise necessary to evaluate the information that it is enabled to acquire. Given the advantages of supra-state cooperation, it may be preferable to accept the short-run loss of informational efficiency entailed by transferring some discovery and monitoring powers from the state-based agency to the supra-state agency.

Of course, such decisions are not mere technical abstractions. Before delegating power to a supra-state agency, it would be wise to be confident that the state's other political institutions (including the state's regulatory agency) will honor that delegation. If the coordinating body is continually challenged and thwarted by the state's legislature and regulatory agency, it makes little sense to delegate to the outside body. Situation-specific political dynamics will undoubtedly dominate this aspect of the decision process.

Second, the state or Federal government might value diversity and experimentation for its own sake. This has been a recurrent theme in the recent literature on deregulation and the new federalism: phrases like "laboratories of democracy" are frequently bandied about.[12] Political rhetoric aside, it is not clear that decentralization equals experimentation in any strong or direct fashion: some states simply replicate Federal ossification on a smaller scale. Further, with regard to the specific case of electricity, we face once again the fact that a number of electricity systems cross state borders. It is not at all clear that the "laboratories" logic applies when a host of states "experiment" on a single electricity producer. In fact, the likely outcomes— regulatory inconsistencies among states, a consequent overburden on the producer, and so on—are exactly the eventualities and "regulatory externalities" that current efforts at cooperation are intended to reduce or prevent. Still, the movement toward regulatory decentralization maintains some promise of fostering innovation, or at least tailoring policies to specific situations. The successful development of regional transmission groups would be a good example of the benefits this strategy might someday provide.

Finally, the state or nation might be concerned about the possibility of regulatory "capture." Although there is a large literature on capture (Stigler, 1971, is the cornerstone), its conclusions offer no easy guidance in resolving the question of which level of government is least susceptible to undue influence. Part of the problem lies in defining the relevant political groups: do electricity producers struggle against all consumers for control of the regulatory agency, or with commercial customers against residential customers, or against state regulators directly? Or are some few producers so dominant that they can capture the agency, not only from consumers, but from all other producers as well? Are electricity producers so homogeneous that what benefits the Tennessee Valley Authority (TVA) also benefits a mom-and-pop co-generator? The answer to the last question may be *no* for most eventualities, but for electric power, the answers to all of the questions are clearly issue and situation specific.

Moving from the Federal to the state (or supra-state) level changes all of these configurations and potentialities for capture, but it does not change them in any clear and uniform direction. Regional differences apply (due to systematic differences in energy sources, size and configuration of producers and consumers, etc.), and intra-regional differences may apply as well, in, for example, the homogeneity of the population with respect to issues such as the desired percentage of production from nuclear power. Since decentralization is already underway, the question of whether it is a good idea from the capture perspective is moot. Still, capture theory suggests some important concerns for state regulators and officials attempting to honor the public trust by ensuring a level playing field for all stakeholders in the electricity regulation process. As states attempt to design new or changed regulatory regimes, for example, they may wish to pay close attention to balancing constituencies in the regulatory process in such a way that information flows to the regulatory entity are free, full, cross-checked, and consequently more likely to be unbiased. Such attention to proper design, we submit, will be rewarded by the creation of a more equitable, more credible regulatory system.

CONCLUSIONS

There are, of course, other factors than the ones mentioned here that regulators should consider carefully when formulating regulatory policy for the new electricity environment. But we hope that at least four central points from this chapter are clear. First, fiscal federalism provides a large, well-developed body of literature with which to address the core concerns of electricity regulation. It is particularly helpful in identifying key aspects of jurisdiction, allocation of authority, mobility, and the sensitivity of planning to assumptions about inputs and outputs. But it is by no means the only body of literature, even in economics, to address concerns of relevance to the new theory of electricity regulation, nor is it alone sufficient to the design of adequate regulatory structures and processes.

Second, the political process is a valuable as well as an inescapable part of the dynamics of forthcoming regulatory change. Political systems aggregate multitudes of individual values and priorities in an authoritative way and provide regulators with essential guidance in choosing among competing goals, values, and approaches for the regulatory process. This benefit does not accrue without cost, however; political systems allow winners and losers in regulatory reform a venue from which to attempt to change the rules of the game in their favor. "In politics," the aphorism says, "nothing is ever resolved; instead, it is 're-solved' over and over again." Astute regulatory designers must take into account not only present political configurations, but also the political lessons of the past and the probable political trends of the future (including the configurations that regulatory reform itself will produce), if their efforts are to meet with long-term success.

Third, the technically efficient allocation of regulatory authority within the federal system is at best difficult, and perhaps effectively impossible. The best hope for technical efficiency in regulation lies at some supra-state level, in the form of informal or formal cooperation/coordination. But the political realities of state control over the regulatory process, political constraints on the abilities of states to enter into long-term cooperative relationships, and constitutional limitations (in some states) on the abilities of states to delegate power or authority outside their borders all work to make interstate cooperation difficult. Perhaps the best hope lies in the proliferation of early, creative efforts at informal cooperation. The successes among these early efforts can be extended incrementally into more formalized regimes as circumstances demand and public acceptance permits.

Finally, and most importantly, there exists no single set of ideas or of research that can provide the regulator with the tools necessary to predict the future of electricity regulation and meet it adequately. Our efforts here only skim the surface of the issues, yet we draw on research from at least three distinct schools of economic thought as well as studies from political science and organization theory. Similarly, there is no single solution that will fit every situation. Instead, regulators must proceed cautiously: weighing evidence from a number of sources, encouraging market forces where feasible, protecting consumers and smaller producers where necessary, eliminating artificial bumps in the playing field at every opportunity, and remaining sensitive to the particular sets of goals and priorities that characterize the citizens they serve.

NOTES

1.   For clarity in this work, we use "federal" to refer to the system of distributed and shared authority characteristic of the United States and several other governments around the world. The capitalized "Federal" refers solely to the U.S. national government.

2.   Such models have been contested by scholars outside of economics as excessively cynical. John DiIulio (1993) for example, notes that organizational

cultures, professional socialization, and a range of other norms act to produce
"principled agents"; that is, they constrain the tendency of governmental
agents to "shirk" their public duty by providing reinforcing norms of duty, professional obligation, agency mission, and the like. But even these scholars
argue that such forces serve at most to *reduce* the tendency of public servants
to pursue their own interests—they do not eliminate shirking altogether. One
need not consider bureaucrats to be evil in order to recognize that they hold
strong economic and psychological investments in their agencies and their
careers, and tend to resist the attenuation of their authority. Note the com-
plaint, elsewhere in this volume, that Federal regulators continue to use their
authority to overrule state-level regulatory innovations and other decisions
that states (at least nominally) are responsible for making. In the case of electricity deregulation, the resistance of Federal regulators is undoubtedly
strengthened by their recognition that blanket delegation of agency authority
to the states is not a technically optimal move. But it remains, nonetheless, an
example of what this literature would call "shirking."

3.   For a useful discussion of the role of ideas in stimulating regulatory
change, specifically the spate of Federal deregulation decisions in the 1970s,
see Derthick and Quirk (1985). Quirk (1988) is a journal-length treatment of
the same subject.

4.   Policy issues focus overwhelmingly on negative externalities, such
as air pollution. But the reasons for this focus are political, not technical: positive externalities are equally legitimate concerns when evaluating the technical efficiency of an economic system. Reliability, for example, might be
conceptualized as a positive externality; other authors in this volume argue
that its spillover benefits may not be fully appreciated until they are lost to
deregulation and a consequent degradation of service quality.

5.   Since a systematic application of this principle would lead to an infi-
nite number of overlapping jurisdictions, a more pragmatic vein in the same
literature argues that one should factor the costs and benefits of electricity
production in both the Ohio valley and Canada into one's production and consumption functions and thus "automatically" attain the socially efficient levels
of electricity production and environmental degradation. Tradable emissions
permits are one of the policy manifestations of this theoretic approach.

6.   An entire economics literature on the theory of organization
addresses the potential efficiencies of such "relational contracting" as compared to more rigid or less routinized forms of interaction. Oliver Williamson's
The Economic Institutions of Capitalism (New York: Basic Books, 1985) provides the best and most comprehensive introduction to the efficiency issues.

7.   Typically, the empirical literature looks at social security funding or
assistance to families with dependent children (AFDC), but the principles
apply just as well to cross-subsidization in electricity policy. Johnson (1988) is
one treatment among many of the redistribution issues.

8.   See, for example, Greenwood and Hunt (1984) and Day (1992).
"Mobility" in this sense may seem to be implausible: How many of us have
ever moved because of a change in tax policy or local service levels? But the

more accurate conception recognizes that there is a relatively high level of "structural" mobility in the U.S. economy—many people move every year, for a wide variety of reasons. When choosing a new location, the empirical literature demonstrates persuasively that people pay attention to both taxation and service provision (e.g., families choosing locations with good schools; retirees seeking low crime rates, both groups wanting low property and income taxes, etc.). These people do not move *because* of government policy change, but they factor policies into their decisions once they decide to move for other reasons. Governments are thus forced to pay attention to the consequences of their policies lest they experience net out-migration. The fiscal federal model itself is agnostic on the subject of individual motives: as long as individuals are sensitive to fiscal policies as part of their relocation decisions, the policies need not directly stimulate mobility—the model still holds.

9.   When considering issues of mobility and competition, it is important to remember that proximity alone is no measure of competitiveness. Although the literature typically abstracts away from specific policy areas, it is obvious that issue specificity also matters. From a state perspective, for example, Connecticut and New Jersey may be competitors for housing the bedroom commuter from New York City. But they are in no meaningful sense competitors for electric power distribution, and peculiarities of transmission siting may make them non-competitors in electricity production as well. Large electrical consumers located in New Jersey may thus gain no necessary benefits from innovations developed in Connecticut.

10. The scenario is more often discussed in terms of states exercising monopoly powers over firms wishing to locate within their borders, but the logic is fully symmetrical. See, for example, Kolstad and Wolak (1983) on strategic, predatory tax behavior among Western coal states.

11. Since the majority of externalities of any policy significance are negative, and since the vast majority of all new discoveries of policy externalities are negative, we can state with some confidence that the market will usually miss efficiency in the direction of overprovision and/or underpricing of electricity. But this should not necessarily be taken to imply that today's real-world electricity price is too low. For example, the real-world regulatory system permits firms to recover sunk costs; such costs can easily exceed forward-looking (total social) costs, and consequently increase the price of electricity above the efficient social optimum.

12. The phrase was originally popularized by Osborne (1988).

REFERENCES

Brennan, G., and J. M. Buchanan. "Towards a Tax Constitution for Leviathan." *Journal of Public Economics* 9 (Fall, 1977): 301–318.

Day, K. M. "Interprovincial Migration and Local Public Goods." *Canadian Journal of Economics* 25 (February, 1992): 123–144.

Derthick, M., and P. J. Quirk. *The Politics of Deregulation*. Washington, DC: The Brookings Institution, 1985.

DiIulio, J. "Principled Agents." Unpublished manuscript, 1993.

Epple, D., and A. Zelenitz. "The Implications of Competition among Jurisdictions: Does Tiebout Need Politics?" *Journal of Political Economy* 89 (December, 1981): 1197–1217.

Greenwood, M. J., and G. L. Hunt. "Migration and Interregional Employment Distribution in the United States." *American Economic Review* 74 (December, 1984): 957–969.

Johnson, W. R. "Income Redistribution in a Federal System." *American Economic Review* 78 (June, 1988): 570–573.

Kolstad, C. D., and F. J. Wolak. "Competition in Interregional Taxation: The Case of Western Coal." *Journal of Political Economy* 91 (June, 1983): 443–460.

Niskanen, W. A. "Bureaucrats and Politicians." *Journal of Law and Economics* 18 (December, 1975): 617–643.

Oates, W. E. "The Theory of Public Finance in a Federal System." *Canadian Journal of Economics* 1 (February, 1968): 37–54.

Oates, W. E. *The Political Economy of Fiscal Federalism*. Lexington, MA: Heath-Lexington, 1977.

Oates, W. E. *Studies in Fiscal Federalism*. Brookfield, VT: E. Elgar Publishing Co., 1991.

Osborne, D. *Laboratories of Democracy*. Boston: Harvard Business School Press, 1988.

Quirk, P. J. "The Politics of Ideas." *Journal of Politics* 50 (February, 1988): 31–41.

Stigler, G. "The Theory of Economic Regulation." *Bell Journal of Economics and Management Science* 1 (Spring, 1971): 3–21.

Tiebout, C. "A Pure Theory of Local Expenditures." *Journal of Political Economy* 64 (October, 1956): 416–424.

Wildasin, D. E. "Theoretical Analysis of Local Public Economics." Chapter 29 in E. S. Mills (ed.), *Handbook of Urban and Regional Economics,* vol. II. Amsterdam: Elsevier Science Publishers, 1987.

Williamson, O. E. *The Economic Institutions of Capitalism*. New York: Free Press, 1985.

6

Planning versus Competition and Incentives: Conflicts, Complements, or Evolution?

Kenneth Rose

State and federal regulators have a variety of options for overseeing electric utility decision making. This chapter characterizes and compares traditional, planning-based, and market-based approaches.

INTRODUCTION AND BACKGROUND

There is little doubt that the structure of the future electric services industry will be significantly different than that of two decades ago or, most likely, even today. The current structure and regulation of the industry can at best be described as being in a state of transition; that is, from vertically integrated electric utilities that are cost-of-service regulated to more market- and incentive-based arrangements. Examples include competitive bidding in generation, market-based rates for wholesale power now being used by the Federal Energy Regulatory Commission (FERC), and the national allowance trading program created by the Clean Air Act Amendments of 1990 to reduce and limit sulfur dioxide (SO_2) emissions in environmental regulation of the industry.

The industry's structure and its federal and state regulation remained unchanged from what was established at the time the Public Utilities Holding Company Act of 1935 (PUHCA) was enacted by Congress until the early 1970s. The 1970s, however, proved to be a watershed period for the industry. The period began with sharply rising energy costs in the early part of the decade, progressed through higher capital costs, and ended with a leveling out of demand for electricity. Disallowances of power-plant capital costs (mainly nuclear, which continued into the 1980s) and calls for regulatory reform were the results.

The federal response to the rising fuel costs and concerns about fuel supply availability (primarily oil) began with the Public Utility Regulatory Policies Act of 1978 (PURPA). PURPA and resulting FERC rule making encouraged cogeneration and small power production of electricity by creating a new category of power producer, the qualifying facility (QF). States were required to establish "avoided-cost" rates for power purchased from QFs by utilities. Originally, states determined avoided-cost rates based on the incremental cost of power of the utility, calculating a separate rate for capacity and energy costs "avoided" because of the QF.

THE STATE RESPONSE

In 1985, states, starting with Maine, began to use competitive bidding as a means to determine avoided-cost rates and find lower-cost sources of generation. Although some state and utility competitive bidding programs remain limited to QFs only, many now permit other non-utility power producers.[1] Also at this time, some states turned to incentive mechanisms to encourage cost control,[2] and FERC began using market-based pricing to determine some wholesale power rates.[3] In general, these approaches can be characterized as market- or incentive-based approaches.

Also in response to the 1970s tumult, state public utility commissions became more involved in the forecasting and planning process of regulated utilities. This was the beginning of a second path to regulatory reform that runs parallel to, but distinct from, the increased use of markets in utility regulation. Currently, over half the states now use what has become known as integrated resource planning (IRP). Generally, this approach can be characterized as a planning approach.

Often the two newer approaches are intertwined in the IRP process; for example, competitive bidding is often conducted within an IRP process. Traditional cost-of-service rate regulation, however, has remained as the predominant form of rate regulation for electric utilities. As a result, at this time, many public utility commissions employ some combination of the three regulatory approaches; for example, cost-of-service rate regulation (traditional) with an IRP process (planning) and, in some cases, competitive bidding and performance incentive mechanisms for some power plants (competitive/incentives).

The most recent federal legislation aimed at the electric service industry, the Energy Policy Act of 1992 (EPAct), embodies both of these newer regulatory approaches that public utility commissions have been considering and utilizing in recent years. Title I of EPAct requires commissions to consider adopting a planning-type regulatory approach, whereas Title VII promotes changes to the industry that will significantly alter its structure and increase competition. Specifically, Title I amends section 111 of PURPA and requires states to consider

- requiring utilities to adopt integrated resource planning;
- allowing investments in conservation and demand-side management (DSM) to be at least as profitable as supply-side resources; and
- encouraging utilities to make investments and expenditures for improvements in power generation, transmission, and distribution.

State commissions can, after some consideration, accept or reject any or all three.

Title VII of EPAct, on the other hand,

- creates exempt wholesale generators (EWGs) that are exempt from provisions of PUHCA and
- provides FERC with broad authority to require more open access to utility transmission.

Both of these changes are designed to encourage more competition in electricity generation and supply. Although many details of Title VII's implementation will be determined by FERC and are beyond the control of the states, there are several consequential issues that states will have to resolve. These include whether to allow retail wheeling and the best way (if at all) to foster a more competitive generation sector.

It was not until fairly recently that some involved with the electric services industry began to recognize a possible inherent conflict between the two newer approaches.[4] This has occurred primarily because some regulators and utilities have realized that commissions cannot continue to be involved, sometimes heavily, in the planning or decision-making of electric utilities and then expect the same utilities to behave as nimble competitors in bulk power markets and in supplying generation capacity within their own service territory.

THREE REGULATORY APPROACHES

Both the planning and competitive/incentives approaches evolved, in part, as a response to the perceived limitations of traditional regulation of electric utilities, which became apparent to many during the events of the 1970s and early 1980s noted above. These limitations include a lack of incentive for utilities to minimize operating costs, conduct careful long-range planning for new sources of supply, adopt innovative techniques (for example, in supply or demand resource planning and environmental compliance), and pursue opportunities to reduce demand.[5]

Although both of the relatively new approaches to regulation have been evolving simultaneously for the last ten or fifteen years and in response to the same conditions, they do have somewhat different goals and objectives. The planning approach's emphasis is on the planning process, including: how electricity demand will be supplied or reduced, the range of resources considered and the criteria for their evaluation, forecasting methods, and participation by the public in the process. The market or incentives approach, in contrast, emphasizes economic efficiency, rate impacts, incentives for the utility to minimize its costs, and the administrative resources required for implementation. Both of the newer approaches are concerned, of course, with all of these considerations in one way or another. However, the differences lie in where the emphasis is placed and the degree of the commission's involvement in the planning decisions of the regulated utility.

All three regulatory approaches are used to address major regulatory problems such as ratemaking, adding capacity, environmental control, and so on. Table 6.1 outlines major regulatory issues and the means of addressing them under the three different approaches. Each approach is sufficiently developed so that a distinct means of addressing each issue is available. Not all means described are widely used in electric utility regulation. For example, price caps and deregulation of competitive services have become common in telecommunications (Davis, 1993) but are only now beginning to be suggested for electric utilities (Rose, 1992; Lowry, 1991).

WHICH REGULATORY APPROACH IS BEST SUITED FOR THE FUTURE?

Will traditional regulatory processes be able to cope with the changes occurring in the industry and take full advantage of competitive opportunities? If not, which of the alternative regulatory approaches is best suited for the future? As noted, many commissions currently use a combination of traditional, planning, and competition/ incentives. However, because of the increasing level of competition in the industry, which EPAct will likely accelerate, commissions will need to address the advantages and disadvantages of each approach for specific issues as well as determine which alternative is the appropriate response overall. Table 6.2 outlines the advantages and disadvantages of the different regulatory approaches.

Traditional Approach

The traditional regulatory approach, or cost-of-service approach, is probably the best known of the three. It is characterized by ratebase/rate-of-return regulation, with utility decisions subject to review by the commission after-the-fact. Both state and federal regulators have used and are currently using this cost-based approach extensively.

Traditional ratebase/rate-of-return regulation of electric utilities has held sway as the leading state regulatory paradigm since the 1920s. Traditional approaches may be favored, therefore, because there is an existing and well-known infrastructure. Another possible advantage is that the short-term outcome is known in advance.[6]

Criticism of this approach began with the seminal article by Averch and Johnson[7] in 1962 and increased in the 1970s and early 1980s when sharply rising fuel prices, capital costs, and excess capacity resulted in higher rates to customers.[8] As a result, utility regulators began to consider improvements in or alternatives to the traditional approach.

As noted, a significant and often cited limitation to this approach is that it provides inadequate incentives to a utility to minimize cost. Advocates of the planning approach also note that the traditional approach does not consider external social costs. It has been argued by some[9] that after-the-fact prudence reviews are unfair because they are sometimes applied asymmetrically; that is, if a utility makes a decision that turns out in hindsight to be a bad one, the utility suffers a loss; if, on the other hand, the utility's decision is a good one it can only retain up to its allowed rate of return.[10]

Planning Approach

Advocates for a planning approach stress the need to consider the social costs or externalities that are associated with electricity production. Because, they believe, markets cannot solve these problems alone, state and federal regulators must intervene to see that these factors are considered. As a result, this approach often includes removing disincentives for utilities to invest in DSM programs, incorporating into the planning process environmental "externality" considerations,[11] and increasing the level of public participation. In

Table 6.1.
Regulatory Issues and Three Regulatory Approaches to Address Them

Regulatory Issues	Traditional	Planning	Markets/Incentives
Ratemaking	• ratebase or rate-of-return regulation • past or future test year to determine revenue requirement	• generally, same as traditional, but modified to encourage (or not discourage) utility demand-side management (DSM) programs • modifications include uncoupling utility rates from sales, compensating utilities for lost revenue, allowing a higher rate-of-return for DSM investment in rate base, and sharing the savings	• price caps • retrospective ratemaking for some performance-type incentives • revenue sharing • deregulation of competitive services
Capacity Additions	• utility capacity ratebased • purchased power costs passed through to ratepayers	• supply resources considered simultaneously with demand resources	• competitive bidding • incentives for purchased power
Environmental Control	• command-and-control • implemented by environmental regulators	• environmental externalities considered in planning for new resources • quantitative ("adders") or qualitative • implemented by public utility commissions	• emission trading • emissions taxes • hybrid systems of both trading and taxes • implemented by environmental regulators

Demand-Side Management	• voluntary utility programs (but little incentive for utility to consider)	• supply and demand resources considered together in planning • specific incentives or removal of disincentives for DSM investments or both	• customer and utility discretion • utility may offer programs voluntarily
Commission Review	• prudence or retrospective reviews	• preapproval or prior approval of utility plan often used	• commission monitoring of competitive bidding process and incentive programs
Wholesale Customer Options	• captive of utility • no choice of supplier • options are purchase, self-generate, or conservation	• captive of utility • choice of energy demand-management provider	• can access other suppliers • retail wheeling • conservation at customer discretion
Retail Customer Options	• captive of utility • no choice of supplier • options are purchase or conservation	• captive of utility • choice of energy demand-management provider	• can access other suppliers • retail wheeling • conservation at customer discretion
Transmission Pricing	• embedded-cost pricing	• regional plan, if considered • cost-based pricing	• market-based or incentive pricing
Transmission Access	• voluntary	• regional plan, if considered • voluntary	• access may be required • retail wheeling
Bulk Power Rates	• cost-based	• may be provisions for buying and selling power in regional plan • cost-based	• market-based when competition is demonstrated

Table 6.2
Advantages and Disadvantages of the Regulatory Approaches

	Traditional	Planning	Markets/Incentives
Advantages	• existing or well-known infrastructure • short-term outcome is known in advance	• increases public participation • provides a means to include social costs • provides a basis for improved planning	• can encourage cost-minimizing behavior • lower costs to ratepayers • lower administrative costs
Disadvantages	• perceived to provide inadequate incentives to utility to minimize cost • does not consider external social costs and benefits • prudence reviews considered unfair by some	• process has become cumbersome in some states • may still provide inadequate incentives to minimize cost • conservation savings have not been as expected, and cost may be higher than expected in some cases • treatment of environmental externalities is subjective and can be costly • may be incompatible with competitive markets	• skepticism about competitive markets developing • fear of market power and self-dealing • incentives thought to be a bribe to the utility for doing what it should be doing • possible unanticipated results • possible cross-subsidization

the mid-1970s, some states, beginning with California and Wisconsin, became more involved in the demand forecasts and other planning processes of utilities and began to use what has become known as least-cost planning or IRP.

The distinguishing feature of planning approaches across states is the varying level of commission involvement in the utility's decision-making process. Some states prefer to only review a plan submitted by a utility with no commitment from the commission as to the future rate-making treatment of resources in the plan. At the opposite end of the spectrum are states that prescribe detailed rules for utilities to follow and either approve the overall plan or, in the most extreme cases, approve specific details of a plan such as expenditures.

This approach is very process oriented, and often the development of the process itself requires a considerable expenditure of resources for all parties involved. Critics note that this process has become cumbersome in some states. It requires considerable time and effort by commission staff to review the substantial amount of information filed by utilities as well as the comments from third parties. The information required by the commission is directly proportional to the level of prior review from the commission: the more up-front the review, the more information required.[12]

This information requirement can make the process inflexible and difficult for utilities to respond to more dexterous competitors which are not faced with the same regulatory responsibilities. This lack of flexibility may be the planning approach's most significant drawback in a more competitive environment. Planning advocates argue that the process can be made more flexible. However, state experience in recent years has shown that the process can proceed for one to two years (or more if a particularly contentious issue is involved), generate thousands of pages of testimony and commission staff and intervener reports, and, as a result, require all involved parties to incur significant direct monetary expenses.

Once a utility has successfully negotiated the planning process it is unlikely to return to the commission afterward to modify the plan in response to changing economic conditions or other critical assumptions. Commissions, of course, can require some change, but this depends on the commission having and maintaining the same level of information and analytical ability as the utility to recognize when change is needed.

Ratemaking under the planning approach is still, with some modifications, the same as the traditional approach; that is, rate-base, rate-of-return regulation. This, of course, may still not provide a utility with an economic signal to minimize its cost. In addition, another serious drawback to pre-approval of a plan is that, to the extent a commission guarantees recovery of a utility's cost, pre-approval reduces further the utility's incentive to minimize cost.[13] If there is pre-approval of a plan, therefore, not only does it fail to solve the problem of lack of incentive to minimize cost associated with traditional regulation, but it may intensify the problem.

The ratemaking modifications to traditional regulation that have occurred under the planning approach, primarily to encourage conservation investment, are themselves under attack from critics who believe the savings from DSM programs have been less than expected (NERA, 1992, 1993) and costs may actually be higher than reported (Joskow and Marron, 1992).

As noted, a goal of the planning approach is to correct the problem of non-market considerations, primarily environmental externalities. Supporters of public utility commission consideration of environmental externalities point out that current federal and state legislation may not take adequate consideration of local environmental conditions. Also, currently there is no restriction on some greenhouse gas emissions such as carbon dioxide (CO_2). The proponents have argued that public utility commissions, which are charged with protecting the public interest, should consider the environmental damages that result, or could result, during the entire fuel cycle (NARUC, 1993). This includes the mining of coal, the disposal of nuclear waste, the transportation of natural gas, and the emissions of greenhouse gases.

Critics of these commission considerations, however, believe that environmental regulation is best conducted at the federal level or by the environmental authority at the state level.[14] This diminishes the problem of utilities avoiding those jurisdictions having more stringent environmental regulations and locating in areas where there are fewer environmental restrictions, but perhaps at a higher overall cost. This will become more critical as competition increases in the industry because unregulated suppliers may have an advantage over regulated utilities when the commission requires utilities to consider externalities, but has no authority over unregulated sources. Restrictions at the federal level by environmental authorities applied to all suppliers— existing, as well as new sources—would avoid these problems.

Another point critics make concerning environmental externality consideration by state commissions is that there are other sources of pollution and other environmental damage that can be reduced (or reduced further) at a lower cost than in the already regulated electric utility industry, such as the transportation sector (e.g., Joskow, 1992). The Clean Air Act and its amendments and state legislation have already, in effect, internalized much (but perhaps not all) of the environmental externalities from electric power production.[15] Moreover, the critics also note that, as commissions only control the selection of new resources, this policy may inadvertently be giving utilities an incentive to keep older, less-efficient, and more-polluting plants in operation.[16] As a result, these policies may actually have a negative, albeit unintentional, impact on environmental quality.

Finally, the use by commissions of environmental "adders" in the IRP process are criticized because of the difficulty in establishing precise numbers for the value of the externalities. These numbers are, they argue, often arbitrary and not a reflection of the actual cost to society. Moreover, these additional costs can distort the price of electricity, creating an additional burden for ratepayers that exceeds the benefit to the environment.

Markets and Incentives Approach

Advocates of increased use of markets and incentive regulation often point out the efficiency gains and lower rates which should result from their increased use.[17]

Passage of PURPA in 1978 and subsequent FERC rule making allowed QFs that were cogenerators (facilities that simultaneously generate electrical and thermal energy) and small power producers that use certain resources (solar, wind, biomass, and geothermal) to interconnect and either receive back-up power at non-discriminatory rates or sell power back to an electric utility at the utility's avoided cost. Although the original intent of PURPA was to conserve energy, events subsequent to the passage of PURPA have demonstrated that competition is possible and potentially beneficial.

Markets are now being used by state and federal regulators that permit competition where traditionally it was prevented, such as in generation with competitive bidding or in transmission with more open access. In addition, regulators are creating new markets which did not exist previously. For example, markets have been created for environmental protection that internalize external social costs through emissions-trading programs, such as the national SO_2 allowance trading system created by the Clean Air Act Amendments of 1990.

Regulatory incentives can be used when the existing markets are not sufficiently competitive or cannot be created. In the electric utility industry, performance standards (for example, rewarding a utility for capacity-factor or heat-rate improvement at a power facility) have been the most common type of incentive used. These performance standards usually employ a benchmark to judge utility performance, based on a target set by the commission, or an industry index or average. When a utility is able to outperform the benchmark, it is rewarded with, for example, a higher rate of return. If, on the other hand, it falls short of the target, it may be penalized in some way. Overall productivity measures, or yardstick incentives, have been discussed as a means to provide an incentive to improve a utility's overall performance (Diewert, 1992). Price caps, as noted earlier, are used extensively in telecommunications regulation and may have some application in the electric industry as well,[18] such as for pricing transmission service.

By one survey, approximately thirty states now use some type of incentive mechanism for electric utility regulation (NERA, 1985). These mechanisms include incentives to encourage investment in DSM programs[19] and incentives to minimize operating costs, such as power plant performance or benchmark standards.

As noted, the primary advantage to using competitive markets is that it encourages utilities to minimize their costs. There is more motivation for the utility to control costs and innovate since it retains part or all of the profit from good decisions or incurs the loss from faulty ones. As with unregulated firms, utilities which are unable to compete with others will lose market share to the lower-cost suppliers. This should result in lower costs to ratepayers and lower administrative costs to commissions.

Incentive programs can also encourage cost-minimizing behavior by rewarding utilities for good performance or penalizing them for unsatisfactory performance. There is evidence that utilities do respond to incentive mechanisms. For example, the over 1,300 individual DSM programs nationwide can largely be attributed to the recent increased use of incentives by commissions to encourage utilities to adopt DSM measures.[20] Also, there is some evidence to suggest that the use of price-cap regulation in the telecommunications industry has resulted in significantly lower customer prices.[21]

Some, however, are skeptical about competitive markets developing in either bulk power markets or for supplying capacity in the utility's service territory. They argue that, although there may be competitors, this does not necessarily mean there would be effective competition.[22] Utilities with significant market power could sustain higher prices and earn monopolistic profits. This may be a problem if a utility's subsidiary is allowed to supply power in the parent company's own service territory. This "self-dealing" can be avoided, however, if the utility is only allowed to participate in a bidding program as a regulated firm in its own service area.

Some critics of incentive programs often consider them nothing more than a bribe to the utility for doing what it is required to do already (Anderson, 1991). Also, some improperly designed programs have led to some unanticipated results, such as deferring maintenance on power plants with performance-based incentives. In general, broader-based programs, such as price caps, yardstick incentives, or where there is a competitive market to provide cost evaluation, have performed better than narrowly focused programs, such as when a particular power plant is the object of the program (Joskow and Schmalensee, 1986). As experience increases, as with telecommunications regulation, commissions should be able to determine which programs are suitable and which are not.[23]

If competitive markets exist or can be developed, then deregulation of that service may be appropriate. As noted, however, deregulation is rejected by some because of possible monopoly profits. Monopoly profits, of course, are avoided if the market is in fact competitive. Another problem with deregulation is that a utility may cross-subsidize an unregulated subsidiary with profits from a regulated service or shift costs from the unregulated to the regulated service and recover those costs from ratepayers. Problems such as this have been encountered in the telecommunications industry as it moved toward a more competitive structure and are likely to be faced by public utility commissions in the restructuring of the electric service industry as well.

CONCLUSIONS

Is there a conflict between these approaches? Are they complementary? Are the changes in the industry structure already so far along that planning options will become obsolete and inappropriate? Commissions currently use elements of traditional, planning, and competition/incentive approaches. As a result, it would appear that they are able to find ways to integrate them. However, with the substantial changes that are now likely because of EPAct, states will have to review some very fundamental regulatory procedures, such as franchise rights granted to utilities and the regulatory compact. It is possible that these reviews will lead states to rethink their mix of regulatory approaches. In some instances, they are likely to substitute market and incentive approaches for traditional and planning approaches. Some utility representatives, either out of fear of competition and being prevented from responding or anticipating the benefits of competition, are already beginning to ask for more flexibility from regulators.

Although these approaches are perhaps not mutually exclusive or in conflict, a choice will have to be made by commissions to determine the best way, in their view, to handle the issues outlined in Table 6.1

and elsewhere. Although it was not originally intended to be, it could be argued that IRP is a transitory approach to the increased use of markets. Legislative and regulatory actions have been evolving toward more market-based solutions for the last fifteen years. It is likely that competition will continue to increase in generation and wholesale power markets with the introduction of EWGs and the transmission-access provisions of EPAct. As a result, regulatory changes by state commissions will be required to enable them to take full advantage of these changes as the limitations of the traditional and planning approaches become more apparent in a more competitive environment. In general, this will likely mean a move away from cost-based regulation and toward more market- and incentive-based mechanisms. For utilities, this will mean more flexibility to respond to changing market conditions, increased opportunities for financial gain, and less regulatory risk. However, they will also then be expected to incur more market risks in exchange.

An example of the choices that commissions will have to make and one that shows the contrast in the approaches is the issue of environmental regulation. Commissions, in an effort to be proactive on the environment, are likely to persist in their efforts to internalize environmental costs. To date, this has occurred through qualitative or quantitative consideration during the planning stage of an IRP-type process. However, emission taxes and trading systems to reduce emissions may be able to achieve the desired emissions level at a lower cost than these planning methods. California (the South Coast Air Quality Management District) has used an emissions offset program for volatile organic compounds for over ten years and for other pollutants more recently (Hahn and Hester, 1989) and is currently considering a modified trading system (RECLAIM, 1992). Also, eight states in the Northeast have proposed a multi-state trading system (NESCAUM, 1992), and a trading system is being considered for at least two urban areas (Chicago and Houston-Galveston). Preliminary indications are that the national trading system for SO_2 emissions is developing and has demonstrated that these types of programs can work in the electric industry and can be beneficial.

Commissions, however, may be limited statutorily from implementing such measures. If so, commissions will be required to cooperate with the environmental agencies in their state to develop and implement these types of programs. Historically, with some exceptions, these two state agencies have not always worked well together. Also, many of these programs would require multi-state cooperation, something that is also without a great deal of precedence in this industry.[24] The potential environmental benefit and cost savings, however, which could occur from such cooperation, could be considerable and worth the effort to pursue. This is just one example of the new challenges states will face in the coming years as the industry is transformed to a more competitive condition.[25]

NOTES

1. See survey and discussion of bidding participants in Rose, Burns, and Eifert (1991) or Edison Electric Institute (1992).

2. Incentive programs actually go back to the early days of regulation. Laffont and Tirole (1993) note that in the nineteenth century "price caps were not uncommon" (p. 13) and cite an incentive mechanism used from 1925 to 1955 for an electric utility (p. 16).

3. Recently, FERC has allowed, when adequate basis for competition has been found, market-based pricing of wholesale power transactions and open access of transmission service (Henderson, 1992). At this time, however, most of FERC's cases are still cost-of-service determined.

4. See, for example, "A Colloquy on DSM and IRP."

5. These limitations are summarized in Rose (1992).

6. Over the short term the utility knows its revenue, price structure, load, and so on. Over the long term, however, as has been seen with fuel prices, these become less assured.

7. See Averch and Johnson (1962). This article began the more recent strain of criticism of the traditional approach, which first occurred in the early days of regulation (Shepherd, 1992, p. 2). More recent criticism and suggestions for improved approaches are considerably more complex (Laffont and Tirole, 1993).

8. The most commonly cited limitation to the traditional approach is the lack of incentive to minimize operating and capital costs (Rose, 1992).

9. For example, see Kolbe and Tye (1990).

10. Defenders of prudence reviews point out that, if warranted, the review should be a retrospective evaluation of the utility's decision based on the information available at the time the decision was made. Therefore, the utility is being penalized for an imprudent decision, not the outcome. For a discussion, see Burns et al. (1985).

11. Externalities are costs or benefits incurred or acquired by society but not the firm or individual producing the product or service. Examples of external environmental costs from producing electricity are sulfur dioxide, nitrogen oxides, carbon dioxide, and other forms of pollution occurring during the fuel cycle. A report prepared by ECO Northwest for the National Association of Regulatory Utility Commissioners (1993) describes in six state case studies how these costs are considered.

12. Planning advocates often suggest prior or pre-approval of a plan by commissions. For a recent example, see Hirst, Driver, and Blank (1993).

13. This is basically the "moral hazard" argument. This and other limitations of pre-approval are discussed in the context of Clean Air Act compliance planning in chapter 6 of Rose et al. (1992).

14. See, for example, Joskow (1992).

15. For example, CO_2 is not currently restricted at the federal level; however, at this time, there is interest in Congress to do so, and the Clinton administration has released *The Climate Change Action Plan* (October 1993), which relies largely on voluntary action to reduce greenhouse gas emissions.

16. See Andrews (1992) and Joskow (1992).

17. For example, see Dasovich, Meyer, and Coe (1993).

18. For a discussion of a price cap proposal by an electric utility see Maine Public Utilities Commission (1993).

19. For a detailed discussion of these methods, see Moskovitz (1989). For a recent survey of these methods, see Reid, Brown, and Deem (1993).

20. See RCG/Hagler, Bailly, Inc. (1992). While Table 6.1 categorized DSM incentives under the planning approach, the responsiveness of utilities to such programs is of interest here.

21. Mathios and Rogers (1989) found, in an econometric analysis comparing long-distance telephone service in states that allow pricing flexibility (price caps) with states that do not, evidence which suggests rates were significantly lower in states that allowed price flexibility than states that used rate-of-return regulation.

22. Hempling (1993) argues that the potential for utilities to gain at their ratepayers' expense is significant and requires state public utility commission "protections" to guard against, for example, cross-subsidization of expenses.

23. Jones (1991) suggests experimentation and critical evaluation by public utility commissions of incentive programs.

24. For a discussion of two exceptions, see Chapter 4, "Two Major Regional Initiatives and the FERC," in Jones et al. (1992).

25. The views and opinions of the author do not necessarily state or reflect the views, opinions, or policies of The National Regulatory Research Institute (NRRI), the National Association of Regulatory Utility Commissioners (NARUC), or their contributors.

REFERENCES

Anderson, John. Presentation at *The Future of Incentive Regulation in the Electric Utility Industry.* Sponsored by School of Public and Environmental Affairs, Indiana University and PSI Energy, Indianapolis, Indiana, November 18, 1991.

Andrews, Clinton J. "The Marginality of Regulating Marginal Investments: Why We Need a Systemic Perspective on Environmental Externality Adders." *Energy Policy* 20 (May 1992): 450–463.

Averch, H., and L. L. Johnson. "Behavior of the Firm Under Regulatory Constraint." *American Economic Review* 52 (December 1962): 1052–1069.

Burns, Robert E., et al. *The Prudent Investment Test in the 1980s.* Columbus, OH: The National Regulatory Research Institute, April 1985.

Clinton, William J. et al. *The Climate Change Action Plan.* Washington, DC: White House, October 1993.

Dasovich, Jeffrey, William Meyer, and Virginia A. Coe. *California's Electric Service Industry: Perspectives on the Past, Strategies for the Future.* San Francisco, CA: California Public Utilities Commission, Division of Strategic Planning, February 1993.

Davis, Vivian Witkind. "Summary of the Status of Alternative Regulation in Telecommunications." *NRRI Quarterly Bulletin* 14 (June 1993): 161–167.

Diewert, W. Erwin. "Summary of Index Number Issues in Incentive Regulation." Chapter 3 in Sanford V. Berg, et al. *The Potential for Using Performance Indices to Provide Regulatory Incentives.* Final Report to the New York Public Service Commission, Performance Incentives Consultants, December 30, 1992.

Edison Electric Institute. *Competitive Bidding in the Investor-Owned Electric Utility Industry,* Vol. 3. Washington, DC: Edison Electric Institute, 1992.

Hahn, Robert W., and Gordon L. Hester. "Where Did All the Markets Go? An Analysis of EPA's Emissions Trading Program." *Yale Journal on Regulation* 6 (Winter 1989): 109–153.

Hempling, Scott. *Reducing Ratepayer Risk: State Regulation of Electric Utility Expansion.* Washington, DC: American Association of Retired Persons, 1993.

Henderson, J. Stephen. "FERC Criteria for Evaluating Transmission Tariffs and market-based Bulk Power Contracts." In *Proceedings of Seminar on Power Contracting in a Competitive Market.* Held by ECC, Inc. Arlington, Virginia, October 7–8, 1992.

Hirst, Eric, Bruce Driver, and Eric Blank. "Integrated Resource Planning: A Model Rule." *Public Utilities Fortnightly* (March 15, 1993): 24–28.

Jones, Douglas N. "Old Style and New Style Regulation of Electrics: The Incentives Connection." Presented at The Future of Incentive Regulation in the Electric Utility Industry, sponsored by School of Public and Environmental Affairs, Indiana University and PSI Energy, Indianapolis, Indiana, November 18, 1991.

Jones, Douglas N. et al. *Regional Regulation of Public Utilities: Opportunities and Obstacles.* Columbus, OH: The National Regulatory Research Institute, December 1992.

Joskow, Paul L. "Weighing Environmental Externalities: Let's Do It Right!" *The Electricity Journal* 5 (May 1992): 53–67.

Joskow, Paul L., and Donald B. Marron. "What Does a Negawatt Really Cost? Evidence from Utility Conservation Programs." *The Energy Journal* 13 (1992): 41–74.

Joskow, Paul L., and Richard Schmalensee. "Incentive Regulation for Electric Utilities." *Yale Journal on Regulation* 4 (1986): 1–49.

Kolbe, A. Lawrence, and William B. Tye. *The Fair Allowed Rate of Return with Regulatory Risk*. Cambridge, MA: Putnam, Hayes & Bartlett, Inc., March 1990.

Laffont, Jean-Jacques, and Jean Tirole. *A Theory of Incentives in Procurement and Regulation*. Cambridge, MA: The MIT Press, 1993.

Lowry, Mark Newton. "The Case for Indexed Price Caps for U.S. Electric Utilities." *The Electricity Journal* 4 (October 1991): 30–37.

Maine Public Utilities Commission. "Hearing Examiners' Report on Alternative Rate Plans." Prepared by Kenneth W. Costello and Wayne Olson. Docket No. 92-345, November 3, 1993.

Mathios, Alan D., and Robert P. Rogers "The Impact of Alternative Forms of State Regulation of AT&T on Direct-Dial, Long-Distance Telephone Rates." *Rand Journal of Economics* 20 (Autumn 1989): 437–453.

Moskovitz, David. *Profits and Progress Through Least-Cost Planning*. Washington, DC: National Association of Regulatory Utility Commissioners, November 1989.

National Association of Regulatory Utility Commissioners (NARUC). *Environmental Externalities and Electric Utility Regulation*. Washington, DC: NARUC, September 1993.

National Economic Research Associates, Inc. (NERA). *Estimating the Net Benefits of Demand-Side Management Programs Based on Limited Information*. Revised draft, prepared for the Office of Policy, Planning and Evaluation of the U.S. Environmental Protection Agency, January 25, 1993.

National Economic Research Associates, Inc. (NERA). *How Much Energy Do DSM Programs Really Save: Engineering Estimates and Free Riders*. Revised draft, prepared for the Office of Policy, Planning and Evaluation of the U.S. Environmental Protection Agency, December 23, 1992.

National Economic Research Associates, Inc. (NERA). *Incentive Regulation in the Electric Utility Industry*. Cambridge, MA: National Economic Research Associates, Inc., 1985 (mimeo).

"The Next Frontier for Integrated Resource Planning and Demand-Side Management." *The Electricity Journal* 6, no. 1 (January/February 1993): 44–50.

Northeast States for Coordinated Air Use Management (NESCAUM). "Development of a Market-Based Emissions Cap System for NO_x in the NESCAUM Region, Project Summary for Section 105 State Air Grant Funds for Market-Based Initiatives." Boston, MA: NESCAUM, submitted to U.S. Environmental Protection Agency, September 1992.

RCG/Hagler, Bailly, Inc. "Comments on Incentives for Purchases of Non-Utility Generated Power." In the *Proceeding to Consider the Reauthorization of the Texas Public Utilities Commission*. Sunset Review Commission of Texas, June 1992.

Regional Clean Air Incentives Market (RECLAIM). "South Coast Air Quality Management District, Summary Recommendations." Diamond Bar, CA: RECLAIM, Spring 1992.

Reid, Michael W., Julia B. Brown, and Jack C. Deem. *Incentives for Demand-Side Management*. 2nd ed. Washington, DC: National Association of Regulatory Utility Commissioners, March 1993.

Rose, Kenneth. "Price-Cap Regulation: Some Implementation Issues." In *Regulatory Perspectives on Price Caps*, R. W. Lawton and K. Rose (eds.). Columbus, OH: The National Regulatory Research Institute, February 1992.

Rose, Kenneth et al. *Public Utility Commission Implementation of the Clean Air Act's Allowance Trading Program*. Columbus, OH: The National Regulatory Research Institute, May 1992.

Rose, Kenneth, Robert E. Burns, and Mark Eifert. *Implementing a Competitive Bidding Program for Electric Power Supply*. Columbus, OH: The National Regulatory Research Institute, January 1991.

Shepherd, William G. *Regulation and Efficiency: A Reappraisal of Research and Policies*. Columbus, OH: The National Regulatory Research Institute, July 1992.

7

Network Oligopoly Regulation: An Approach to Electric Federalism

Richard P. O'Neill and Charles S. Whitmore

The Energy Policy Act of 1992 (EPAct) increased the pace of change in the American electric power industry. Traditional regulatory theory and practice no longer match the industry and are clearly ill-equipped to achieve the simple objective of EPAct: "to provide for improved energy efficiency." The time has come to reconsider *who* can best regulate *which* parts of the industry and *how* they can best regulate it. This chapter considers:

- ways in which the current system no longer works well. Today's regulation rests on theoretical underpinnings that are no longer true or relevant. It forces parties into badly framed debates; fails to account for the realities of the modern marketplace; and resolves disputes in ways that are polarizing, costly, and technically unsophisticated.

- an outline of a new approach: spin off and deregulate generation; make transmission regulation federal; leave distribution regulation to the states; and change the way both levels of regulation work. This would use competition where it can work, create better incentives for regulated firms, and reduce the costs of regulation.

- how the new approach would affect major issues facing the industry: retail access, demand-side issues, power markets based on auctions, the Public Utilities Holding Company Act (PUHCA), and mergers.

OUTMODED ASPECTS OF TRADITIONAL REGULATION

Today's electric regulatory system grew up in the 1930s, when inflation and competition were absent (see Stalon, 1990). It still reflects the industry and economy of that time, not the industry it now regulates:

- The state-federal split of jurisdiction reflects an electric industry composed of many, largely isolated systems. Regulators did not need to be too concerned with long-distance transmission or a strongly integrated grid. Today, the combination of State control over new transmission construction and federal regulation of generation can impede efficient interstate markets.

- Today's large and expanding markets have all but eliminated the scale economies in generation which justified regulating that sector.

- Inflation mattered little. This (and the presumption that utilities would build, not buy) made original cost of service rate-making seem more reasonable than it does now.

- The economy moved much more slowly. The regulatory compact seemed a reasonable way to find fairness. In today's faster-moving, more fluid economy, the regulatory compact creates needless—and costly—uncertainty.

An Obsolete Theoretical Base

Most regulatory practice rests on theories developed for monopolies (see Phillips, 1988). However, generation markets are now partially competitive and can be highly competitive, both for new generating plants and for existing plants which are spun off from their host utility. Transmission is a partly competitive, partly cooperative oligopoly. Only distribution still fits a traditional natural monopoly. Traditional regulation for generation can mean foregoing very large benefits from competition. For transmission, it means missing the key problem: finding the right balance for oligopolists between cooperation (to gain the large value of an integrated grid) and competition (tempting to companies and potentially of great value in lowering prices to customers).

Even for distribution, traditional regulatory approaches are obsolete. Original cost of service (COS) rate-making has enjoyed more than fifty years as the main approach to utility regulation. It has shown four gaping weaknesses: a bias to over-capitalize; a lack of management incentives; outdated approaches to risk and uncertainty; and a dispute resolution mechanism which is formalistic, uncertain, and long.

False Dichotomies

Traditional regulation rests on highly developed methodologies and a largely static notion of efficiency. So the very language of regulation creates false problems. Competition and monopoly become literary foils with no middle ground. Perhaps the largest myth is that efficiency and equity must be traded off.

Efficiency means creating the largest bundle of benefits (maximizing social welfare). Equity (fairness) deals with distributing benefits once created.[1] Many different distributions can be efficient. But inefficient solutions are wasteful—by definition, more total benefit could have been created. No one receives the benefit that inefficiency wastes, and it is surely fairer that someone receive it than that no one does. Seen in this light, a truer relationship between efficiency and equity emerges: *Efficient solutions may be fair or unfair, but inefficient solutions must be unfair.*

Increasing efficiency is a positive-, not a zero-sum game. In theory, a proposal improves efficiency only if one could make some people better off while hurting no one—that is, a Pareto improvement is possible. This test is also called the "no losers" or "hold harmless" test. Pareto changes are a key point where efficiency and equity converge— and should be far more central to regulation than they are.

Practical Problems

Traditional regulation also leads to practical problems. Under the regulatory compact, regulators act as shepherds for the industry and its customers, fixing problems as they arise. This makes key aspects of the business either vague or absurdly absolute: The rights of entitle - ment holders are unclear; arrangements to bear risk are decided largely after the fact; and the obligation to serve, reliably, seems so absolute as to justify massive over-building.

The regulatory compact may once have been sensible. Today, it leads to waste, lack of accountability, and needless uncertainty that are increasingly hard to justify. Four major examples are:

- *Over-capitalization.* COS rate-making reflects regulatory (not market) asset values and offers few rewards for efficient asset management. It often leads to excessive capital programs.

- *Direct regulatory overhead.* Formal regulatory hearings are now costly, highly scripted, multi-act plays. They have trouble dealing with technical issues since the central players (judges and attorneys) are highly trained as litigators and mediators but usually lack technical skills.

- *Bad risk management.* The electric industry requires inherently risky, large capital outlays. The regulatory compact usually handles risk only after the fact, spreading pain *after* decisions turn out poorly. This works badly. As independent generators play a larger part in the industry, it will become incompatible with the larger commercial realities (e.g., the capital markets) which developers face.

- *Incentives.* Traditional COS regulation is notoriously poor at giving firms incentives to operate efficiently.

Information, Models, and Predictions

Traditional regulation gets the strengths and weaknesses of the information age backward. It depends heavily on forecasting (rates almost always depend on forecasts) and uses little of the information technologies available for modern market trading.

Information is Key

Today, a single analyst can now have more computer power and data storage than a major university had twenty years ago. Market participants adapt to changing conditions by weighing a vast array of information and responding very quickly. Industries under traditional regulation are slow to use such information, relying instead on, for example, occasional rate cases that reach decisions in years, not weeks (or hours).

Two types of information should be critical for regulated industries: price information to promote competition and yardstick information to create incentives by decoupling rates from the seller's cost. Competitive markets depend on good, timely price information. In most industries, good information lets firms run more efficiently, handle risk better, and lower transactions costs. The same can be true in electricity. New technology (e.g., flexible AC transmission systems) could change how networks are controlled, lower reliability costs, promote creation of property rights, and change the nature of regulation. Good yardstick information can make non-competitive sectors more efficient (see later section on distribution).

Forecasting Isn't

Almost all traditional ratemaking relies on forecasting. Even when rates rest entirely on prior test period data, ratemakers tacitly assume a forecast (that the future will be the same as the recent past). Firms in all industries base decisions on their own forecasts. But forecasting plays a different role in regulated industries because:

- the company is not accountable for the accuracy of the forecast since the forecast is inherent in the ratemaking process. In other industries, companies are accountable for their assessments of the future and their responses to those assessments.

- the results are inflexible. Rates are in effect for some years (usually). Other industries can change their pricing as the projected future unfolds.

- regulating mechanisms leave little scope for companies with different perceptions to make different bets on the future. Mistakes tend to be laid off on captive customers, not on other parties who are willing to take the risk.

Relying on forecasts to make authoritative regulatory judgments has always been dangerous. Increased computing power has led to little improvement.

The mismatch between computer capability and good forecasts became clear in the 1960s when the "Club of Rome" model predicted worldwide disaster. (Slight changes in parameters to include "technological progress" eliminated the disaster.) Models grew more complex in the energy debates of the 1970s. They, too, produced bad forecasts because they missed "technological progress," seriously misjudged future oil and gas prices, and underestimated the demand response to higher prices. More recently, climate models have brought small, controlled laboratory results to large-scale interactive "reality" but have yet to include the effect of clouds, oceans, or other realities and have shown little predictive power.

Forecasts fail to predict not only general trends but also specific matters used in policy-making. The Clean Air Act limits overall sulfur dioxide (SO_2) emissions and then lets markets price the rights to cause such emissions. Many models calculated that a ton of SO_2 emissions would cost more than $1,000. First indications are that these estimates may have been off by an order of magnitude. Among other things, they seem to have missed the social pressure which buying local coal and the right to pollute locally creates. Scrubbers can let local coal be consumed, even if they are inefficient. On the other hand, the local public is often unwilling to accept higher pollution even in return for lower electric rates, making emissions rights much less valuable than predicted.

Vastly larger, more complex models have not improved forecasts. Risk is unavoidable. This is why a key function of markets is not to predict the future but to accommodate risk-taking and risk-shedding. Parties in regulated industries should focus on unavoidable risk up front and make provision for it. So should regulators (see Harris, 1979; Harris and Raviv, 1981).

ONE APPROACH TO REFORM: AN OUTLINE

EPAct offers the electric industry (including regulators) a chance to reform itself to the benefit of all. The benefits can be enormous. But to make the reforms politically palatable—and to keep the reformers honest—the process needs one basic recognition: Real benefits can be managed so that there need be no forced losers.

The modern approach to regulation is to decide whether a market failure is likely, identify the type of market failure, and apply an appropriate remedy. Several market failures are possible. Public goods and goods produced from natural monopolies may be undersupplied. Externalities may not be included properly in decision-making. Markets may be incomplete—for example, they may lack good information or arbitrage mechanisms. Remedies for a specific failure are much less intrusive than older regulatory schemes. If the market failure results from a lack of information, the remedy is to supply information (not to impose COS regulation). A crucial step is often to move to ex ante regulation rather than trying to cure problems after the fact. An ex ante approach lets planning and competition coexist peacefully and efficiently. The industry plans public goods aspects of the business jointly, then lets competition achieve efficiency in building and operating the system.

What Might a New Regulatory World Look Like?

Consider three changes in the regulation and structure of the electric industry:

- Generation is spun off and deregulated. Traditional utilities sell off all or most existing generation assets (perhaps sometimes to affiliates). Spot and market-based contract markets grow.

- All regulation of transmission (including construction approval) moves to the federal level; traditional regulation is superseded by a form of club regulation that better recognizes the partly competitive, partly cooperative nature of the transmission grid and the role of states as key players.

- All regulation of distribution stays with the states, but state regulators largely replace COS regulation with yardstick regulation, which promotes efficiency at lower regulatory cost. Yardstick regulation applies wherever a distributor has market power: distribution itself (the wires) and power sales unless there is retail wheeling.

Generation Market Reform

The usual rationale for regulating generation is its supposed status as a natural monopoly.[2] But generation today is almost certainly not a natural monopoly because:

- electric generation markets are much larger now. An integrated grid lets many participants access each other. Individual plants, even very large ones, are not large relative to today's markets.

- technology has cut the cost of smaller gas turbines compared to larger plants.

- large-scale plants with subadditive costs on the drawing board have often not realized them in practice. One reason is reliability. If measured by first and second contingencies, reliability costs for large plants may offset scale economies.

- larger plants are often riskier. They take longer to build and their capacity is more likely to overshoot an uncertain future demand. Should such a plant run into problems (e.g., nuclear plants), the results can be severe. When risk is properly accounted, expected costs may no longer be subadditive.

- today's communications and control technologies make it possible to realize many coordination economies across several companies.

Often overlooked in discussing natural monopoly is the inefficiency of having many small, local monopolies. Today, each utility (or small group of utilities) plans, builds, and operates generation plants. The generation business has hundreds of independent builders, operators, and owners. How many wholesale manufacturing industries have hundreds of firms under local ownership? Many electric generators may be inefficient. One utility can—and often does—pay far more than another to build what is essentially the same plant and operate it to generate what is the same electricity. Much of the difference is pure waste that ratepayers pay for. The industry would be better served by having suppliers chosen by their ability to build and operate efficiently rather than by their franchise.[3]

Since the traditional arguments for seeing generation as a natural monopoly no longer apply, the major reason for market power in this sector today is simply the existence of local monopolies which have outlived their justification. Today, it is feasible to create a competitive market for existing as well as new plants if utilities spin off their generation assets. Doing so would lead to benefits because it would create competition to operate and maintain existing plants more efficiently.[4]

This process can benefit all parties. Utilities could take existing power plants out of rate base and sell them to the highest bidder. Usually the new owner (perhaps the old owner in a new corporate form, if local public utility commissions [PUCs] allow) could operate and maintain the existing asset more efficiently—that is, at costs under the current COS. Bidders could be required to reflect the savings they offer by structuring their bids to include both:

- premium over book value (to benefit the utility's stockholders) and

- an offer to sell the power back under contract (for say five to ten years) to its current owner at rates lower than those that would be expected for the plant if it continued under COS (to benefit current customers by lowering the costs included in their rates). The power could come from the existing facility, or the new supplier could buy power elsewhere and resell it.

Bids that do not reflect such savings can be rejected—the lack of such bids would suggest that the incumbent is also the most efficient operator.[5] Utilities could sell off even the most costly plants this way. If the new owner can operate the plant less expensively, it can sell power (or capacity) back for less than the plant would have cost ratepayers otherwise. The regulator can share the benefits between the utility's stockholders and ratepayers. One key here is to understand that everyone benefits as *compared with continuing the status quo*, not as compared with some other possible outcome.[6]

Of course, this is not the only arrangement. The asset could be sold outright if the power is not needed (see Rothkopf et al., 1987; Vickrey, 1961). If the current owner does not need the asset, its value to ratepayers may be zero or even negative (if site cleanup is needed, for instance). Any bid above that value is acceptable. In any case, a major advantage of selling off generation assets is to address biases inherent in most COS ratemaking.

Local commissions or regulators would control the spin-off process and the distribution of resulting revenues, except possibly for multi-state utilities. The Federal Energy Regulatory Commission (FERC) would step out of generation regulation, first through lighter-handed regulation, then perhaps through a change to the Federal Power Act (FPA). Because of the size of an orderly asset transfer, it could take ten years or more to complete—all the more reason not to delay starting the process.

The potential for achieving efficient competition is high if care is taken to create a reasonably diffuse set of non-affiliated (with the buyer) generating companies. In time, electric generation would resemble any other heavy manufacturing industry. It is a source of jobs and uses the State's other resources. An efficient operation will survive in the long-term and even export its product.

Using asset spinoffs and contracts to sell power back to the utilities allows a smoother, gradual, and predictable transition to a deregulated generation market. Prices would be lower but not volatile. The transition would follow a path where expectations would deter excess capacity (beyond reliability needs) from being built.

In any event, spinoffs should be a quid pro quo for any special treatment for stranded investment. Any special treatment for stranded investment must be considered transition costs. Transition costs imply a new set of institutions that correct the root cause of stranded investment. Without a long-term solution, there is reason to expect those paying transition costs to ask why.

Transmission Regulatory Reform

Why Regulate Transmission?

Unlike generation, transmission is subject to a real, continuing market failure. Not only are the costs subadditive, but reliability is a quasi-public good, and externalities abound (for instance, siting and loop flow). Even conservative market-oriented analysts have not proposed physically separate competing grids. Regulation is the sensible answer. But the current approach is too simple. For example, corporate postage stamp ratemaking reduces the spatial geometry of each intra-corporate transaction to a single two-bus system. The rest is covered by the "gentlemen's agreement."

In transmission pricing reform, both long- and short-term pricing signals matter. Long-term pricing should send the price signal to site new assets efficiently. Short-term pricing should promote efficient use of the existing system. Long- and short-term signals can conflict when there are significant sunk costs. For sunk assets, pricing based on efficient location comes too late—sunk assets cannot change location at any price. Price signals for efficient location can only be relevant for new assets. Fairness may play a key role in pricing sunk assets.

The transmission network presents an important, possibly the most important, state-federal interaction. EPAct lets FERC order service, but states control the construction of transmission assets. This creates the potential for problems.

Why Regulate at the Federal Level?

Almost all electric markets cover at least several states. If states regulate transmission (e.g., new construction), the temptation can be overwhelming to adopt mercantilist solutions which consider only benefits to the state regardless of the effects on others. Parties can easily create games with no stable outcomes (empty cores) that lead to vast uncertainty and even greater delay. This could greatly weaken the chance of expanding and increasing the efficiency of markets through the new federal access authority. Pursued generally by all states, the result is to harm each because coordination and reliability issues leave little room for parochial solutions. Regulation will work best at the federal level to realize the greatest efficiency benefits.

What Form of Regulation?

This does not imply full-blown, traditional regulation. Electric transmission is a network oligopoly. Individuals own and maintain separate parts of the system. Players who are net buyers of electricity at some times are net sellers at others. Electric transmitters have much more complex incentives than traditional monopolists. Cogent regulation for a network oligopoly must go far beyond simply ensuring that companies do not exercise market power to earn excessive profits. It must both use competitive forces that exist in the network and ensure that companies cooperate as necessary to reach efficient results.

Since the industry is an oligopoly, some competition exists to provide transmission service. Today, this competition is based on "contract" path rather than physical flows. The result easily resembles a market that has incentives to undermine every deal (the empty core again). But since it is also an integrated network, the companies must spend much of their time cooperating. "Gentlemen's agreements" keep the system from falling apart. Failure to cooperate could destroy many of the benefits of an integrated system.

Since Congress is unlikely to address electric regulatory reform again soon, any transition needs to start under existing legislation. Partly for that reason, a new regulatory approach—club regulation in the form of regional transmission groups (RTGs)—could build on present approaches. Club regulation brings interested parties together in an open setting, provides voting rules for making decisions, and uses more formal regulation only to handle exceptional issues.

Since club decisions would govern many or most of the contentious issues the industry faces, the clubs themselves would need inclusive membership (so all those affected would be represented), good voting rules (to ensure against the exercise of market power), technical expertise (to focus discussion on technical issues), and a fairly wide mandate (to handle issues of new construction and planning, power trading, accounting for transmission transactions, etc.).

Although clubs would handle many issues on their own, regulators would remain crucial. They would provide an appellate process. Their decisions would also provide the basic structure of outcomes that parties could expect by going outside the club. This is especially important at the start. Clubs will form only if all parties think they will benefit. Regulation would form the baseline against which the parties would judge their individual benefits. Thus, the expected course of future regulation forms an indispensable backdrop if clubs are to form.

Clubs are not new in the electric industry. A restricted form of club has traditionally provided transmission access and helped resolve many coordination problems. This provides an example for the future. But today's form of club governance in the electricity sector cannot serve the purposes of future club regulation. Both membership and the scope of issues addressed are too narrow. For instance, entrance to the governing club often requires ownership of transmission assets. Further, some clubs focus only on reliability (the North American Electric Reliability Council [NERC] and its regional siblings), whereas others focus only on trading (Mid-America Power Pool [MAPP], Procedure to Optimize Economy Transactions [POET], the Florida "broker," and Western System Power Pool [WSPP]). So today's forms of clubs and club governance are probably not well suited to the problems RTGs will face, though some existing clubs could serve as the basis for further development. For instance, NERC and its siblings with expanded membership could form the technical backbone of the new clubs.

Many other parties will be important for any future form of club regulation in the industry. Similarly, transmission regulation (a combination of traditional COS, nuclear licensing, joint ventures, public projects, and antitrust law) will need to change. EPAct and market developments are forcing a more active approach. Still, with good rules for membership and voting and a well-defined regulatory role, the industry may find that negotiation among club members can be cheaper than traditional regulation, but at least as effective in checking abuses of market power (see Jones et al., 1992).

Why might new approaches to club regulation succeed? A major reason is technical expertise. Understanding transmission, beyond some analogies to hydraulic systems, requires a background in complex mathematics, physics, electrical engineering, and computer simulation. Delegating primary supervision of technical matters to regulators (typically lawyers with backgrounds in the social sciences and humanities) raises form over substance and makes technical mistakes more likely. Regulators need to focus on more important issues such as fairness and guidelines for resolving disputes.

Technical expertise must play the dominant role in resolving technical issues. Today's regulatory system is not up to the job. For instance, the cry of degraded reliability sends regulators into disorganized retreat.[7]

Club regulation requires that the regulators set admissions requirements and voting rules and then let club members who have technical expertise work out settlements, subject to regulatory review and less formal, more technical (e.g., special masters) dispute resolution. The public choice and cooperative game theory literature provides insights and guides to this new approach (see, e.g., Owen, 1982; Mueller, 1979; Littlechild, 1970; Luce and Raiffa, 1957; von Neumann and Morgenstern, 1944).

Rules for each club may differ, but one would expect all clubs to converge on rules that rely on a superauthority to resolve disputes. States need to be active participants to make the approach work.[8] FERC's job would shift to a role between the one it plays now and that the Commodity Futures Trading Commission plays—less direct regulation, more monitoring, and oversight. The test of any approach must be that it preserves both the competition in generation markets and the benefits to consumers promised by reform.

One potential arrangement is that transmission owners cede control to a central operating authority. Non-owners (or those with less valuable assets) pay a fee to the club based either on a reservation of peak capacity or on actual usage. Owners get similar rights and compensation for the use of their assets. The club members plan the system jointly and those who need more capacity pay for any network expansions. All club members share reliability costs. The operating authority runs spot markets which optimize the short-run efficiency of the system and shares the additional benefits among the club members (see Hogan, 1993; Schweppe et al., 1988).

Some analysts advocate restructuring the industry by spinning off the transmission function into separate corporations. For now, the alternative suggested here (spinning off generation) may remove many of the problems that suggest the need for separate transmission companies. Also, the industry can achieve many of the scope economies which could come from large, separate transmission companies through joint operation and planning, that is, through RTGs. The assets of the RTG are likely to be geographically dispersed. Since utility companies must already maintain the distribution system in each area, it may be efficient for the same companies to continue to own and maintain the transmission grid. Without reorganizing the transmission function, asset construction, ownership, and maintenance could remain in separate hands and be subject to yardstick regulation. Or the companies could form a joint venture that would gain the benefits of unitary ownership while preserving existing stakes in the system.

Distribution

A Bastion of Traditional Regulation?

Strung off the network at hundreds of buses or nodes are the distribution systems. Distribution (the wires business) usually still qualifies as a natural monopoly. But this does not imply continuing COS regulation (see Demsetz, 1968; Joskow, 1989). The inefficiencies of such regulation can so compromise economies of scale or scope that entry and competition become a real possibility where in theory none should exist. If generation is spun off, a regulated distribution company's (disco's) costs will consist mostly of power purchases. Without good management incentives, the result could become a regulatory nightmare. Yardstick information on other discos' purchasing combined with visible spot and long-term markets are key to creating benefits for the regulated firm and its customers.

Yardstick Incentives

Yardstick regulation consists of developing indexes from industry data and using them to discipline rates and services for individual companies. The indexes can be general, covering all business expenses, or specific, covering particular kinds of cost (power purchase, operation and maintenance, etc.) Either way, yardstick regulation:

- decouples any single company's rates from its own costs (almost all of the index reflects other companies' costs.) This gives a strong incentive to greater efficiency, since costs are no longer simply passed through. It also gradually creates what might be called "virtual competition." Discos would begin to compete with each other to lower costs, even though each retained its local monopoly.

- uses indexes that track the industry and are less likely to diverge from a company's experience. That implies fewer · periodic rate reviews and puts the burden on parties who wish to change rates to show why a given disco differs enough from others to warrant extraordinary treatment.

With hundreds of distribution systems, yardstick regulation/competition has much to offer in incentives to be efficient. Information technology is available both to implement yardstick regulation and to unbundle the wires business (the transmission of electricity at distribution voltages) from the commodity business (the sale of electricity).

Yardstick regulation is both cost based and a form of incentive regulation. Incentive regulation has provoked much debate. It has several parts: decoupling costs and rates (typically by indexing rates), creating incentives to be efficient, and allowing negotiating flexibility. The best approach to indexing is to create a set of indexes which track costs of similar but spatially dispersed activities. A side benefit of such an approach is that it produces "best practice" information.

Another form of incentive regulation pegs rates to a much more general index, such as producer or consumer prices across the whole economy. (This is the RPI-X approach used in Britain. A yardstick approach was not feasible there since the regulated firms are monopolies over the entire country.) In terms of severing the link between a company's costs and rates, such an approach is a mirage. Finding the index is easy, but it is not likely to track utility costs. For example, health care and food costs—likely parts of a general index—are not well correlated with utility costs. As a result, the index is likely to need frequent review. In England, such reviews begin to resemble a COS rate case. Without good yardstick comparisons, this process could quickly become a traditional rate case with new arguments about "X" replacing arguments about throughput and rates of return.

The main argument against yardstick regulation is that it is information intensive. But the costs may well pale compared to traditional cost-based regulation. Anyone who is familiar with the discovery process of a formally litigated rate case will grasp a basic point: Even very small savings in the number of rate cases or the intensity of the administrative and information burden in each case will produce benefits that outweigh the costs of yardstick regulation. Moreover, many regulators already collect much of the needed information—it needs only minor changes to become useful.

Incentive Regulation Miscellany

Any incentive proposal (whether using yardstick regulation or not) should include incentives on each rate. Tariffs often contain multiple pricing and penalty components. Each part or margin should include incentives—that is, each should have ex ante profit margins for a company that performs well. Similarly, penalties should be set to induce good behavior. One key part of incentive rates should be to encourage efficient dispute resolution. This suggests using a form of yardstick regulation for legal fees, regardless of any other changes in ratemaking. Basing allowable legal fees on an industry average rather than on the company's actual expenses encourages managements to find the most efficient ways to resolve disputes.

Fairness: The Importance of Contracts and Property Rights

In any reform, ensuring that results are fair and that most parties see them to be fair will be crucial. Beyond the general need to find solutions which share benefits widely (Pareto improvements), two key elements of ensuring fairness are:

- to rely more on contracts. When parties agree before a deal, the results are much more likely to be fair. This is especially true for agreements on how to share risk.

- to define entitlement and property rights much more specifically. This can prevent many later disputes. Here, legal expertise is particularly important.

Contracts and Fairness

Many fairness problems can be short-circuited at the beginning. Relying far more on contracts can avoid laying offintractable problems for the future. Decisions about risk and uncertainty (a critical underlying problem for the industry) ought to be made before, not after, the events happen.

In general, the industry seems to be relying more on contracts and less on the regulatory compact, moving away from the ex post/prudence approach to an ex ante approach. Integrated resource planning (IRP) and competition-based regulatory contracts may be moves in this direction. In any transition, ex ante contracts will be especially important. They help avoid fruitless, prolonged litigation later, and the process of reaching mutually agreeable initial contracts can work powerfully to prevent the tradeoffs inherent in any transition from being lopsided.

Property Rights and Fairness with Competition

More competition requires well-defined property rights. Further, the entitlement must be accompanied by more explicit obligations. Currently, the utility makes long-term investments and accepts a deal to collect an income stream from a presumed captive customer. This customer is often not bound legally to pay the income stream. This loose arrangement is called the regulatory compact. This incomplete contract is often silent on many aspects of the deal such as risk bearing, implicit length, and reassignment.

With more competition and a continuing inability to forecast accurately, the regulatory compact must become the regulatory contract. The major difference is more ex ante specificity. Those who assume the risks of a project must be rewarded or accept the losses. If the native load ratepayers are the residual risk bearers, they should take the reward if the future favors the investment. The same holds for the asset owner. As a matter of practical historical fact, the risks have (implicitly) been shared. The process must be much more specific. If the risks are shared, so must be the rewards.

Well-defined property rights are also critical for secondary markets. Secondary markets matter—they can lead to much greater efficiency in allocating scarce resources. With competition, the ability to reassign existing rights and substitute when new opportunities arise is crucial. Since the ability to forecast with any accuracy is not yet within reach, secondary markets (and well-defined entitlement) are critical to adjustments for failed forecasts.

REGULATORY REFORM AND MAJOR CURRENT ISSUES

Many key problems now facing the industry will challenge whatever regulatory system is in place: retail access, integrated resource planning, and demand side management, auctions for both generating capacity and energy, PUHCA issues, and mergers.

Retail Access

The technological gates to retail competition are now open. Modern information technology makes it possible—and probably cost effective—to send price signals directly to households as well as to larger customers. These signals could trigger control mechanisms that change temperature settings and reschedule discretionary activities like washing.

EPAct forbids FERC from ordering retail access. Some believe this will solve the retail bypass problem. It won't. As Tip O'Neill was fond of saying, "All politics is local." Pressure for retail access will come from the bottom up. Once wholesale access and spot markets are established, marketers will offer retail customers (not just the large industrials) much better deals for power than they have now. This will focus local political pressure on local regulators, regardless of current federal law. A major advantage to spinning off generation is that it provides an orderly way to deal with transition costs before the fact.

Retail wheeling may change the focus for regulating distributors. There would be less reason to regulate power purchases (customers could make their own choices). But the need to regulate distribution itself (the wires business) would remain.

IRP and Demand-Side Management (DSM)

An efficient electric industry requires efficiency on both demand and supply sides. Electric customers can sometimes spend far less to lower their peak loads or overall usage than it costs to build more capacity. That is the basic economic case for IRP (considering both supply- and demand-side options together) and DSM. But getting an efficient mix of demand and supply options requires new demand side approaches which rely more, not less, on better-structured market mechanisms.

The three biggest market failures in the demand side of the electricity market have been bad price signals, lack of good information, and lack of interest or discount rate arbitrage. In each case, the utility is the most likely party to fix the problem. But each fix can and should work outside traditional monopoly regulation.

Bad Price Signals

Bad price signals are an artifact of traditional regulation (see Bonbright et al., 1988; Sherman and Visscher, 1978; and Ramsey, 1927 for other approaches to pricing even within a traditional setting). They arise from marginal prices that reflect average historical costs. Rate designs that set marginal rates at marginal opportunity costs and are better understood by customers may largely correct this problem. Fixed charges or initial block rates can allow for adjustments in the overall bill.

Lack of Good Information

Lack of good information can prevent customers from choosing efficient electric equipment. This problem is not solved by any amount of traditional regulation, but by producing and distributing good information. The principal-agent problem is related: Builders install appliances, but home buyers buy a complete house. Builders have less reason to install the most efficient mix of appliances if customers buy houses mostly for other reasons. Again, no amount of traditional regulation will solve the problem. No matter how traditional regulation tries to attack the problem, it ends up sending price signals that are likely to be at least as distorted as any effects from the principal-agent problem. Customers need the information to make the most efficient decisions, and building codes may need to be revised.

Better Arbitrage

Better arbitrage is needed if many electric customers require very short payback periods to install efficient equipment. The best answer is probably a market to let others arbitrage the difference between the implicit discount rate customers insist on and those prevailing in the broader economy. For instance, an arbitrager might contract with a home owner (or builder) to pay for a conservation measure in return for some or most of the energy savings over (say) a five or seven year period. The contract could cover future owners of the home as well as the current owner.

Solving demand-side market failures would solve many of the problems considered under IRP. The market will often determine the best level of demand-side investment and obviate the need for detailed central planning. However, some parts of IRP will remain important. For instance, demand-side measures could affect the transmission grid (and any need for expansion) either by reducing demand for power generation in some areas or freeing up generation for sale elsewhere. This sort of planning would be a natural subject for RTGs and club regulation.

Power Auctions

For power markets to reach full potential, good access for both short- and long-run sales with efficient price signals is vital. Although bilateral trading may remain the norm, systematic multi-player auctions can achieve even greater efficiency. Such auctions can capture additional efficiencies that are difficult, if not impossible, to obtain in bilateral trading.

Multi-player auctions must evolve for sales on all time scales: long term (through procurement processes), short term (through spot markets), and intermediate term (through processes which combine features of the first two). These markets may grow in parallel with RTGs, so that regional transmission groups become regional trading groups. The initial institutions could be established by taking dispatch software and replacing cost information with bids and posting the resulting spot prices which clear the short-term market. Next, demand schedules could be included. This would substitute for the traditional central dispatch and system lambda approach.

Long-Term Procurements

As energy and power transactions become market driven,

procurement processes become more important. More and more new long-term power needs are being procured through processes that range from formal auctions to structured negotiations. The logic of competitive generation would lead to a great expansion of such long-term auctions.

Short-Term Spot Markets

Short-term energy auctions can extract efficiencies not achieved in other transactions. These auctions must rest on computer algorithms that optimize benefits while honoring reliability constraints. Agreements on how to distribute benefits from the auctions are also needed. Spot electric markets need more technical coordination than classic spot markets. Those that exist today (NEPOOL, MAPP, Florida) lack key elements of complete markets. For instance, they generally do not have visible prices. Without good spot prices, forward contracts and hedging markets operate less efficiently.

Intermediate-Term Auctions

These would also be valuable for spinning reserves and maintenance scheduling. The latter would look more like a long-term capacity auction, and the former would resemble short-term energy auctions. The auctions cascade into each other and price information flows in the other direction as information for informed decisions in "up-stream" auctions.

PUHCA Problems

Although EPAct gives only partial solutions to PUHCA problems, there is enough to start fashioning remedies to long-standing problems. With good open-access transmission, FERC can allow states greater input, control, and responsibility in decisions of multi-state holding companies. Securities and Exchange Commission (SEC) oversight can be reduced to the same responsibility it has over other public corporations. Finally, greater market discipline will be possible.

For instance, suppose a holding company had a large coal plant that does not comply with SO_2 regulations. The state with the plant in it wants to scrub local high-sulfur coal, but other states where the holding company operates believe using low-sulfur coal or natural gas is more economical. Traditionally, the company and its regulators would guess at the future and decide which action is better. Later, FERC would decide the prudence of the decision and then split the cost among the states.

Cooperative approaches can give states more input. They would let conflicting views of the future benefit if realized. In the example, if scrubbers are installed, the transfer price of power could be set based on the price of low-sulfur coal to satisfy the wishes of the neighboring state. The state advocating scrubbers would recover the cost of scrubbers from within the state and benefit or lose based on the accuracy of its projection. The state advocating low-sulfur coal or natural gas would receive power based on a yardstick price of these fuels. The utility could earn its rate of return based on an indexed cost for scrubbers. The decision calculus is changed. Open access that lets each company and its state commission (or local regulatory body) examine more substitutes gives each participant more options and lets each pursue benefits based on its view of the future, unencumbered by federal rules for holding companies. With the incentive and reward structure changed, decisions may change. The need for holding companies and/or separate rules for them would be brought into question. Eventually PUHCA could be unnecessary.

Mergers

With new market structures, FERC could cut administrative overhead by changing its approach to mergers. It could allow mergers whenever the merged company offers good open-access and a commitment to hold existing customers harmless. Good open-access transmission tariffs enhance competition for energy and power. Merging firms often claim that the merger benefits ratepayers. FERC can take this claim at face value and condition the merger on the guarantee that the benefits will be realized without harm to any existing captive customer.

Finally, in the new electric world, a typical reorganization may differ from the traditional combination of neighboring integrated utilities. For example, combinations of generating assets into national companies may be more common. Eventually FERC merger authority could disappear, except possibly for transmission companies.

CONCLUSIONS

The industry and regulatory structure proposed here can benefit all parties compared to the status quo. If transition costs result from outmoded institutions, any transition must change the existing institutions. If transition costs are a random event or due to other outside one-time changes, existing regulatory approaches need not be changed. We subscribe to the former assessment. Any reasonable approach to transition costs must stop the problems from recurring and should be subject to a no-forced-losers test. The structural changes in regulation proposed here do that. Major features include:

- providing better information to the market and to regulators.

- promoting competition in generation by creating arm's-length competition, putting more competition in the market, and letting the most efficient suppliers operate the plants. Of the industry's costs, 50 to 70 percent would be returned to the market discipline from their present regulated status.

- using new regulatory forms to improve technical dispute resolution and cooperation among players. The new approach to the problems of network oligopolies permits greater ex ante input from all players including states.

- using yardstick incentives for non-competitive services.

- creating a better state-federal locus of authority. States have more control over power purchases, and the federal government no longer needs to oversee energy and power transactions.

NOTES

1. The fact that simple approaches to efficiency often imply a particular distribution of goods creates much of the confusion between efficiency and fairness.

2. That is, production costs are subadditive so that it is more costly for two or more firms to provide a service than for a single firm to do so.

3. Whether many small non-generating distribution companies can be efficient is a separate issue—local knowledge may matter more for local distribution service.

4. If competitive generation markets produce benefits for society, why wait? Over the last decade, the most profitable (possibly the only profitable) diversification activity for electric utilities has been independent power producers (IPPs).

5. A variation on this approach would have the local regulator and utility design a contract to buy power and accept bids for the assets.

6. One can debate the fairness of the status quo, but it usually offers the only practical point against which to judge change. Thus sharing benefits from selling expensive plants can probably occur only after disposing of all issues of prudence. Until then, no one knows what the starting distribution of cost and benefit is, so it is hard to share an improvement in the overall result equitably.

7.   The classic example is the Hush-a-phone case (see Kahn, 1971). There, AT&T argued successfully that a plastic device attached to a telephone receiver to ensure privacy for conversations was an "alien attachment" that degraded service quality—despite the fact that many thousands of customers bought the device and preferred the "degraded" service. Although the Federal Communications Commission (FCC) initially agreed with AT&T, a federal circuit court eventually struck down the ruling. The formal legal system must be used as a last resort as it often involves exchanges among the technically ignorant.

8.   Although we recommend shifting all jurisdiction over transmission to the federal level, state policies will remain crucial in other ways. For instance, the state policy toward power procurement will affect the demands placed on transmission systems, and state policy may greatly affect the nature of power trading.

REFERENCES

Alger, Daniel R., Richard P. O'Neill, and Michael A. Toman. "Gas Transportation Rate Design and the Use of Auctions to Allocate Capacity." Washington, DC: Federal Energy Regulatory Commission, July 1987.

Baumol, William J. *Superfairness*. Cambridge, MA: MIT Press, 1986.

Baumol, William J., and David Bradford. "Optimal Departures from Marginal Cost Pricing." *American Economic Review* 60 (June 1970): 265–283.

Baumol, William J., John C. Panzar, and Robert D. Willig. *Contestable Markets and the Theory of Market Structure*. New York: Harcourt, Brace, Jovanovich, 1982.

Bonbright, James C., Albert L. Danielsen, and David R. Kamerschen. *Principles of Public Utility Rates*. Arlington, VA: Public Utility Reports, 1988.

Braeutigam, Ronald R. "An Analysis of Fully Distributed Cost Pricing in Regulated Industries." *Bell Journal of Economics* 11 (Spring 1980): 182–196.

Braeutigam, Ronald R. "Optimal Pricing with Intermodal Competition." *American Economic Review.* 69 (March 1979): 38–49.

Brown, Stephen J., and David S. Sibley. *The Theory of Public Utility Pricing*. Cambridge: Cambridge University Press, 1986.

Coase, R. H. "The Nature of the Firm." *Econometrica* 4 (1937), reprinted in American Economic Association. *Readings in Price Theory*. Chicago: Irwin, 1952, p. 331–351.

Coase, R. H. "The Regulated Industries–Discussion." *American Economic Review* 54 (May 1964): 194–197.

Demsetz, Harold. "Why Regulate Utilities?" *Journal of Law and Economics* 55 (1968): 62–63.

Federal Energy Regulatory Commission (FERC). *The Transmission Task Force's Report to the Commission–Electricity Transmission: Realities, Theory and Policy Alternatives.* Washington, DC: FERC, 1989.

Goldberg, V. "Regulation and Administered Contracts." *Bell Journal of Economics* 7 (1976): 426–428.

Goldberg, V. "Toward an Expanded Economic Theory of Contract." *Journal of Economic Issues* 86 (June 1976): 256–277.

Harris, Milton. "Optimal Incentive Contracts with Imperfect Information." *Journal of Economic Theory.* 20 (April 1979): 231-259.

Harris, Milton, and Arthur Raviv. "A Theory of Monopoly Pricing Schemes with Demand Uncertainty." *American Economic Review* 71 (June 1981): 347–365.

Hogan, William W. "Electric Transmission Capacity: What it Costs Depends on What it is." Presented at American Bar Association Sixth Annual Conference on Electricity Law and Regulation, 1993.

Hogan, William W. "Transmission Pricing: It's Not Brain Surgery." *The Electricity Journal* 6 (March 1993): 18–29.

Jaffe, Adam B., and Joseph P. Kalt. "Incentive Regulation for Natural Gas Pipelines." Discussion draft, financial support provided by Transcontinental Gal Pipeline Corp., Cambridge, MA: Harvard University, November 1991.

Jones, Douglas et al. *Regional Regulation of Public Utilities: Opportunities and Obstacles.* Columbus, OH: National Regulatory Research Institute, 1992.

Joskow, P. "Asset Specificity and the Structure of Vertical Relationships: Empirical Evidence." *Journal of Law, Economics, and Organization* 4 (1988): 95–117.

Joskow, P. "Regulatory Failure, Regulatory Reform, and Structural Change in the Electric Power Industry." In *Brookings Papers: Microeconomics* 1989. Washington, DC: Brookings Institution, 1989.

Joskow, P., and R. Schmalensee. "Incentive Regulation for Electric Utilities." *Yale Journal of Regulation* 4 (1986): 1–50.

Joskow, P. and R. Schmalensee. *Markets for Power: An Analysis of Electric Utility Deregulation.* Cambridge, MA: MIT Press, 1983.

Kahn, Alfred E. *The Economics of Regulation.* New York: John Wiley & Sons, 1971.

Kelly, Kevin, J. Stephen Henderson, and Peter A. Nagler. *Some Economic Principles for Wheeled Power.* Columbus, OH: National Regulatory Research Institute, 1987.

Landes, W. M., and R.A. Posner. "Market Power in Antitrust Cases." *Harvard Law Review* 94 (March 1981): 937–996.

Littlechild, Stephen C. "A Game-Theoretic Approach to Public Utility Pricing." *Western Economic Journal* 8 (June 1970): 162–166.

Luce, R. D., and Howard Raiffa. *Games and Decisions*. New York: John Wiley and Sons, 1957.

Mankiw, N. G., and M. D. Whinston. "Free Entry and Social Inefficiency." *The Rand Journal of Economics* 17 (Spring 1986): 48–58.

McCabe, Kevin, Steven Rassenti, and Vernon L. Smith. "An Experimental Examination of Competition and 'Smart' Markets on Natural Gas Pipeline Networks." Federal Energy Regulatory Commission Technical Report, July 1988.

Miller, Robert H. *Power System Operation*. New York: McGraw-Hill, 1970.

Mueller, D. C. *Public Choice*. Cambridge: Cambridge University Press, 1979.

National Grid Company. *Seven Year Statement for the Years 1992/93 to 1998/99*. Coventry, United Kingdom: National Grid Company, 1992.

Oi, Walter. "A Disneyland Dilemma: Two-Part Tariffs for a Mickey Mouse Monopoly." *Quarterly Journal of Economics* 85 (1971): 77–96.

O'Neill, Richard P. "Competition, Efficiency and Equity in Commission Regulation." Discussion paper. Washington, DC: Federal Energy Regulatory Commission, April 1990.

O'Neill, Richard P., and William R. Stewart. "Auctions with Incentives for Fair and Efficient Pricing of Public Utility Services." Discussion paper. Washington, DC: Federal Energy Regulatory Commission, March 1990.

Owen, Guillermo. *Game Theory* 2nd ed. New York: Academic Press, 1982.

Phillips, Charles F., Jr. *The Regulation of Public Utilities: Theory and Practice*. Arlington, VA: Public Utility Reports, 1988.

Raiffa, Howard. *The Art and Science of Negotiation*. Cambridge, MA: Harvard University Press, 1982.

Ramsey, F. P. "A Contribution to the Theory of Taxation." *The Economic Journal* 37 (March 1927): 47–61.

Roth, Alvin E., and Marilda A. O. Sotomayor. *Two-Sided Matching*. Cambridge: Cambridge University Press, 1990.

Rothkopf, M. H., E. P. Kahn, T. J. Teisberg, J. Eto, and J. M. Notaf. *Designing PURPA Power Purchase Auctions: Theory and Practice*. Berkeley, CA: Lawrence Berkeley Laboratory, August 1987.

Schmalensee, R. "Another Look at Market Power." *Harvard Law Review* 95 (June 1982): 1789–1816.

Schmalensee, Richard, and Robert Willig. *Handbook of Industrial Organization*. New York: North Holland, 1989.

Schweppe, Fred C., Michael C. Caramanis, Richard D. Tabors, and Roger E. Bohn. *Spot Pricing of Electricity*. Boston: Kluwer Academic Publishers, 1988.

Sherman, Roger, and Michael Visscher. "Second Best Pricing and Stochastic Demand." *American Economic Review* 68 (March 1978): 41–53.

Stalon, Charles G. "Feasible Regulatory Objectives for Weak Monopolies." Washington, DC: Federal Energy Regulatory Commission, September 11, 1990.

Stalon, Charles G. "Paths Out of the Maze." *The Electricity Journal* 6 (June 1993): 29–35.

Stalon, Charles G. "Pricing Transmission Network Services." Presented at American Bar Association, The Sixth Annual Conference on Electricity Law and Regulation, 1993.

Stiglitz, Joseph E. *Economics of the Public Sector*, 2nd ed. New York: W.W. Norton, 1988.

Telser, L. A. *A Theory of Efficient Cooperation and Competition.* Cambridge: Cambridge University Press, 1987.

Tenenbaum, Bernard W., and Henderson, J. Stephen. "Market-Based Pricing of Wholesale Electric Services." *The Electricity Journal* 4 (December 1991): 30–45.

Vickrey, W. "Counterspeculation, Auctions, and Competitive Sealed Tenders." *Journal of Finance.* 16 (March 1961): 8–37.

von Neumann, John, and Oskar Morgenstern. *Theory of Games and Economic Behavior.* Princeton NJ: Princeton University Press, 1944 (1st ed.), 1947 (2nd ed).

Williamson, Oliver E. "Franchise Bidding for Natural Monopolies–In General and With Respect to CATV." *Bell Journal of Economics* 7 (1976): 73–104.

Williamson, Oliver E. "Transaction-Cost Economics: The Governance of Contractual Relations." *Journal of Law and Economics* 22 (October 1979): 233–261.

Williamson, Oliver E. *The Economic Institutions of Capitalism.* New York: The Free Press, 1988.

Willig, Robert D. "Pareto-Superior Nonlinear Outlay Schedules." *The Bell Journal of Economics* 9 (1978): 56–69.

Willig, Robert D. "Consumer Surplus Without Apology." *American Economic Review.* 66 (September 1976): 589–597.

8

Inter-Jurisdictional Economic Cooperation: Regional Power Markets

Kevin A. Kelly

James Madison, arguing in *The Federalist Papers* (1788) for adoption of our Constitution to replace the original Articles of Confederation, wrote:

> The powers delegated by the proposed Constitution to the federal government are few and defined. Those which are to remain in the State governments are numerous and indefinite . . . If the new Constitution be examined with accuracy and candor, it will be found that the change which it proposes consists much less in the addition of new powers to the Union than in the invigoration of its original powers. The regulation of commerce, it is true, is a new power; but that seems to be an addition which few oppose and from which no apprehensions are entertained.

Today, Mr. Madison would likely share our apprehensions about federal and state regulation of regional commerce in electric power.[1] The focus of this chapter is whether federal and state regulatory authorities will cooperate or clash with one another as the electric power industry evolves toward larger regional markets. Federal-state relations have frequently been strained in the area of electricity regulation. Yet both classes of regulators have the same goal of ensuring adequate and reliable electric service at the lowest cost in a simply configured industry. As the configuration of the industry becomes more complex, the goal of merging market and planning concepts may be pursued differently by federal and state regulators. Regulatory jurisdictional tensions will increase unless new means of sharing regulatory responsibilities are worked out.

HISTORICAL INTRODUCTION

During its first half-century, the electric power business, where it was regulated at all, was regulated by state and local governments. From the early 1880s to the early 1930s, electric companies were mostly local businesses serving local needs.

In the second half-century, from the early 1930s to the early 1980s, the influence of the federal government in the electric power business grew.[2] No longer a novelty, electricity became a necessity of modern life and an engine of the economy. Privately owned electric companies struggled for control of the lucrative industrial markets in densely populated urban areas. Many rural areas were ignored. Urban areas became more tightly interconnected, interstate electricity commerce increased, and much electric corporate power was concentrated in a few national holding companies. State utility regulatory commissions complained that the resulting problems were outside the power of any one state to control.

For the most part, federal solutions were designed to complement, not supplant, state regulation. The new federal laws solved problems that the states could not. This is particularly apparent in the 1935 Public Utility Holding Company Act (PUHCA) in its system of exemptions from Securities and Exchange Commission regulation of holding companies. The principle underlying the exemptions is that the SEC cannot regulate corporate structures which the states can reach. PUHCA created strong measures to break up most then-existing holding companies into single-state entities subject to state regulation.

The 1935 Federal Power Act gave the Federal Power Commission the authority to regulate prices for interstate power sales, thereby filling a "regulatory gap." The act was in large part a response to a 1927 Supreme Court ruling that a state could not constitutionally regulate the price of power generated in one state and sold in another.[3] The most serious clash between federal and state electricity regulators during the second half-century of U.S. electric power involved the intent of Congress in filling this regulatory gap. Before 1960, each state believed it had the authority to set rates for all the electricity generated in the state and sold to a buyer in the state, regardless of whether the sale was a retail sale to a consumer or a wholesale sale to a power distributor.

In the early 1960s, the Federal Power Commission claimed exclusive authority to regulate the price of power generated in a state and sold at wholesale to a distributor in the *same* state over transmission lines that are part of an interstate network. The Supreme Court affirmed the Commission's view that such a sale is in interstate commerce and subject exclusively to the jurisdiction of the Commission under the Federal Power Act.[4]

As the second electric century began in the early 1980s, first the Federal Energy Regulatory Commission (FERC, which took over most FPC responsibilities), then the Department of Energy, and now the Congress have taken a new interest in the regulation—or deregulation—of the electric power sector of the economy. Much of this interest stems from the increasingly multi-state regional economic character of the business, which creates new "regulatory gaps"—areas of public interest that neither federal nor state regulators can address adequately acting alone.

For example, states have always had exclusive authority over the relations between the local electricity distributor and its retail customers. In the 1970s and 1980s, customer conservation and other so-called demand-side management (DSM) programs became an integral part of generation supply planning, and states took increasing interest in how best to balance the utility's future electricity supply and demand. As the federal interest in supply and transmission planning for multi-state entities grows, the question of who—if anyone—has the authority to oversee all aspects of multi-state utility planning, including DSM programs, keeps coming up. DSM programs are inherently local and retail, and seemingly not subject to federal review. A regulatory gap may exist if regulatory oversight of integrated supply and demand planning is needed, and neither federal nor state authority alone is adequate.

An open question still is whether this new federal interest will result in new federal authorities which complement state regulation or whether it will further supplant state authority, either immediately by design or eventually by erosion.

WAYS OF REGULATING REGIONAL MARKETS

The original rationale for state regulation of electric companies still holds. States are closer to the electricity customers, sensitive to local economic and environmental concerns, the source of electric company franchises and rights of way, and—unless many more mergers occur in the electric sector to reduce the number of U.S. companies and hence the regulatory work load—staffed sufficiently to regulate hundreds of electric companies. Retail rate regulation is safely in state hands. In the Energy Policy Act of 1992, Congress in many ways affirmed the exclusive authority of state regulators over retail electricity sales. At the same time, however, Congress increased federal authority in new areas, creating new opportunities for federal-state jurisdictional disputes.

Congress created new federal authorities because the electric power business is more than ever in interstate commerce, and even international commerce. Also, federal lawmakers and regulators look to new ways of regulating electric utilities as they consider new actions and treaties to control global climate change. How can these national interests be best coordinated with state regulation?

Several important electricity decisions regarding federal and state regulatory authorities were made—and others avoided—in the Energy Policy Act of 1992. The way we implement this act over the next few months and years will profoundly affect the relative ease or difficulty with which regional power markets work. Federal and state decision makers need to examine how their authorities can best be coordinated in regulating the rapidly evolving electric power industry. If they do this successfully, regional markets can operate effectively to lower regional costs. Otherwise, the outcome may satisfy neither side and generate years of litigation to reset the so-called "bright line" between federal and state electricity jurisdictions.

Several approaches to regulating regional electricity markets are possible. No single approach is necessarily the best: The various approaches to cooperative regulation may not work equally well for different regional issues.

No Change

Some would argue that no new approach is needed at all. Existing ways work, and anything new would create a new "layer of regulation" by adding to existing federal and state procedures. This, it is said, would impede instead of help regional market development.

State Cooperation

A second option is to rely on the states in a region to regulate cooperatively without any federal role. Cooperative state regulation can take any of several forms. An informal mechanism such as that employed recently in New England and the West is a weaker form. Also, states could engage in voluntary agreements under which they would coordinate their activities and consider regional needs in their planning and pricing activities. States could also create formal interstate compacts for regional regulation with formal rules and procedures to be followed by participants.

Federal-State Joint Board

Most often, FERC and the state commissions each treat the other as they would any other intervener with no special standing, although each is a government agency which decides rate base, rate of return, and allowable expenses, often for the same assets and operating costs. Once a matter is before the FERC, commissioner and senior staff communications with anyone—including state regulators—about the case are cut off, except for formal filing of comments. State commissioners treat federal officials the same way. This is not a retaliation: The federal government is one of the nation's largest electricity consumers, and the Department of Energy—of which the FERC is a part—frequently intervenes in state rate cases to seek favorable electricity retail rate treatment for federal facilities.

This separatist approach may work poorly as multi-state regional markets grow. Various forms of cooperative federal-state regulation are possible. For example, the Federal Power Act permits the FERC to establish a joint board of federal and state regulators to handle multi-state regional issues. This requires a formal agreement defining the duties and obligations of each agency.

There are less formal ways of regulating cooperatively. At a minimum, the FERC and state public utility commissions could exchange and compare the information and statistics they receive about firms they regulate.

Federal Preemption

Congress could decide that, for some issues, simple federal preemption is preferable to a complicated system of cooperative state-state or federal-state regulation. In other areas of the electric power business and for other energy businesses, federal agencies frequently have preemptive authority. For example, the FERC has preemptive authority over most aspects of hydroelectric facility licensing and over oil and gas pipeline siting, and the Nuclear Regulatory Commission is the sole judge of nuclear power plant safety issues.

Federal electricity regulation could be extended to some or all multi-state regional activities of the electric power business. Some state officials have suggested, for example, that there may need to be a federal role in siting electric transmission lines that traverse more than one state.

Although some industry analysts favor simple federal preemption, others would allow federal preemption only if the states involved cannot agree among themselves, formally or informally, about the best policy for the region.

Industry Self-Regulation

Voluntary associations among industry participants could be used to resolve some regional issues without primary reliance on regulators. The electric power industry has taken this approach before: It created the North American Electric Reliability Council and the Institute for Nuclear Power Operations at least in part as alternatives to increased federal regulation of grid reliability and nuclear plant operating practices.

A private-sector agency composed fairly of all regional industry players could address many regional technical and planning issues, subject to either state or federal regulatory oversight.

REGIONAL ISSUES

Federal-state coordination is important because of recent regional issues of concern to both federal and state authorities. Some current regional issues relate to the growing reliance on market forces to reduce the cost of electricity. Others concern increased reliance on government oversight of industry planning for lowering costs or reducing the environmental effects of electricity generation. Let us consider some of these regional market and planning issues.

Market Issues

International Relations

Increasingly, electricity trade issues are of federal interest because they occur in regions which extend into another country. Therefore, they affect U.S. relations with neighboring countries.

U.S. electric transmission grids are international.[5] There is great potential for economies in joint planning between U.S. and Canadian utilities, which are interconnected at many points along our common border. International purchases and sales of electric power are likely to grow, leading to growing federal interest in these two-country regional power markets.[6]

State regulation of utilities that participate in two-country regional markets may need to be coordinated with federal trade initiatives and diplomatic efforts. Could a state's integrated resource-planning order, for example, conflict with a free trade agreement? We need to develop a system of federal-state cooperation that fits with the increasingly international character of the business.

Would a two-country regional transmission group partly outside FERC jurisdiction be discouraged or disapproved by the FERC as too difficult jurisdictionally for the commission to monitor? The governments of the two countries might choose some cooperative joint oversight rather than forego the benefits of an industry association which reflects the physical and economic characteristics of the regional power market.

Wholesale Power Price Deregulation

The FERC has granted many requests for market-based rates for wholesale generation by electric utilities.[7] It does so only where it finds that a market exists and the power supplier lacks the market power to control the price of electricity. Then the FERC does not set the price through the traditional method of calculating in detail the supplier's production cost. Instead, the FERC lets the market regulate the price. In effect, the price is deregulated, but only if the FERC finds on a case-by-case basis that an adequate market exists.

Both federal and state regulations affect the development of these deregulated power markets and the existence or absence of market power. States approve the competitive means of selecting new supply resources and demand control strategies. Conflicts could arise because of a state's use of non-market factors in its generation resource selection process. Restrictions on market participation or fuel use could conflict with the FERC's need to find that the power price is set by an unconstrained market before it allows the winner of a state-approved resource competition to charge market-based rates. Some vehicle for federal-state dialogue is needed to avoid these potential conflicts.

Externalities

State commissions efforts to "internalize the externalities" associated with electricity production may attract increasing regional or federal attention.[8] Use of externality adders by only some states or inconsistent use of externality ideas among states would skew investment decisions by power producers. If a state uses unusual externality values in choosing a source of electricity in a competitive market, the FERC may not allow the winner of the price competition to charge a market-based rate. A regional approach to externalities would reduce these electricity market distortions.

Alternatively, a state which ignores environmental externalities could find itself at odds with future federal regulations. Congress considered requiring states to include environmental costs in resource plans during the development of the Energy Policy Act, and although this requirement was not included in the act, the issue may come up again. Also, state efforts to control the state "fuel mix," that is, the ratios of various fuels for generating electricity, may conflict with future federal rules to control national greenhouse gas emissions.

SO₂ Allowance Trading

The allowance trading provisions of the Clean Air Act Amendments are intended to reduce a utility's SO_2 emissions in the lowest cost way. Whether it results in least cost reduction for a multi-state region depends in part on state regulatory policies. A least-cost solution is likely to involve several utilities and states, but a regional least-cost solution may create winners and losers within the region. A state may act to minimize a utility's compliance cost or the state's cost instead of the region's cost.

Transmission Pricing

Transmission pricing is a difficult federal-state jurisdictional issue. In the Energy Policy Act of 1992, Congress gave the FERC authority to order transmission service and restated (in new language) FERC's authority to set wholesale transmission prices. States retain authority over transmission siting and over recovery, in retail rates, of most of the utility's transmission capital investment and transmission expenses.

This split jurisdiction over transmission prices can result in considerable federal-state conflict if a means of cooperative regulation is not developed. A state places great importance on protecting its utility's native load customers from having to subsidize the transmission costs of the utility's wholesale transmission customers. To promote an efficient regional power market, the FERC places great importance on setting the transmission price for wholesale transmission customers at the lowest reasonable rate.

Transmission costs must be allocated between FERC-regulated and state-regulated transmission services. But economists contend that there is no theoretically correct way to allocate common costs: The allocation of the common transmission costs is inherently arbitrary. The cooperative development of an agreed-upon cost allocation procedure accepted by both regulators is necessary to avoid conflict. The recent FERC inquiry on transmission pricing must recognize this.

Although cost allocation can be a problem for either existing or new transmission capacity, it will be particularly difficult where new transmission capacity is needed just to comply with a FERC transmission order. Will the cost of the extra capacity go into the retail or the wholesale ratebase? What if economies of scale require construction of a large line with more capacity than is needed to comply minimally with the FERC order: Who pays for the extra capacity?

Planning Issues

Regional Integrated Resource Planning

Integrated resource planning (IRP) has been done mostly for individual utilities. Some states, particularly Wisconsin, have begun to develop an integrated least-cost plan for the state as a whole. The larger the integrated planning region the more opportunities for savings.

Electricity is likely to be produced at the lowest cost if the planning region is as large as possible and federal interest in developing integrated regional plans may grow.[9] A principal example of federal interest in regional cost minimization is in the Northwest.[10] However, although the total regional cost may go down, the costs of individual utilities or states may go up. For example, a state with low-cost hydroelectric resources is likely to experience a cost increase as its neighbors share access to these resources. Federal regulators may be at odds with state regulators if federal policymakers' interest in regional cost minimization grows while state policymakers' interest remains focused on state cost minimization.

The public policy issue is whether it is possible to coordinate the integrated resource plans of many utilities subject to several state jurisdictions without running into federal-state jurisdictional conflicts. How can several utilities coordinate the planning of new generation and transmission capacity additions or demand-side management activities so that the costs and benefits are allocated fairly?

Multi-State Holding Companies

A multi-state utility holding company comes under the regulatory authorities of the FERC and the SEC. It consists of several subsidiary companies operating in several states and subject to the regulation of several state commissions. The holding company system operates and plans to minimize costs throughout the system, not on an individual operating company basis. As such, it challenges federal and state regulators to develop cooperative ways to regulate it while retaining the economies it offers. The holding company situation is a kind of case study of future federal-state conflicts as federal interest in regional planning grows. Indeed, most of the federal-state issues that can arise in regional markets, such as allowance trading, integrated resource planning, and transmission planning, can and have been issues for holding companies.

The electric business opened its second century with a contentious court case involving a registered holding company and another "regulatory gap" in federal and state authority. Here the gap involved a lack of regulatory authority to require and enforce integrated resource planning for the integrated system, stimulating a proposed federal law.[11] The proposal raised several questions. Are changes in federal or state laws needed to enable states to regulate cooperatively and enforceably? If the states cannot agree on the best plan for the multi-state system, should FERC decide the integrated resource plan? If so, does this undesirably take the FERC beyond wholesale power regulation into demand-side regulation? Is the best plan the same as the least-cost plan? The proposal was viewed cautiously not only by some federal regulators but also by holding companies and regulators in other regions.

CONCLUSIONS

Resolving the federal-state jurisdictional disputes that arise in regional regulation will not be easy. Yet, cooperation among the states, between the states and the federal government, and among the United States, Canada, and the Canadian provincial governments is necessary if multi-state regional markets are to realize the possible benefits. Today's holding company regional issues may foreshadow federal-state jurisdictional issues that can arise for unaffiliated companies as regional markets, and federal interest in them, develop further.

Although cooperation is needed, there is not necessarily a "right" way to do it that works for every regional issue. Perhaps—and this is purely by way of providing examples—no new cooperative mechanism may be needed for treating allowance trading issues, federal preemption may be appropriate for determining if market conditions allow wholesale price deregulation, state-to-state joint regulation might work best for regional IRP, industry self-regulation could be used for regional grid planning, and a federal-state joint board could be used for multi-state transmission line siting decisions. The structure of the industry and the nature of the issue ought to guide us to the appropriate federal-state regulatory approach.

NOTES

1.   The electric power business today is more than ever concerned with regional markets and regional planning. Markets imply competition, and government oversight of anti-competitive activities. Planning implies cooperation and government monitoring of industry plans. Whether regional industry participants can cooperate with one another, for example, in transmission planning, as they compete with one another in wholesale power sales, is one key issue. Another is how government during this period of change relates to

industry, whether more as a partner or an overseer.

2.   In the federal government, executive and legislative branch leaders looked for federal solutions. In the mid-1930s, this led to the creation of the Federal Power Commission (FPC), the Securities and Exchange Commission (SEC), the Rural Electrification Administration (REA), the Tennessee Valley Authority (TVA), and the federal power-marketing administrations such as the Bonneville Power Administration (BPA).

3.   This *Attleboro* ruling denied the Rhode Island Public Utilities Commission the right to set the rates for power generated by a utility in Rhode Island and sold to a distributor in Massachusetts. Because Massachusetts could not constitutionally regulate the Rhode Island generator, and no Federal power regulator existed at the time, the ruling was said to create a "regulatory gap," which Congress had to fill. Congress (1935) authorized the FPC to regulate interstate electricity commerce, but provided in the Federal Power Act that "such federal regulation, however, [is] to extend only to those matters which are not subject to regulation by the states." See U.S. Supreme Court (1927).

4.   This *Colton* decision gave the FPC jurisdiction over almost all U.S. wholesale power sales, except for most of Texas, where the transmission grid remains electrically isolated from grids in other states. A series of subsequent decisions clarified the broad scope of the commission's authority, covering not only rates but also all the attendant terms and conditions of wholesale service. See U.S. Supreme Court (1964).

5.   The Eastern Interconnection is a synchronously operated transmission network that runs from Key West, Florida to New Brunswick, Canada and extends some two thousand miles westward from the east coasts of both countries. The Western Interconnection extends into resource-rich British Columbia and a small portion of Mexico.

6.   The Free Trade Agreement with Canada and the North American Free Trade Agreement with Canada and Mexico apply to trade in electricity. Unintended power flows around Lake Erie are already the subject of U.S.–Canadian discussions. Because many Canadian utilities are part of the provincial governments, relations between U.S. and Canadian utilities have a diplomatic dimension. Several North American Electric Reliability Council regions encompass parts of the United States and another country. The emerging regional transmission groups may also extend into Canada or Mexico.

7.   The first thirty FERC cases involving market-based rates are reviewed in Tenenbaum and Henderson (1991, p. 30).

8.   Some states have used externality "adders" to alter the prices of electricity from various potential sources, based mostly on the fuel used, before the lowest-cost option is determined. The adders are intended to reflect the environmental costs and benefits of each option which are not reflected in the supplier's bid price. In some states, economic and other factors may also be accounted for.

9. If the "plan" is to rely on a competitive market to minimize costs, the market should be as large as possible.

10. The Bonneville Power Administration operates over a large region under the requirements of the Northwest Power Planning Act. BPA's IRP follows a regional approach that allows BPA to capture economies that might not be available if it minimized the costs of smaller segments of its system.

11. Over the objections of state regulators, the Supreme Court upheld a FERC order allocating the costs of the Grand Gulf nuclear power plant among utilities in three states. As a result, the Arkansas Commission, Entergy, and the City of New Orleans proposed a federal law setting up a procedure for states and the FERC to do integrated resource planning for a multi-state holding company.

REFERENCES

Madison, James. "The Federalist No. 45." In James Madison, Alexander Hamilton, and John Jay, *The Federalist Papers*, Isaac Kramnick (ed.). New York: Penguin Books, 1988 (first published, 1788).

Tenenbaum, Bernard W., and J. Stephen Henderson. "Market-Based Pricing of Wholesale Electric Services." *The Electricity Journal* 4 (December 1991).

U.S. Congress. *Federal Power Act.* §201(a), 16 U.S.C. 824, 1935.

U.S. Supreme Court. *Federal Power Commission v. Southern California Edison Co.* 376 U.S. 205, reh. denied, 377 U.S. 913, 1964.

U.S. Supreme Court. *Rhode Island Public Utilities Commission v. Attleboro Steam and Electric Co.* 273 U.S. 83, 1927.

9

Inter-Jurisdictional Environmental Cooperation: Regional Emissions Trading

Praveen K. Amar, Michael J. Bradley, and
Donna M. Boysen

Environmental problems spill across jurisdictional boundaries to a much greater extent than the electric power systems which help cause them. In recognition of this fact, responsibilities for environmental regulation in the United States are shared by the state and federal levels of government, with an increasing trend toward regional entities. This chapter examines an ongoing initiative in regional cooperation initiated by Northeast States for Coordinated Air Use Management (NESCAUM).[1] This regional agency was created in 1967 by the environmental administrators of eight Northeastern states from New Jersey through Maine, in recognition that they share a common airshed. The initiative involves creating a regional market-based emissions cap system for oxides of nitrogen (NO_x).

BACKGROUND

The pattern of U. S. environmental regulation has evolved over thirty years from a focus on plant-specific impacts to a more system-wide view, as embodied in the sulfur dioxide emissions trading scheme of Title IV of the 1990 Clean Air Act Amendments (1990 CAAA). This has occurred in part because the worst local environmental impacts by now are coming under control, and the remaining challenges involve longer-range pollutants and longer-term planning issues. During this period, a national "floor" of environmental standards has been put in place by Congress, but much regulatory implementation is performed by the states under the eye of the U.S. Environmental Protection Agency (EPA). The system-wide perspective adopted in recent legislation encourages states to cooperate with their regional neighbors in order to cost-effectively meet federal mandates.

The 1990 CAAA also strongly encourage the design and application of market-based approaches to control air pollution.[2] NESCAUM has been exploring the feasibility of a market-based emission trading program (ETP) since April 1992. More recently an Ozone Transport Commission has begun examining the same questions for a larger portion of the Northeast.[3]

In order to meet ambient air quality standards for ground level ozone, Northeastern states must dramatically reduce emissions of ozone precursors, chiefly NO_x and volatile organic compounds (VOCs).[4] The potential for interstate/regional trading of VOCs is diminished by variations in toxicity, reactivity, exposure, and added difficulties in enforcement; therefore emissions trading proposals have focused on NO_x. Two major challenges in creating a market-based regional emissions cap system are (1) creating a viable trading scheme and (2) achieving regional cooperation. We address each topic in turn.

CREATING A VIABLE TRADING SCHEME

There is a modest amount of experience in creating emissions trading schemes. Here we briefly sketch the likely advantages of a NO_x emissions cap system relative to traditional regulatory approaches, the lessons from other recent experiments with emissions trading, and the technical components needed in such systems.

Expected Advantages of a NO_x Emissions Cap System

An emissions cap system offers two primary advantages: clear goals and compliance flexibility, as well as other benefits.

Clear Goals

An emissions cap system provides the air pollution control agencies with increased certainty of achieving environmental results, while at the same time providing the affected industry with increased certainty in its environmental planning process. It does so by setting clear goals for emission reductions and by setting the time deadlines by which they need to be met.[5] It is expected that these types of caps, by providing well-defined goals in terms of region-wide limits on daily and annual emissions as well as limits on NO_x emissions per unit of electric output, will help the regulated industry in the NESCAUM region in its long-term environmental and resource planning.

Compliance Flexibility

An emissions cap system provides an increased level of compliance flexibility to industry as compared to the more traditional command and control alternative. Using the market-based cap approach, sources may choose the method of compliance that best suits the source's unique combination of needs, available resources, and long-term planning goals. Some potential compliance options include fuel switching, repowering, or application of control technology to existing equipment, measures to improve efficiency of electricity production and use, and the purchase of emissions allowances. Under an emissions cap system, sources will have the ability to choose the lowest-cost option available to them to meet the requirements of the NO_x emissions reduction targets for their facilities. Past clean air laws and policies in the United States have sometimes impeded the search for least-cost approaches to air quality.[6]

Other Benefits

The use of a market-based cap system may provide environmental benefits in addition to NO_x reductions. A properly implemented emission cap system has the strong potential to also deliver emission reductions of SO_2, particulates, air toxics, and carbon dioxide via the implementation of demand-side management measures, energy efficiency and conservation measures, increased reliance on renewable sources of energy, and switching to cleaner fuels. Use of such options could also result in the generation of lower amounts of solid waste (ash) as compared to a more traditional command and control program.

Past and Existing Emissions Cap Programs

Any emission cap system for NO_x for the NESCAUM region will need to consider the experience gained in similar programs across the United States. Precedents for the use of a cap have been established by the gasoline lead program of the last decade, and more recently by the national SO_2 cap system being implemented for acid rain control, the utility-wide NO_x emission caps in California's South Coast Air Basin, and by the NO_x and SO_2 cap system proposed under the South Coast Air Quality Management District's (SCAQMD) Regional Clean Air Incentives Market (RECLAIM) program in southern California. A brief discussion of the three more recent programs follows.

Title IV Acid Rain Program

The overall goal of this program is to significantly reduce SO_2 and NO_x emissions, the two precursors to acid rain. SO_2 reductions of 10 million tons below 1980 levels will be achieved through a market-based approach.[7] The program establishes an innovative, market-based allowance trading system to reduce SO_2 emissions. Under this system, power plants will be allocated tradable allowances based on their past fuel usage and statutory emission limitations. An allowance authorizes a unit within a utility or industrial source to emit one ton of SO_2 during or following a given year. At the end of each year, the unit must hold an amount of allowances at least equal to its annual emissions; otherwise stringent penalties will apply. After the year 2000, the total number of allowances allocated each year will be half of what the source emitted in 1980.

Allowances may be bought, sold, traded, or banked for use in future years like any other fully marketable commodity. A unit with allowances that do not cover its emissions has a number of options. These include transferring allowances from other units within its utility system, buying allowances on the open market from another utility, or buying allowances through EPA auctions. More importantly, a unit may choose to reduce its emissions, thereby reducing the number of allowances needed. Note that many utilities may be required to set lower emissions under the ambient air quality provisions of the CAA than under the acid rain provisions. Emissions reduction options include energy conservation and efficiency measures, and switching to lower-sulfur fuels. Auctions and sales of emission allowances started in 1993 and are conducted by the Chicago Board of Trade under delegation from the EPA.

South Coast's RECLAIM Program

RECLAIM is a marketable permits program for stationary source emissions of NO_x and SO_2. It is a major departure from the current technology-based regulations which have driven the control program in the Los Angeles Basin, the region with the highest pollution levels in the United States. Under RECLAIM, stationary sources will be allowed to achieve their required emission reductions of NO_x and SO_2 through their choice of add-on controls, use of reformulated products, purchasing "excess" emission reductions from other sources at their "free-market" value, or some combination of all of these approaches.

RECLAIM goes far beyond the Title IV emission allowance approach for SO_2 in that it covers two pollutants instead of one and is applied across many different types of industries.[8] For example, in its present design, RECLAIM will cover about 2,700 stationary sources of NO_x and SO_2, compared with 110 utility sources of SO_2 covered under Phase I of Title IV.

One way to understand the key differences between RECLAIM and the current command and control approach is to note that

RECLAIM replaces equipment permits by facility-wide permits, and current emission rate limitations (in lb/MMBtu input) by mass emission limits (quarterly), with annually declining emission limits for all sources. It also replaces current retrofit control rules with rules mandating annual emission reductions and requires high-tech monitoring of emissions for compliance verification.

SCAQMD's rationale for adopting the market-based approach to meet the clean air objectives is that additional incremental emission reductions required to meet the ozone standards in the South Coast Air Basin are extremely difficult to achieve after requiring stringent controls for many sources, large and small, over many years. It appears that the current and future control measures included in the district's 1991 Air Quality Management Plan will not provide sufficient emission reductions to achieve the ambient ozone standard. The control measures recently evaluated by the district were expected to provide only marginal emission reductions and were forcing the district to "micromanage" the industry.[9] All of these reasons are believed to have led the district to radically change its direction.

In spite of ground-breaking progress in the development of the concept, a number of outstanding issues remain before RECLAIM can be successfully implemented. The district is working on a number of rules that will address the issue of enforceability,[10] determination of baseline emissions from which all progress toward required emission reductions will be measured, and the issue of equity among sources.[11] Additionally, there appear to be a number of issues that still need to be resolved before the program is found approvable under the 1990 Clean Air Act (Title I, nonattainment provisions).[12]

SCAQMD Emission Cap System for NO_x from Utilities

SCAQMD recently modified its emission cap system under which the local utilities[13] have operated for the last ten years. It established a novel cap system measured in terms of pounds of NO_x per unit of electric output.[14] The more traditional approach has been to set limits based on pounds of emissions per unit of heat input. However, by requiring an emission cap based on useful output of the system, utilities are encouraged to produce their electric output in the most efficient way possible, thereby minimizing their emissions for a given amount of output. SCAQMD believes that a tightening of caps will give the utilities an additional reason to seriously consider wind, solar, geothermal, fuel cells, demand-side management, conservation, and low- and no-emission resources in their future resource plans.

Technical Components of a Cap

In order to develop a cap system which meets standards of accountability, quantifiability, enforceability, and environmental integrity, a number of fundamental issues need to be addressed.

Baseline Emissions

Before a cap system can be implemented, the baseline emission level for each source affected by the cap must be established. Normally, baseline emissions for a given source are defined as that level of emissions below which any additional reductions may be counted (credited) for use in trades. Different approaches to baseline emissions calculations exist: actual versus allowable emissions, selection of a specific baseline year or the average of several years' emissions, and credit provided to sources with stringent controls already in place. All of these issues and their resolution in other programs need to be examined for their applicability to the NESCAUM cap system as a means for establishing a consistent method for setting baseline emission levels for sources.

Emissions Analysis

Establishing a cap system will require that an appropriate methodology be adopted for measuring the existing levels of NO_x emissions from stationary sources and for quantifying the subsequent reductions made to conform to the cap. Accurate emissions analysis is critical to the ability of a cap system to deliver improvements in air quality.

Allowance Scheme

One of several ways sources can meet their requirements under an emissions cap system is by buying and selling "emission allowances" in a format similar to the Title IV SO_2 allowances. Successful implementation of the cap system will require translating baseline emission levels for sources into emissions allowances. The use of alternative ways to equitably assign NO_x allowances to the sources included in the cap program needs to be evaluated.

Target NO_x Reductions

The current NESCAUM NO_x control strategy is based on the need to meet the NAAQS for ozone for various nonattainment regions. Percentage reductions in NO_x emissions have been determined and are currently being refined using regional photochemical models (ROMNET II, urban airshed model [UAM], etc.). These NO_x reduction targets predicted from the photochemical modeling approach need to be "converted" into a state- or region-wide emissions cap that provides equivalent air quality benefits. Issues of significant concern include the impact of region-wide caps on urban ozone levels as well as long-range transport of ozone and its precursors across adjacent modeling domains.[15]

ACHIEVING REGIONAL COOPERATION

The design of the NESCAUM emission cap system draws on the experience gained in previous experiments.[16] In its broadest terms, the emissions cap system requires an upper bound on NO_x emissions on a regional or sub-regional basis[17] that will need to be met by a certain date in the future. Unlike previous experiments, implementing the NESCAUM system requires close cooperation among multiple jurisdictions. Regional cooperation is most challenging in defining source populations, the geographic scope of the cap, and the type of administrative and enforcement mechanisms. Key points follow.

Source Population

For NO_x emission caps, a number of options exist to determine which sources should be included. The initial source population is still under discussion by NESCAUM members.

- Only utility boilers could be under a region-wide cap.
- Incorporate all fossil-fired units owned by utilities, including internal combustion engines and combustion turbines. These options would result in a cap for about 20 percent of NO_x emissions in the NESCAUM region.
- All major stationary sources, including independent power producers and industrial boilers, could be included under a region-wide cap. This would cover about 35 percent of the NO_x emissions in the region.
- Only by including mobile sources and small area sources as well could the program include a majority of regional emissions.

Geographic Scope

A credible cap system will need to cover an appropriate geographic range. Four main options are available:

State-Wide

The development of state-specific caps has the advantage of ease of integration with SIPs and state-specific request for proposals (RFP) requirements. It may be possible to design state-wide emissions caps to operate effectively within a regional or multi-state emission cap.

Region-Wide

A cap covering a larger region provides a greater level of flexibility to industry in meeting both the cap and NSR requirements; that is, it makes a stronger market. However, the likelihood of some local areas experiencing some degradation in air quality is also increased. The potential for such an adverse impact would need to be factored into the design of a regional cap.

Urban Airshed Model Domain

Establishing a cap for the air corridor extending over the existing UAM domains presents the advantage of dealing with a regional air quality problem in a consistent manner, without unnecessarily burdening those areas where the NO_x problem is of a much smaller magnitude. It requires a higher level of interstate cooperation, however, than a system of state-wide caps.

Electric Power Pool-Based Domain

A cap covering an existing power pool has the distinct advantage of overlaying the cap requirements on a system that is already well integrated.

Administrative/Enforcement Mechanisms

A key implementation issue is how marketable emission allowances under a NO_x emissions cap will interface with other requirements of the 1990 CAAA, including the following concerns.

Title V Operating Permits

These permits can serve important administrative functions of helping to ensure the environmental integrity of a cap system, tracking allowance transactions, and providing sources with clear compliance schedules. The design will need to focus on developing the most effective and administratively efficient means for integrating the tracking and compliance features of a NO_x emissions cap program into the Title V Operating Permit Program.

State Implementation Plans

The adoption of a NO_x emission cap system by a state would be an important component of that state's SIP. The application of a declining cap system would be determined based on the state's RFP requirements and attainment deadlines.

RACT Determination

The consistency in RACT determination by individual NES-CAUM states will serve to greatly reduce inconsistencies and inequities in the generation of the baseline emission levels that will be required under a cap system.[18]

Enforcement Protocols

Consistent enforcement protocols will need to be developed among NESCAUM states to implement the region-wide emission cap system. Interstate protocols which provide clear lines of communication among states, and ensure consistent enforcement among states would be key to successful implementation of the cap system.

Use of Banking/Clearinghouse

To the extent that a cap system results in the generation of emission allowances, sources would rely on the use of banking and clearinghouse/information systems to store and exchange emission allowances. Such systems would need to be publicly or privately created.[19]

NESCAUM members routinely coordinate administrative mechanisms through various sitting committees. For example, RACT determinations are becoming more consistent across the region. Uniform enforcement protocols and a banking or clearinghouse system have not yet been established.

CONCLUSIONS

The recent legislative emphasis on market-based incentives for improving air quality has encouraged unprecedented interactions among government, utilities, environmental groups, and the private sector. To help states within our regional airshed to achieve goals set forth by this legislation, a market-based emissions cap system for NO_x is under development.

A successful and effective emissions cap system needs to have solid technical foundations that take advantage of previous experience. Yet a multi-jurisdictional system has an additional requirement: It must contend with the issue of state sovereignty. It appears that an inter-jurisdictional market must evolve from a coordinated set of intra-jurisdictional markets. Regional cooperation on innovations in environmental protection will only slowly move from an informal to a formal level.

NOTES

1.   NESCAUM (Northeast States for Coordinated Air Use Management) is an interagency association of eight states: Connecticut, Maine, Massachusetts, New Hampshire, New Jersey, New York, Rhode Island, and Vermont.

2.   This push for economic incentives is clear not only in the Title IV (Acid Deposition Control), but also in Title I general provisions for state implementation plans (SIPs) for achieving the National Ambient Air Quality Standards (NAAQS) for ozone. Title I encourages and, in certain cases, mandates market-based approaches for both stationary sources and mobile sources through the use of economic incentive programs. The EPA has recently proposed a set of Economic Incentive Program rules that promote market-based approaches to meet Title I requirements.

3.   As a part of this process, NESCAUM sponsored three roundtable discussions with representatives of state departments of environmental protection, industry, utilities, energy agencies, environmental groups, and EPA. A subsequent effort, initiated by the Ozone Transport Commission (OTC; comprised of above states and the states of Delaware, Maryland, Pennsylvania, Virginia, and Washington, DC) in June 1992, has investigated the need for and structure of an interstate emissions offset/trading program. Both the NESCAUM and OTC efforts share the primary goals of developing an ETP to help provide emission offsets for new growth and to demonstrate required "reasonable further progress" in the SIPs.

4.   The need to reduce NO_x emissions in the Northeast in a cost-effective manner is both a critical and a problematic component of meeting the requirements of the Clean Air Act (CAA). In 1987, NO_x emissions from all sources in the NESCAUM region totaled approximately 1.6 million tons. About 40 percent of the annual NO_x emissions are from stationary sources, and the remaining 60 percent are from mobile sources. A substantial portion of the stationary source component of NO_x (about 80 to 90 percent) is emitted by four major categories of stationary sources: utility boilers, industrial and commercial boilers, combustion turbines, and large internal combustion engines. Some or all of these source categories could be considered under an emissions cap system. Based on the results of the most recent regional ozone modeling (ROMNET) analysis, the northeast states will require NO_x emissions reductions which are far more extensive than was first thought in order to comply with the NAAQS for ozone. To begin to address this concern, in 1992 the NESCAUM Stationary Source Committee developed recommendations on Reasonably Available Control Technology (RACT) for NO_x emissions from the four categories listed above. Each of the eight NESCAUM states is in the process of adopting these RACT measures, which are expected to provide approximately 35 percent reduction in NO_x emissions from these sources. Region-wide NO_x emission reductions are also necessary to provide for NO_x emission offsets triggered by New Source Review (NSR) requirements for ozone nonattainment areas. This mandate of providing offsets for new growth poses the most immediate concern for economic growth in the Northeast. A properly

designed and executed market-based NO_x emissions cap system can provide for the additional NO_x reduction necessary to meet NAAQS and provide an effective process for the generation of NO_x emission offsets for new sources.

5.   During the ratcheted phase-out of lead from gasoline in the 1980s, an emissions trading system provided clear goals and significant transition cost savings. A more recent example is the emerging experience with Title IV of the 1990 CAA, where a nationwide cap of 8.9 million tons per year (TPY) cap for SO_2 is believed to have brought a high level of certainty to the regulated industry. Another example is the utility-wide NO_x emissions caps for California's South Coast Air Basin. Over the last ten years, electric utilities in the South Coast Air Basin have successfully designed their future resource plans under a system of emission caps and emission rate caps (daily emission caps, annual emission caps, and daily emission rate caps in pounds of NO_x per megawatt-hour of output [lb/MWh]).

6.   Perhaps the most egregious example pertains to the emissions limitations for sulfur dioxide on new coal-fired power plants under the Clean Air Act Amendments of 1977, which required the sources to meet the prescribed emission standards in only one particular way through application of flue-gas desulfurization equipment (SO_2 scrubbers).

7.   The 1990 CAAA also calls for a two-million-ton reduction in NO_x emissions by the year 2000, a significant portion of which will be achieved through application of control technology to utility boilers.

8.   VOCs have presented additional difficulty because of many dispersed sources of emissions which are difficult to quantify and enforce. Targeted industries include electric utilities, petroleum refineries, chemical manufacturers, cogeneration projects, furniture manufacturers, and the like. SCAQMD decided to start the program in 1993 without including sources of VOCs. They are expected to be added later, after issues of enforcement and quantification are addressed.

9.   Even the traditional measures included in the 1991 plan would have required over 130 command and control rules during the next three years, with an uncertain chance of adoption by the SCAQMD Board because of intense industry opposition.

10.   Enforceability is the key threat to RECLAIM's success and approvability, especially in the case of VOCs emissions from 2,000 facilities containing 10,000 separate permitted emission sources.

11.   To provide equity among sources, specific rules will need to be developed to implement RECLAIM that consider their effects on sources that are already well controlled, on large and small sources, and on employment.

12.   For example, the expected extent to which sources may trade emissions may be limited by EPA's interpretation of provisions of the 1990 CAAA, which set forth requirements for Reasonably Available Control Technology, New Source Review Programs, and attainment demonstrations.

13.   Utilities under SCAQMD jurisdiction include Southern California Edison (SCE), Los Angeles Department of Water and Power (LADWP), and

three small utilities.

14. Under the revised Rule 1135 (adopted on July 19, 1991), the district adopted a system-wide NO_x emission rate of 0.15 lb/MWh for SCE and LADWP, and a slightly higher emission rate of 0.2 LB/MWH for three smaller utilities. For SCE and LADWP, the rate of 0.15 lb/MWh will need to be met by the year 2000 and will represent an approximately 85 percent reduction from the current rate of about 1.0 lb/MWh. There are similar requirements for daily and annual emission caps for individual utilities. For example, SCE will be required to meet a daily emission cap of 13,400 lb/day from its current level of about 30,000 lb/day. Also, the annual cap for SCE will be reduced from the current level of approximately 5,000 tons per year to 1,640 tons per year starting in the year 2000.

15. This transport can occur in the Northeast over distances of 500 miles and time periods of two to seven days.

16. To the extent the NO_x issues (Title I ozone nonattainment, ozone health-base standard, mid-range transport, relative roles of hydrocarbons and NO_x in ozone formation) are different from acid rain issues (Title IV, regional transport, ecological impact-based issues), the acid rain model is not entirely applicable to a NESCAUM NO_x emission cap system. Moreover, whereas the acid rain program is mandated in federal legislation, no such direct requirement exists in the federal or state laws for the NESCAUM NO_x emission cap. The major difference between a potential NESCAUM cap system and SCAQMD utility cap system (or for that matter, the RECLAIM program) is the large geographic (and equally important, political) extent of the NESCAUM region, covering eight states and hundreds of miles, as compared with the regional extent of the South Coast region (approximately 100 miles).

17. The basis could be all of the NESCAUM states as one region, individual states as sub-regions, or some other boundary defined by consideration of transport of air pollution and source-receptor relationships. It could also be based on existing power pool structures, specifically the New England Power Pool, New York Power Pool, and the Pennsylvania-Jersey-Maryland Interconnection.

18. NESCAUM's recent recommendations for NO_x RACT for four major categories—utility boilers, industrial boilers, combustion turbines, and large internal combustion engines—are examples of the consistency needed among states to have a workable and equitable NO_x emissions cap system.

19. A bank could serve as a central source to facilitate the exchange of allowances, as well as provide information to buyers and sellers on market rates, pricing, credit requirements/certification, availability, discounting, and restrictions. The banks could be state run or privately owned. A clearinghouse system could be a preferable alternative to a bank if it becomes apparent that the pool of allowances is relatively small, or if the number of trades is expected to be too small to require a banking system. In this case, the clearinghouse could still serve the important purpose of tracking the information necessary to facilitate those trades which do occur and to ensure that state and federal regulations are being met.

10

Inter-Firm Cooperation: Maintaining Reliability of Electricity Supply

Michehl R. Gent

The North American Electric Reliability Council (NERC) has long been the "keeper" of electricity reliability in the United States and Canada and will be looked to by governments, electricity suppliers, and indirectly by consumers to continue to ensure a reliably operated bulk electric supply system. To carry out this assignment, NERC is changing. NERC intends to facilitate. This chapter discusses the changes under way. As expected, there is not unanimity among principals.

WHAT IS NERC?

Almost every electric utility in the United States and Canada is in one of nine Regional Councils. The Councils are organized to meet the needs of the utilities in that region. Each is different. They vary from formal power pools to loose confederacies. These nine Regional Councils are the owners of NERC, a not-for-profit corporation.

It needs to be emphasized that NERC is not an electric utility, an association, an institute, or a government agency. NERC is a company owned and operated by the regions. Many non-electric utilities and would-be electric utilities often complain that they are precluded from being a member of NERC. Strictly speaking, they are correct. By charter, only Regional Councils can become members of NERC. Individual utility membership is only available at the regional level. The members of the Regional Councils include utilities of all different ownership types: investor owned, federally owned, rural electric cooperatives, provincial, state owned, and municipally owned. Some of the regions also include independent power producers (IPPs) in their membership. These Regional Council members account for virtually all of the electricity supplied in the continental United States, Alaska, Canada, and the northern portion of Baja California, Mexico.

HISTORY OF NERC

Utilities have cooperated on reliability issues since the inception of the industry. For example, the pre-1930 inauguration of the Pennsylvania-Jersey-Maryland Interconnection was motivated by economic and reliability goals. As interconnections increased, so did the need for uniform engineering standards and operating principles. Much was achieved in a piecemeal fashion through professional societies, standards organizations, and inter-utility operating agreements. Periodic surveys by the federal government reviewed the overall status of reliability in the industry, but standards were largely self-enforced.[1]

NERC was formed after the Northeast blackout of November 9, 1965. If you were not there, it is hard to imagine what it was like. It was 5:16 P.M. when an improperly set relay in Canada, near Niagara Falls, worked properly and started a cascading failure of electrical circuits that left thirty million people in the dark and caused economic losses estimated at $100 million. Those were 1965 dollars! Major portions of the Northeastern United States and Canada were without electricity, and hundreds of thousands of people were inconvenienced for days.

The Federal Power Commission [FPC] (1967) investigated the blackout and recommended ways to ensure that it would never happen again.[2] After a federal investigation which lasted nearly two years, the FPC proposed the Electric Reliability Act of 1967 to Congress.[3] The industry clearly was surprised by the FPC's proposal. The proposed act would have created a federal system of regional reliability councils. Instead of this federally mandated program to coordinate electric power, electric utility representatives from twelve regional and area organizations argued persuasively before Congress that the electric utility industry could better maintain the reliability of electric supply than a watch-dog agency. The regional representatives signed an agreement creating NERC on June 1, 1968. The twelve councils were later reduced to the nine we have today. See our annual reports (1968-present) for further historical details.

ACTIVITIES

In the simplest of terms, NERC helps electric utilities work together to prevent blackouts. We have a committee structure and processes which require us to critique the past for lessons learned, monitor the present to ensure system security, and to assess the future to identify threats and the degree of risk to reliability.[4]

The way we accomplish this is by creating criteria and guides—the "rules of the road" for operating and planning the bulk electric systems.[5] NERC does not impose sanctions or penalties. We rely on peer pressure to achieve utility management commitment to reliability. The physics of the system will simply not allow "bad actors."

ORGANIZATION

NERC is governed by a twenty-seven-member Board of Trustees that includes two utility executives from each Regional Council plus others to ensure representation of at least two from each segment of the industry and one from Canada. Observers from government and industry trade associations attend NERC Board meetings.[6]

NERC's strength lies in our ability to call on the unmatched expertise and experience from member utilities. Our staff, located in Princeton, New Jersey, works with the Board of Trustees, the Regional Councils, and various committees and their sub-groups to provide project coordination, facilitation, and support. Each Regional Council also has its own staff. Involvement in NERC and commitment to reliability does not stop there. Each Regional Council has its own committee structure and active participation by representatives of its members. About 2,500 individuals in the regions join with the 230 that are directly involved on NERC committees to protect and promote reliable electric systems.

Control areas are the operating entities which have the hardware, computers, and communications to match total tie-line actual flow to an agreed-on schedule. The only moment-to-moment control available to the interconnection is the control of each generator's output. The measure of how well the control areas collectively accomplish this goal is the interconnection frequency (60 Hz in the United States and Canada). Although it is beyond the scope of this chapter, this control and feedback scheme is unique to the United States and Canada and allows for a huge number of participants on any interconnection.[7]

CHANGE HAS BEEN EVOLUTIONARY

The proper role for NERC has been debated since its formation in 1968. All participants agreed that the purpose was "to promote the reliability and adequacy of bulk power supply by the electric systems in North America." There was rarely unanimous agreement on how that was to be done.

In the late 1970s, draft legislation surfaced that implied the United States' electric systems needed "help" with their future resources. Federal legislation in 1978 gave us a ban on the burning of natural gas in electric utility boilers, a non-utility generating industry called qualifying facilities (QFs), a National Electric Reliability Study, and a National Power Pooling Study.[8] It is not a coincidence that NERC expanded its role to address many of the provisions of this legislation. The "new" NERC of the late 1970s and early 1980s was characterized by new objectives, a doubling in the size of the staff, a full-time president, and a huge new data base of electric generating units in North America called the Generating Availability Data System.[9] Finally, and most significantly, NERC merged with the premier operating organization in North America, the North American Power Systems Interconnection Committee (NAPSIC). The "new" NERC now had both operating and planning reliability functions.

Legislative interest in electric utility matters continued to increase through the 1980s. This interest was at first sparked by sharply higher rates—accusations and rebuttals abound, but the rates did go up, sharply. Then, the electric utility industry claimed it was not being allowed to build enough capacity to meet future needs. Congress heard that as a plea for help, and gave us help. Somehow, natural gas was back in plentiful supply, and it seemed that Congress and regulators were saying that the United States' future electricity needs could best be served by IPPs and demand-side management (DSM).

In 1992, the NERC Board started earnest discussion on what NERC's future role should be relative to current and future legislative proposals.[10] The board was concerned that such proposed legislation intended to make the Federal Energy Regulatory Commission (FERC) the arbiter of reliability, a role NERC had fought for and won in the late 1960s and has performed well since. The job is so well done that nearly everyone in the United States and Canada takes a reliable supply of electricity for granted.

The Energy Policy Act of 1992 grants new powers to the FERC. The FERC may now require any electric utility in the United States to provide "transmission access" to a party wishing to sell or purchase electricity at the wholesale level. NERC's concern during the debate prior to passage of the act was for the reliability of the electricity system. Congress addressed our concerns by requiring FERC to consider "consistently applied regional or national reliability standards, guidelines, or criteria" so that FERC orders would not "unreasonably impair the continued reliability of electric systems affected by the order." However, at some point, we will still need FERC to recognize NERC's criteria as *the* criteria.

THE "NEWER" NERC EMERGES

With the new law comes new challenges. It is clear that the "new" NERC of the 1980s must become the "newer" NERC of the 1990s. The organization is in transition, several outcomes have already been determined, and other proposals are being considered: The "newer" NERC will redefine its scope to include operating policies, planning policies, dispute resolution policies, and membership recommendations. The keys are that all interested parties will be afforded some type of membership and peer pressure will continue to be the basis of enforcement.

In January 1993, the board approved "NERC Policies for Interconnected Systems Operation." These operating policies are much more than a restatement of the existing procedures. They are based on "control area" concepts and the principle that all control areas enjoy the benefits of interconnected operations and need to operate in a manner which promotes reliability and does not burden other control areas. In other words, with the benefits come obligations.[11]

THE RULES OF THE ROAD

The new operating policies will be backed up by criteria, requirements, standards, guides, and instructions. The criteria and standards will detail the control area's obligations. In many cases, the new "standards" will be the old "requirements" that have ways of being measured or accounted for. In some instances, totally new procedures will be developed. The old "guides," which suggested "good operating practice," will probably retain the label "guides." All changes, even changes in terminology, will be done slowly because thousands of operators and dispatchers are involved.

A control area that cannot comply with the conditions and terms of a particular NERC criterion or standard, must notify other affected control areas and its Regional Council, which will report it to the NERC Operating Committee. In addition to this "self-confession," there are established survey and monitoring procedures to periodically evaluate control area operations and compliance. New to these operating policies is a well-defined peer review scheme that can traverse the committee structure clear to the board.

Although the entire process is still being refined, we think we have answered the accusation that "some consider conformance with the NERC and Regional Council reliability criteria and guides to be optional"—they are not.

STRENGTHENING INTER-REGIONAL COORDINATION

NERC has developed and is about to adopt new planning policies as well. We have always been cautious about using the word "planning" because of the possibility a lay person would think NERC committees were actually doing top-down, central planning. At best, we are acting to coordinate the plans of the regions.[12]

In September 1993 the board approved new policies[13] that provide a framework for Regional Councils and others to develop their own more detailed planning criteria or guides which reflect the diversity of individual system characteristics, geography, and demographics. This type of diversity cannot be tolerated in operations, but can be accommodated in planning and, in fact, is desirable.

The planning policies also have a formal issue resolution process. The procedures are similar to those of the operating policies, stressing the importance of resolution at the lowest possible level, but providing a clear understanding of the path to the top.

Conformance to the planning policies is through peer review. The beginning step is again "self-confession." In addition, regional reviews will be augmented by the Reliability Criteria Subcommittee's periodic review and analysis of the regional planning criteria or guides; as well as the Reliability Assessment Subcommittee's annual assessment of the adequacy of the regional plans.

WHOSE CLUB IS THIS?

Detractors perceive NERC to be a "private club." It is true that NERC is not a government agency or sponsored by the governments of the United States and Canada. Admittedly, if we are not public, we must be private. The board is sensitive to this issue and addressed it with its new membership recommendations.

NERC is a not-for-profit corporation owned by the nine Regional Councils. Only Regional Councils can be "members" of NERC. However, Regional Council membership is open to nearly everyone in some fashion. The NERC Board recently approved the concept of electing two "additional" trustees to the Board of Trustees from the exempt wholesale generator (EWG) sector. To further ensure representation, the board also recommended that an observer be appointed from one of the EWG trade associations.

Regarding regional membership, the Membership Subcommittee recommended to the regions that they provide membership to virtually anyone with an interest in the bulk electric supply systems in North America. This will not be readily accepted and will probably be implemented in nine different ways. It is encouraging to note that several regions have already implemented this type of membership policy and others have always been open.

WILL IT BE DIFFERENT?

NERC is changing, but will it be effective? The Board of Trustees and the committees certainly think the "newer" NERC will be effective. They have designed their policies and procedures to be fair, effective, and to provide a way to solve disputes. The key to maintaining a reliable electric supply system, while providing the myriad of choices foreseen by the futurists, is to live up to our own rules while relying on peer pressure rather than sanctions for enforcement. Should NERC fail, the FERC, the DOE, or some new agency will be looked to for restoring order.

NOTES

1. See the U. S. Federal Power Commission's *National Power Survey*, various years.

2. Leading that investigation was Joe Swidler, then the chairman of the FPC and formerly the head of the New York State Public Service Commission. Mr. Swidler practices law today in Washington, DC. He has had a big effect on NERC throughout its history.

3. By this time the FPC was led by someone other than Mr. Swidler.

4. In addition to seasonal assessments which examine short-term issues, there is an annual long-term assessment, most recently our *Reliability Assessment 1993–2002*, and its companion volume, *Electricity Supply and Demand 1993–2002*.

5. For operational issues, see the *NERC Operating Manual*. For planning issues see the *Overview of Planning Reliability Criteria of the Regional Reliability Councils of NERC* and *Discussion of Regional Council Planning Reliability Criteria and Assessment Procedures*.

6.   These observers at NERC Board Meetings include: U.S. Department of Energy (DOE), U.S. Federal Energy Regulatory Commission, Canadian National Energy Board, Edison Electric Institute, American Public Power Association, National Rural Electric Cooperative Association, Electric Power Research Institute, Canadian Electrical Association, and the National Association of Regulatory Utility Commissioners.

7.   See the *NERC Operating Manual* for more details.

8.   Relevant reports inspired by the Public Utility Regulatory Policies Act of 1978 include U.S. Department of Energy (1981) and U.S. Federal Energy Regulatory Commission (1981).

9.   A recent summary of the data is available in NERC's *1986–1990 Generating Availability Report*.

10.   These included the proposed Electric Power Fair Access Act of 1991 (Markey) or Electricity Policy Act of 1991 (Sharp).

11.   For details see NERC's *Control Area Concepts and Obligations (1992)*.

12.   That is probably the reason we have an "Engineering" Committee and not a "planning" committee. The board instructed the Engineering Committee to develop planning criteria and to do so with all deliberate speed. That was in 1979. As recently as April 1993, members of an Engineering Committee Task Force told the board that "the development of common NERC Planning Criteria is not appropriate because it would lead to a "lowest-common-denominator approach" to reliability."

13.   These new policies are summarized in *NERC 2000: The Future Role of the North American Electric Reliability Council*.

REFERENCES

North American Electric Reliability Council (NERC). *Annual Report*. Princeton, NJ: NERC, 1968 to present.

North American Electric Reliability Council (NERC). *Control Area Concepts and Obligations*. Princeton, NJ: NERC, 1992.

North American Electric Reliability Council (NERC). *Electricity Supply and Demand 1993–2002*. Princeton, NJ: NERC, 1993.

North American Electric Reliability Council (NERC). *1986–1990 Generating Availability Report*. Princeton, NJ: NERC, 1990.

North American Electric Reliability Council (NERC). *NERC Operating Manual*. Princeton, NJ: NERC, 1991.

North American Electric Reliability Council (NERC). *NERC 2000: The Future Role of the North American Electric Reliability Council*. Princeton, NJ: NERC, 1993.

North American Electric Reliability Council (NERC). *Overview of Planning Reliability Criteria of the Regional Reliability Councils of NERC, and Discussion of Regional Council Planning Reliability Criteria and Assessment Procedures.* Princeton, NJ: NERC, 1988.

North American Electric Reliability Council (NERC). *Reliability Assessment 1993–2002.* Princeton, NJ: NERC, 1993.

U.S. Congress, *Public Utility Regulatory Policies Act of 1978.* P.L. 95-615.

U.S. Department of Energy. *The National Electric Reliability Study: Final Report.* DOE/EP-0004. Springfield, VA: National Technical Information Service, 1981.

U.S. Federal Energy Regulatory Commission (FERC). *Power Pooling in the United States.* FERC-0049. Washington, DC: FERC, 1981.

U.S. Federal Power Commission (FPC). *National Power Survey.* Washington, DC: FPC, various years.

U.S. Federal Power Commission (FPC). *Prevention of Power Failures.* Washington, DC: FPC, 1967.

11

Bottom-Up Analysis for Utility Decisions: Company, State, and Regional Models

Benjamin F. Hobbs

The purpose of this chapter is to review the principles and uses of engineering economic models for utility operation, planning, and policy analysis. The "bottom-up" approach to policy modeling that engineering economic models represent is contrasted to the "top-down" approach of national energy models. Recommendations for improvements in engineering economic models conclude the chapter.

THE ENGINEERING ECONOMIC APPROACH TO UTILITY MODELING

Planning and operating modern electric power systems involves several interlinked and complex tasks (Figure 11.1). Accomplishing each so that consumers receive power reliably at an acceptable economic and environmental cost is hugely difficult for several reasons. First, the electric system itself encompasses an interconnected array of a large number of electrical machines and circuits. Maintaining acceptable voltages and frequency in such systems under rapidly changing circumstances is by itself a daunting task. Second, scheduling short-run generation and load management to minimize costs is complicated because of the sheer number of alternative schedules that are possible and uncertainties in load and equipment availability. Finally, long-term planning involves sorting through a wide range of possible resources and in-service dates, while keeping in mind the implications of each for short-term schedules and costs (Hirst and Goldman, 1991).

Figure 11.1
Overview of Utility Planning and Operations Problems
(adapted from Talukdar and Wu, 1981)

Resource and Equipment Planning

Resource Planning and Production Costing (10–40 year horizon)

- Given forecasts of loads, construction costs, fuel prices, and regulations, find the least-cost mix of generator additions and retirements, power purchases and sales, and demand-side management. Risks and multiple objectives should be considered.

- Models: mixed integer, dynamic, and linear programming models and screening models, with production costing and financial/corporate models to assess impacts of alternative plans. Decision trees and multi-objective methods increasingly used.

Long-Range Fuel Planning (10–20 years)

- Given generating plants, find the least-cost sources of fuel and schedule deliveries. Regulatory and environmental policy constraints are important.

- Models: mathematical programming optimization methods for national- and state-level analyses; but tariff, contractual, and regulatory intricacies make optimization difficult and inappropriate for individual utilities.

Transmission and Distribution Planning (5–1 years)

- Given load forecasts and planned generation additions, design circuit additions that maintain reliability and minimize costs and environmental effects.

- Models: load flow models for simulation, but not optimization; utilities instead use automated "rules of thumb."

Demand-side Management Implementation Planning (3–15 years)

- Given base load forecasts and market opportunities, identify cost-effective DSM programs to target at particular markets, and design marketing and financing programs.

- Models: DSM screening methods, sometimes using production costing methods; market penetration and energy utilization models.

Figure 11.1 (cont.)

Operations Planning

Maintenance and Production Scheduling (2–5 years)

- Given load forecasts and available equipment, schedule interutility sales of energy and routine equipment maintenance to maintain reliability and minimize costs.

- Models: optimization methods proposed, but most utilities use simple scheduling heuristics.

Fuel Scheduling (1 year)

- Within limitations of long-term fuel contracts, schedule fuel deliveries and storage to meet plant requirements.

- Models: usually handled informally.

Unit Commitment (8 hours to 1 week)

- Given load forecasts and available generators, decide when to start up and shut down generators so as to minimize costs and maintain reliability. Plant ramp rates and minimum down and up times must be respected, and fixed start-up costs must be considered.

- Models: often "priority list" techniques, which are heuristics for defining priority-of-shutdown rules. Optimization methods starting to see some use.

Real-Time Operations

Dispatching (1 to 10 minutes)

- Given the load, schedule committed generators and load management to maintain voltages and frequencies, while minimizing cost and avoiding undue equipment stress. Air pollution sometimes considered.

- Models: automated non-linear programming methods.

Automatic Protection (fractions of a second)

- Design protection schemes to minimize damage to equipment and service interruptions resulting from faults and equipment failures.

- Models: automatic control methods.

To cope with this complexity, the industry has developed and applied a wide range of conceptual and mathematical tools (EPRI, 1990; Stoll et al., 1989; Talukdar and Wu, 1981; Turvey and Anderson, 1977). Figure 11.1 briefly describes how they are used to attack each of the short- and long-run tasks. Most of the tools are "bottom-up" engineering economic models. These models represent the process of electricity production in some detail, considering, for example, generation unit dispatch, forced outages, minimum-output constraints, and interconnections. Examples include the generation expansion model EGEAS (Stone and Webster Management Consultants, 1991) and the production costing model PROMOD (EMA, 1993). "Bottom-up" models can be contrasted with "top-down" models. The latter omit details on power generation and instead attempt to encompass larger geographical regions or more markets (Hutzler, this volume; Wilson and Swisher, 1993).

Engineering economic models share the following structure:

- *A cost objective*, such as "minimize the variable cost of generation" in a dispatch model or "minimize the present worth of capital costs, operating costs, and outage costs" in a resource planning model. Other objectives, such as financial or environmental goals, can also be included.

- *A set of decision variables* representing the design and/or operating options open to the utility. For a dispatch model, these would be the loads carried by each generating unit and the amount of load curtailment. In a planning problem, resource amounts and timing, fuel sources, environmental control measures, and simplified dispatch variables might all be included.

- *A set of constraints* defining what values of the decision variables are feasible. The set almost always includes constraints derived from physical processes and capacity limitations, along with the requirement that generation be sufficient to meet customer demands. Other possible constraints include regulatory limitations on where, when, and how generation can take place, along with financial and economic constraints that relate expenditures, prices, and demands.

"Optimization models" and "mathematical programs" are other terms used to describe models that attempt to find the best combination of decision variables (Hillier and Lieberman, 1990).

What distinguishes engineering economic models from other types of models, such as econometric models, is their explicit representation of the physical processes that determine how electricity is produced and what its cost will be. For example, an econometric model of electricity supply might relate the quantity and cost of output to capital, labor, and fuel inputs by statistically fitting a smooth function (e.g., Huettner and Landon, 1978). In contrast, an engineering model would deduce this relationship from fundamental physical quantities, such as heat rates, fuel costs, and unit capacities. Although statistically estimated relationships such as demand curves can be included in an engineering economic models, at the core of these models is an explicit representation of physical processes.

Engineering economic models have two advantages for operations and planning:

- *They explicitly represent the decisions that are to be made to achieve an objective*, so that a model solution unambiguously indicates what is to be done to minimize cost.

- *They permit introduction of new technologies, demands, and regulations*, which gives operators and planners many more "handles" to play with when asking "what if" questions. In contrast, statistical models assume that past relationships among variables will hold in the future. Such models cannot be trusted to extrapolate beyond the historical range of these variables, or if the nature of those relationships change.

POLICY ANALYSIS USING BOTTOM-UP ENGINEERING ECONOMIC MODELS

For these same two reasons, engineering economic models also attract policy analysts. If the analyst is willing to assume that utilities will choose from among the modeled options in order to minimize cost, then the reactions of utilities to alternative policies can be projected, along with the resulting impacts on costs, emissions, and other variables of interest.

Government policies can be simulated in engineering economic models in several ways:

- *By altering objective function coefficients* via, for instance, fuel taxes or price regulations. For example, the impact of increases in energy taxes on a utility's optimal short-run dispatch and long-run fuel mix could be analyzed by appropriate changes in the objective functions of engineering economic models.

- *By adding or deleting decision variables* as a result of, for example, government research into new technologies or prohibitions of certain fuels. For instance, what cost savings and emission reductions, if any, would result if increased research and development (R&D) spending moved up the date of commercial availability of molten carbonate fuel cells?

- *By modifying constraints.* As an example, tighter NO_x limitations may limit dispatch or fuel options, resulting in an increase in cost and, prayerfully, an improvement in environmental quality. Alterations in cost recovery rules could affect prices and, ultimately, loads in planning models.

Pure statistical models do not and cannot offer the same richness or flexibility.

Examples abound of the use of engineering economic models for policy analysis. I review several applications here. Many policy studies adopt the same models that utilities have used for resource planning and dispatch. Other studies apply state or regional models that encompass several utilities simultaneously. These larger-scale models generally assume that the utilities involved cooperate to minimize costs or, equivalently, engage in perfect competition wherein prices are set equal to marginal cost, and no one exercises market power (Takayama and Judge, 1971). From those models, it is a small logical step (but a huge practical jump!) to models, such as the National Energy Modeling System (NEMS), that use the engineering economic approach to simulate the national electricity market (Hutzler, this volume).

Emissions Reduction Policies

Engineering economic models are particularly useful for analyzing tradeoffs between costs and environmental impacts because of the detail with which they can model fuel choices and emissions control measures. For instance, Krause et al. (1992) use the production costing module of UPLAN, a capacity expansion model, to examine how much it would cost New England utilities to reduce CO_2, SO_2, and other air pollutants. They conclude that inexpensive alternatives exist and that a policy mandating a significant reduction in CO_2 would not be as expensive as some top-down studies imply.

Krause et al. (1992) also clarify a policy debate regarding the effectiveness of emissions dispatch, in which cleaner units generate more energy and dirtier units generate less. Bernow et al. (1991) had proposed that utilities use externality "adders," not just to choose new resources, but also to dispatch generation; they concluded that large reductions in emissions were possible. However, industry representatives disagreed (Browne, 1991). Using UPLAN, Krause et al. (1992)

find that some emissions dispatch is possible, although the magnitude of reductions is much less than Bernow et al. (1991) imply. UPLAN's results are more conservative because that model explicitly represents operating constraints such as generator minimum-run levels.

The Spatial Dimension of Energy and Environmental Policies

Most policy analyses define environmental impact in terms of total emissions. Yet, aside from CO_2, such numbers are insufficient for credible environmental assessments. This is because environmental impacts depend on where and when emissions take place, where pollutants are transported, and who is exposed to what concentrations. Generation expansion models are excellent candidates for bridging the gap between general energy system scenarios, on the one hand, and pollutant transport models, on the other.

In particular, versions of such models that choose location of generation facilities can be used for this purpose. Examples of policy analyses of this type include an evaluation for the New Jersey Department of Energy of the merits of siting power stations in an offshore industrial complex in the New York Bight (Meier, 1982) and a study of tradeoffs between transmission costs and population proximity to nuclear plants in the mid-Atlantic region (Cohon et al., 1980). The explicit consideration of the spatial dimension by these models sometimes results in conclusions that more aggregate analyses would miss. For instance, Meier (1979) finds that stricter New Source Performance Standards (NSPS) in New York could result in greater population exposure to SO_2, primarily because the cost advantage of rural sites would diminish. As another example, Hobbs and Meier (1979) conclude that stricter regulation of thermal discharges in coastal areas could yield greater water consumption in drought-prone river basins in the Pennsylvania-Jersey-Maryland (PJM) power pool.

Price Regulation

Engineering economic models have been utilized to assess the simultaneous effect upon costs and consumer welfare of alternative power pricing policies. For instance, Scherer (1977) applies a mixed-integer capacity expansion model and Lo et al. (1991) use a linear programming production costing model to examine different marginal cost pricing structures for retail power sales. The pricing of utility purchases of cogenerated power under the Public Utility Regulatory Policy Act (PURPA) is examined by Haurie et al. (1992) using mathematical programs imbedded in a game-theoretic framework.

Wheeling and Regional Cooperation

Engineering economic models have been used to examine the economic consequences of policies encouraging bulk power exchanges and wheeling. The analysis by Gately (1974) of the benefits of coordination among India's state power boards is the classic study of this type. He used a mathematical programming-based generation expansion model to calculate the costs for each board if they operated autonomously, and then their costs if they cooperated. Those results allowed him to calculate a "core" of solutions that would result in all parties being better off. As another example, Hobbs and Kelly (1992) scrutinize alternative Federal Energy Regulatory Commission (FERC) policies concerning transmission access and pricing. The policies they consider include the status quo (as of 1990), in which transmission is neither unregulated nor fully regulated; mandatory access with prices based on embedded cost; and contract pricing, in which wheeling rates for non-firm power would be unregulated in some cases. A linear programming model of system operation is used to define losses and gains to sellers, buyers, and wheelers of power, and to determine if efficient transactions, and only efficient transactions, take place.

BOTTOM-UP VERSUS TOP-DOWN POLICY MODELS

"Bottom-up" modeling is so called because it simulates the particular capacity, fuel choice, and dispatch decisions made by individual utilities. It is a partial equilibrium approach that assumes that the utility cannot affect prices in bulk power or fuel markets. Regional and national trends can then be calculated by aggregating the actions of individually simulated utilities. In contrast, "top-down" modeling considers all utilities in the region or nation simultaneously. In addition, top-down models often explicitly consider the interactions of the power sector with fuel markets or, in some cases, the entire macro-economy. The structure of the power sector in many top-down models is inspired by the engineering economic approach, in that they simulate least-cost acquisition and operation of resources.

The bottom-up approach has several advantages. Its focus on a particular utility allows for detailed representation of state regulations in addition to federal ones. As pointed out earlier, its detailed output on timing, location, and amounts of emissions makes credible environmental analysis possible. Detailed operational constraints can be included, increasing the realism of the results, so, too, can multiple scenarios of future demand, price, and regulatory conditions within a decision-tree framework, which better characterizes the problem faced by utility planners.

In contrast, top-down modeling must simplify utility decisions in order to be tractable. It treats planning and operation decisions in a highly aggregate form by lumping together utilities within the same region and combining resources with similar characteristics. Operating constraints, such as minimum run levels or transmission bottlenecks, are simplified or neglected. So too are uncertainties.

The most aggregate top-down models, based on macroeconomic theory, omit technology choice variables entirely. As Krause et al. (1992) and Wilson and Swisher (1993) point out, macroeconomic models assume that each economic sector is already using energy, labor, and capital in a welfare-maximizing mix. Consequently, these models disregard possible microeconomic improvements in efficiency that could result from correcting market failures. In particular, Krause et al. (1992) complain that macroeconomic models will therefore underestimate the potential for demand-side management (DSM) to lower emissions and costs.

But the simplifications that top-down models make may, in many cases, be a small price to pay for the top-down approach's advantages. Its major strength is its comprehensiveness and consistency. A single set of macroeconomic and fuel market assumptions can be imposed on all utilities simultaneously. Also, the amount of power that utility X sells to utility Y will be the same as the amount utility Y buys from X, whereas those two quantities can differ in the bottom-up approach. Macroeconomic feedbacks, such as the effect of higher CO_2 taxes or energy prices on regional economic growth, are captured.

To highlight the differences between the two approaches, I review what they have to offer for three different problems: determination of net air emissions, forecasting prices for bulk power purchases and sales, and analysis of the flexibility of utility plans under uncertainty. In each, top-down and bottom-up models have complementary advantages that suggest that both have their uses.

Calculating Net Emissions

Many utilities use engineering economic models to project the emissions of their facilities. Because of the detail with which these models represent fuel choice and dispatch decisions, relatively sophisticated environmental analyses can be undertaken. As an example, the owners of the Centralia plant in western Washington state can differentiate between SO_2 emissions from that facility, which may affect visibility in Mt. Rainier National Park, and SO_2 released from other plants, which would have little or no such effect. The benefits and

costs of emissions dispatch, temporary fuel switching during the summer, and other intermittent strategies for visibility improvement can
be assessed by appropriate engineering models and compared to other
policies, such as scrubbing or plant retirement. Top-down models cannot hope to include such detail.

However, because of the ceteris paribus nature of engineering economic models, they can overlook important interactions of the utility
with regional power and fuel markets that can result in additional or
offsetting environmental effects. For instance, approval by the Seattle
City Council of Seattle City Light's (SCL's) plans to participate in the
third Pacific AC intertie would result in more generation and emissions by that utility, because it would sell more power to California.
Those increased emissions might be viewed as a drawback of participation. Yet, in reality, the net effect on air quality might be zero or
even positive. A zero effect might occur if, as is actually the case, the
line is going to be constructed anyway and if SCL's share would be sold
to other northwestern utilities with similar generation mixes, should
SCL decide not to buy it.

However, air quality impacts would actually be positive if the
effects of SCL's sales on other utilities' emissions are considered. Such
sales will lower California's CO_2 and NO_x emissions. Those decreases
are several times SCL's emission increases. Moreover, the NO_x reductions in California are especially valuable because they would occur
during the summer smog season. These are interactions that could
automatically be captured by a regional or national top-down model.

As another example, several states such as California and
Nevada use adders of $1500/ton or more to penalize SO_2 emissions
from new resources (Wiel, 1991). These adders are not actually paid by
the utility; rather, they are an accounting device that is used to correct
a perceived bias against DSM and renewables in the resource acquisition process. However, even though an engineering economic model of
that utility may show that a new coal plant would increase that utility's emissions, a national top-down model would reveal that the net
national increase is zero.

The reason that the net effect is zero is the SO_2 allowances system set up by Title IV of the 1990 Clean Air Act. The system caps
national emissions at 8.9 million tons/year after 1999. As a result, any
utility that wishes to increase its emissions must purchase allowances
from other utilities who, in turn, must lower their releases by an equal
amount. Regulations that discourage local emissions of SO_2 will
merely shift that pollution elsewhere, raising costs (Hobbs, 1992).
Moreover, average national environmental quality may actually
worsen because it is not Nevada or California where SO_2 emissions do
the most harm; rather, it is the high-sulfur coal states in the Midwest

whose emissions are downwind of the sensitive ecosystems and populations of the northeastern United States and southeastern Canada. Because midwestern states are unlikely to adopt adders that discourage use of their coal reserves, adoption of SO_2 adders elsewhere would likely increase Midwestern emissions, causing average national damages to increase. Top-down models are the best way of projecting the between-region shifts of emissions that result from state regulation.

Another advantage of top-down models is that their inclusion of other fuel markets allows analysts to trace the environmental effects that occur because power price changes will induce consumers to alter their use of fuels. As an example, aggressive DSM programs will increase electric rates for most utilities. This will, in turn, encourage some end-users to switch from electricity to other fuels, such as natural gas and, for some industrial users, coal. Wood and Naill (1992) use the U. S. Department of Energy (USDOE) national energy model FOSSIL2 to project the effect of including externalities in utility planning. The 10 percent or more rate increases that result will, in the long run, encourage more industrial self-generation. For instance, utility CO_2 emissions were projected to decrease by 393 million tons in the year 2010, but partially offsetting this will be a 22 million-ton increase in nonutility (primarily industrial) emissions. This market interaction would be missed by engineering economic models.

Bulk Power Prices

As utilities rely more on purchased power, their resource plans will become more sensitive to assumptions regarding its price. This is true also of utilities who hope to expand their sales. Engineering economic models normally take those prices as a fixed input and then solve for the least-cost resource plan. The difficulty with this approach is that bulk power prices depend on fuel market conditions, interregional transmission capabilities, and regional supplies and demands for bulk power. Unless a utility possesses the capability of modeling the entire bulk power market within which it participates, it may be very difficult to derive scenarios of bulk power prices that are consistent with other assumptions, such as fuel prices.

As an example, Seattle City Light uses an engineering economic model called ANN (Annual Optimization Model) for resource evaluation and marginal cost calculations (Wilson, 1989). An input to the model is a set of prices at which SCL can sell its excess hydropower within the Northwest and outside of the region. These prices must be specified for a range of hydrologic flow conditions. This is accomplished by assuming that Northwestern utilities are subjected to the same hydrologic conditions (which is generally, but not always, true) and by guessing what type of generation source will be the marginal power supply in California under each set of conditions. Although these assumptions are based on many years of experience and insight, inconsistencies can easily sneak in, especially when projecting prices for future conditions quite unlike the present.

An alternative is to use a top-down model. Top-down models would impose consistent hydrologic conditions on all utilities within a market, while accounting for the cumulative effect of their demands on fuel prices. The Power Market Decision Analysis Model (PMDAM) is such a top-down model. Its development was sponsored by the Bonneville Power Administration (BPA) for the purpose of analyzing bulk power markets (Cazalet, 1991). It solves for generation levels and prices in each location in the western United States at each time under each hydrologic condition by explicitly calculating supply-demand equilibria. From the output of such a model, a utility can derive price scenarios that are consistent with its projections of hydrological and fuel market conditions. Indeed, this is the major use that BPA foresees for the model. Individual utilities would not run it, because it requires twenty-four hours or more of computer time to execute; rather, BPA would make available output files from a standard set of runs. BPA's hope is that PMDAM's forecasts of prices will improve the consistency of the planning assumptions used by the region's utilities.

Uncertainty

Utilities increasingly recognize that they need to explicitly consider uncertainty if they wish to develop robust and flexible strategies (Hirst and Goldman, 1991; Merrill and Wood, 1991). I've already pointed out that some engineering economic models can explicitly model risk, along with available recourse actions. The Electric Power Research Institute (EPRI) product, Multiobjective Integrated Decision Analysis System (MIDAS; Farber et al., 1988), is an example. It allows an analyst to explicitly lay out how uncertainties are resolved over time and what decisions can be made in response. Hirst's (1993) analysis of the relative flexibility of DSM versus supply-only resource strategies is a good illustration of the application of decision analysis.

However, risk analysts have the headache of having to develop consistent scenarios for the future (Chapel, 1989). For instance, in a study of SO_2 compliance strategies, we considered uncertainties in prices of natural gas, low-sulfur coal, and emission allowances (Hobbs et al., 1992). We polled experts in order to quantify probability distributions for each variable over the period 1995–2010. This task was difficult enough; coming up with correlations among those uncertain variables was even tougher. To what extent are allowance prices linked with the fuel variables? "Somewhat" was everyone's answer, because the price a utility could demand for allowances is logically linked to national costs of alternative means of emissions control. But it was impossible for the experts to be more specific.

Top-down models can be helpful in this situation, because they explicitly model linkages among the different markets. Sensitivity analyses of an appropriate top-down model can form a credible basis for making assumptions about the correlations of uncertain variables. For instance, a variety of assumptions concerning, say, mining costs, gas discovery rates, control technology developments, and economic growth, could be fed into the top-down model. Each run of that model would result in a set of fuel and allowance price estimates. These could be plotted for a number of runs and then correlated. Of course, the input assumptions to the top-down model too must be consistent; for example, low economic growth and high gas discovery rates might not be logically consistent assumptions.

It is humbling to note, however, that both top-down models and expert polls of the type used in Hobbs et al. (1992) have grossly over-predicted the price of allowances. The recent Environmental Protection Agency (EPA) auction resulted in prices below the lower bound assumed in Hobbs et al. (1992), even when escalated to account for the time value of money. Top-down models might enforce more consistency among scenarios, but they do not necessarily correct the problem that experts tend to underestimate the range of uncertainty and thus specify confidence bands that are too narrow (Kahnemann et al., 1982).

Another reason to be humble about the value of models is the optimistic bias of optimization models. It can be shown that if there are random estimation errors in the objective function coefficients, then an optimization model will, on average, overestimate the performance of the optimal solutions it yields (Hobbs and Hepenstal, 1989). That is, if the optimal solution is implemented, its actual cost or net benefits will likely be worse than the model predicts. There may also be a bias in the solution toward technologies or fuels whose prices are highly uncertain. This result is related to the "winner's curse" phenomenon of bidding, wherein the lowest bidder has probably underestimated his or her costs. The optimistic bias of optimization arises from its fundamental mathematical properties, not from any biases an analyst might have. There is no easy cure for this bias; therefore, for this and other more familiar reasons, model users should take optimal solutions with a grain of salt—if not a shaker full.

CONCLUSIONS

Bottom-up engineering economic models are indispensable for certain types of policy analyses. For instance, questions concerning the impact of state or local regulations on particular resource acquisition and system operation decisions are best analyzed by models that include detailed descriptions of options and operating constraints. As another example, environmental assessments are more credible if based on descriptions of where and when residuals are disposed. Bottom-up models can include the necessary detail.

However, the engineering economic models that were developed for an era when competition was closely regulated and environmental restrictions were relatively insignificant may be irrelevant to the questions policymakers ask today. Competition in the power industry is sharpening at the same time that the public and regulators demand that utilities be more environmentally responsible. Given these trends, how ought we improve bottom-up engineering economic models so that their results are useful and trustworthy for planning and policy analysis? Here are a few suggestions:

- *Include price responsiveness.* Most engineering economic models assume fixed demands. However, utility customers are price responsive, and will become more so as transmission policies move towards retail wheeling. Higher price elasticities will alter business strategies and make it more difficult to subsidize DSM and environmental improvements (Kahn, 1992). Elastic loads can and ought to be included in planning models so that the effect of policy changes on loads, consumption of rival fuels, and value received by customers can be gauged (Hobbs et al., 1993).

- *Consider multiple objectives.* The various parties involved in utility planning have different and often conflicting objectives. Rather than subsume all impacts into a single metric such as "net benefits," models should be used to generate tradeoffs among the objectives. In this manner, the advantages and disadvantages of different alternatives can be discussed by the interests, allowing negotiations to focus on the most important issues (Andrews, 1992).

- *Consider risk.* Competition and the possibility of additional regulations designed to lower, for instance, CO_2 emissions, all increase uncertainty. Although some engineering economic models accommodate multiple futures, most utilities and policy analysts do not take advantage of those capabilities. The result may be brittle plans that cannot adapt to changing circumstances, and unrealistic policy conclusions.

- *Use consistent scenarios.* In decision tree studies and sensitivity analyses, it is important that logically consistent scenarios of future loads, prices, and regulations be constructed (Chapel, 1989). Otherwise, the risks facing utilities and policymakers will be mischaracterized. Top-down models can help create consistent scenarios.

- *Quantify market failures.* Engineering economic models generally optimize system design and operation subject to assumed prices. Biases in those prices due to regulation, taxes, market power, or externalities are not recognized. As a result, social costs can diverge from private costs (Fisher and Rothkopf, 1989). Unless this divergence is recognized, solutions may be suboptimal, and erroneous policy recommendations may result. But quantifying the degree of market failure is difficult and contentious, as the debate over the external effects of power production proves (Joskow, 1992; Wiel, 1991).

However, my recommendations should not be interpreted as a call for ever larger and more complex models. The most useful models are usually those that address issues of concern with a minimum of fuss. Small, nimble models encourage analysts to "play," trying various scenarios and investigating a wide range of alternatives. Through such an interactive process, users gain insight—and insight is usually far more valuable to them and policymakers than particular numerical results (Liebman, 1976).

REFERENCES

Andrews, C. J. "Spurring Inventiveness by Analyzing Tradeoffs: A Public Look at New England's Electricity Alternatives." *Environmental Impact Assessment Review* 12 (March 1992): 185.

Bernow, S., B. Biewald, and D. Marron. "Full-Cost Dispatch: Incorporating External Costs in Power System Operations." *The Electricity Journal* 4 (March 1991): 20–33.

Browne, G. R. "A Utility View of Externalities: Evolution, Not Revolution." *The Electricity Journal* 4 (March 1991): 34–39.

Cazalet, E. G. "Power Market Decision Analysis Model Methodology Report." Draft report submitted to the Bonneville Power Authority. Consulting Decision Analysts, Los Altos Hills, CA, July 24, 1991.

Chapel, S. "CATALYST: Designing Flexible Business Strategies." *EPRI Journal* (October/November 1989): 46–49.

Cohon, J. L., et al. "Application of a Multiobjective Facility Location Model to Power Plant Siting in a Six-State Region of the U.S." *Computers and Operations Research* 7 (1980): 107–123.

Electric Power Research Institute (EPRI). *TAG, Technical Assessment Guide*. Palo Alto, CA: EPRI, 1990.

Energy Management Associates (EMA). *PROMOD model*. Atlanta, GA: EMA, 1993.

Farber, M., E. Brusger, and M. Gerber. *MIDAS, Multiobjective Decision Analysis System*. Palo Alto CA: Electric Power Research Institute, 1988.

Fisher, A. C., and M. H. Rothkopf. "Market Failure and Energy Policy: A Rationale for Selective Conservation." *Energy Policy* 17 (1989): 97–108.

Gately, D. "Sharing the Gains from Regional Cooperation: A Game Theoretic Application to Planning Investments in Electric Power." *International Economic Review* 15 (1974): 195–208.

Haurie, A., R. Loulou, and G. Savard. "A Two Player Game Model of Power Generation in New England." *IEEE Transactions on Automatic Control* 37 (1992): 1451–1492.

Hillier, F. S., and G. J. Lieberman. *Introduction to Operations Research*. New York: McGraw-Hill, 1990.

Hirst, E. "Do DSM Programs Increase Risk?" *The Electricity Journal* 6 (May 1993): 24–31.

Hirst, E., and C. Goldman. "Creating the Future: Integrating Resource Planning for Electric Utilities." *Annual Review of Energy* 16 (1991): 91–121.

Hobbs, B. F. "Environmental Adders and Emissions Trading: Oil and Water?" *The Electricity Journal* 5 (Sept. 1992): 26–34.

Hobbs, B. F., and A. Hepenstal. "Is Optimization Optimistically Biased?" *Water Resources Research* 25 (February 1989): 152–160.

Hobbs, B. F., J. C. Honious, and J. Bluestein. "What's Flexibility Worth? The Enticing Case of Natural Gas Cofiring." *The Electricity Journal* 5 (March 1992): 37–47.

Hobbs, B. F., and K. A. Kelly. "Using Game Theory to Analyze Electric Transmission Pricing Policies in the United States." *European Journal of Operational Research* 56 (1992): 154–171.

Hobbs, B. F., and P. M. Meier. "An Analysis of Water Resources Constraints on Power Plant Siting in the Mid-Atlantic States." *Water Resources Bulletin* 15 (1979): 1666–1676.

Hobbs, B. F., H. B. Rouse, and D. T. Hoog. "Measuring the Economic Value of Demand Side Resources in Integrated Resource Planning Models." *IEEE Transactions on Power Systems*.(August 1993): 979–987.

Huettner, D. A., and J. H. Landon. "Electric Utilities: Scale Economies and Diseconomies." *Southern Economic Journal* 44 (1978): 883–912.

Hutzler, M. J. "Top Down: The National Energy Modeling System." This volume.

Joskow, P. L. "Weighting Environmental Externalities: Let's Do It Right!" *The Electricity Journal* 5 (1992): 53–67.

Kahn, E. "Integrating Market Processes into Utility Resource Planning." *The Electricity Journal* 5 (November 1992): 12–23.

Kahnemann, D., P. Slovic, and A. Tversky. *Judgment Under Uncertainty: Heuristics and Biases.* New York: Cambridge University Press, 1982.

Krause, F., J. Busch, and J. Koomey. *Incorporating Global Warming Risks in Power Sector Planning: A Case Study of New England.* LBL-30797. Berkeley, CA: Energy and Environment Division, Lawrence Berkeley Laboratory, 1992.

Liebman, J. C. "Some Simple-Minded Observations on the Role of Optimization in Public Systems Decision Making." *Interfaces* 6 (1976): 103–107.

Lo, K. L., J. R. McDonald, and T. Q. Le. "Time-of-Day Electricity Pricing Incorporating Elasticity for Load Management Purposes." *Electrical Power & Energy Systems* 13 (1991): 230–239.

Meier, P. M. "Energy Modelling in Practice: An Application of Spatial Programming." *OMEGA* 10 (1982): 483–491.

Meier, P. M. "Long-Range Regional Power Plant Siting Model." *Journal of the Energy Division, ASCE* 105 (EY1, 1979): 117–135.

Merrill, H. M., and A. J. Wood. "Risk and Uncertainty in Power System Planning." *Electrical Power and Energy Systems* 13 (April 1991): 81–90.

Scherer, C. R. *Estimating Electric Power System Marginal Costs.* New York: North Holland, 1977.

Stoll, H. G., et al. *Least-Cost Electric Utility Planning.* New York: John Wiley and Sons, 1989.

Stone and Webster Management Consultants. *EGEAS: Elective Generation Expansion Analysis System.* Englewood, CO: Stone and Webster, 1991.

Takayama, T., and G. Judge. *Spatial and Temporal Price and Allocation Models.* Amsterdam: North Holland, 1971.

Talukdar, S. N., and F. F. Wu. "Computer-Aided Dispatch for Electric Power Systems." *Proceedings of the IEEE.*69 (October 1981): 1212–1231.

Turvey, R., and D. Anderson. *Electricity Economics: Essays and Case Studies.* Baltimore, MD: The Johns Hopkins University, 1977, Ch. 13.

Wiel, S. "The New Environmental Accounting: A Status Report." *The Electricity Journal* 4 (1991): 46–54.

Wilson, A. F. 1989 *Marginal Value of Energy Study.* Seattle, WA: Seattle City Light, 1989.

Wilson, D., and J. Swisher. "Exploring the Gap: Top-Down versus Bottom-Up Analyses of the Cost of Mitigating Global Warming." *Energy Policy* 21 (March 1993): 249.

Wood, F. P., and R. Naill. "Externalities in Utility Planning: What Would It Cost?" *The Electricity Journal* 5 (1992): 35–43.

12

Top-Down: The National Energy Modeling System

Mary J. Hutzler

The Energy Information Administration has a legislated responsibility to provide independent information and analysis to support public decision making. This chapter provides an overview of the structure and purpose of the electricity module in the National Energy Modeling System (NEMS). It describes how legislative initiatives, such as the Clean Air Act Amendments of 1990 (CAAA) and the Energy Policy Act of 1992 (EPAct), and modeling issues such as new technologies, have motivated the development of NEMS. It indicates how NEMS is expected to perform, nationally and regionally, and how it will contribute to policy formulation in the areas of new technologies, demand-side management, and environmental controls.[1]

MODEL CHARACTERISTICS

The NEMS is a partial equilibrium model of energy markets that includes a detailed structural representation of energy supplies, conversion processes, and consumption. The mid-term NEMS is designed to provide annual projections of energy markets over a twenty- to twenty-five-year horizon. It has been used to prepare the projections for the 1994 *Annual Energy Outlook* (AEO); the Outlook is required annually for the U.S. Congress. NEMS is also intended to be an analysis tool for policymakers and analysts in the Department of Energy and elsewhere. The solution algorithm uses prices and quantities of energy commodities subject to environmental constraints and other regulations as the vehicle for achieving equilibrium in energy markets. Energy markets in NEMS are modeled in a variety of ways.

NEMS uses five linear programing formulations to represent certain supply markets and a variety of heuristic algorithms to represent other energy markets and their interactions.

The Electricity Market Module (EMM) of NEMS includes a representation of capacity planning, production costing, and plant dispatching, and a pricing mechanism that determines average prices that consumers pay. The capacity planning submodule is a multi-period linear program that includes a representation of new generating facilities in fifteen regions for both traditional utilities and non-utilities.

Decisions to construct various capacity types are based on expected electricity demand over a six-year horizon and the need to comply with the Clean Air Act Amendments. The planning submodule considers investments in emission control equipment as well as low or non-polluting technologies (e.g., renewable) as options to comply with environmental regulations. It also uses a simplified production costing representation to determine how potential investments would be utilized. New technologies are explicitly considered and adjustments are made to account for uncertainties in cost and performance. Non-traditional sources of supply in the form of demand-side management programs and non-utility power production are also represented in the planning process. The use of transmission facilities to market wholesale power in adjacent regions is also addressed.

For each year the model is executed, capacity expansion plans are made for all of the options discussed above; then the production costing submodule determines how plants are dispatched in the current year.[2] In both the capacity expansion and production costing sub-modules, demands for electricity are represented by a load duration curve that includes seasonal and daily variations in discrete steps where the time-related variations are preserved.[3]

The costs of providing electricity service are determined by a regulatory accounting framework that uses information on investments and fuel consumption provided by the capacity expansion and production costing sub-modules, respectively. The costs of providing electricity are developed in a submodule that emulates the decision-making process of state regulators. It establishes a rate base and develops revenue requirements using endogenously determined cost of capital. Options for alternative pricing methods such as levelized-cost pricing are provided to address prices that consumers would experience given competitive wholesale markets for generation and transmission services.

The EMM has fifteen regions based on North American Electric Reliability Council (NERC) regions and sub-regions. The rich structural detail of the EMM is supported by copious data. For example, cost, performance, and environmental characteristics for generating capacity are based on unit-level data that are aggregated into the various plant types for a particular NERC region or sub-region.

MOTIVATION FOR NEMS

The development of NEMS was prompted by the need to support policymakers by expanding the scope and structural representation of the existing energy market modeling framework, known as the Intermediate Future Forecasting System (IFFS).[4]

Consequently, these enhancements require new model structures. For example, since new technology cost and performance characteristics are subject to considerably more uncertainty than existing technologies, a "level playing field" needs to be established where they can be competed against existing technologies whose characteristics are known with a far greater degree of certainty. A modeling construct is required that eliminates technological optimism (the tendency of developers to understate realized costs because of optimism and lack of real data). This construct must also address learning effects, where the cost and performance of new technologies are refined as they penetrate the marketplace and benefits of replication are realized. There is also the need to evaluate the financial risk associated with large irreversible investments where there is economic value associated with delaying investment decisions in order to gain additional information which lowers the riskiness of new construction. The impacts of new technologies in the marketplace are of interest to policymakers because they face decisions about allocating resources to facilitate their development.

Similarly, demand-side management (DSM) programs require new modeling structures because these programs impact both electric utilities and consumers. Investments made by utilities to accelerate the penetration of efficient technologies, such as lighting programs or efficient refrigerators, result in changes in electricity consumption that need to be reconciled in the consumption models. The changes in demand levels and load profiles that result from utility DSM programs require adjustments to the load shapes used in the electricity module. These interactions need to be addressed in the modeling framework to ensure consistency between the technologies assumed in the demand models and the electricity model.

Another policy issue that motivated the development of NEMS is environmental concern. In order to capture the impacts of the Clean Air Act Amendments of 1990 NEMS explicitly represents the investment decisions to retrofit plants with emission control equipment, switching to lower-sulfur fuels, banking and trading allowances, and determining allowance prices as part of compliance strategies. Inter-temporal decisions about the disposition of allowances are reached within the Electricity Market Module.

Because the impacts of the CAAA were relatively modest on electric utility costs, market interactions were not significant issues. However, future environmental policies such as carbon stabilization or carbon reduction could have significant economic impacts. In order to analyze these policies, an integrating model is required to capture responses across all energy sectors and markets as well as the associated macroeconomic feedbacks.

IMPACTS OF THE ENERGY POLICY ACT OF 1992

The Energy Policy Act of 1992 (EPAct) is a comprehensive initiative that affects many energy markets. The Energy Information Administration (EIA) has represented many of the EPAct provisions in its integrated modeling work to date. For example, provisions that mandate efficiency standards, streamlined licensing activities for new nuclear plants, and requirements for integrated resource planning either had been addressed in IFFS or are directly addressable in the NEMS structure.

Other provisions that require a more detailed analysis, such as transmission access and pricing, can not be represented in an aggregate modeling framework. Transmission questions require a detailed representation of the transmission system to capture first contingency limits that may restrict flows to below capacity; the loading of transmission lines, which is governed by the physics of power flow and subject to Kirchhoff's laws;[5] and investments in transmission equipment and control such as solid-state relays. However, the results of a detailed transmission model can be incorporated into NEMS by adjusting aggregate parameters to capture regulatory policies. For example, if a detailed transmission study using alternative pricing policies resulted in different levels of utilization of the transmission system, then constraints and cost parameters in NEMS could be adjusted selectively to mimic the results of the detailed model in order to project impacts of policy alternatives on energy markets.

The legislation also creates a new group of players in the electricity supply industry called exempt wholesale generators (EWGs) who own or lease generating capacity and generate power for wholesale purchase only. EWGs are represented in NEMS as an extension of the non-utility generator category.

As the electric utility industry becomes more deregulated, analysis of alternative pricing methods for electricity will need to be addressed. To this end, the electricity pricing methods in NEMS have been revised to account for costs on a functional basis consistent with movements toward vertical disaggregation. Separate accounting information is being accumulated for generation, transmission, and distribution services so that providers of these services can be distinguished and competition in these markets can be analyzed. Alternative pricing methods are permitted within each functional category as well. In addition to the traditional cost of service calculations that have been used under ratebase regulation, alternative pricing methods such as levelized costing are being incorporated. This added capability will allow policymakers to examine an array of pricing alternatives that may be used in a competitive environment.

CONTRIBUTIONS TO POLICY FORMULATION

NEMS is designed to analyze a variety of alternative policies, such as taxes, investments to develop new technologies, conservation initiatives, and environmental regulations. It is being built to assist policymakers in their evaluation of alternatives by providing quantitative measures of policy impacts. For example, NEMS can address policy initiatives that would limit any of a variety of pollutants from electric utilities. In particular, the model is structured to accept explicit constraints on carbon emissions from electric utilities. Invoking this constraint is expected to result in changes in both the choices for new capacity and the dispatching patterns of plants to meet load requirements.

EIA models, such as NEMS, provide both a documented structure and a set of assumptions that can be discussed and modified in response to critical review. Hence, the model imposes discipline. Scenarios can be constructed and analyzed to develop preferred policies. Scenario analysis frequently results in insights that would not be realized outside of a modeling framework because the complexities of market interactions are not always apparent.

REGIONAL ISSUES

DOE's Office of Domestic and International Energy Policy has a national-level, integrating model called IDEAS (previously known as FOSSIL 2), which it uses to provide quick turnaround analysis. IDEAS is calibrated to EIA's *AEO* Reference Case through 2010 and develops its own baseline beyond that to 2030. It has been used for the National Energy Strategy resulting in the Energy Policy Act of 1992 and for President Clinton's energy tax analysis. Calibration to EIA's forecasts is necessary to capture the details of the CAAA and for other policy analyses where regional results affect the forecasts.

Because there are significant variations that exist in the regional mix of electric generating stock in the United States, EIA uses a regional electricity model. Regional conditions can result in plans to meet future demands that differ from a typical national strategy.

An example of a regional analysis performed by EIA dealt with a request from the Army Corps of Engineers. A user fee of $1 per gallon on towboat fuel was proposed to pay for the maintenance and operation of the U.S. barge system. EIA analyzed the problem using the IFFS system. U.S. coal production and electricity consumption was essentially unaffected, but coal-producing states on barge routes lost production to states on rail routes. Coal prices to utilities increased 3 percent in the state most affected. An analysis using a national energy model could not have captured these regional details.

LIMITATIONS AND BIASES

Although the NEMS electricity model is a regional model of electric utility operations, aggregation could still cause bias in the results. For example, aggregation of data assumes that utilities within a region operate their facilities on a cooperative basis with their neighbors. While this assumption is generally valid based on history, it is not clear if it will be appropriate as utilities respond to pressures created by an environment of increased competition. Another aggregation issue is the merging of the financial conditions of individual utilities. Although a given utility may have inadequate interest coverage that would preclude it from making capital investments, this condition may be masked when the firm's data are merged with those of neighboring utilities, whose financial conditions are sufficient to support investments in new equipment. Aggregation may also affect the representation of the load faced by utilities. Company-level load data are merged for each region, which may result in overoptimization.

Similarly, the model does not address existing constraints that limit transmission within a given region. It is implicitly assumed that transmission of power within a region will occur as needed. Because of the aggregation to the regional level, it is possible to project generation levels for various capacity types that are not achievable given the intra-regional transmission network.

Another limitation is the ability of the model to adjust to changes that result from behavior other than that assumed. For example, dispatching plants based on least cost may not represent how an individual utility will manage emission constraints. Concern about not achieving emission limits and incurring penalties could lead individual utilities to overcompliance, which is not economic. Another behavior that is not part of the current model is the value of waiting. Utilities may choose to defer investment in expensive baseload facilities in order to minimize the risk associated with the uncertainty of demand growth.

Consumer behavior is also difficult to capture when historical observations are not available. For example, if electricity is priced so that the quality of service is differentiated, then consumer responses to price variations could be different from those that result when electricity is perceived as a homogenous commodity. How customers would group into various categories that are based on quality of service is unknown and their responsiveness to price changes within and among categories is also unknown due to lack of similar past circumstances. Also unknown is how various pricing methods would change responses of both electric utilities and EWGs in developing supplies needed to meet demand growth.

Although there are limitations to the application of aggregate models to the analysis of energy issues, models such as NEMS can be applied to a wide variety of policy and regulatory initiatives that are important at the national level. They can also use the results of more detailed models such as a transmission model or a more detailed regional model.

CONCLUSIONS

The NEMS model is being developed with sufficient flexibility, such as in electricity pricing, so that a wide range of policy alternatives can be examined with minimal analyst interaction. The structural detail chosen for NEMS represents a balance of regional specificity sufficient to provide a regional capability while being able to maintain and operate the model. The structural enhancements that are included in NEMS capture the impacts of the CAAA and those provisions of EPAct that can be analyzed in an aggregate model.

NOTES

1.   See U.S. Department of Energy, Energy Information Administration, Documentation of the Electricity Market Module, 1994.

2.   This heuristic (line-search) algorithm uses merit-order dispatching constrained by environmental regulations as the basis for allocating capacity

to meet required levels of electricity demand.

3.   This detailed approach includes twenty-two vertical load segments designed to ensure that nondispatchable generating sources such as wind and solar and demand-side management programs compete in the appropriate load segments. Because nondispatchable units have limited time periods during which they can be relied on, load segments are chosen to correspond to their availability.

4.   NEMS was designed to support electric utility policymakers' need to address such issues as emerging technologies, demand-side-management programs, and environmental requirements, none of which were incorporated in IFFS.

5.   See McGraw-Hill (1992), p. 330.

REFERENCES

Encyclopedia of Science and Technology, 7th ed., Vol. 5. New York: McGraw-Hill, 1992.

U.S. Department of Energy, Energy Information Administration. *Annual Energy Outlook* (AEO). Washington, DC: U.S. Department of Energy, 1994.

U.S. Department of Energy, Energy Information Administration. Documentation of the Electricity Market Module. Washington, DC: U.S. Department of Energy, Energy Information Administration. Documentation of the Integrating Module of the Intermediate Future Forecasting System, 1992.

PART II

CASE STUDIES AND ANALYSIS OF REGIONAL SYSTEMS

13

Northwest Power Planning Council Case Study

Richard H. Watson

The Northwest's experiment in electricity and federalism began with the creation of the Bonneville Power Administration and was modified more than forty years later with the passage of the Pacific Northwest Electric Power Planning and Conservation Act of 1980. The Northwest Power Planning Council, created by that act, gives a state-appointed body unique powers relative to the federal Bonneville Power Administration. This chapter reviews the factors that led to the creation of the council, its authorities, its planning methods, its accomplishments, and the challenges it faces. The implications of the continuing technological, regulatory, and financial changes in the utility industry for the future of this experiment are explored.

THE BONNEVILLE POWER ADMINISTRATION— THE FEDERAL PRESENCE IN THE NORTHWEST'S ELECTRICITY SYSTEM

The Northwest is an appropriate case study of electricity and federalism. The federal Bonneville Power Administration is the single largest presence in the Northwest's electricity system. It was created in 1937 to market power from the federal Columbia River dams. The first of those, Bonneville Dam, was completed in that year. Today, there are eight federal projects, owned by the Army Corps of Engineers and the Bureau of Reclamation, on the Columbia and Snake River systems.

These dams and the Bonneville Power Administration were part of an explicit federal strategy to bring economic growth to the Pacific Northwest. Irrigation, barge transportation, and most importantly, low-cost electricity were seen as the engines of economic development for the region. The heroic spirit of the time made it the stuff of song and populist myth.[1]

Today, the Bonneville Power Administration markets about 39 percent of the approximately 19,000 average megawatts of firm electricity consumed in the Pacific Northwest.[2] It sells that electricity to over 100 publicly owned utilities (municipalities, public utility districts, cooperatives) and seventeen direct service industries (DSIs). About half of the direct service industries are aluminum plants that consume about 90 percent of the electricity sold to DSIs. In addition, Bonneville markets "secondary" or non-firm power (power that can be produced by the regional hydro system when water conditions are better than historic lows) to direct service industries, Northwest utilities— both public and private—and to utilities in California and the Desert Southwest. The web knitting this all together is 14,000 miles of high-voltage transmission systems owned and operated by Bonneville, including majority ownership of three high-capacity lines to the Southwest. This is by far the majority of the high-voltage transmission in the region.

Hydropower provides 62 percent of the firm energy resources in the Northwest. In reality, its contribution is typically greater because of the non-firm power usually available. In an average water year, this non-firm power amounts to about 4,100 average megawatts. In a very wet year, the non-firm energy can be as much as 7,500 average megawatts. This year-to-year variability adds another dimension of uncertainty to electricity planning in the region. Few, however, would trade the region's system for one with greater certainty. The Northwest continues to enjoy electricity rates that are roughly half the national average.

The ownership of the hydroelectric power is concentrated (about 60 percent) within the federal agencies—the Corps of Engineers and the Bureau of Reclamation—and marketed by Bonneville. As a result of the public preference provisions of the Bonneville Project Act, publicly owned utilities have first access to that power. In contrast, less than 25 percent of the region's hydropower is owned by private utilities.

In the first few decades of Bonneville's existence, the agency saw its mission not merely as the supplier of power to public agencies and direct service industries. It saw itself as a catalyst for the region's economy through the coordinated development and operation of the regional electrical supply and distribution system—whether the utilities involved were public or private. Even though Bonneville's early years were marked by conflict between public and private utilities, the system that evolved by the 1950s and 1960s was characterized more by cooperation than conflict. Bonneville was the glue that held it together.

The End of Hydroelectric Innocence

Today, the low-cost federal hydropower marketed by the Bonneville Power Administration is generally acknowledged as one of the major factors in the economic development of the Northwest. It is not, however, an unlimited resource. During the late 1960s and early 1970s, it seemed clear that growth in the Northwest was going to outstrip the capacity of the federal Columbia River system and other existing utility resources. Demand was forecast to grow at rates of 5 to 7 percent per year and all the economically and environmentally feasi-
 large dam sites on the Columbia River system had been developed.
 tor-owned utilities, restricted in their access to federal power by
 blic-preference provisions of the Bonneville Project Act, were
 to turn to developing their own thermal generation. Soon,
 blicly owned utilities came to believe that they too would
 l resources to meet their growing needs.[3]
 me, Bonneville had no authority to acquire new
 backing of a federal agency would result in lower-
 Bonneville's involvement would provide a mecha-
 e risks of resource development around the
 Bonneville's mission as a catalyst for coordi-
 e thinkers sought a way in which Bonnev-
 ment of new thermal resources. The
 The public utility owners of planned new
 d provide the *capability* of that plant
 duced power) to Bonneville at the cost of
 lants. Bonneville would sell power back
 plus thermal) system cost. The public
 be credited with the cost of the capabil-
 cash would actually change hands.
 ities were to be credited with the capa-
 e region, through Bonneville, absorbed
 ance.[4] This mechanism put the backing
 istration behind a portion of the Trojan
 anford Generating Project (a civilian
 eapons production reactor on the Han-
 Washington Public Power Supply Sys-
 NP-2, and WNP-3.

The net-billing arrangement, however, was self-limiting. Even then, the cost of power from the new thermal plants was expected to greatly exceed the cost of power from the federal Columbia River System. Consequently, there was only so much new power that could be absorbed without getting to the point where an actual exchange of dollars would be required. As public utility plans for WPPSS plants WNP-4 and WNP-5 firmed up, spurred on by a "notice of insufficiency" from Bonneville, it was clear that another arrangement would be required if the advantages of Bonneville backing were to be maintained.

At the same time, as the region's investor-owned utilities planned for additional coal and nuclear plants, they too saw advantages in Bonneville being able to back their development of resources. Investor-owned utilities also had another interest. Without ensured access to power from the federal Columbia River System, they were seeing a growing disparity between their rates and the rates of their public utility neighbors. Add to this the interest of the region's aluminum companies in securing new supply contracts, and you had the ingredients necessary to seek congressional approval for increasing Bonneville's authorities.

Throughout the mid-1970s, Bonneville and the region's utiliti worked at developing new legislation that would meet their aims. T legislation would have increased Bonneville's powers to acq resources and would have guided the new Bonneville through a of utility representatives. At the same time, as the costs of the W plants began to spiral upward, it became apparent to some t nuclear option was proving to be an expensive one and that, a new Bonneville with expanded powers might need more ch balances than would be provided through the utility plan.

THE NORTHWEST POWER PLANNING COUN AN EXPERIMENT IN "NEW FEDERALISM"

The efforts to create a new Bonneville attracted the northwestern states and the environmental co legislation, significant compromises were going to months of negotiations, the result was The Pacific Power Planning and Conservation Act of 198 Regional Act, as it is commonly called, gave Bor to acquire the "actual or planned" capability of The direct service industries got the right to ne from Bonneville. Investor-owned utilities (

exchange power for their residential and farm customers with Bonneville—a paper transaction in which Bonneville purchases the power at the IOU's average system cost and sells it back to them at Bonneville's lower average system cost.

At the same time, however, the Regional Act created a new institution and new mandates. The new institution was the Northwest Power Planning Council. The council is composed of two representatives of each of the governors of Washington, Oregon, Idaho, and Montana appointed pursuant to legislation passed in each of the states. Appointment of the members constituted an agreement of the states consented to by Congress—an interstate compact. The council was given two primary charges:

- the development and maintenance of a twenty-year conservation and electric power plan for the region that was to guide the resource acquisitions of the Bonneville Power Administration; and

- the development of a program to protect, mitigate, and enhance the fish and wildlife populations of the Columbia ⋯n that had been affected by hydroelectric develop-

⋯institution marked a major experiment in fed-
⋯body with members appointed by the states
⋯e actions of a federal agency. Moreover,
⋯vas that of "one big utility," that is, a
⋯s would be developed with backing
⋯on. Consequently, it was antici-
⋯ave sway over many of the
⋯all.

⋯ly quite limited,[5] its first
⋯ington, noted that its
⋯and politically per-
⋯consensus, the
⋯ontrary to the
⋯uently, the
⋯credible

⋯wer
⋯ublic
⋯expect
⋯o comply
⋯charge has
⋯been imposed,
⋯it should have.

⋯o
⋯on-

⋯rator
⋯gional
⋯rams to
⋯e future
⋯o impor-
⋯g)(1)).
⋯e prescription for
⋯council's initial
⋯he country.

⋯anning Methods
⋯of 1983. The plan was
⋯ouncil was generally per-
⋯d—its planning was more
⋯issues of the day than was
⋯me. Some of the key innova-
⋯ogy are:[6]

And, with respect to the region's investor-owned utilities, what power the council has is the result of the council's relations with their states' regulatory commissions rather than any powers granted in the act.

In addition to the institutional innovations of the Regional Act, the act also brought some significant substantive changes to electricity planning in the Northwest:

- The act specified that conservation, defined as improved efficiency of electricity use, is to be treated on a slightly more-than-equal basis with generation; that is, conservation is to be considered cost-effective if it has an incremental system cost up to 10 percent greater than the next least costly non-conservation alternative (Section 3(4)(C)).

- The act established resource priorities. The highest priority is conservation followed by renewables, high-efficiency generation and, finally, conventional generation. Although these priorities are really only "tie-breakers," they set a vision for the overall planning framework (Section 4(e)(1)).

- The council's plan is to ensure the region adequate power at the lowest probable *societal* system cost—costs define broadly to include total resource costs, regardless w pays them, as well as any associated quantifiable envir mental costs (Section 3(4)(B)).

- The act mandated that the council and the adminis broadly involve the public in the formulation of r power policies and maintain comprehensive prog facilitate this involvement. The decisions about t of the region's electricity system were deemed tant to be left solely to the utilities (Section (4)

In short, the Regional Act laid down a reasonabl least-cost or integrated resource planning, and t planning efforts were among the first examples in

The Northwest Power Planning Council's P

The council adopted its first plan in Apr subsequently revised in 1986 and 1991. The ceived as capturing the planning high grou sophisticated and more responsive to the typical of northwestern utilities at the t tions in the council's planning methodo

- The council's plans focus on the inherent uncertainty of the future.[7]

- The council fully integrated demand-side efficiency resources into the planning process.[8]

- The council developed the concept of a frozen efficiency demand forecast in order to ensure that efficiency improvements made by consumers in response to price would not also be double-counted as efficiency resources on the supply side.[9]

- The ISAAC (Integrated System for the Analysis of Acquisitions) Monte Carlo simulation model was developed to allow the council to better evaluate risk mitigation strategies.[10]

- The concept of resource "options" was identified as an important opportunity to reduce the lead time of electricity resources and, thus, help respond to uncertain future resource needs.[11]

- Finally, an "action plan" was included in the council's least-cost plan to explicitly chart a course for the plan's implementers to follow for the first couple of years following adoption of the plan. The action plan is critical to being able to achieve the goals of the plan and provides a means of tracking progress and identifying problems.

The council's overall planning process begins with the development of a family of demand forecasts spanning the probable range of future demand trajectories. These forecasts are built up by demand sector and, in many instances, by specific end use. Detailed "supply curves" estimating the potential resource available as a function of cost are developed in parallel for both supply-side and demand-side resources. The supply curve from the 1991 plan is shown in Figure 13.1. These data, along with the basic information regarding the existing system, are analyzed using the ISAAC model to determine both the expected costs and the variability of those costs for a variety of resource portfolios under conditions of uncertainty regarding loads, water conditions, and fuel prices. The council's judgment is key in selecting the preferred resource portfolio. The council then identifies the near-term actions necessary to translate the preferred portfolio into reality.

All through the planning process, the staff's data and analysis and the council's judgments are subject to intense scrutiny from the various interests—Bonneville, other utilities, major industries, environmental groups, state and local governments, and others. The net result is a plan that has been tempered by exposure to additional

Figure 13.1
Resource Supply Curve — 1991 Plan

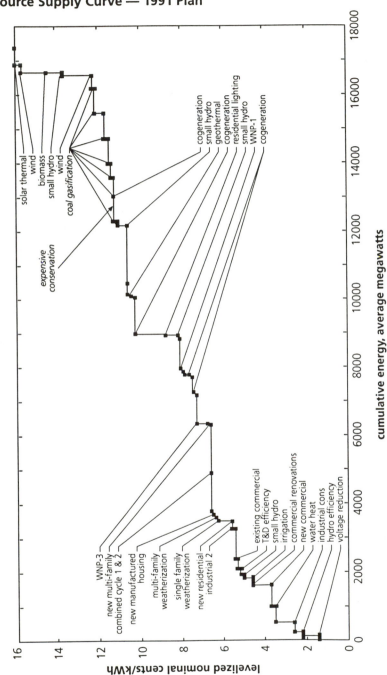

information and criticism. If not universally accepted, it is at least well understood.

A Funny Thing Happened on the Way to Implementation

The bane of all planners is the future. In the case of the council's first plan, it is not that the future was different than the plan anticipated, but that future was at least temporarily one in which resource planning was not an interesting or timely topic. The council's first plan was, however, groundbreaking in at least two ways. First, it forecast electricity needs increasing at far smaller rates than the utility forecasts of a few years before. The lower ranges of growth in the council's forecast actually showed stable or slightly declining electricity demands through much of the decade of the 1980s. This view was thought to be heresy by many during the planning process.

Second, the plan relied heavily on conservation, the more efficient use of electricity—another heretical thought. The council's analysis found this conservation to cost, on average, half as much as the power from the standard for new generating facilities at the time—large scale coal-fired plants. Conservation was planned to be a significant contributor under any growth scenario. Under conditions of very low growth, the council's plan showed that the region's resource needs could be met with very modest amounts of conservation and virtually nothing else.

The future that actually unfolded was at least temporarily close to a low-growth scenario. The rapid run up in electricity rates brought about by the addition of expensive new thermal resources to the system and the payments on yet unfinished nuclear power plants combined with the general economic slowdown of the period to make demands nearer the low end of the council's forecast range a reality. New plants were coming on line but, far from needing vast amounts of new resources, the region was in surplus. The early 1980s saw the cancellation of plans by investor-owned utilities to build two nuclear plants; the termination of two of the five Washington Public Power Supply System Nuclear Plants already under construction, triggering the largest municipal bond default in history; and the "moth-balling" of two more of the WPPSS plants that were between 60 percent and 70 percent complete.

Despite the surplus, the council believed it was essential that at least a modest level of effort be expended to develop the conservation resource. There were two kinds of conservation actions that the council believed prudent. The first was "capability building." It was recognized that the surplus would not last forever. Since the region was relatively inexperienced in developing the efficiency resource, it was believed prudent to develop the capability to develop the resource through modest pilot efforts in a variety of demand sectors.

The second was "lost opportunity resources"—the efficiency savings that would effectively be lost if efficiency were not built into new structures at the time of construction. This translated into a major effort to incorporate high levels of efficiency into the building standards of the states and local governments of the region—model conservation standards. As a consequence, the states of Washington and Oregon have among the most stringent energy codes in the country. Several local governments in Idaho and Montana have also followed suit.

Two other types of conservation programs were carried out. Residential weatherization programs, initiated prior to the council's plan, proved to be a popular customer service in response to rapidly rising rates. In light of the surplus, the council urged reducing these programs to minimum levels, with little consequence. Later in the decade, concerns about maintaining the viability of the regional aluminum industry (without whose load the regional surplus would have been much greater) in the face of rock-bottom aluminum prices brought about the Conservation-Modernization Program. Bonneville paid the aluminum companies for the electricity saved in their processes. The energy saved was quite cheap for Bonneville and did improve the market situation for the industry at least modestly.

In total, despite the surplus, the Northwest achieved an estimated 660 average megawatts of conservation savings through 1992, half from residential programs and the remainder from commercial, industrial, and governmental programs, including the Energy Code (NPPC, 1993).

In the course of the decade, conservation achieved a measure of credibility in the region. Whether it was through experience or through constant repetition, conservation became accepted as a resource in the minds of many, if not most, utility managers in the region. It would be naive, however, to assume that conservation is now on an equal footing with generating resources. Since retail rates in the region are typically greater than the short-run marginal cost of power —Bonneville's wholesale rate for the public utilities—conservation leads to a loss of net revenues, at least in the short run. The resulting upward pressure on rates, even though it is small, is a major concern for some of the utilities in the region. And, despite the numerous evaluations which have significantly reduced the uncertainty regarding the reality of the conservation resource, there are still those who, lacking a "negawatt" meter, remain dubious of the resource.

A Plan for "One Big Utility"?

One casualty of the 1980s was the concept of "one big utility," that is, the notion that most resource development, whether by public or investor-owned utilities, would take place with the backing of Bonneville. The investor-owned utilities generally decided that they would go it alone rather than develop resources through Bonneville, despite the fact that they would be needing new resources sooner than Bonneville's public utility customers. The council, in the preparation of its 1986 plan, did an analysis of the potential benefits of "regional cooperation," another way of saying one big utility (NPPC, 1986, p. 2-1). That analysis found that as a result of a number of factors, the expected net present value cost to the region would be less by about $2.2 billion (1985 dollars) if resource development were to occur in a coordinated fashion. The benefits came about from better use of non-firm hydropower, the preservation of the two moth-balled nuclear plants to meet IOU needs (buoyed by an optimistic view of the viability of those plants), and the ability to carry out conservation in public utility service territories to provide resources to the IOUs. The council openly questioned whether Bonneville's role was to be a catalyst for regional cooperation or just another utility.

Despite the apparent magnitude of the benefits, Bonneville and its public utility customers were not interested in special overtures to the IOUs and/or the IOUs weren't buying. The hypothesis of one observer of the period is that Bonneville management, under the cost pressures of the Washington Public Power Supply System debt, consciously abandoned the traditional Bonneville mission of catalyst for regional cooperation (Merrill Schultz, 1993). For the council, this raised the question of the relevancy of their regional plan when a large part of the region was deciding not to behave in the ways contemplated by the Regional Act.

As it became clear that the one big utility concept was becoming seriously out of date, the council sought ways to make their planning relevant to the entire region even without the leverage provided by a Bonneville that is primary acquirer of new resources for the region. One avenue was to disaggregate the planning analysis to address the major subgroups of the region separately as well as in regional aggregate. Consequently, analysis was carried out for the IOUs as a group, for Bonneville and its customers as a group, and for the region as a whole. This did not result in resource portfolios that were different in character for one group from another. It did, however, affect the timing of resource development for the different groups.

The other element of the council's strategy was to work with and through the public utility commissions of the states of the region to influence the planning of the investor-owned utilities. The commissions were all at one stage or another of requiring least-cost plans of their utilities. By participating in those commission-mandated planning processes and by actively addressing issues of importance to the utility commissions, the council was able to provide a service to the commissions. The commissions, in turn, typically used the council's plan as a bench mark for evaluating the adequacy of the utility least-cost plans, giving the council's plan leverage it would not otherwise have had.

The council has continued to make working with the utility commissions a major priority. The council members maintain a liaison with the commission members of their states; meet annually as a group with the states' utility commissioners to discuss issues of common interest; and the staffs of the commissions and the council meet quarterly. Council staff continue to participate in the least-cost planning processes of each of the investor-owned utilities. Even though the council has no authority relative to the investor-owned utilities of the region, the council believes that it has been relatively successful in influencing the actions of those utilities.

A Time for Action—the 1991 Plan

The council's 1991 plan marked the end of the Northwest's supply surplus and the beginning of a period for which the council had actually been created—a period in which the council's plan would guide the resource acquisition activities of the region's utilities. Even with modest rates of growth in the 1990s, the region was facing significant firm energy deficits in the absence of aggressive resource development.

In developing the 1991 plan, the council examined a number of different scenarios, searching for the combination of resources that was both low cost and risk resistant. Among the variations explored were limitations on the penetration of conservation, faster than expected increases in the price of natural gas, and limitations on the availability and/or acceptability of coal and nuclear power plants. The plan identified a least-cost resource portfolio heavily weighted toward conservation, cogeneration, gas turbines used in a hydro-firming mode (the gas turbines being run when secondary hydropower is unavailable—in effect, firming that non-firm hydropower), and in the event of high load growth, possible completion of the two moth-balled Washington Public Power Supply System nuclear power plants and/or building of coal-fired generation (NPPC, 1991). The 1991 plan laid out four main objectives for the region's utilities in its action plan:

- *Acquire low cost resources*: 1,500 average megawatts of conservation and 800 MW of low-cost generation (anticipated to be hydro and cogeneration) by the year 2000.

- *Reduce resource lead times:* Acquire the necessary siting, licensing, and other approvals necessary to be able to quickly develop an additional 100 average megawatts of hydropower, 750 average megawatts of cogeneration, and 1500 of combustion turbines for hydro-firming.

- *Determine the cost and availability of resources*: Carry out demonstrations of geothermal and wind resources on the scale of tens of average megawatts and resolve the remaining financial, legal, and institutional uncertainties regarding completion or termination of the moth-balled nuclear power plants.

- *Encourage actions supporting implementation*: For example, development of a system to track conservation implementation region-wide, continued support of least-cost planning activities by the region's utilities, regulatory actions like decoupling to remove disincentives to utility investment in conservation, reforms to state siting processes, and implementation of multi-level wholesale rates by the Bonneville Power Administration to encourage resource development by its customer utilities.

Soon after implementation of the 1991 plan began, it became apparent that the region's resource situation was to become even more precarious. First, environmental groups filed petitions to declare certain salmon species endangered under the Endangered Species Act. A major part of any strategy to help the salmon recover is to increase flows in the river during the late spring and early summer to help the juvenile salmon migrate out to sea. To provide these flows, it is necessary to forego electric generation in the winter, when Northwest loads are highest, to store water in the reservoirs. Under some proposals, the loss in firm energy load carrying capacity of the hydro system would have been as much as several thousand average megawatts.

The governors of the region asked the council to take the lead in preparing a recovery plan with the aim of keeping decisions critical to the future of the region in the hands of the region. The strategy developed by the council keeps the average impact on the hydro system to 50 to 100 average megawatts while providing flows for the salmon. This is in addition to approximately 300 average megawatts lost to earlier fish flow requirements. Along with this loss, however, are losses in the operational flexibility and capacity of the hydro system. In addition, there are concerns that future salmon recovery measures may require further impacts on the hydro system.

The second and much larger impact on the power system occurred in January 1993 when Portland General Electric made the decision to close the Trojan Nuclear Power Plant in the face of increasing costs and the risks of even greater future costs for the replacement of the reactor's steam generator. This represents a loss of approximately 726 average megawatts from the regional system, 30 percent of which was net billed to Bonneville by its public utility owner. The decision was based on the determination that it would be possible to develop alternative resources at less cost than continued operation of the plant. Adding another 700 average megawatts to the region's already significant new resource needs was not, however, inconsequential.

The ultimate test of a plan is whether it is being implemented. The council recently sought to answer this question by undertaking a "mid-course review" of implementation of the 1991 plan (NPPC, 1993). This review was generally encouraging. The early results indicate that conservation acquisitions by both Bonneville customer utilities and investor-owned utilities appear to be on a pace of acceleration sufficient to achieve the council's goal of 1,500 average megawatts by the year 2000. And with respect to generating resources, the pace of development is such that the council's overall resource goals for the year 2000 appear likely to be met.

CENTRALIZED PLANNING FOR A DECENTRALIZED WORLD?

The council recently marked the tenth anniversary of its first plan. Despite this milestone, the continuing evolution of the utility world is causing council members and others to ask whether the institution will continue to be relevant in the years ahead. The concept of "one big utility," a major reason for the council coming into being, was largely discredited in the 1980s when investor-owned utilities decided to undertake resource development without the involvement of the Bonneville Power Administration. Only the council's relationship with the states' regulatory commissions and, more importantly, the credibility and public support of the council's plan, provided leverage for influencing the plans and actions of the investor-owned utilities.

Today, continuing regulatory and technological changes, combined with increasing costs and perceived risks associated with the Bonneville Power Administration, are beginning to call into question whether even the region's publicly owned utilities will rely on Bonneville for new resource development. For example:

- Deregulation of wholesale power production and the opening up of wholesale transmission access in the National Energy Policy Act of 1992 have opened the door for independent power producers (IPPs) to supply individual customer utilities.

- Deregulation of natural gas production and transport has resulted in a more competitive market—apparently more secure supply and lower prices—giving utilities greater confidence in moving toward reliance on gas-fired resources for their own development or purchase from IPPs.

- Advances in gas turbine technology in terms of efficiency and low air emissions along with low gas prices have made relatively small-scale generation projects feasible and cost-effective.

- The potential for retail wheeling, which might allow large retail consumers to shop for their power supplier, is raising utility concerns about losing loads.

- Advances in the development of even smaller-scale technologies (e.g., fuel cells) could make self-generation by large retail customers feasible in the not too distant future, further raising utility fears of losing major loads.

- The costs and risks associated with doing business with the Bonneville Power Administration are perceived to be growing.

    - The effects of a prolonged drought and low prices in world aluminum markets have weakened Bonneville's financial condition. These factors in combination with the costs of new resources have resulted in prospects for an increase of as much as 20 percent in Bonneville's wholesale rates.

    - The risk of congressionally imposed changes in the terms of the repayment of Bonneville's debt to the U.S. Treasury could sharply further increase Bonneville's rates.

    - The risk of additional fish and wildlife restoration and mitigation costs could put further upward pressure on Bonneville's rates.

    - Being tied to a slow moving giant in a fast moving age may entail even greater costs and risks— Bonneville is a large, bureaucratic federal agency, sometimes wasteful and always subject to legal requirements which tend to increase their cost of

doing business. For example, Bonneville is subject
to compliance with the National Environmental
Policy Act, whereas an independent developer is
not.

The direction of these changes would appear to be toward greater
independent action for new resource development on the part of Bonneville's customer utilities. The idea that Bonneville will be the
resource acquirer of choice for its public utility customers, let alone for
the region, seems to have little currency.

Bonneville, for its part, is attempting to respond to the challenges
by becoming "more like a business." It is focusing on what it takes for
them to become more competitive (although some cynics have
observed that this is akin to teaching an elephant to dance). They are
talking about unbundling and differentiating the pricing of their services. The ability of Bonneville to use the hydro system and its transmission system to provide services like storage, shaping, transmission,
and automatic generation control will be important to utilities developing their own resources. And, absent the cost pressures of large-
scale new resource acquisition, the power from the Federal Columbia
River system should continue to be a relatively low cost resource of
tremendous value. Still, for those who still hold to the old federalist
model of Bonneville as an agent of regional development, the idea of
Bonneville becoming more like a business is not encouraging.

What value is the council's plan in a future like this? The council
has no authority relative to the public utilities absent implementation
through Bonneville. Unlike investor-owned utilities, the public utilities are not subject to regulation by the states. More fundamentally, do
we need to have a plan if resource development is taking place in a
market-driven environment?

If that market environment can be expected to lead to the same
kind of future that the Regional Act created the council and its planning function to produce—that is, a long-term, least *societal cost*
future—there would be no need for the council or its plan. There may,
however, be market factors which may tend to discourage utilities
from pursuing this goal. For example, markets, by definition, do not
consider environmental externalities. Markets also have imperfections
that most observers agree prevent an economically efficient level of
investment in conservation. If utilities are concerned about their competitiveness with competing fuels, competing electricity suppliers or
self-generation, how will they try to compete? Will they focus on providing electricity *services* at the lowest possible cost, that is, by investing in the efficient use of electricity which reduces total bills even
though it slightly increases rates? Or will they focus on electricity as a
commodity to be delivered at the lowest possible rate? The former will

lead toward the conservation goals of the Regional Act, the latter quite possibly will not.

Many of the region's public utilities can be expected to pursue the goals of the Regional Act, regardless of the council and its plan. Others might not. In either event, the value of the council's plan as a vehicle for reaching public consensus and as a benchmark against which the plans of individual utilities can be judged may continue to have value even in the brave new world of independent resource development.

There are also a number of emergent problems and issues in the Northwest's electricity system on which the council could provide important leadership:

- The region is increasingly becoming capacity constrained. Whereas in the past, the hydro system could be counted on for load following, the combination of growing peak loads and increasing constraints on the hydro system are such that this may soon no longer be the case. Should utilities go it alone in planning to meet capacity needs, or are there advantages to regional planning cooperation to meet these emerging needs?

- How should the issue of fuel choice be addressed? In an era when gas-fired generation is being developed, the fact that direct use of natural gas is likely to be more cost-effective for the regional electricity system in many applications is difficult to ignore. But electric utilities still locked in a decades-old competition with gas utilities have difficulty recognizing this. Could the council bring some rationality to the fuel choice issue in the Northwest?

- How should utilities take environmental externalities into consideration in their planning, acquisition, and operational decisions? Should this be decided piecemeal, jurisdiction by jurisdiction, or could a regional body like the council bring some coherence to this issue?

- The problem of restoring endangered runs of salmon remains. Can this responsibility be left to the federal agencies, or is there the need for a regional body like the council to attempt the thankless task of balancing competing interests?

- Are the current critical water hydro planning and operating criteria still adequate, or could the region save a considerable amount of money by moving to a probabilistic hydro planning model? Is the council the appropriate institution to address this issue? If not, who is?

The Northwest's experiment in federalism in electricity has been evolving continually since it was initiated. Although this experiment has added value to the Northwest, it is clear that today's world is not the world for which the experiment was designed. Whether the experiment will have value in the years ahead is an open question.

NOTES

1. For example, see Woodie Guthrie's "Roll on, Columbia," quoted in Springer (1976, epigraph).

2. An "average megawatt" is equivalent to 8,760 MW hours. The annual electricity use of the city of Seattle is approximately 1,100 average megawatts.

3. The Hydro-Thermal Power Plan of 1968 foresaw the need for over 21,000 average megawatts of new thermal generating capacity by 1990, more than double the existing firm hydropower. See Lee et al. (1980, p. 69).

4. For a complete discussion of net billing, see Lee et al. (1980, pp 75–82).

5. The actual authority of the council over Bonneville's actions are limited to: (1) Bonneville's major resource acquisitions (greater than 50 MW for five or more years) are to be consistent with the council's plan. If the council finds a proposed resource acquisition inconsistent with its plan, Bonneville can only proceed with acquisition with explicit approval of Congress (Section 6(c)). (2) The council may at any time review the actions of the administrator to determine whether those actions are consistent with the plan and program and the extent to which the plan and program are being implemented (Section 4(i)). (3) The council may request the administrator to take actions to carry out his or her responsibilities under the act. While the administrator is not compelled to take those actions, he or she must make a formal determination of why the requested action would not be consistent with the plan, or the administrator's obligations under the act or other provisions of law (Section 4(j)). (4) The council was directed to establish model conservation standards for new construction (i.e., building standards) and for utility conservation programs. The council was authorized to request the administrator to impose a surcharge of up to 10 percent on Bonneville's wholesale rate for utilities that do not comply with the model conservation standards (Section 4(f)(1)).

6. Adapted from Morlan and Nybo (1992).

7. In the council's first plan, there was no medium or best guess forecast, but rather a range of four forecasts with an estimated probability distribution. The intention of this focus on uncertainty was to shift planning objectives from meeting a best guess forecast of electricity requirements to one of developing a risk-averse strategy for meeting an uncertain future requirement.

8. Conservation supply curves are developed to be consistent with the demand forecasts, from the number of houses and appliances available to the technological assumptions behind both estimates. Conservation resources

compete directly with generating resources in developing a least-cost mix of choices. The costs of resources, both supply and demand side, affect the forecast price of, and demand for, electricity. These aspects of the planning process are iterated until a balance is found. The degree to which the council consistently integrates demand-side resources into the plan is still unmatched by most integrated resource planning efforts.

9.   Two other demand forecasting concepts were used to complete the demand characterizations. These were a forecast of demand if consumers responded to prices but no conservation programs were in place, and a forecast of what actual electricity sales would be with all planned resources in place, including conservation programs.

10.   A Monte Carlo simulation model, ISAAC enables the council to look at the expected value as well as the variance implications of alternative resources over a wide range of futures involving combinations of future loads, water conditions, and fuel prices. It can evaluate the worth of risk-reduction strategies such as shorter lead times, smaller unit sizes, and different resource cost structures.

11.   The most familiar form of an option would be a pre-designed and pre-sited power plant that is held in inventory until the time the plant is needed. The reality of such options remains to be proven due to the regulatory procedures now in place, but Bonneville is currently soliciting resource option bids in an effort to push the concept to fruition. Other forms of options, such as flexible power export contracts with recall provisions, have been successfully implemented.

REFERENCES

Guthrie, Woodie. "Roll on, Columbia." Quoted in Vera Springer. *Power and the Pacific Northwest*. Portland: Bonneville Power Administration, 1976, epigraph.

Lee, Kai N., and Donna Lee Klemka with Marion Marts. *Electric Power and the Future of the Pacific Northwest*. Seattle, WA: University of Washington Press, 1980.

Morlan, Terry, and James Nybo. *Conservation Planning and Accomplishments in the Pacific Northwest*. Unpublished paper, 1992.

Northwest Power Planning Council (NPPC). *1986 Northwest Conservation and Electric Power Plan*. Vol. 1. Portland, OR: NPPC, 1986.

Northwest Power Planning Council (NPPC). *1991 Northwest Conservation and Electric Power Plan.*, Vol. 1 and 2. Publication 91-04. Portland, OR: NPPC, April, 1991.

Northwest Power Planning Council (NPPC) and Conservation Monitor (CM). Survey of utilities. Portland, OR: NPPC, 1993.

Northwest Power Planning Council (NPPC). *Draft "Mid-Course" Review of Implementation of the 1991 Power Plan* Publication 93-7, Portland, OR: NPPC, March, 1993.

Schultz, Merrill. Personal communication. June 1993.

U.S. Congress. *Pacific Northwest Electric Power Planning and Conservation Act of 1980.* PL 96-501.

14

Comment on the Northwest Power Planning Council Case

Kenneth W. Costello

Any discussion of the electric power sector in the Pacific Northwest must begin with the Bonneville Power Administration (BPA). This federal agency, which is one of five federal power marketing administrations, was established by Congress in 1937 to market and transport power from the Bonneville Dam on the Columbia River. The BPA's mission was to promote economic development in the Northwest by delivering low-cost hydropower, particularly to rural areas. During the 1930s, there was a belief that privately owned utilities were unwilling or simply could not be trusted to provide power to scarcely populated areas. Today, the BPA's objectives extend to promoting conservation, irrigation, and fish and wildlife protection.[1]

Preference customers comprise the BPA's largest class of customers. These customers, namely municipalities, public utility districts (PUDs), and rural electric cooperatives, have first-access rights to the low-cost hydropower. BPA also sells non-firm power to investor-owned utilities (IOUs) located both within and outside the Northwest and directly to regional aluminum producers.

THE UNIQUENESS OF THE PACIFIC NORTHWEST POWER SECTOR

The prominent features of the Pacific Northwest power sector make the sector somewhat unique in the Untied States. The sector is dominated by a federal agency which has no authority to build new generating capacity (unlike, for example, the Tennessee Valley

Authority [TVA]). Federal law prohibits BPA from owning generating capacity.

The federal agency sells to both publicly owned and privately owned entities. The passage of the Pacific Northwest Electric Power Planning and Conservation Act of 1980 (Regional Act) actually weakened the preference rights of publicly owned utilities in order to arrive at a political compromise aimed at stabilizing conditions in the Northwest power sector. The fundamental problem addressed by the Regional Act was how to introduce economical new power sources and, simultaneously, keep the basic preference rights of publicly owned utilities.

The Northwest has placed great emphasis on the environmental and ecological considerations of power generation. During the 1970s, new power supplies in the form of additional dams were precluded from consideration because of the damaging effect on the salmon population on the Columbia River system. Hydropower generation, which varies with annual and seasonal river flow, is affected by decisions made in the region relating to alternatives to power uses such as irrigation, recreation, upstream storage, and fish conservation. It is probably correct to say that regional environmental and ecological concerns relating to power generation are more, or at least as, pronounced in the Pacific Northwest than in any other region in the United States.

The high historical dependence of the Northwest on low-cost hydropower (which today provides two-thirds of the region's power needs), together with the ecological constraints on increasing hydropower production and capacity, foretells of a future where the average cost of regional power production would rise. This reality explains much of the political backing of the Regional Act and the formation of the Northwest Power Planning Council.

Terms such as "net billing" and "residential exchange programs" are singular to the Pacific Northwest. Net billing, as discussed by Mr. Watson in this volume, was a way for the BPA to provide financial backing for new thermal resources. In one sense, it reflected the extension of federal ownership of generating facilities in the manner of TVA. On the negative side, some analysts view net billing as a device used to circumvent the legislative prohibition against BPA owning generating facilities. For example, net billing allowed the BPA to acquire most of the generation capacity of the five Washington Pacific Power Supply System's (WPPSS) nuclear projects. This was accomplished by shifting the risks of construction failure to the BPA and its customers. For example, a large portion of the construction costs would be charged to the BPA, including debt service, whether or not the projects were completed. As almost everyone knows, the $2.25 billion default of the

WPPSS soon followed, which was the largest municipal default in history.

Residential exchange programs were a mechanism aimed at dispersing the preference rights to low-cost hydropower to the customers of the regional investor-owned utilities. In effect, these customers were able to continue receiving low-cost hydropower by having industrial customers pay much of the costs associated with new thermal capacity. In return, industrial customers received power supply guarantees.

The gap between marginal cost and price for power may be greater in the Pacific Northwest than in any other region of the country. Residential electrical rates in Washington, Idaho, and Oregon are the lowest in the country. Yet, marginal costs for many periods during a typical year are more comparable to those in other regions. A study applying 1980 data showed that the BPA sold power at an average price equal to only 13 percent of its marginal cost (Levy, 1990).

Finally, with the possible exception of the TVA, no one electric utility dominates a region as the BPA does. In addition to falling outside the jurisdiction of state public utility regulation, the BPA has much discretion over its own pricing and transmission-access practices. As a federal agency, especially before the passage of the Regional Act, the BPA was held accountable for little of its activities and policies. Even today regulation of its prices by the Federal Energy Regulatory Commission is best characterized as light-handed.

WHAT HAPPENED DURING THE 1970s?

Starting in 1973, the BPA stopped supplying firm power to investor-owned utilities. Further, during the 1970s, it became more clear that the BPA could not extend the contracts of industrial customers in the absence of additional power resources. Preference customers hoped to capture additional hydropower at the expense of investor-owned utilities and industrial customers. The 1970s, more than anything, illuminated the real objective of the BPA—serving regional *consumers'* interests.

In an attempt to increase new power supplies, the BPA agreed to sign take-or-pay (net billing) contracts to help fund new thermal generating facilities, especially nuclear power plants. Net billing allowed the BPA to play a major role in the development of new power resources in the Pacific Northwest. Partly because of the default of WPPSS bonds, consumer-interest groups turned to Congress for a legislative remedy. The Regional Act was subsequently enacted.

Although presenting a historical overview of the 1970s may seem like second-guessing the major players in the Northwest power sector, it can provide some insights into the sources of the problems that can conceivably recur. One major source of the problems that started to emerge was the preference clause of the Bonneville Project Act of 1937. The clause attempts to allocate the low-cost hydropower to certain consumers, originally to customers of publicly owned utilities. Its effect has been:

- too low prices are established for power (namely, prices lie below marginal costs);

- U.S. taxpayers have been deprived of the economic rent that would otherwise be associated with the hydropower facilities;

- hydropower is not distributed to those who value it the most; and

- considerable rent-seeking costs have been incurred by different consumer groups over time to gain preference rights to the hydropower.

The threats from aluminum smelters and the customers of investor-owned utilities to gain legal access to preference power compelled a political deal that would appease all consumer-interest groups. Passage of the Regional Act embodied that political compromise.

Another problem, related to the preference provisions, revolved around the BPA marketing electricity at subsidized prices (which can be attributable to federal subsidies in the form of direct appropriations, low-interest loans, and flexible amortization schedules on outstanding debt). Low prices, assuming other things remain the same, imply underinvestment in energy conservation, overinvestment in power capacity, and excessive environmental costs. BPA's survival has largely depended on its ability to hold down prices to politically influential consumers who over time have convinced themselves, as well as others, that they have a permanent right to low-cost electricity.

An additional problem that arose in the 1970s was the inability of WPPSS to accurately forecast demand for electricity. (Of course, investor-owned utilities throughout the country were subjected to the same criticism.) The municipal agency, which was responsible for building five nuclear plants in the Northwest, was criticized for underestimating construction costs and their effect on demand; WPPSS assumed, for example, that price elasticities of demand were zero. A recent study suggested that WPPSS' problems could have been avoided with better management (Fisher et al., 1992). Specifically, given the evidence that was available to WPPSS about price elasticities and the likelihood of cost overruns at the time the nuclear plants were being constructed, there was substantial uncertainty over whether WPPSS management would be able to meet its debt obligations. In any case, whether or not the WPPSS management was at fault, the debt default that subsequently took place sparked consumer groups in the Pacific Northwest to push ahead for electric planning reform.

THE REGIONAL ACT

The Regional Act, which was passed in 1980, intended to join together the activities of the federal government and the states in a way that would create a more accountable and efficient electric power sector in the Pacific Northwest. The act responded to two major issues debated during the 1970s: the preference provisions and the BPA's role as the manager of the regional power resources. For preference customers and small customers of IOUs, the act substantially limited the amounts they had to pay for new high-cost thermal resources.[2] For other customers such as direct service industries, the act helped assure reliable sources of power supplies. These customers, however, paid a high price for this reliability. For example, electricity rates for aluminum smelters rose from 0.35 to 2.45 cents per kilowatthour over the period of 1979 to 1984 (Spies, 1990).

As a major objective, the Regional Act created the Northwest Power Planning Council. The major activity of the council, which is comprised of state representatives from Oregon, Washington, Idaho, and Montana, involves the development of a twenty-year power plan for the Pacific Northwest. Under the act, BPA is required either to carry out the plan or obtain congressional approval for an alternate plan. Under the act, the council is mandated to give priority to energy conservation and renewable energy resources.

One of the objectives of the act is to ensure public participation in the creation of an electric plan, and a fish and wildlife program. The act reflects the belief that a broad regional consensus regarding the expansion of the electric power system in the Pacific Northwest was necessary in light of the high costs of thermal generating facilities on both power consumers and the environment.

The act mirrors the reality that most of the electric energy questions facing the Northwest were political in nature. Consequently, it recognized the importance of giving the states a larger voice in charting the region's energy future.[3]

QUESTIONS RELATING TO THE EFFECTIVENESS OF THE COUNCIL'S PLANNING ACTIVITIES

Many experts have pointed to the council's activities over the last ten years as an example of how electric power planning should be carried out in the United States.[4] The council's initial planning was a forerunner to the planning activities incorporating the principles and components of what has become known as integrated resource planning (IRP). The emphasis on energy conservation, accounting explicitly for environmental effects, and applying advanced techniques to address uncertainty are all features of the council's twenty-year electric plans. Another characteristic of the council's planning activities is the high degree of public involvement in the creation of plans.

For those skeptics of IRP, the council's activities represent centralized planning where political pressures and the use of nonmarket mechanisms guide the formation of electric power plans. For example, they ask how the council can develop a sound and economically rational plan when it has no ratemaking authority and the BPA's existing rates are highly inefficient. The U.S. Office of Management and Budget (OMB, 1992) has criticized the council's most recent plan because it does not include the benefits of household energy consumers switching from electricity to natural gas for space heating and water heating purposes and for not considering the effects of more economically efficient pricing on encouraging energy conservation. Overall, OMB characterizes energy planning in the Pacific Northwest as a "hodgepodge" of activities that generally increase the demand for electricity, unnecessarily increase costs to ratepayers and taxpayers, and are not unlikely to produce adverse environmental activities. For example, it has described many of the BPA's energy conservation programs as simply subsidies aimed at discouraging residential consumers from switching to natural gas for specific end-use purposes.

Critics of command-and-control planning practices such as those engaged in by the council have recently pointed to several problems and questions related to such practices.[5] The major ones are as follows:

- Market failures are less serious than they are claimed to be by conservationists and other demand-side management (DSM) supporters.

- IRP, as practiced throughout the United States, incorporates central planning tenets whereby utility's plans are subject to political review and approval. Although markets are imperfect, aggressive regulatory intervention is even more imperfect because of the high costs associated with micromanagement of utility activities.

- IRP will result in energy consumers being forced to pay higher prices in order to fund utility activities advocated by special-interest groups such as conservationists and environmentalists. In other words, subsidies paid to certain consumers for promoting energy conservation result in taxing other consumers.

- IRP is contrary to promoting competitive markets. Consequently, IRP will likely fade away as electric power and natural gas industries become more competitive. When treating electricity as a commodity, utilities should be in the business of providing highly reliable energy at the lowest possible price. Doing anything else is either counterproductive or peripheral to achieving this objective.

- DSM should extend beyond promoting conservation to encompass market-based pricing and aggressive marketing activities. Utilities can best promote DSM by efficient pricing, in addition to dispensing consumer information regarding the benefits of conservation and other DSM activities. Any additional utility DSM activities should be done through an unregulated subsidiary in the absence of ratepayer funding.

- Before investing more in DSM programs, energy savings from existing programs should be measured by applying well-grounded statistical techniques. Based on current evidence, many conservation programs have been oversold: Their actual costs were higher than what was initially projected, and their actual energy savings were less.

In sum, although advocates of the IRP process such as the council's were successful in gaining political acceptance, hard empirical evidence supporting their position awaits further work. The most fundamental question regarding IRP centers on whether it represents the most appropriate institutional arrangement for achieving such desirable outcomes as economic efficiency, promotion of energy conservation, and a cleaner environment. As the electric power industry becomes more competitive, greater reliance on market forces, deregulation, or light-handed regulation will likely replace the current form of the IRP process for both economic and political reasons. What this implies for the Pacific Northwest is that the planning activities of the council will undergo an intensive review during the next few years. Mr. Watson acknowledged this possibility when he questioned whether the council should continue to develop plans, especially in their present form, in a market-driven environment.

REVAMPING THE NORTHWEST COMPACT

Changes in the electric power industry along with the recent problems of the BPA call into question the regional desirability of staying with the current institutional arrangement. Specifically, with the movement of the electric industry toward robust competition and the BPA's current financial problems (caused in large part by several years of low water conditions), the time may be ripe for revamping the structure and modus operandi of the Pacific Northwest electric power sector. The real issue today is whether the public policy toward the electric power sector in the Pacific Northwest serves the region's interest.

A key feature of any reform of the electric power sector in the Pacific Northwest should entail the nurturing of market forces. Movement in this direction would parallel the evolution of the U.S. electric power industry and, more importantly, would allow power consumers to avail themselves of the benefits that are likely to arise from a more competitive, decentralized, and efficient electric power industry. One new reality is that utilities will need to transform their traditional function from generating and delivering power to providing whatever services consumers demand.[6] The pertinent question today is not whether the current balance of power between the federal government and the states is appropriate, but rather, how the electric power sector in the Pacific Northwest can be restructured and governed in a way that relies more on and accommodates market forces. A market-driven electric power industry will diminish the role of both the BPA and the council. At the minimum, it will cause both entities to reassess their activities and, perhaps, to reshape their missions in light of a new U.S. electric power industry.

It is questionable whether the Pacific Northwest, given the dominance of the BPA and the role of the council as a centralized planner, will be in the position of "being on the train" instead of "left at the station." Whether the Northwest moves in line with the rest of the country depends on several factors. First, the BPA should establish prices that are compatible with market realities. Subsidized pricing of bundled electric services makes no sense in a competitive environment where power consumers would have access to various electrical services at affordable prices.[7]

The BPA, as well as investor-owned utilities in the Northwest, should open their transmission systems to all power producers requiring access to market their power to anyone willing to pay the market price, including the BPA's preference customers. As mentioned by Mr. Watson, preference customers may oppose continued restrictions on their ability to purchase power from suppliers other than the BPA.

Although new federal legislation will expand transmission access on privately owned networks, it is uncertain what effect this will have on publicly owned networks such as the BPA's.[8]

Because abolishing preference rights may not pass the political test, those customers who benefit from subsidized prices should be allowed to resell their allocated power to whomever is willing to pay the highest prices. The Clinton Administration's *Vision of Change* recommends reselling rights be granted to preference customers with the profits shared between them and the U.S. Treasury. Reselling would improve efficiency in accordance with the Coase theorem idea that, when transaction costs are minimal, efficiency does not depend on the initial allocation of property rights.

The existing planning activities of the council may not be compatible with tomorrow's competitive electric power industry. It seems logical to believe that the IRP practices of the council and many of the states will lose ground, as they probably should, as the environment in the electric power industry becomes more market driven. For government planning to survive in such an environment, at the minimum, it must change in a way that avoids the tenets of highly politicized centralized planning.[9] Mr. Watson alludes to this likely conflict between IRP and a competitive electricity market when he comments that, in pursuing the market-driven objective of providing different electrical services at the lowest possible prices, utilities may forego DSM activities that are compatible with the goals of the Regional Act.

NOTES

1. The major asset of the BPA is its extensive transmission network, the Intertie, which comprises approximately 80 percent of the Northwest's high-voltage transmission capacity, with over 14,700 circuit miles of lines (with a replacement value of around $10 billion) and almost 400 substations. BPA markets the power for the Federal Columbia River Power System, which consists of the Pacific Northwest generating facilities, operated by the Army Corps of Engineers, and non-power related projects of the Bureau of Reclamation. The BPA has increasingly transmitted power from thermal generating facilities that were built to meet the growing demand for electricity in the Northwest. As discussed by Richard Watson, this provided much of the impetus for the formation of the Northwest Power Planning Council (NPPC).

2. The act rejected marginal or replacement cost pricing in favor of historical or embedded cost pricing. Politically, marginal-cost pricing was unacceptable since power rates would have increased significantly in the Northwest. Almost from its beginning, the BPA had opposed marginal-cost pricing on the grounds that it would reduce the aggregate usage of power in the region and, thereby, adversely affect the region's economic growth. The

cross-subsidized pricing structure that has transpired is being funded from the pocketbooks of both U.S. taxpayers and BPA's non-preference customers.

3.   The act included other major provisions. First, it codified the net-billing program by which the BPA can purchase the output or capacity of new energy resources that are owned by other utilities. Second, the act placed a price cap on power sold to preference customers, in order to make them no worse off than during the period prior to the act. Third, the act guaranteed energy supplies to direct service industries, but at a cost. For at least five years after passage of the act, higher prices charged to industrial customers were to offset the increased costs to the BPA and small customers of investor-owned utilities. Fourth, the act established a residential exchange program which extended the preference clause of the Bonneville Project Act of 1937 to the residential and small farm customers of investor-owned utilities.

4.   See, for example, Hirst et al. (1990) and Jones et al. (1992, pp. 93–106).

5.   See, for example, Taylor (1993), Houston (1992), Ruff (1988), Kahn (1992), and Joskow (1988).

6.   Many electric utilities have already begun to prepare themselves for the new environment by downsizing and repositioning their assets in markets where they expect to earn the highest rates of return. As transmission access broadens, the distinction between wholesale and retail transactions will likely blur. Industrial, electric rural cooperative and municipal customers will have powerful incentives, if they do not already, to drive ahead for retail transmission access and wholesale pricing of electricity. To survive and prosper, traditional utilities will have to change with the times by becoming leaner and more competitive.

7.   The Clinton Administration's *Vision of Change* recommends lower subsidies in its endorsement of standard depreciation practices for the federal power marketing administrations. If nothing else, efficient pricing would end the high rent-seeking costs that various groups have incurred since the inception of the BPA for the purpose of gaining or retaining access to low-cost hydropower.

8.   As a matter of economics, the BPA should begin considering unbundling electricity from transmission and other electrical services in both its pricing and accounting. One important benefit from unbundling would be to bring the BPA's prices closer to competitive levels by giving power consumers in the Northwest more choices. Government-owned firms have generally less incentive and freedom than their private counterparts to restructure or reorganize their assets when warranted by market and technological conditions. The importance of reorganizing the BPA's assets during this period of fundamental change in the U.S. electric power industry underlies the case for considering privatization.

9.   Incentive payments or what some would call subsidies paid to power users for energy conservation, for example, may not be defensible or even feasible in a world where prices are more compatible with economic costs, and consumers have choices among power suppliers. Consumers who pay for

conservation that benefits others may decide to buy their power from someone else. Conservationists and other advocates of IRP are beginning to realize the devastating effect competition in the retail markets could have on utility-funded energy conservation activities and IRP as a whole.

REFERENCES

Fisher, Franklin M., et al. "Due Diligence and the Demand for Electricity: A Cautionary Tale." *Review of Industrial Organization* 7 (1992): 117–149.

Hirst, Eric, et al. *Assessing Integrated Resource Plans Prepared by Electric Utilities*. Oak Ridge, TN: Oak Ridge National Laboratory, 1990.

Houston, Douglas A. *Demand-Side Management: Ratepayers Beware!* Houston, TX: Institute for Energy Research, November 1992.

Jones, Douglas N., et al. *Regional Regulation of Public Utilities: Opportunities and Obstacles*. Columbus, OH: The National Regulatory Research Institute, 1992.

Joskow, Paul L. *Testimony before the Subcommittee on Energy and Power.* Washington, DC: Committee on Energy and Commerce, March 31, 1988.

Kahn, Alfred E. "Least-Cost Planning Generally and DSM In Particular." *Resources and Energy* 14 (April 1992): 177–185.

Levy, Yvonne. "Pricing Federal Power in the Pacific Northwest: An Efficiency Approach." *Federal Reserve Bank of San Francisco Economic Review* (Winter 1980): 40–63.

Ruff, Larry. "Least-Cost Planning and Demand-Side Management: Six Common Fallacies and One Simple Truth." *Public Utilities Fortnightly* (April 28, 1988): 19–26.

Spies, Paul. "Variable Electricity Prices for Aluminum Smelting in the Northwestern USA." *Energy Policy* 18 (March 1990): 162–169.

Taylor, Jerry. "Energy Conservation and Efficiency: The Case Against Coercion." Cato Policy Analysis No. 189. Washington, DC: Cato Institute, March 9, 1993.

U.S. Office of Management and Budget (OMB). "BPA Proposed Resource Program Plans." Internal Memorandum, July 31, 1992.

15

New England Case Study

Stephen R. Connors

The New England electric service industry is unique in that it has developed tightly knit communities of electric utilities, utility regulators, environmental regulators, and industry interveners. Although cooperation and coordination are a hallmark of the six-state region, initiatives to increase competition within the industry are straining these relationships. This chapter outlines the industry's structure, with its multitude of players, and the evolution of these industry and regulatory structures, and discusses recent trends in the industry's transformation.

INTRODUCTION

The institutional arrangements that comprise an electric service industry are a curious arrangement of interconnected electrical equipment, corporate entities, governmental bodies, and societal interests. The industry is in turn intimately linked with the oil, natural gas, and coal supply industries. On the physical side of things, the industry is dominated by the New England Power Pool (NEPOOL), which oversees the dispatch and maintenance scheduling of all but seventy of the region's roughly 25,000 MW of generation capability (EIA, 1991; NEPLAN, 1993). New England is in turn part of a supra-regional power system encompassing the northeastern United States and Eastern Canada. Although this implies centralized control, nothing could be farther from the truth, since the rules under which NEPOOL operates are arrived at via a consensus of utility members, agreed on before a background of pressures from state, regional, and federal regulatory agencies and interest groups.

Industry stakeholders fall into five functional categories independent of geographic purview and range. These categories are:

- electric utilities (publicly held and investor owned),
- non-utility resource providers (generation and demand-side alike),
- public utility regulators (state and federal with regional coordination),
- environmental regulators (state, regional, and federal), and
- sanctioned interest groups (business, environmental, and local issue constituencies).

Within each of these categories are numerous sub-categories, which are outlined in the following discussion. Legislatures and lawmakers also play a role in shaping industry decisions, but do so on only an intermittent basis. Each sub-category, while grouped by institutional function, often competes with or will be at odds with another both within and across categories.

INSTITUTIONAL OVERVIEW OF THE NEW ENGLAND ELECTRIC SERVICE INDUSTRY

This section outlines the major sub-categories and stakeholder groups that comprise the New England electric service industry.

Electric Utilities

The New England region's electric utilities encompass a diverse group of corporate and municipal entities. These include:

- single-state investor-owned utilities;
- multi-state investor-owned utilities (including wholesale power divisions);
- municipal electric companies, and municipal cooperatives;
- jointly owned generation (including short- and long-term capacity purchases);
- the New England Power Pool; and
- the Northeast Power Coordinating Council (NPCC).

Single-state investor-owned utilities are one of the simpler sub-categories, as state regulatory agencies wield almost exclusive power over them. These utilities are often small (< 1,000 MW) but can be relatively large as with Boston Edison (3,200 MW of committed resources). Multi-state investor-owned utilities are substantially more complex with service territories and generation in several states, often with wholesale power divisions. In these instances, FERC plays a major role in setting wholesale electric rates and reducing the leverage of state public utility commissions to allow or disallow certain costs, implement integrated resource planning, or institute competitive bidding mechanisms for resource selection. Multi-state investor-owned utilities need not be large organizations. Eastern Utilities Associates (EUA) has two service territories each in Massachusetts and Rhode Island but has exclusive ownership of only 240 MW of its 1,270 MW of generation capability. In contrast, Northeast Utilities (NU) with its recent acquisition of Public Service New Hampshire (PSNH) operates in three states with a generation capability totaling nearly 8,800 MW. Municipal electric companies and their cooperatives such as the Massachusetts Municipal Wholesale Electric Cooperative (MMWEC) and the Connecticut Municipal Electric Energy Cooperative, round out the combined generation/service territory entities within the electric utilities category.

In addition to these groups are the utility affiliated generation companies, NEPOOL, and the regional reliability council. Joint ownership of nuclear units, such as Seabrook, and fossil units, such as Wyman 4 and Canal 1 and 2 allows investor-owned and municipal electric companies to share risk in power plant ventures. Such ventures are particularly interesting in two ways. Their formation is indicative of how closely the individual utilities within the pool work together and how even such ventures are prone to multi-jurisdictional competition among state and federal agencies. The Seabrook nuclear power plant is the most prominent example of these two factors. Continual intervention by anti-nuclear and environmental groups and Massachusetts state and local lawmakers at the Nuclear Regulatory Commission (NRC) and in New Hampshire sufficiently delayed unit completion so that the increased interest costs, in addition to already substantial construction cost overruns, put the final nine investor-owned utilities and municipal cooperatives investing in the project in financial peril. NU's takeover of Public Service of New Hampshire is a direct result of PSNH's bankruptcy at the hand of Seabrook.

The New England Power Pool encompasses seventy-eight of the region's investor-owned and municipal utilities (not counting multi-state utilities' subsidiaries). As mentioned, it has no true corporate identity, being managed by consensus agreement of its member utilities. NEPOOL's genesis is a direct result of the great northeastern blackout of 1965 when it became apparent to the region's electric utilities that a faster transmission system control structure employing computerized relaying of power flows was required. This brought together what had before been loosely coordinated regional control centers. Upon this foundation of daily coordination of resource allocation grew a larger system of negotiated contractual agreements which allocated the reduced costs of power plant operation, scheduled unit maintenance, guaranteed transmission system access to smaller utilities, and distributed the costs of transmission system investments. Developed over nearly a decade, with state and federal regulators keeping careful watch, NEPOOL evolved into an institution with divisions in operations (NEPEX), billing, and planning (NEPLAN), overseen by an elaborate committee and sub-committee structure (Browne, 1993; NEPOOL, 1993). Finally there is the North American Electricity Reliability Council's (NERC) regional coordinating body, which oversees transmission system reliability issues, the NPCC.

Non-Utility Resource Providers

In addition to the preceding companies are those corporations, not (majority) owned by New England utilities, that provide electric service to the region—currently via the utilities. These entities can be grouped into the following categories:

- independent power producers (IPPs, and their industry organizations),
- demand-side management (DSM) resource providers (and their industry organizations and interest group allies), and
- true cogenerators and other available sources of generation.

The first two sub-categories are those in business to provide either generation or conservation and load management services to the utilities and their customers. The third, such as cogenerating pulp and paper mills, or hospitals and large industrial customers—which might have emergency generation or load relief capabilities—play a substantially smaller role than the IPP and DSM industry groups.

Born of the Public Utility Regulatory Policies Act (PURPA) legislation in the late 1970s, independent power producers play an ever increasing role in providing electrical generation to New England customers. In many utilities' opinions, independent power producers have succeeded in gaining favor with the region's utility regulators for not only the quantity of capacity and generation contracted, but the terms of the contracts as well. Such practices have led to such perverse operational practices as ramping down baseload nuclear generation in order to meet contractual obligations with IPPs (Kansas, 1993). Organizations such as the New England Cogeneration Association actively petition state agencies on the behalf of IPPs, and host conferences and seminars on Clean Air Act compliance and other issues. Although some utilities do not mind letting someone else run the gauntlet of new units' siting and licensing, the prospect of accelerated erosion of the utilities' power plant assets, as IPPs try to displace existing utility generation with their own (as a Clean Air Act compliance measure) is causing trepidation in some utility circles.

DSM resource providers are hoping to attain similar leverage with respect to the Clean Air Act. Environmental regulators' consideration of emissions offsets from DSM is an example of how industry groups such as the Massachusetts Energy Efficiency Council hope to build on their already considerable influence with state regulators. Long standing support from regional environmental and consumer advocacy groups has strongly assisted their efforts over the past half a decade as well.

Utility Regulators

Numerous state, regional, and federal agencies oversee the economic, commercial, and reliability aspects of utility operation. Such organizations include:

- state public utility commissions,
- state facility siting boards,
- regional-state utility coordinating organizations,
- national-state utility coordinating organizations, and
- numerous federal agencies.

Each state has its own utility regulatory agency. Although the titles might differ, as with the Vermont Public Service Board and the Connecticut Department of Public Utility Control, their functions are nearly identical. These agencies oversee utility expenditures and decision making, guarding the consumer against surprise or hidden costs. These functions have become more expansive and complicated over the years as commissions seek to introduce competitive-like practices, such as bidding for new resources, or broader considerations in resource choice, such as the inclusion of environmental externalities in resource evaluation. These new practices, although well intentioned, may not produce the intended result, as the preceding IPP contracting issue indicates. Often closely associated with the state utility commissions are the licensing boards that oversee the siting and permitting of large industrial establishments such as refineries and power plants.

Helping New England utility commissions coordinate their actions are groups such as the New England Governors' Conference (NEGC), whose Power Planning Committee routinely provides commissioners and senior regulatory staff the opportunity to discuss issues of regional importance. The New England Conference of Public Utility Commissioners (NECPUC) plays a supporting role in this regard as well as hosting conferences and seminars each year on various topics. On the national level is the National Association of Regulatory Utility Commissioners (NARUC). NARUC hosts numerous meetings and conferences each year, which allow state utility commissioners and senior staff to interact and discuss recent experiences and industry topics. Eighteen of New England's utility commissioners are currently members of NARUC's committees on electricity, energy conservation, finance and technology, gas, and others.

Finally there are the federal agencies such as the Federal Energy Regulatory Commission (FERC), the Nuclear Regulatory Commission, and to some extent, the Department of Energy (related to the nuclear fuel and waste issues). Foremost, however, is the Federal Energy Regulatory Commission, which regulates interstate wholesale electric rates and oversees industry impacts on market structure, which can result from wholesale pricing policies and issues related to transmission system access. Jurisdictional conflicts associated with utility regulation are becoming more frequent as state agencies want greater leverage over multi-state utilities, and commissions strive to implement more competitive and broader industry practices.

Environmental Regulators

State, regional, and federal environmental agencies exhibit many of the features utility regulatory agencies have. These include:

- state departments of environmental protection (DEPs) (including air, water, and soil subdivisions),
- regional environmental quality coordinating agencies and
- the United States Environmental Protection Agency.

Environmental agencies commonly follow the same sort of geographic arrangements as the utility regulatory agencies, with overlapping state, regional, and federal jurisdiction. They are dissimilar, however, in two substantial ways. Although there is usually one central decision-making forum in utility regulation, this is not so in the environmental arena. Different departments in environmental agencies independently formulate rules and issue permits related to air quality, water quality, and solid waste issues. Fractionated purview is therefore substantially greater on the environmental side. In contrast with utility regulation, state environmental regulation is closely linked with federal action. State agencies' requirement to develop state implementation plans (SIPs) for the 1990 Clean Air Act implementation is one such example. With the realization that air emissions (and therefore air quality issues) cross boundaries, arises the role of the regional environmental coordinating agencies. The most long-standing is Northeast States for Coordinated Air Use Management (NESCAUM), which encompasses all of New England, New York, and New Jersey. Although it has no true authority to impose decisions or rules, with its board comprised of the directors of each state's air quality agency, NESCAUM strives to attain consistent state air regulations by considering alternatives beforehand and providing a consensus recommendation upon which individual state DEPs can act. The more recently formed Ozone Transport Commission (OTC) plays a more decisive role, as its existence is called for under the 1990 Clean Air Act to help implement regional ozone attainment measures, encompassing an area from northern Virginia to coastal Maine.

Unlike the utility regulatory structure, the U.S. EPA oversees the activities of the state and regional agencies to see if their efforts will satisfy the federal mandate. State agencies must also implement measures that satisfy air quality provisions put forth by their respective state legislatures, such as with the Massachusetts Acid Rain law, passed prior to the 1990 Clean Air Act. These measures are stricter than federal measures (states are not allowed to usurp federal jurisdiction by passing less stringent standards).

Sanctioned Interest Groups

Finally there are the various business, environmental and consumer advocacy groups that play a role in public hearings and as interveners in regulatory proceedings. This is a rather diverse group that often includes other government agencies. Sub-categories include:

- state and local government interveners,
- environmental and conservation groups, and
- business and industry consumer groups.

Common government agencies that intervene on behalf of the general population are the attorney generals' offices, state energy offices, and local and state housing authorities. Participation of these groups in rate hearings is especially common as the attorney generals' offices seek to ensure that costs are minimized and rates are designed equitably. Housing authorities will often focus on the development and availability of rates for low-income residents, bill averaging, and measures to protect residents from cessation of service during wintertime.

In New England, as elsewhere, environmental and conservation groups are very influential. Many groups currently play a dual role of promoting environmental protection and energy conservation, lobbying for demand-side management as low- or negative-cost pollution prevention options. The most influential group of this sort is the Conservation Law Foundation (CLF) of New England, which in the mid-1980s was sanctioned by state regulatory agencies to negotiate with the electric utilities the structure of utility-sponsored DSM programs. Other groups commonly active in the conservation arena are the respective state public interest groups such as MassPIRG, the National Consumers Law Center, and the Natural Resources Council of Maine. Other environmental groups are also prevalent, such as the Sierra Club and the Audubon Society. Local issue groups, often formed to confront specific projects, also play an important role, such as the No-Coal Coalition in southeastern Massachusetts. This group was formed by local residents to combat proposals for several coal-fired power plants in the area, including a cogeneration facility.

Then there are the business groups and industry advocates. These groups encompass concerns ranging from the general climate for business growth to utility rate structures and DSM program availability. Groups such as The New England Council, The Massachusetts Business Roundtable, and The Business and Industry Association of New Hampshire generally focus on issues such as economic development rates. Other groups like The Energy Consortium (TEC) and TEC-RI (Rhode Island) are comprised of various companies' facilities managers and focus on more specific issues like DSM rebate structures, and energy and load factor charges in rate design. Other business and consumer groups may arise after an unfavorable ruling has been passed. Such was the case in Massachusetts when the Department of Public Utilities eliminated the subsidy for electric heat customers in a rate decision. As one among several groups formed to combat the decision, "IRATE" was founded and fought successfully for a legislative rollback of the "economically efficient" new rates. Such is the diversity, and complexity—geographically and institutionally—of the New England electric service industry.

COMPETITION AND COORDINATION IN THE NEW ENGLAND ELECTRIC INDUSTRY

Prior to the pervasiveness of independent power producers, competition between New England utilities could be considered a form of sibling rivalry among the children of divorced parents—the individual state regulatory agencies. As competitive bidding for new generation sources continues, however, cooperation will become further strained as individual utilities compete amongst themselves for IPP resources and the transmission rights to transfer that power. Transmission access issues have been particularly important in New England since the high-growth period of the mid-1980s. Although the region is currently in a capacity glut—as a result of the economic downturn—transmission access continues to be an important issue.

When in the late 1980s Northeast Utilities bid to purchase bankrupt Public Service of New Hampshire, other New England utilities went scrambling—to NEPOOL and the FERC—to ensure that the resulting NU/PSNH merger would not inhibit their transmission system capabilities or their ability to deliver power to native load customers. On a regional basis the discussions continued until 1993 when the Regional Transmission Agreement (RTA) was finalized, which not only dealt with the native load issues but also addressed transmission system ownership concerns regarding the allocation of future transmission system capital costs. Although some of this agreement's provisions have been eroded by recent FERC rulings, the concerns that facilitated the development of the RTA were ones primarily of "operational reliability," and the need for utilities to guarantee transmission system access, rather than strict economic concerns over market power.

With the general push toward a restructuring of the industry, the issue of transmission system access and ownership is also changing. With the passage of the Energy Policy Act of 1992 and more recent FERC rulings, issues of transmission system access and utilization have shifted from the issues of native load access and "operational reliability" to those of "economic/market efficiency." With open access for IPPs and wholesale wheeling of power across service territories, generation and transmission changes are likely to be the first incarnation of the competitive industry structure. Issues related to transmission system access are quickly overtaking traditional utility transmission system concerns of power system dynamics and voltage control. Such traditional issues are not less important—as the system would cease to operate if they are not addressed—but they are diluted to some extent as the utility regulatory community focuses on market-based issues rather than purely technological ones.

Failure to address technological issues when breaking down the present system's vertically integrated structure could lead to substantial service inadequacies. Generation does not operate isolated from transmission and distribution functions. Planned and unforced outages—at all three levels—require pre-arranged backup procedures and obligations. From an operational perspective, where is spinning reserve generation controlled? Is it bundled with the wheeling requirements? How are unforced outages dealt with? If limited retail wheeling exists, with whom does the "commitment to serve" requirement for non-participating native load customers rest? Similarly, for industrial customers playing the market, who, if anyone, guarantees power—and at what price—should the electricity provider be unable to deliver electricity for technological or financial reasons. Technologically, a competitive electric power market entails some serious forethought if reliable service is to be maintained.

Competition and coordination do not always march hand-in-hand in the regulatory arena either. States, through the legislative process and regulation, also compete. A recent example of this is where Massachusetts, Connecticut, and Rhode Island sued the state of New Hampshire, challenging the constitutionality of the property tax levied on the Seabrook nuclear power station. In the New Hampshire rules, a special property tax was levied on the power station's assets. Although the property tax was levied on all owners equally, New Hampshire owners could deduct their contribution in other tax categories (Milne 1992). The U.S. Supreme Court eventually ruled against the New Hampshire tax.

Another area of competition, or at least poor coordination, is in utility integrated resource planning. Several states, Massachusetts in particular, have passed regulations instituting a process of integrated resource planning, approval, solicitation, and acquisition. Such a strong centralized planning approach is immediately in conflict with the alleged efficiencies of multi-state utility operations. State regulators lament their inability to influence decision making in other states or FERC jurisdictions. Multi-state utilities also dislike the structure because of the increased overhead of having different reporting requirements in each state. To alleviate at least some of the timing problems associated with jurisdictional issues, two New England utilities, New England Electric and Eastern Utilities Associates, recently requested an exemption from Massachusetts Department of Public Utilities' Integrated Resource Management (IRM) provisions. They recommended establishing in its place a corporate—as opposed to service territory—level integrated resource planning arrangement with concurrent, coordinated state reviews. Although this might be a step in the right direction with respect to integrated planning, how will it interact with an increasingly competitive system comprised of short-term bidding for generation and other services?

Other factors likely to make corporate-based planning difficult arise from the disparities among state utility regulators' respective rules. In New England, there are significantly different approaches to utility regulation based on the size and composition of the regulatory staffs. Smaller staffs, such as Rhode Island's, invest significantly less time in developing new rules and procedures. With a smaller number of utilities to regulate, they can negotiate the desired agreements. Although this also occurs in larger states such as Massachusetts, there is a greater impetus to develop generalized rules such as the IRM in order to maintain continuity in utility-regulatory dealings. Superimposed on these different institutional arrangements is the fact that many of the region's state regulatory agencies—both utility and environmental—tend to be progressive, expanding beyond traditional realms of regulation to influence broader issues. Inclusion of environmental factors in utility resource choice, such as with the introduction of "externality adders" in the Massachusetts IRM regulations, is an example of this. However, to this date, none of the other state commissions have jumped on the "adder" bandwagon, although each wants to see environmental consideration included in some fashion. How individual states will handle utilities' voluntary actions, such as New England Electric's CO_2 offsets and "Green RFP," also complicates matters. These factors will make the analytic tasks involved with multistate corporate-based planning difficult.

CHALLENGES IN THE FORTHCOMING COMPETITIVE INDUSTRY STRUCTURE

As the preceding discussion indicates, competition and coordination are, in many respects, two sides of the same coin. With this realization enters the discussion of the role centralized planning plays in a competitive market. As introductory economics students learn, functioning markets require good, if not perfect, information. Coordination occurs because each player recognizes and accepts his or her role in the marketplace. Market structure focuses more on the transaction itself than those doing the transaction.

With a competitive market structure, centralized resource control may become a thing of the past; however, centralized coordination may not. Technologically the system will have the same basic components. It is the ownership and control structures that will change. Some of these aspects will be reflected in the technological makeup of the system as distributed control systems are introduced. "Transaction rules" will undoubtedly be contained within some of these decentralized decision-making and control structures. The primary task of the utilities, regulators, and other industry stakeholders will be to develop these passive systems, the transactions by which producers and consumers operate. This is where centralized planning continues to play an important role. It can be used to identify where operational linkages need to be maintained, so that the rules of the game allow competitive flexibility without destroying the structure of the game. Identification of the end-game, the ultimate structure that industry is likely to take, will go a long ways toward making the transition go smoothly.

This shift heralds the greatest underlying challenges of industry restructuring; the coordination of a large technology-based infrastructure with a decentralized market structure. This decentralized coordination goes well beyond the basic generation, transmission, and distribution of electric power. We see similar trends toward decentralized coordination in the environmental regulatory arena as well, with the development of markets for sulfur dioxide allowances and potentially NO_x and CO_2 offsets. The transition from a command and control, to a competitive—or at least command and compliance—market structure also relies on decentralized control and predetermined transaction rules. A greater challenge on the environmental side may well be in the verification of the transactions. Note that in a competitive system, it is the parameters of the transaction, not the transaction itself, which is regulated.

FEDERALISM AND COMPETITION

Generation, transmission, spinning reserve, environmental compliance, billing! How can and how will these disparate functions hold together in a competitive, federalist system? Who is responsible for establishing the system of allowable transactions and overseeing their use? It is unlikely, given the institutional inertia of today's regulatory structure, that a single transaction-monitoring regulatory body will evolve. State and federal agencies will remain. Utility and environmental regulatory functions will remain separate. What we are seeing with groups such as NESCAUM and the New England Governors' Conference is that regulators are needing and will need to coordinate more.

Regulators in a competitive electric power industry must coordinate to be effective. Relatively stable transaction systems must be constructed and maintained, if not nationally, then at least regionally.

Such coordination appears to be working well in the telecommunications area, even with rapidly evolving types of services. This illustrates that for a rather tightly defined class of transactions, state and federal regulatory agencies can coordinate. Electric power, unfortunately, is not like telecommunications. In telecommunications the service is, technologically, the connection. The generation component—the actual service in the electric power system—is missing in the telecommunications example. Understandably, telecommunications lacks the heavy environmental regulatory component as well. These factors will make regulatory coordination in the electric sector much more difficult than in the telecommunications case.

Critical to the formulation of an electric sector transaction-regulation system will be the ability of the utility regulators and the environmental regulators to work together, coordinating their actions. Although only in its infancy, these two disparate groups of regulators are beginning to work together. With the environmental regulators' focus on market mechanisms to meet Clean Air Act compliance, utility and environmental regulators are starting to talk the same language. Utility regulators are moving in the environmental regulators' direction as well, as they attempt to build into their integrated resource planning processes features that ensure capital expenditures for Clean Air Act compliance are least-cost, and that resource plans themselves mitigate the possible impacts of future environmental regulation, such as with carbon dioxide. In order for a robust competitive system to evolve, utility and environmental regulators, as well as state and federal regulators, must coordinate and cooperate.

CONCLUSIONS

The New England electric service industry has evolved into a highly coordinated technological structure which ensures reliable service and economies of scale to its customers. Overseen by a broad range of regulatory agencies and private sector interests, the industry is becoming more complex as independent power producers and demand-side management providers enter into an increasingly competitive system. The history of coordination among New England's various stakeholder groups will serve the region well as the challenges of breaking up the vertically integrated system continue.

Key to the successful transition to a competitive structure will be the identification of the rules and obligations the newly transformed players must meet. Many of the operational parameters necessary for the transformation are in place, as the utilities, NEPOOL, and NERC have worked over the years to establish operation and reliability criteria. Many of the requisite decentralized and passive systems necessary for a competitive system to operate need to be developed, however. On the economic and environmental transaction side, utility and environmental regulators will need to coordinate much more than in the past, with both their state and federal counterparts. Only by such coordination at the outset can a stable competitive system be constructed that meets consumers' needs.

REFERENCES

Browne, G. Director of External Coordination, NEPOOL. Personal communication, 1993.

Kansas, D. "Power Glut Jolts Northeastern Electricity Producers: Large Utilities Buy Out Contracts with Independents to Reduce Costs." *The Wall Street Journal* (April 20, 1993), B4.

Milne, J. "Mass., Conn. and R.I. try to recoup their cut of Seabrook property tax," *The Boston Globe* (December 9, 1992), 39.

NEPLAN. *NEPOOL Forecast Report of Capacity, Energy, Loads and Transmission 1993–2008*. Holyoke, MA: New England Power Pool, 1993.

NEPOOL. *New England Power Pool 1992 Annual Report*. Holyoke, MA: New England Power Pool, 1993.

U.S. Department of Energy, Energy Information Administration (EIA). *Inventory of Power Plants in the United States 1990*. Washington, DC: EIA, 1991.

16

Comment on the New England Case

Barry D. Solomon

The New England electric service industry, as discussed in the chapter by Connors, has developed into a relatively small, generally cooperative, open, well-managed and coordinated structure. This proud region has been a national leader in demand-side management and energy efficiency. It was also the setting for an interminable controversy between the affected states and the Nuclear Regulatory Commission, known as the Seabrook nuclear power plant, that stretched our federalist system of electric power regulation to its limits. According to Connors, competition is also straining some of the Yankee traditions in this industry, and better coordination is required among regulators to avoid or resolve the inevitable conflicts. Although I agree that more coordination is important, I argue that he has misdiagnosed the problem and is unnecessarily pessimistic about its resolution.

To begin with, I was surprised that Connors ignored the strain that the severe recession that began in the late 1980s placed on New England. Economic recession, competition, conflict, and uncertainty are assuredly closely linked. These conditions inflicted enormous stress and pain on the utility industry, which has been mitigated somewhat by the recent economic recovery. The recession also influenced and limited the ability of economic and environmental regulators to do their respective jobs. Even the sanctioned interest groups could not ignore the serious economic hardship that enveloped the whole region for over five years.

In the long run, what is more important to successful restructuring of the electric service industry is the region's leadership and innovation on several fronts—integrated resource planning (IRP); energy efficiency; demand-side management (DSM); and environmental

issues such as acid rain, NO_x trading, global warming, and environmental externalities. Although many of these issues are controversial,
regional decision makers generally have debated the issues in open
forums with considerable public and interest-group input. The recent
NEESPLAN 4 crafted by the New England Electric System (NEES)
and the Conservation Law Foundation is a case in point, one which is
visionary on environmental problems (NEES, 1993). NEES is one of
only a handful of utilities that has voluntarily begun a *major* reduction in its CO_2 emissions through cost-effective measures. And even
though Central Maine Power's experiment in decoupling profits from
electric sales fell victim to the recession, the program became a model
for DSM advocates and has been emulated and improved upon in several utility systems throughout the nation. This all bodes well for New
England's ability to cope with whatever challenges electric utility market competition may bring.

THE COMPLEMENTARITY OF PLANNING WITH MORE COMPETITIVE ELECTRIC SERVICE MARKETS

The U.S. economy has combined a generally successful mixture of
private markets and government planning for sixty years, through initiatives such as the New Deal employment programs and agencies,
and a more activist monetary policy. The electric service industry has
similarly acquired a mixed structure, with regulators and investor-
owned utilities as well as public-power producers. This does not mean,
however, that regulatory responsibilities should necessarily be re-
aligned. State public utility commissions (PUCs) and environmental
regulators have limited resources to cope with problems that accompany competition, while regional regulators are even weaker, and federal regulators have a poor track record in resolving state and local
conflicts. For example, the U.S. Environmental Protection Agency
(EPA) has been notoriously slow in developing Federal implementation plans (FIPs) for air pollution control when states have failed to
develop adequate State Implementation Plans, and the EPA has a
very limited ability to implement FIPs. Moreover, the Federal Energy
Regulatory Commission (FERC) lacks authority over non-hydro generating facilities but regulates transmission rates. The PUCs, in turn,
have jurisdiction over transmission line and power plant sitings. The
answer is not federal preemption but a fine-tuning of regulation.

The region has been improving on the IRP model, for example,
through integrated resource management in Massachusetts and more
recently limited regional IRP. IRP in New England and elsewhere

needs to better capitalize on market forces to achieve real least-cost planning, which will strengthen it in turn. Fair competition between fuel and power service providers (including DSM and competitive bidding) while systematically accounting for externalities, can improve service to customers, keep electric rates in check, and enhance the financial status of the utility. Retail wheeling that allows industrial customers to leave a utility system, however, while increasing the embedded costs to captive customers, is inconsistent with this goal.

Environmental protection is a special case where resource and compliance planning can be compatible with market approaches. In this case, the jury may still be out, depending on how well the environmental planning is implemented and merged with markets. At the federal level, EPA has implemented a thus far successful SO_2 allowance trading system for acid rain control under the Clean Air Act Amendments of 1990, serving as "banker" for tracking allowance trades between electric utilities. Over thirty inter-utility trades have been made since 1992. Only one so far has involved a New England company (United Illuminating), although other utilities have received bonus allowances for energy efficiency and renewable energy generation. Importantly, transaction costs for this program are less than 10 percent because of the active involvement of brokers and consistent EPA requirements for continuous-emissions monitoring. I am concerned, however, that Massachusetts is leading the region hastily toward NO_x and Volatile Organic Compounds (VOC) trading where transaction costs probably will be higher because of information and emissions monitoring costs for generally smaller sources. Furthermore, New England's utilities and regulators may not fully appreciate the allowance trading experience and regulatory requirements. Although trading may well succeed for NO_x, and perhaps be extended to CO_2, it is important for New England to jump into the SO_2 trading market to bolster existing least-cost planning procedures.

I agree with Connors that better coordination between and among state and federal economic and environmental regulators is important under the new market conditions, but this will be limited by regulatory culture and sometimes conflicting laws. The new FERC has signaled its willingness to be more responsive to state PUC concerns, while the EPA's Region 1 office in Boston is typically the first point of contact with state environmental agencies and utilities in the region. My office at EPA headquarters even sponsored a workshop in Portsmouth, New Hampshire, in January 1993 to coordinate implementation of the Acid Rain Program with the New England State PUCs and air agencies. Attendance by the air officials was half of what was expected because of a hastily called meeting of the Ozone Transport Commission on the same days. Clearly, if coordination is to improve, all parties with a stake in electric power issues need to make a better effort to communicate.

CONCLUSIONS

My perception of the New England situation leads me to conclude with guarded optimism that the region's electric utilities have demonstrated a robust ability to resolve conflicts and positively respond to and anticipate increasingly competitive electric service markets. Barring any more surprises on the scale of Seabrook, the appropriate administrative machinery is in place (including regional environmental agencies) to efficiently regulate a restructuring industry, as long as state and federal officials remember to talk to each other. Regulators and electric utilities in the New England region are leaders, and I do not foresee increased federal preemption of the region's authority and responsibilities during the Clinton Administration.

Although increased competition is certainly no panacea for the problems and challenges facing the electric service industry, it is already happening and is in the best interest of cost-conscious utility ratepayers. Therefore, the nature and level of competition that is anticipated and desirable needs to be carefully charted out by the region's decision makers, and then acted upon. NEES has already started this task with NEESPLAN 4, with planning initiatives "designed to enhance flexibility and foster a diverse resource supply at the lowest cost" (NEES 1993, p. 16). These initiatives include a new resource selection process that explicitly quantifies flexibility, hedges against risks, and preserves diversity in its energy mix; development of short-turnaround resource options; planning for a phased retirement of aging fossil generating units; natural gas fuel switching; hydro relicensing; and DSM. Hopefully, the other utilities will follow this promising lead into the next century.

REFERENCE

New England Electric System (NEES). *NEESPLAN 4: Creating Options for More Competitive and More Sustainable Electric Service.* Westborough, MA: New England Electric System, 1993.

17

American Electric Power Company Case Study

Raymond M. Maliszewski

Each utility organization is a unique product of its history, experiences and circumstances, and if history had been different, the current organizational framework and composition would likewise be different. To put it another way, if the forces that are paramount today—competition in generation and the move toward open transmission access, to name just two—had been drivers during the evolution of the electric utility industry over the last fifty to sixty years, the shape of the industry today would no doubt be noticeably different. With this in mind, the present chapter develops a case study of decision making in a multi-jurisdictional environment—the American Electric Power (AEP) System.

Key elements of this story are the cohesiveness of the AEP System, the forces that influenced its development, and the wide-ranging benefits that have been achieved. This chapter includes a brief description of the physical characteristics of the AEP System and a discussion of the AEP Interconnection Agreement and Transmission Agreement—the mechanisms that bind the members of the AEP Pool together. It also includes a discussion of the flow of benefits among the members of the AEP family and the responsibilities that are incumbent on each member. Given that the operating subsidiaries of the AEP System operate in the context of a multi-jurisdictional environment—seven state regulatory commissions and the Federal Energy Regulatory Commission (FERC)—the influence that such an environment has had on the development of the AEP System is emphasized.

This chapter provides two illustrations of the impact of a multi-jurisdictional regulatory environment:

- the development of the AEP Transmission Agreement in 1984; and

- the development of the AEP System compliance strategy relative to the Clean Air Act Amendments of 1990.

It also examines a regulatory innovation—the AEP Regional Coordinating Committee—developed in response to this environmental legislation. The committee consists of representatives from each of the seven state regulatory commissions that have jurisdiction in the AEP service area.

DESCRIPTION OF THE AEP SYSTEM

The AEP System consists of seven electric operating companies whose generation and transmission facilities are planned and operated so as to function as a single, wholly integrated power system. These operating companies collectively serve a population of about 7 million people in 3,200 communities located in a 46,000 square-mile area in parts of seven states, including Michigan, Indiana, Ohio, Kentucky, Tennessee, Virginia, and West Virginia.

The five largest operating companies in the AEP System own and/ or operate generation and transmission facilities, and include Appalachian Power Company (APCo), serving in the states of Virginia and West Virginia; Ohio Power Company (OPCo) and Columbus Southern Power Company (CSP) in Ohio; Indiana Michigan Power Company (I&M), in Indiana and Michigan; and Kentucky Power Company (KPCo) in Kentucky. The remaining two operating companies receive all of their power requirements, at wholesale, from one of the other five, namely, Kingsport Power Company (KgPCo), serving in Tennessee, from APCo and Wheeling Power Company (WPCo), serving in West Virginia, from OPCo.

The AEP System's service area is primarily rural and small community in character, with the exception of the City of Columbus, Ohio, which has a metropolitan population of over one million people. A substantial number of industrial facilities, including primary metal, petroleum refining, and chemical processing plants, among others, are located within the AEP System territory, creating a heavy concentration of electric load in certain areas of the system.

At the end of 1992, the AEP System supplied the electric power requirements of approximately 2,800,000 retail customers, including about 2,470,000 residential, 300,000 commercial, 20,000 industrial, and 10,000 miscellaneous customers. Total energy sales to these customers amounted to about 89 billion kilowatthours, with the residential sector accounting for about 30 percent, commercial 22 percent, industrial 46 percent, and miscellaneous the remaining 2 percent. In addition, about 22 billion kilowatthours were supplied to wholesale (sales for resale) customers, including municipals, cooperatives, and non-affiliated electric power systems. The peak system demand in 1992, including sales to other utilities, was 20,474,000 kW, which occurred in January of the year. If sales to other utilities are excluded, the corresponding peak internal demand on the AEP System was 17,499,000 kW. During 1992, about 90 percent of AEP System's total generation was produced from coal, 5 percent from nuclear energy, and the remaining 5 percent from other energy sources.[1]

The AEP System's transmission system, which is comprised of a 765-kV, 500-kV, and 345-kV extra-high-voltage network, together with an extensive underlying 138-kV transmission network, provides the means for integrating the system's major power generating plants with its principal load centers.[2] In addition, the AEP System has 143 transmission interconnections with twenty-eight neighboring electric utilities in ten states.

The five major operating companies of the AEP System are directly interconnected with a multitude of neighboring utilities whose aggregate installed generating capacity amounts to about 160,000,000 kW. These neighboring utilities, along with the AEP System, account for a major portion of the Eastern interconnected network of electric utility systems.

THE INTEGRATED SYSTEM

The AEP System is planned and operated as a wholly integrated system. The term "integrated system" means an electric power system where the generation and transmission facilities are planned and operated on a single-system basis—one that is fully interconnected and coordinated from the standpoint of power supply. It means a system in which the generating facilities are operated on a minute-to-minute basis under the direction of a single control center. The integrated system concept enables each local service area to gain the economic advantages of the latest developments in the state-of-the-art in size, design, and efficiency of generating units, even though such units may be widely separated geographically. The transmission network is the integrating medium which binds the generating sources to the load centers, making it possible for each service area to share in the benefits of the economical operation of the entire system and, in the process, to enhance reliability and continuity of power supply to each local area.

The basic principle underlying the integrated system concept is that "the whole is more than the sum of its parts." This means that because of the intrinsic synergism of integration, the individual operating companies of the AEP System, and their customers, can and do achieve more by being part of the AEP System than they could possibly achieve individually.

The relationships that exist among the operating companies of the AEP System, from both an electric facilities planning and an operating point of view, reflect the integrated system concept. The operating companies are each franchised in their respective service areas to furnish electric power to their customers and, together, form the AEP System. The AEP System, as such, does not own any power supply facilities. All facilities are owned and/or operated by the individual operating companies that comprise the AEP System. The AEP System is merely the mechanism through which the benefits of integrated planning and operation can be achieved. The effective functioning of this mechanism depends on the recognition by each member company, and by their regulatory commissions, that the benefits and the responsibilities of integrated system planning and operation must be shared by all participants.

This concept of integrated development did not come about by chance, but was a carefully designed strategy that was crafted during the formative years of the AEP System. It simply was a recognition that through centralized planning and operation the individual members could benefit greatly—more than they could if they were independent—from the economies of scale that were thus available. Furthermore, this allowed for the application of the most up-to-date technological improvements and, in many cases, was the very impetus behind such technological developments.

As a result of this concept, the AEP System has been able to advance the state-of-the-art of the technology of power generation and delivery systems, thus providing benefits to the members of the AEP System and to their customers, far beyond what they could achieve if they operated as independent utilities. In addition to pursuing the state-of-the-art to its limit, the AEP System concept also provides the means to take advantage of the economies of scale to the greatest extent possible, again achieving economic advantage for the individual operating companies and, in turn, for their customers.[3] Innovations have included ways of producing more electricity from less fuel, thus reducing emissions; transmitting more electricity across greater distances while using less land (and other resources); and distributing electricity more efficiently.

This integrated system concept has served the AEP member systems well over the years and has resulted in the customers of the

AEP System companies having the advantage of the lowest cost of power supply achievable. Indeed, for half a century the average cost of electricity on the AEP System has been consistently about 20 percent lower than the average cost for the United States as a whole.

Mechanisms for Achieving Integrated Planning and Operation

The instruments for achieving integrated planning and operation are the Interconnection Agreement and the Transmission Agreement among the five operating companies (member companies) which own generation and bulk transmission facilities (namely, APCo, CSP, I&M, KPCo, and OPCo) and which comprise what is often referred to as the AEP System Pool. The Interconnection Agreement, commonly referred to as the "Pool Agreement," provides the basis for the day-to-day operation of the AEP System as an integrated system and, as will be explained later, establishes the planning responsibilities of the member companies. It has been modified and supplemented from time to time since its original signing in 1951. Both the Interconnection Agreement and the Transmission Agreement are subject to the jurisdiction of the FERC.

The electric facilities of the operating companies of the AEP System have been interconnected for many years and were functioning under interconnection agreements between certain of the companies dating back many years. Through cooperation with each other, the companies were successful in achieving substantial economies in the conduct of their business by coordinating the expansion and operation of their power supply facilities. In 1951, so as to enhance further the integrated planning and operation of their systems, the companies of the AEP System then owning generation facilities entered into an "Interconnection Agreement." In 1962, it was revised to include Kentucky Power Company. In 1975, several rate adjustments were introduced, and on November 1, 1980, it was modified, effective January 1, 1981, to include the Columbus and Southern Ohio Electric Company (later renamed Columbus Southern Power Company), which became one of the operating companies of the AEP System in May 1980.

The Agreement recites that the pool member companies believe that a fuller realization of the benefits and advantages through coordinated operation of their power supply facilities will be better ensured and more efficiently and economically achieved by having the operation directed by a central organization skilled in large-scale system operation and familiar with the generating facilities of the companies, and that the participation of the members in the coordinated operation and expansion of their facilities will be simplified by having such

procedures conducted by a single clearing agent. The agreement desig-
nates the AEP Service Corporation as that agent.

The basic principles of operation of the AEP Pool, as provided by
the Interconnection Agreement, are summarized as follows:

- Each member of the pool is responsible for a proportionate
  share of the aggregate AEP Pool generating capacity. Such
  sharing is done on an after-the-fact "member-load-ratio"
  (or MLR) basis.[4]

- Operation of the pool is predicated on the basis of optimum
  minute-by-minute central dispatch of all of the AEP System's capacity without regard to individual company ownership, so as to meet the overall system demand.[5]

- System transactions with non-affiliated neighboring utility systems are likewise carried out on an optimum,
  minute-by-minute basis, without regard to the individual
  members' proximity to the neighboring systems or to ownership of the generation facilities dispatched to provide the
  power sold.[6]

Responsibilities of Integrated System Planning and Operation

Membership in an integrated system such as the AEP System
includes two distinct responsibilities, shared by each of the member
companies, namely:

- the responsibility of each member company to provide sufficient generation facilities to meet its internal load
  requirements plus an adequate reserve margin, and

- the responsibility of each member company to provide, for
  the use of all the member companies, those transmission
  facilities that lie within its jurisdiction.

In addition, in a broader sense, each member company must
comply with certain general obligations that are implied in any
meaningful pooling arrangement among several electric utilities. The
most fundamental obligation in this regard is the understanding and
recognition among all the participants that the entire pooling
arrangement must be based on mutuality—mutual benefits, mutual
sharing of costs and benefits, mutual trust, and mutual
accommodation to each participant's needs. This may require, on
occasion, a member utility to subordinate its individual interests to
the interests of the group. On the other hand, the group must also be
willing to accommodate the interests of the individual participant.
This mutuality is essential to ensure the continuation of the pooling
arrangement and the flow of its associated benefits to the participants.

Benefits of Integrated System Planning and Operation

The individual member companies of the AEP System receive significant benefits as a result of integrated planning through:

- very substantial economies of scale in generation and in bulk transmission facilities,

- greater flexibility in the siting of new generation, and

- opportunity for greater optimization in the development of the overall generation-transmission system, in terms of transmission network configuration and its interrelation with the siting of new generation and the establishment of new interconnections.

Benefits accrue to the individual member companies as a result of integrated operation through:

- greater access to emergency support from neighboring utilities;

- greater opportunity for sales of capacity and energy to neighboring utilities, when such capacity and energy is available for such sales; and

- more efficient operation of the available generating capacity.

These benefits are reflected in greater economy and reliability of power supply than would otherwise be possible to the customers of each of the individual member companies.

Examples of Benefits of Integrated System Planning and Operation

To begin with, the AEP System has realized and demonstrated significant savings from economies of scale in generation and transmission. The costs were significantly less—in terms of dollars per kilowatt of installed capacity—to build the larger generating units that were able to be accommodated on a system the size of AEP, rather than the smaller units that would have been built by the individual operating companies if they planned and operated their facilities on an entirely independent basis. Thus, the AEP System member companies were able to achieve very substantial economies of scale through the installation of the largest generating units in the world, such as the 1,300-MW units at APCo's Mountaineer Plant and OPCo's Gavin Plant. The largest generating unit represents only 7.4 percent of the AEP System's aggregate peak internal load for the year 1992, whereas it represents 22.0 percent and 26.0 percent, respectively, of APCo's and

OPCo's peak internal loads.

The average installed cost per kilowatt of the steam generating capacity by operating company ranges from 226 to 704 $/kW, and is 428 $/kW for the AEP System, as of December 31, 1992. This embedded cost is the basis on which the capacity equalization charges are determined under the Interconnection Agreement. Thus, while OPCo and I&M are today, and are expected to remain for many years into the future, "surplus capacity" companies within the AEP Pool, they are being compensated for the capacity they make available to the "deficit capacity" companies—namely, APCo, CSP, and KPCo—at a rate that fully recognizes the associated costs. As OPCo's and I&M's internal loads increase over time, they will be recapturing this temporarily surplus capacity for their own use, at a cost that could not possibly be duplicated either today or in the future. In the meantime, the other member companies of the AEP System have the benefit of using—for some period of time—this capacity to meet their requirements, again at a cost that just could not be duplicated.

Somewhat similar analyses with respect to economies of scale could be carried out for the AEP System's transmission system: None of the AEP System's operating companies could have supported on its own the installation of 345-kV transmission back in the early 1950s or the 765-kV transmission in the late 1960s, when these voltage classes were introduced on the AEP System.

Another benefit accruing to each of the AEP operating companies from being part of the AEP System is the reduced capacity requirements resulting from the load diversity that exists among the operating companies. During 1992 the average of the monthly peak load diversities among the operating companies amounted to 304 MW. In other words, the sum of the non-coincident monthly peaks of the individual operating companies was 304 MW more than the coincident monthly peaks. This means that the AEP System operating companies, in the aggregate, needed to have installed about 304 MW less capacity (excluding provision for reserve capacity) than they would have needed to have installed if they operated independently.

This reduction in capacity requirements translates into an avoided investment, or provided savings, of $130 million if the capacity is valued at the embedded cost of AEP System steam capacity as of year-end 1992 (428 $/kW), or $269 million at the per-unit cost of one of the more recent 1,300-MW generating unit installed on the AEP System (I&M's Rockport Unit No. 1, at 884 $/kW).

Another very significant benefit of integrated planning and operation of the AEP System is the system's ability to utilize temporary capacity surpluses for sales to non-affiliated utilities. Each member company receives benefits from such sales, including sales to non-affiliated utilities with whom it is *not* directly interconnected, but has access to the use of the transmission facilities of its sister companies within the AEP System. Such opportunities help to increase the utilization of generating facilities that are already in service, thus reducing costs to the member companies and electric bills to their customers. Overall net revenues from sales to non-affiliated utilities aggregated to about $783 million, or about 13.5 percent of total AEP pre-tax operating income, during the five-year period 1988–1992.[7]

Observations

It is clear from the foregoing discussion that the development of the AEP System in an integrated manner has resulted in significant benefits to its members. These benefits did not come about without concurrent responsibilities, including the recognition that in some instances the parochial interests of each member might need to be subordinated for the good of the overall system. An example of this is the development of the AEP Transmission Agreement, which is discussed in the following section.

FUNCTIONING UNDER A MULTI-JURISDICTIONAL ENVIRONMENT

Example 1: The AEP Transmission Agreement

The construction and ownership of the system's power supply facilities is the responsibility of each of the major operating companies. The transmission network is planned as a single integrated network, and all members of the AEP System have "access" to every part of the integrated transmission network. Unlike the generation system—whereby, through the mechanism of the AEP Interconnection Agreement, the members equalize their participation in the generation resources by means of an equalization formula based on each party's member load ratio—no such mechanism was in place for the transmission network prior to 1984.

Prior to 1984, although a member company did not receive compensation for the use of its bulk transmission facilities by the other member companies, it—in return—had the benefit of being able to use bulk transmission facilities of all the other member companies, without having to share in the payment of carrying charges on such facilities. Experience had shown that, in the past, the investment in transmission by each member relative to its load responsibility more or less balanced over a period of time, thus maintaining—within the bounds of practicality—the basic equity among the member companies of the AEP System Pool.

In the late 1970s, and particularly continuing into the 1980s, the expansion of the system slowed down due to the significant downturn in load growth—a trend experienced not only by AEP, but by the industry in general—leading to repeated modifications in system plans for major generation and transmission facilities. Notwithstanding these modifications in plans, several major transmission projects were required to integrate new generation resources into the system and also to integrate certain sections of the system. This totaled over 350 miles of new 765-kV transmission lines concentrated in two of the system's operating companies. These projects resulted in a significant imbalance in the relative levels of transmission investment among the system's operating companies. Further, it was recognized that this imbalance would grow as a result of the increasing costs of new bulk transmission facilities due to inflation and other factors. This led to the conclusion that a transmission equalization process was required similar in concept to the sharing of responsibility for generation resources installed on the AEP System. The outcome was the creation of the AEP Transmission Agreement, which was filed with the FERC in 1984. The fundamental concept underlying this agreement is to provide a mechanism whereby equity with regard to investments in bulk transmission facilities can be assured continuously.

The approach for allocating bulk transmission equalization credits and charges among the member companies is based on the principle of sharing among the member companies the cost of ownership and operation of the bulk transmission network in proportion to their respective member load ratios. The members which contribute more than their respective transmission investment responsibilities (the surplus members) receive monthly equalization payments from the members which contribute less than their respective transmission investment responsibilities (the deficit members). The monthly payment to each surplus member reflects the product of that member's transmission investment surplus and an appropriate monthly carrying charge rate. Such payments are made by the deficit members in proportion to their respective transmission investment deficits.

The filing of the AEP Transmission Agreement with the FERC attracted widespread intervention by all the state regulatory commissions in each of the jurisdictions in which the AEP System operates. In addition, many other interested parties filed intervention, including consumer advocates and industrial groups in each state, as well as other advocacy organizations. It was obvious that each party had specific issues that it planned to pursue. However, the interveners fell into two camps. Those interveners associated with transmission surplus members (who anticipated receipts due to transmission investment being higher than their MLR share) sought changes to the transmission equalization methodology to maximize to the greatest extent the new-found revenues. The other interveners, that is, those associated with transmission deficit members (who found themselves to be in a paying mode) sought ways to reduce to the greatest extent such payments. In this connection, these are transfer payments among the member companies, and, therefore, the net effect is a zero-sum game—where deficit members are paying surplus members.

During the course of these proceedings, which covered well over a year of hearings, many suggestions were made by the FERC Administrative Law Judge that the parties seek to arrive at a mutually agreeable solution among themselves. It was clear that in attempting to negotiate a settlement, the parties were not willing to compromise their established positions, the result being a deadlocked position among the intervening parties.

Given the positions of each of the parties, this impasse—between those seeking to maximize their advantage versus those seeking to minimize their disadvantage—was not surprising. In general, these jurisdictional parties took positions aimed essentially at shifting as much of the perceived burden as possible to other jurisdictions while holding onto all the perceived benefits.

In 1987, the FERC approved the basic concept of the AEP Transmission Agreement, with some modifications in the methodology to determine the allocation of transmission investment responsibility. This case clearly demonstrated the difficulty of achieving consensus in a multi-jurisdictional environment where there are clear "winners" and "losers."

Example 2: Acid Rain Compliance on the AEP System

With the passage into law in late 1990 of Title IV of the 1990 Clean Air Act Amendments (CAAA), the development of a compliance strategy to meet the requirements of this new legislation became the most complex issue the AEP System has ever had to address. Not only were there a myriad of assumptions that had to be made, but compliance planning was complicated by the jurisdictional issues associated with the multi-state nature of the AEP System's operation. A further complication was the fact that compliance decisions had to be made on the basis of limited information and prior to the promulgation by the U.S. Environmental Protection Agency (EPA) of final regulations and regulatory guidelines. This section examines the process used by AEP (rather than the analytical details of the compliance strategy) in dealing with this complex issue and, in particular, on the interaction that took place with the regulatory and other parties that had interest in this subject.

The goal of Title IV of the Clean Air Act Amendments is to reduce the annual emissions of sulfur dioxide (SO_2) from utility boilers by approximately 10 million tons, and oxides of nitrogen (NO_x) by approximately 2 million tons, from the emission levels experienced in 1980.[8] The cornerstone of the SO_2 reduction program is the establishment of the emission allowance as a method of regulating SO_2 emissions in a flexible and least-cost manner.[9]

The provisions of Title IV impose a significant compliance burden on the AEP System. AEP has fifty coal-fired generating units, twenty-one of which are designated as affected Phase I units (six units owned by CSP, two units owned by I&M and thirteen units owned by OPCo). During the 1985–87 base period, these twenty-one units emitted about 1.2 million tons of SO_2 annually, and based on the 2.5 lb./MBtu emission limitation during the Phase I period (January 1, 1995 to December 31, 1999), these units are permitted to emit no more than 554.4 thousand tons of SO_2 annually—a reduction of 54 percent from the base period. Almost 85 percent of the reduction is required at plants owned by Ohio Power. The cornerstone of OPCo's compliance had to be the 2,600-MW Gavin Plant, the largest emitter of SO_2 on the AEP System due to it being fueled by high-sulfur coal produced by local Ohio mines. Almost 40 percent of Ohio Power's SO_2 emissions and 25 percent of AEP emissions are generated by the Gavin Plant.

The Phase II requirements of Title IV apply to all fifty of AEP's coal-fired units. With the emission limits designated for Phase II, the overall SO_2 emissions from AEP's fifty units will be capped at 551.5 thousand tons annually starting on January 1, 2000. This represents a 63 percent reduction in emissions from the 1.5 million tons emitted during the base period of 1985–87.

Considering that the AEP System is planned and operated on a single-system basis, it was obvious that the development of a lowest-cost compliance strategy must be evaluated on a total-system basis. However, given that fifty units on the AEP System are affected, each having multiple compliance options available to it, and with the large number of estimates that had to be made (e.g., alternate fuel costs, flue-gas-desulfurization [FGD] system cost, escalation rates, load levels, emission levels, the availability and value of emission allowances, just to mention a few), it became clear that analysis of compliance alternatives could become incomprehensible because of the very large number of options that could be considered.

To provide a rational sense of direction to the analytical process, it was concluded at the outset that compliance planning should focus on the Gavin Plant, the largest SO_2 emitter on the AEP System. In turn, this could provide direction as to compliance at the other nineteen affected units.

Because of the significant compliance burden AEP has to deal with, the attention of many parties—regulatory commissions and others—focused on AEP's efforts. Naturally, since the Gavin Plant emerged as the cornerstone of compliance planning, and since nineteen of AEP's twenty-one affected Phase I units are owned by OPCo and CSP, the Public Utilities Commission of Ohio (PUCO) had a direct interest in these evaluations. The regulatory commissions in the other jurisdictions were also greatly interested in AEP's compliance planning due to the fact that actions taken to bring OPCo and CSP units into compliance would have an impact operationally and economically on their respective jurisdictions.

The sharing of the compliance responsibilities and costs among the AEP member companies, as well as the resultant emission allowances, is a system-wide issue, of interest to all regulatory commissions having jurisdiction over the AEP operating companies. To provide a mechanism for informing and coordinating the interests of these regulatory bodies, the PUCO took the lead in forming an AEP Regional Coordinating Committee, consisting of representatives of the seven jurisdictional commissions. During the course of its compliance planning, AEP representatives met with this committee frequently to provide updates on work completed and review analyses, and to raise issues of mutual interest and seek a concerted view on issues that have multi-jurisdictional implications.

In examining the compliance options appropriate to the Gavin Plant, it became clear in the early phases of the evaluation that the installation of a FGD system (scrubber) or fuel switching to low-sulfur coal were the two most attractive options to be considered.

The company filed the "AEP System Preliminary Acid Rain Compliance Report" with the PUCO on May 31, 1991. This report was intended to provide an AEP System compliance strategy context to evaluate the merits of fuel switching versus scrubbing at the Gavin Plant. Several technical conferences and local public hearings were held with all parties having an interest in the Gavin issue so as to explain the assumptions, analysis, and other considerations that needed to be taken into account in examining the merits of either option.

In late July and early August 1991, the PUCO held hearings to review the reasonableness and adequacy of AEP's planning process for compliance with Title IV. In September, the PUCO issued its findings. Among other things, the PUCO found that the installation of scrubbers could provide the lowest-cost option, provided AEP receives from EPA its share of the extension reserve allowances. The PUCO also found that AEP should keep both the fuel switching and scrubbing options open until some of the uncertainties surrounding these analyses could be clarified.

From October 1991 through April 1992, the company continued to refine and revise its calculations, explored alternatives to minimize uncertainties and risk, and informed and obtained feedback from regulators in each of the jurisdictions of the AEP service area. Among the many options pursued, the company joined in an allowance pool with other utilities that were considering the installation of scrubbers. This pool would ensure that members would receive a pro rata share of reserve allowances awarded by EPA to winning participants when EPA implemented its allowance lottery. Also, the company pursued alternative means of financing the Gavin scrubbers to reduce the front-end impact and total cost of this capital-intensive option.

In April 1992, the company filed with the PUCO the "AEP System Acid Rain Compliance Report," which outlined a least-cost compliance strategy proposed to be pursued for OPCo Phase I-affected units in the context of overall AEP System compliance planning. Specifically, regarding Gavin, this plan indicated that the installation of scrubbers would be part of a least-cost system compliance program.

Extensive hearings were held by the PUCO in June and July 1992. This proceeding represented the culmination of a process of public input over almost a two-year period in which the PUCO provided clear direction regarding the methodology used by the company in analyzing compliance alternatives and the steps that the company should take to reduce uncertainties and preserve compliance options. In November 1992, the PUCO found, among other matters, that the installation of scrubbers at the Gavin Plant is part of a least-cost strategy, and that the Ohio Power compliance plan is reasonably designed to meet SO_2 compliance requirements and is a reasonably least-cost strategy pursuant to requirements of the Ohio Code.

Even though the company appears to have received a favorable order from the PUCO regarding its proposed SO_2 compliance strategy for the Ohio Power plants, and notwithstanding that this order is now being appealed to the Ohio Supreme Court by the Sierra Club and the Industrial Energy Consumers, a number of issues are still outstanding and need to be resolved. Perhaps the most significant will be the operation of the AEP System in the context of an emission allowance regime. As discussed previously, the AEP Pool Agreement governs the capacity and energy equalization settlement payments among the system member companies. The payments made by deficit members are determined by the embedded cost of capacity of the surplus members.

If a surplus company, such as OPCo, installed scrubbers as a compliance strategy, it would result in a corresponding increase in the capacity settlement payments required to be made by the deficit companies—currently APCo, CSP, and KPCo.

The existing intercompany agreements never contemplated the costs and issues that have been introduced with the acid rain legislation. Even though the AEP companies have adopted an integrated system-wide approach for meeting the requirements of the CAAA, several jurisdictional issues arise, including the determination of:

- each operating company's allocation and entitlement to allowances,[10]

- each operating company's consumption of allowances,[11] and

- transfer payments associated with the purchase (or use) of allowances from affiliated companies.[12]

The issues associated with a multi-state system such as AEP are significantly more complex in view of the interrelationships and transfer payments already established among the affiliated companies. We are hopeful that the commissions from each of the states in which AEP operates may be able to reach consensus on the appropriate allocation concepts for compliance costs and allowances. But even then, it is important to recognize that in the complex world of multi-state operations, such consensus is only the first step. That consensus must then be translated into formal regulatory approval in the course of formal regulatory proceedings—and that means the introduction of numerous interveners with diverse interests and widely varying levels of understanding. Nonetheless, the discussions and analyses that are currently being considered by the Regional Coordinating Committee can significantly contribute to the resolution of these complex jurisdictional issues. It provides an effective forum to define the issues and the jurisdictional concerns, to explore alternatives and potential compromises, and in the end result, to develop a proposal that is well documented, explicitly addresses the issues, and can withstand formal regulatory scrutiny.

WHAT THE FUTURE HOLDS

The development of the AEP System since the beginning of this century, and in particular following World War II, took place during a period of tremendous change. Among other changes, the quarter of a century from the late 1940s to the mid-1970s included the rapid electrification of the U.S. economy, spurring a high growth in electric consumption. Significant advances were brought about in electric power supply technology—in generation, transmission, and distribution systems—resulting in continuous improvements in economies of scale, the outcome of which was a declining cost of electric power supply. Much of the period was marked primarily by concern as to whether sufficient power supply capability would be available to fuel the nation's increasing appetite for electric energy. These technological challenges were coupled with a political and regulatory regime generally supportive of electric utility initiatives. Today, the AEP System and the rest of the electric utility industry face a whole new set of challenges, and the ways of the past may no longer suffice in dealing with the forces of the 1990s and beyond.

The changing complexion of the electric utility industry, with the encouragement of competition in electric generation supply via exempt wholesale generators, independent power producers, cogeneration, transmission access, and perhaps retail wheeling, introduces a vast panorama of forces unlike any the industry has faced in the past. These forces are being encouraged to make electric energy supply more competitive, and the industry more responsive to market forces, like other industries, even though the production of electricity is unlike any other consumer-oriented industry. Coupled with this, regulatory proceedings have become more complex and contentious.

With this backdrop of industry changes, the challenges facing the AEP System are indeed significant. As this chapter has indicated, the strength of the AEP System lies in the recognition that, by coordinating and centralizing the planning and operation of the power supply facilities of its members, the overall system will be more efficiently and economically developed and operated than could ever be achieved on an individual member basis. Therefore, the axiom that "whole is greater than the sum of the parts" is of paramount significance in the case of AEP. This axiom assumes that the regulatory bodies that have jurisdiction over the individual members of the AEP System recognize the beneficial attributes of the integrated system concept—and that the achievement of the benefits of integration also requires certain concurrent responsibilities.

The Regional Coordinating Committee's deliberation with respect to the allocation of emission allowances may be a trial for other complex issues that will have to be addressed on a multi-jurisdictional basis. For example, in dealing with demand-side management (DSM) programs, AEP's state regulatory commissions have not established a common approach to evaluating DSM in terms of judging cost-effectiveness or in determining rate treatment. Nevertheless, DSM evaluations are being conducted on an AEP System basis, as part of an overall integrated resource planning process, consistent with the approach used for the planning of generation resources for the AEP System. Such DSM programs evaluated on an overall system basis will need to be implemented on an individual operating company basis in accordance with the applicable commission's standards for cost-effectiveness and recovery.

With respect to the issue of competitive bidding for new generation resources, some of the state commissions have taken a more aggressive stance than others. When AEP determines that it may need to add additional generating capacity, how will decision making and, if applicable, competitive bidding be treated by the various regulatory commissions?

Another example of issues for the future relates to the need to construct new transmission facilities so that transmission services can be provided to a third party, under the recently expanded powers of the FERC, in accordance with the National Energy Policy Act of 1992. Will the state commissions that have siting and certification authority be receptive to the need for this new construction, and how will cost allocation be decided?

These are but a few of the obvious examples of jurisdictional issues that AEP may face in this emerging new industry environment. Such an environment suggests a need for greater understanding and consensus-building among the regulatory commissions that have jurisdiction over the AEP members, so that resolutions can be reached that will ensure that the benefits of efficient and reliable power supply can be available to all the customers of the AEP System members.

NOTES

1.   The installed generating capacity on the AEP System is 24,084,000 kW, of which 21,120,000 kW is coal-fired and 2,110,000 kW is nuclear. The balance is composed of primarily hydro and pumped storage capacity.

2.   This network consists of 2,022 circuit miles of 765-kV lines, 111 circuit miles of 500-kV lines, and 3,797 miles of 345-kV lines, underlaid by some 8,468 miles of 138-kV transmission.

3.   Examples of these state-of-the-art accomplishments include the first mine-mouth power plant (1917); the first transmission line lightning protection research (1926); the first million lb/hr high-pressure boiler (1937); the first heat rate below 10,000 Btu/kWh (1950); the first 345-kV transmission line (1953); the first heat rate below 9,000 Btu/kWh (1960); the first 765-kV transmission line (1969); the first major research in the United States on pressurized fluidized bed combustion (1976); the first steam-electric generating unit to operate for 607 consecutive days (1987); and the first

conversion of a nuclear facility to a coal-fired generating facility (1991).

4.   A given pool member's proportionate responsibility is determined as the ratio of that member's peak firm load (for the preceding twelve months) to the summation of the corresponding peak firm loads of all the pool members. Each member of the AEP Pool must meet its responsibility for sharing in the pool capacity by providing—over time—sufficient generating capacity to meet its own internal load requirements plus an adequate reserve margin. Compensation for any temporary generation-load imbalances that a member may experience as a result of the installation of discrete-size generating units is provided through appropriate capacity equalization charges and credits among the pool members. The members that contribute more than their capacity responsibility (the capacity-surplus members) receive equalization payments from the members that contribute less than their capacity responsibility (the capacity-deficit members).

5.   Ownership considerations are taken into account on an after-the-fact basis, through appropriate charges and credits, for primary and economy energy transactions among the pool members.

6.   After-the-fact accounting for system sales to neighboring systems compensates each pool member for its out-of-pocket costs associated with such sales and then provides proportionate sharing, on an MLR basis, in the net revenues obtained from such sales. Similarly, after-the-fact accounting for system purchases provides for proportionate sharing of the costs associated with such purchases. The charges and credits associated with capacity equalization, internal energy transactions among pool members, and external transactions with non-affiliated systems are settled on a monthly basis.

7.   Using Appalachian Power Company as an example, of the $27.4 million of net revenues received in 1992 from MLR sales to non-affiliated utilities, $19.4 million was derived from sales to utilities with whom APCo is directly interconnected. The remaining $8.1 million was derived from sales to non-affiliated utilities with whom APCo does not have direct physical connections. This relationship is even more significant for some of the other member companies.

8. SO_2 reductions are to be achieved through the establishment of a new emission allowance program that ultimately will cap utility SO_2 emission at 8.95 million tons per year beginning in the year 2000. The SO_2 reductions are to be achieved in two phases, with a Phase I compliance date of January 1, 1995, and a Phase II compliance date of January 1, 2000. Utility units that emitted SO_2 at rates greater than 2.5 pounds per million Btu (lb./MBtu) in 1985 are designated as affected Phase I units. Such units must institute a compliance strategy to meet the equivalent of about 2.5 lb./MBtu emission limit by January 1, 1995. For Phase II (by January 1, 2000) all utility boilers must meet an aggregate emission restriction of about 1.2 lb./MBtu.

9.   An "allowance" is an authorization to emit one ton of SO_2. Each year, each utility boiler is granted a specific number of emission allowances in accordance with the base-line heat input established for the boiler during the 1985–87 baseline period and the allowable emission rate in lb./MBtu, as

specified in each phase. The CAAA provide a special reserve of allowances—extension reserve allowances—to be made available to Phase I units that reduce emissions through the use of qualifying technologies, such as scrubbers. At the conclusion of each year after 1994, a utility must surrender to EPA the appropriate number of allowances corresponding to the tons of SO_2 emitted during the year or be subject to severe civil and criminal penalties. As opposed to previously enacted environmental legislation, which basically relied on a "command and control" strategy, the 1990 CAAA legislation was a significant departure in that the concept of emission allowances introduced a market-based strategy into environmental control. Thus, emission allowances could be bought and sold or traded (like a commodity) and a combination of strategies could be utilized to achieve least-cost compliance. As a result, some units could be controlled to overcomply, resulting in unused emission allowances for that plant, which could in turn be used for a plant that might undercomply with respect to its allowable annual emissions, or these extra allowances could be sold to another party. As a result, emission allowances will have a monetary value, the value reflecting perceived regulatory risk, resulting in an emerging market operating on the principle of supply and demand.

10. The issue of allocations of allowances raises several questions. First, does the capacity settlement payment by a deficit member entitle that member to a share of the allowances allocated to the units of the surplus member? Second, since the capacity equalization rate will increase when a scrubber is installed on a surplus member's generating unit, should the *increased* capacity settlement payments of the deficit member entitle that member to a share of the extension reserve allowances allocated to the surplus member? And if so, should that entitlement be limited to the extension reserve allowances allocated to the scrubbed unit only or to the transfer units as well? What if a transfer unit is owned by a deficit member? And finally, do energy payments for increased fuel costs potentially associated with fuel switching entitle the purchasing member to any of the allowances allocated to the fuel-switched unit?

11. The generation at each unit is based on an economic dispatch to meet the total system load requirements in the most economic manner on a minute-to-minute basis; thus, the requirements of one company may be met by the generation of an affiliate. It will, therefore, be necessary to define a basis for relating an emissions level to the pool energy. Finally, if it is concluded that overcompliance is an effective strategy and that the allowances that are thereby not required internally should be sold in the market, a mechanism would need to be developed to determine the extent to which allowances should be sold and, therefore, which companies should be credited with the proceeds from such a transaction.

12. Assuming that it is appropriate to track allowances and emissions among the affiliated companies to determine the extent to which allowances are transferred among the affiliates, a major issue is the cost rate that should be assigned to each transfer. It will be important to consider all of the relationships that already exist within the integrated system to ensure that there is

no double-counting. It could be asserted that some of these allowance trans-fers are transactions that are implicitly encompassed by the Pool Agreement as part of the overall economic settlements required among the pool members. Other transactions, particularly between deficit and surplus members, may appropriately require supplemental transfer payments, not presently contem-plated by the Pool Agreement, to equitably allocate costs and benefits among the affiliates.

18

Comment on the American Electric Power Company Case

Jerry L. Wissman

In order for me to place my comments about the regulatory perspective on American Electric Power (AEP) into context, let me begin with a brief discussion of the more theoretical aspects of the regulation of multi-state firms.

The federal system of government in the United States, based on the precept that decentralization of authority is generally the preferred means of making collective decisions, has endured for more than two hundred years. Decentralized political decisions have several advantages: Decisions are made closer to those impacted by them; multiple loci of decision making offer increased opportunities for experimentation and encourage diversity; competition among decision makers may enhance efficiency; and the reduced size of decentralized jurisdictions minimizes and localizes the costs of errors in decision making. However, there is at least one significant disadvantage to decentralized decision making: Decentralized jurisdictions often find it difficult to plan and control for "externalities"—those costs and benefits which cross their geographical and/or administrative boundaries.

Regulatory authority over the U.S. electric industry closely follows the geographical boundaries of the federal/state system. Most regulatory bodies are state-specific, and the majority of the rest are national. Only a handful of governmental authorities, such as the Tennessee Valley Authority (TVA), operate at some geographical level larger than the state but smaller than the nation as a whole. The industry itself, of course, shows no such geographical discipline, as many producers are integrated at the supra-state or regional level. The primary goal of most actors in this regulatory system is economic efficiency in the production, distribution, and consumption of electric service. Given the difficulties mentioned regarding the incorporation of externalities into decentralized (i.e., state-level) regulatory jurisdictions, would it not be surprising if at any point in time the geographical allocation of government authority were exactly appropriate for the efficient economic regulation of electricity? Would it not be even more incredible if this allocation of authority remained appropriate over time?

Historically, a strong case can be made that the mismatch between industry and governmental boundaries did not adversely affect regulatory efficiency to any significant degree. Since all elements of the electric industry were monopolistic, geographical concerns could be addressed through policies such as cross-subsidization, which allowed regulatory planners to address externalities with some precision via both command-control processes and the tailoring of incentives to the electric producers and consumers. But two fundamental changes now occurring in the industry are bringing into question the efficiency of the current allocation of regulatory authority. First, competition has developed in the electricity market, and monopoly status is weakening or vanishing in many segments of the industry. As market forces increase, they work to undermine the incorporation of externalities into electric utility decisions through careful regulatory planning of incentives. Further, they reduce the producer's surplus associated with monopoly, and thus reduce the willingness of firms to incur the costs associated with command-control "regulatory (over)burden." Second, important externalities such as environmental issues have emerged at the regional/sectional level and pose challenges that state-situated regulatory bodies are poorly positioned to address.

For regulation to continue to attain the goal of economic efficiency, changes must take place. If the marketplace approach to electricity production is to prosper, regulatory authorities must work to increase their intramural coordination and communication. But how should such cooperation be structured? There are at least three distinct possibilities: maintain the status quo, increase existing informal communications and coordination channels, or create distinct regional regulatory bodies with formally delegated authority to act. Few knowledgeable people recommend the maintenance of the status quo—there is every reason to believe that the current system is already inadequate to the task of coping with the changing environment and will only become more inadequate as the changes progress.

The second approach poses its own set of challenges. Coordination across states will not be easy since it will require significant consensus-building among actors with very different demographics, interests, and political-regulatory histories and traditions. However, there are precedents for such cooperation, in the form of recently developed regional transmission groups. If such groups can reach consensus and maintain a stable regulatory climate over time, they actually promise a more efficient economic outcome than either the fully decentralized or the fully centralized alternatives, as their "pseudo-jurisdictions" more closely approximate the actual geographic boundaries of the firms they regulate.

The principal obstacles to such long-term stability are threefold: each individual party has a veto power by virtue of the voluntary nature of participation, leading to the types of protracted gridlock that are usually associated with the United Nations Security Council; federal authorities retain sufficient authority that they may preempt regional-level decisions, and thereby undercut the credibility of the associations; and voluntary cooperation will require sets of political skills and attitudes significantly different from those characteristic of the traditional adversarial litigation process.

Finally, the third approach, if rationally implemented, eliminates the problems of veto power and federal preemption, but may create additional layers of regulatory authority (hence additional regulatory burden), and may reduce the authority of existing regulatory entities. It is also much more difficult to implement politically, as it requires overt delegation of authority by the legislatures of every participating state. Such delegation is not only potentially politically unpopular among the legislators and the public, in some states it may also violate state constitutional constraints on the delegation of authority to agents outside the control of the legislative body.

In Ohio, the Public Utilities Commission has made a concerted effort to resolve regional (as well as traditional) issues through expanded coordination, communication, and cooperation at the regional level. The American Electric Power Regional Coordinating Committee (AEPRCC) is a prototypical example of a voluntary body formed to coordinate regulation of a multi-state electric producer. AEPRCC consists of representatives of the state regulatory bodies in the seven states in which AEP operates. Formed in response to the perceived need to coordinate responses to the Clean Air Act Amendments of 1990, AEPRCC has established a dialogue among the state commissions and AEP. As AEPRCC is a voluntary organization, the dialogue is not intended to diminish individual state authority, but rather to provide a vehicle to coordinate regulatory activity.

The committee agreed early in the analysis of AEP's Clean Air Act compliance plan that the goal should be minimization of system compliance costs. The committee, with the cooperation of AEP, is currently analyzing several alternative scenarios allocating the costs and benefits of compliance (including allowances) among the seven states. The final allocation is not yet determined, but continued coordination and communication will be essential to the development of a better understanding of the concerns of each individual state and the AEP region.

19

New York Case Study

William J. Balet and Charles R. Guinn

New York's electrical system and political boundaries are nearly identical. The state's many utilities coordinate their operations through a tight power pool that remains largely within these boundaries, so their activities are regulated chiefly by one state government. Thus in New York, state regulators enjoy relatively concentrated decision-making authority that has supported a tradition of statewide energy planning. Electric power sector decisions are strongly influenced by the state planning process, which reflects diverse policy interests.

The federal government plays a modest role in New York policy-making. Its effect is strongest in the area of environmental regulation, although the Federal Energy Regulatory Commission (FERC) review of international and interstate electricity transactions is also important. Typically, the state has been quite proactive in implementing the policy innovations embedded in the Public Utility Regulatory Policies Act (PURPA) and the 1990 Clear Air Act Amendments (CAAA), and has more often led than followed Federal regulatory cues.

This chapter describes the evolution of the New York electric power system and provides a snapshot of the current regulatory structure. It uses a discussion of the New York energy planning process to illustrate many policy issues and ends with comments on this system's answer to the federalist question.

EVOLUTION OF THE NEW YORK SYSTEM

The electric power industry started in New York City with the construction of Thomas Edison's Pearl Street plant in 1882. It quickly grew.

The first transmission project was a transmission line from Niagara Falls to Buffalo in 1896. Throughout the early part of the century, the various cities began to interconnect their power systems, and thus a basic 115/138 kV network existed throughout the state by the early 1930s.

During and after World War II, first a 230-kV and then a 345-kV network was built through the state. The Power Authority developed the resources on the St. Lawrence River at Niagara, and by the early 1960s, there was a 345-kV system from Niagara to New York City. The development of the statewide power system led to the establishment of the New York Power Pool in 1966.

Today the New York Power Pool (NYPP) is an association of the eight major utilities in New York State. These include seven investor-owned utilities and the New York Power Authority (NYPA). The seven investor-owned utilities have franchise-area load and also generation and transmission facilities. The New York Power Authority has large generating facilities, including the Niagara Project, and also owns a large amount of transmission.

The pool was organized to plan and operate the state's bulk power system in a coordinated manner. Thus, the eight member systems plan on a coordinated basis. The pool operates a control center near Albany from which the bulk power system is controlled to provide for system reliability. In addition, the statewide economic dispatch of the pool's generating resources is coordinated from the control center.

The state's transmission system is interconnected with each of its four neighbors: New England on the east, the Pennsylvania-Jersey-Maryland (PJM) Interconnection on the south, Ontario on the west, and Quebec to the north. The interconnections with the neighboring systems provide for the transfer of sizable amounts of energy. In the case of the American neighbors and Ontario, the transfers are usually fossil-based energy moving for economic reasons, whereas the transfers with Quebec are largely seasonal diversity from which economic advantages accrue. Currently, the state has adequate generation and transmission facilities for the foreseeable future.

The load (26,640 MW in the summer of 1993) is currently growing at a rate of 1.3 percent or about 400 MW per year before demand-side management and about 0.6 percent or 200 MW per year in actuality. The relatively low rate of load growth is due to a combination of a sluggish economy and aggressive DSM programs in the past several years. The generation owned by the utilities includes 5,100 MW of hydro, 4,840 MW of nuclear, 17,800 MW of fossil-fired, and 5,000 MW of combustion turbines, which totals approximately 33,000 MW. Currently, there are 2,720 MW of non-utility generators, which are largely gas-fired, on the New York Power Pool system. This is expected to rise to 6,250 MW by 1998, at which point it should stabilize. This results in 38 percent installed reserve, whereas only 22 percent is required for reliability purposes.

The transmission system is well developed, with adequate capacity to move generation to load and meet the pool's reliability criteria. Thus, with an oversupply of generation and adequate transmission, it does not appear that major additions to the bulk power system are necessary for the next ten to fifteen years unless a significant amount of generation is retired.

REGULATORY STRUCTURE

The New York Public Service Commission is responsible for regulation of retail rates charged to the customers by the utilities in New York State. It also has regulations to promote the public health and safety and thus uses its regulatory authority to monitor the reliability of the Bulk Power System. The Federal Energy Regulatory Commission regulates sales for resale, which are less than 5 percent of electric revenues.

New York State, through its various agencies, has a siting process for generation and transmission facilities, whereas federal involvement is generally limited to obtaining necessary permits. The relations with the neighboring states are carried on by both the state governments and the utilities largely through the Power Pools. Relations with the Canadian provinces are pursued through their provincial utilities.

NEW YORK ENERGY PLANNING

With the transition toward a more competitive industry environment, the points of contact between public policy and private sector energy interests—including electric and gas utilities, independent power producers, energy service companies, and major oil and gas suppliers and distributors—are many and varied. At the same time, from a public policy perspective, there is a growing recognition that energy and environmental policy and planning are inextricably linked and must be conducted in a common forum with a consistent analytic framework.

New York has established an energy planning process that requires energy, regulatory, and environmental agencies to develop jointly a state energy plan that integrates energy planning with environmental and economic competitiveness policy objectives. This public planning process also addresses the linkage between public and private sector planning.

The plans of major energy suppliers are factored explicitly into the public planning process through a set of information filing requirements mandated by the energy planning legislation. Under the information filing requirements of the plan, utilities are required to file the equivalent of an integrated resource plan (IRP) every two years with specific reference to proposed policies, objectives, and strategies for meeting the state's future electricity and gas needs. In addition, the IRPs must examine and report on how their implementation is likely to affect State Energy Plan goals and objectives, and also report on utility efforts to implement the recommendations contained in the previous plan.

The energy plan provides guidance to state agencies on energy and energy-related decisions from environmental regulations to facility siting. For example, the energy plan provides guidance for meeting any future electricity generation capacity needs and, as necessary, the siting of any new facilities whether by independent power producers or utilities. Thus, the public and private sectors are encouraged to work together toward development of an energy plan that provides for an orderly and sustainable energy future for New York.

It should be noted that the marrying of integrated resource plans to the State Energy Plan, so to speak, requires, as do most marriages, a commitment to work together, maintenance of open channels of communication, and, perhaps most importantly, a mutual trust that all involved are working toward a secure, reasonable cost, environmentally sound energy future.

The next sections highlight key features of the New York energy planning process, primary issues, and important conclusions.

The Public Planning Process

In August 1992, Governor Mario Cuomo signed comprehensive energy planning legislation that provided a framework for energy planning with the regulation of utility competitive bidding and the siting of new power projects.[1] The legislation created a State Energy Planning Board, consisting of the commissioners of energy, environmental conservation and the chairman of the State Public Service Commission to oversee the planning process.[2]

The legislation required the State Energy Office and the Departments of Public Service and Environmental Conservation to prepare a periodic State Energy Plan that integrates energy policy with important public policy objectives.

The scope and nature of the state public planning process can best be summarized by examining four important attributes:

- *Integrative*: focusing on the integration of energy, environmental, and economic competitiveness public policy perspectives.[3]

- *Comprehensive*: addressing all energy marketplace fuels and industries.[4]

- *Strategic*: focusing on a limited number of strategic issues.[5] and

- *Longer-range*: assessing the longer-term effects of current decisions.[6]

The plan will present a series of demand and supply assessments of New York State's energy future. These assessments include a reference case forecast and key assumptions, as well as scenarios that examine the sensitivity of the reference scenario to uncertainty and risk. These assessments provide the analytical foundation for the State Energy Plan recommendations. The plan will include at least the following assessments:

- demand forecasts by sector,

- energy efficiency,

- renewable resources,

- petroleum products,

- natural gas,

- electricity,

- economic competitiveness, and

- environmental effects.

These demand and supply assessments are based on an independent analytic capability development by the State Energy Office. This analytical capability includes, among others, a series of energy demand forecast models, PROSCREEN and MAPS electric system planning models, the North American Gas Markets (NARG) model, as well as supportive economic impact and environmental analytical methods and models.

Planning Issues

In the absence of the need for new facilities, the planning issues become more general policy questions rather than issues relating to specific facilities. These issues are addressed in both the political and regulatory arena. The resolution of these issues provides policy guidance to the utilities in planning their systems.

The primary vehicle for the public discussion and determination of issues is the state energy planning process. The utilities submit a planning document, which is then reviewed by the state agencies within the public planning process. The issues that the utilities currently believe to be important are discussed next.

- *Long-run avoided costs (LRACs)*. Past LRACs provided misleading price signals and led to acquisition of new resources in spite of an excess capacity situation. At issue is the potential for distortion of the marketplace by subsidizing selected resources.[7]

- *Demand-side management (DSM)*. DSM is now a mature industry and an important part of the electric utility business. Appropriate approaches and levels of effort need to be fine-tuned to account for economic conditions and rate impacts.[8]

- *Increasing role of non-utility generation*. Most future supply-side additions to the NYPP electric system are projected to come from non-utility generators (NUGs).[9] Although NUGs are expected to make some positive contributions to NYPP's overall resource plans, they carry with them certain reliability, system operating, and economic concerns that must be resolved.[10]

- *Integrated resource plans (IRPs)*. Utilities claim that the State Energy Plan cannot and should not become a substitute for utility-specific IRPs.[11]

- *Environmental quality*. The NYPP member systems' acid rain compliance strategy is based on a nationwide allowance trading system. The effectiveness of the allowance trading system will depend on the establishment of a collaborative and cooperative process with state and federal policymakers, to permit the utilities to achieve compliance with the CAAA at the lowest possible cost to the ratepayers.[12]

- *Environmental externalities*. In 1988, the Public Service Commission (PSC) ordered the utilities to include an estimate of the value of environmental externalities in the evaluation of DSM and for resource capacity bidding evaluations.[13] Their use raises important issues regarding the potential for distortion across sectors and impacts on electric rates.

- *Bulk power transmission access and wheeling.* In 1992, Congress passed the National Energy Policy Act, which will result in significant changes in the wholesale generation and transmission market and in other matters affecting the electric utility industry. There are many issues raised by the Energy Act that must be addressed by the NYPP member systems and the state. These include system reliability, transmission access, wholesale and retail wheeling, intra-state wheeling, regional transmission groups (RTGs), and impacts on transmission planning and financing.

- *Renewable resources.* Renewable resources have an important role in NYPP's resource plan as existing and committed resources.[14] However, based on load and capacity projections discussed earlier, utilities agree that there is no need for additional capacity in NYPP until well into the next decade.

The state's Energy Planning Working Group conducted a series of twenty-five outreach meetings in early 1993. Various participants in these sessions raised additional electric industry issues which are being addressed in the current planning effort. These included the following:

- *Review of all generation.* During a period of excess capacity, planners could conduct a "zero base" review of all system generation (utility and non-utility) in terms of total cost, likely Clean Air Act (CAA) compliance costs and likely expenditures needed to maintain New York's electricity system.[15]

- *CAAA compliance.* Merely meeting national standards for air emissions from either power plants or vehicles will not enable New York to meet the CAAA State Implementation Plan (SIP) emission reduction targets. Careful and consistent analysis is necessary to determine the most cost-effective compliance plan to meet the more stringent SIP targets.[16]

- *Gas-electric system integration.* Planning the interface between the gas and electric industries both in terms of infrastructure development and systems operations is becoming increasingly important.[17]

- *Future DSM programs.* The current utility DSM programs, which rely on broad-based rebate programs for purchase of energy-efficient equipment, appear unlikely to meet the current state energy-efficiency targets. Yet there appear to be ample opportunities for increased efficiency at a cost below the current cost of generation. Perhaps a new approach of a standard DSM offer contract that would be similar to an energy-only supply contract would be the means to achieve the targets in a cost-effective manner.

- *Future structure of the electric industry.* State utility commissions have overseen the deregulation of both the telephone and gas industries and the resulting unbundling of services. The electric industry may follow.[18]

- *Generation fuel diversity.* New York has had a very diverse fuel mix for electric generation; however, the current procurement has been nearly all fossil-fired, predominately gas. The growing share of fossil fuels in the mix raises serious questions about New York's commitment to a sustainable development.[19] The tradeoff between a public desire to move towards a sustainable development future and a public desire for the lowest-cost electric rates is yet to be explicitly addressed.

The Need for Planning

Based on these issues, we suggest that there will continue to be a need for a statewide energy planning effort. Key reasons follow.

- The increasing integration of the energy systems, especially the electric and gas systems, requires comprehensive public and private long-range energy planning, such as is in place in New York.

- Environmental targets, such as those required under the Clean Air Act, must alter the way energy is produced and used. However, greater flexibility to meet these targets has been provided by the regulatory framework. To take advantage of this flexibility and meet the targets in a cost-effective manner requires long-range comprehensive planning among all energy-consuming sectors in a common forum with consistent analysis and assumptions.

- A period of excess electricity generating capacity, a likely changed electric industry structure, a growing number of demand and supply options (each with their own set of zealots), and greater regulatory flexibility requires a working partnership between the public and private sectors to balance near-term and longer-term economic, societal, and environmental goals. As discussed, there is a significant number of issues that must be resolved.

THE FEDERALIST QUESTION

The New York experience indicates that state government will continue to have an important role in the electricity sector, regardless of federal preemption of economic regulatory authority and the evolution of regional electricity markets. One of the key activities of state planners and regulators is to help society make tradeoffs between economic and social objectives (e.g., cents per kilowatthour vs. environmental impacts).

On the other hand, the federal government regulates the use of the bulk transmission system. If a regional transmission group is formed in New York, its primary regulation would come from the federal government. Although regional cooperation is promoted through the Regional Reliability Council, due to the size of New York there is a tendency for the utilities to do things on a statewide basis. Relations with the Canadian provinces tend to be through the provincial utilities.

In New York, there will be a mix of state and federal regulation of the utilities. The state government will have a general overview of utility planning and will regulate the utilities through the retail rate. The federal government will be the primary regulator of the bulk power system, possibly through the establishment of an RTG.

NOTES

1.   Chapter 519 of the Laws of 1992, State of New York.

2.   Chaired by the commissioner of energy.

3.   The planning process provides a public forum for the integration of energy planning with environmental policy and economic competitiveness objectives. The planning process is a multi-agency effort with core participation from staff of the State Energy Office and the Departments of Public Service and Environmental Conservation. Other agency involvement beyond this core group includes the Departments of Economic Development and Transportation and the New York State Energy Research and Development Authority. An inter-agency planning working group meets regularly to review policy and coordinate plan development activities. The Energy Planning Board (EPB) and working group analogy can be compared to the "virtual corporation" in the private sector through which companies contribute what they regard as their core competencies to product development, mixing what one company does best with the best of other companies. The agencies share responsibility for policy and analytical work according to their areas of expertise and/or regulatory oversight. The network structure of the working group is informal and collegial in its deliberations.

4.   The scope of the planning process is as comprehensive as the energy marketplace. It addresses both the demand and supply of energy. It involves those providing all forms of fuel and power, as well as energy services. It involves suppliers of petroleum products, natural gas pipeline companies, regulated investor-owned electric and natural gas utilities, independent power producers, the New York Power Authority, and energy service companies as well as a wide range of public interest groups. One important focus is on public policy issues related to the interdependence of energy supply systems. Another is on the public policy issues associated with the transition to a more competitive marketplace for energy and energy services.

5.   The focus of the energy plan, as well as the process, is strategic in nature. The emphasis of the plan is on providing strategic direction, given a shared vision of how future energy markets may evolve and how government policy and regulation can best assist in the achievement of the plan's goals and objectives. The plan deals with a limited number of strategic public policy issues. The issues identified by the Energy Planning Board for the current planning effort include the following: (1) energy policy and economic competitiveness, (2) future of the electric industry, (3) transportation mobility and demand management, (4) Clean Air Act implementation, (5) public housing and low-income energy efficiency, (6) alternative fuels development, (7) fuel diversity, and (8) externalities in energy decision making. Included in the plan will be series of policy recommendations that represent the energy planning board's strategy for attaining specific planning goals and objectives. Because the plan covers all fuels and end-uses, it is critically important that there be an explicit accounting of the tradeoffs of policy recommendations regarding the balancing of energy, economic, and environmental goals among and between sectors and fuels. An example of an explicit tradeoff might be the competing goals of lowering the costs of energy service consistent with economic competitiveness objectives, while at the same time accounting, as appropriate, for environmental and other externalities in energy decision making. Such balancing is further complicated by the temporal dimension of policy actions, both short-term and long-term.

6.   The plan and supporting analytic framework cover a 20-year time period over which forecasts are made of the state's energy requirements and infrastructure. Scenario analysis is performed both qualitatively and quantitatively to address uncertainty and risk by assessing the effect of a series of possible events or actions on energy demand, supply, and price. In some instances, the scenario analysis is deliberately constructed to evaluate how the energy system might be expected to work under prescribed conditions. In other instances, scenarios are created from analytical model outputs of a number of "what if" cases or optimization algorithms.

7.   LRAC estimates are intended to be a measure of the stream of future resource costs avoided by purchasing additional resources. Their accuracy ensures that the price utilities and their customers pay for a new resource is no greater than the cost of alternative opportunities. Over the next several years, billions of dollars will change hands based on LRAC estimates, even though excess capacity in the state is projected by the NYPP to range

between 3,000 MW and 5,000 MW for at least the next ten years.

8.   Since 1990, NYPP member systems have spent approximately $500 million on DSM programs. The current DSM projection, although still substantial, is somewhat below that projected in the last NYPP Energy Planning Strategy. The reduced levels reflect the impact of lower LRACs, uncertainty regarding the cost-effectiveness of some of the programs, and concern about near-term rate impacts. Given the economic conditions and uncertainty surrounding DSM programs, utilities hope that future State Energy Plans promote the following concepts: (1) cost-effective DSM programs should be selected based on utility IRPs; (2) DSM programs should be flexible to assist utilities in adapting to changing circumstances; (3) the rate impacts of DSM programs on economic competitiveness should be carefully evaluated (many DSM programs currently have benefit-to-cost ratios close to one; these ratios are based on the total resource cost [TRC] test, which includes a benefit of 1.4 cents per kilowatthour for reduced environmental impact; but implementation of programs that pass the TRC but cause rates to increase can reduce economic competitiveness); (4) DSM programs that promote economic efficiency should be incorporated into the resource mix, even though they may increase electric use, because these types of programs will have a favorable rate impact, and (5) efficiency standards and energy codes are free-market mechanisms which should be given priority in achieving energy efficiency goals.

9.   By the year 2000, NUG capacity (including NUG capacity purchased through competitive bidding) is projected by the NYPP to increase to 6,095 MW or 16 percent of total NYPP capacity.

10.   For example, two NYPP members are experiencing or anticipating operational difficulties during light load conditions. In addition, there are rate impact aspects of the competitive bidding process and regulations governing energy-only purchases. Among these is the uncompensated use of the transmission system.

11.   Both federal and state policies support integrated resource planning by the electric utilities. These IRPs strive to balance a wide range of considerations, from price and reliability to fuel diversity and environmental impact, to produce long-range plans that acknowledge the unique characteristics of each utility and its customers' need. The State Energy Plan should provide broad state energy policy direction and ensure consistent state agency and legislative actions that will guide and enable, but not dictate, utility IRPs.

12.   The member systems' emissions of NO_2 are approximately 20 percent of all NO_2 emissions in New York State, whereas mobile sources account for 60 percent. Therefore, careful consideration must be given to how reductions are allocated among the sources of emissions so that compliance can be achieved in the most cost-effective way. New York State has been considering the drafting of regulations aimed at reducing emissions to levels below that required by the federal regulations, further increasing the importance of choosing cost-effective emissions reduction strategies.

13.   Because of the uncertainties associated with valuing environmental externalities, the PSC has ordered the New York utilities to fund and to par-

ticipate in a research study with the Department of Public Service (DPS) staff, the State Energy Office (SEO), the Department of Environmental Conservation (DEC), the New York State Energy Research and Development Authority (NYSERDA) and independent experts to develop an appropriate methodology to estimate the value of such environmental externalities. A PSC proceeding (Case 92-E-1187) was also initiated to consider, among other things, whether and how environmental externalities should be applied to the utility selection process for supply and DSM resources.

14. NYPP members already own and purchase significant amounts of energy from these resources and have commitments to purchase more. In fact, New York utilities are leaders in the country in the use of renewable resources, which account for nearly 19 percent of the state's electric energy needs compared with 10 percent for the nation. In addition, the member systems participate in and sponsor research and development projects on the national and state levels examining and supporting the development of new energy resources, including renewable. The PSC has initiated a regulatory proceeding to examine a 1992 State Energy Plan recommendation to install 300 MW of additional renewable resource capacity by 1998.

15. New York currently has several thousand megawatts of excess capacity on its system. This excess capacity provides New York with an opportunity to study the system and determine whether removal of inefficient or expensive resources from the system is warranted. Much of the state's fossil-fired capacity, built in the 1950s and 1960s, will likely require extensive retrofits to comply with federal and regional regulations governing the emission of SO_2 and NO_2. For some of the less efficient and more expensive units, the relatively short operating lives of ten to twenty years may be insufficient to recover economically the investment in compliance. Similarly, it may not be economic for several of New York's older nuclear plants, requiring substantial investment to comply with federal or operational standards, to continue operating in an era of excess generating capacity. Certain expensive contracts with independent power producers could also be scrutinized in such an effort.

16. Measures beyond the national standards, such as California's low emission vehicle standards have been adopted in New York. Further cost-effective measures will be required, some from the electricity generation industry and the transportation sector.

17. The fuel of choice for new electricity generation and a popular CAA compliance measure is natural gas. First cost, equipment efficiency, and ease of facility siting appeared to be driving this choice. The emergence of the gas-fired combined-cycle technology, with a relatively low capital cost, low emissions, and high efficiency, has greatly changed both the electric and gas industries. Currently there are about 2,045 MW of gas-fired independent power projects in operation in New York. Another 1,930 MW are under construction, and there are some 2,500 MW in the planning stage, expected to be on-line by the mid-1990s. The electric generation sector use of gas could increase by as much as two-thirds from current levels. Federal Energy Regulatory Commission Order 636 will restructure the natural gas industry, providing increased access to pipeline capacity and enhanced competition for gas supplies. When

fully implemented, the responsibility for gas acquisitions will be transferred to local gas distribution companies (LDCs) and end users. The role of interstate pipelines will effectively be limited to gas transportation. A secondary capacity market is being established through an Electronic Bulletin Board System to rationalize and maximize the use of pipeline capacity. The implementation of straight-fixed-variable (SFV) rates under Order 636 will reinforce the establishment of this secondary capacity market. SFV rates will increase the costs (demand charges) of holding pipeline capacity rights. This will encourage power producers to operate at high load factors and contract to share capacity with others when their generators do not run or when they operate on alternative fuels. Prior analysis indicated that future capacity expansion units would operate at load factors that might be too low to support the construction of firm pipeline capacity. In addition, concerns have been raised about potential operational problems (e.g., the needs of the power generation market are instantaneous, where as gas moves 10–20 mph). Quick drawdown storage and high-volume pipeline delivery systems have been proposed to address these concerns. Commonly raised concerns regarding gas for power generation are the adequacy of gas supply (reserves), the adequacy of gas deliverability, and gas price volatility. The IPPs have successfully dealt with these issues. A structural change or incentive approach may be needed for electric utilities to do the same.

18. Perhaps the most significant provisions of the Energy Policy Act of 1992, as they affect electric utilities, are the amendments to the Federal Power Act, which grant to the FERC the authority to require utilities to provide transmission services for the wholesale wheeling of power and for utilities to establish exempt wholesale generation. The relatively high cost of electricity in the Northeast, especially for large customers under economic competitiveness pressures, is a primary concern for energy policy. The available excess capability could spur considerable interest in wheeling among utilities and between customer affiliates. Retail wheeling, which would allow customers to shop around for power within or outside the state, and discounted industrial rates for economic development may not be far behind.

19. How should fuel diversity be treated in a competitive market, and should New York let the market decide which fuels to pursue? Should New York continue to maintain a policy of reducing petroleum product dependence in all sectors? When does too much natural gas become a problem for price, supply, or security? Should the State Energy Plan continue to set forth energy efficiency and renewable resource planning targets; and if so, should the targets be retained or modified, and should flexibility be added to reflect differences throughout the state? The competitive procurement of new generation places a high premium on low capital costs and proven technology. Potential fuel price risks are not explicitly accounted for in the procurement process.

REFERENCE

New York State Energy Office (NYSEO). *New York State Energy Plan*. Draft. Albany, NY: NYSEO (February 1994).

20

Comment on the New York Case

Richard E. Schuler

By most forecasts, ample electricity supplies are currently available in New York State (NYS) to serve the state's needs for at least a decade. Furthermore, the composition of those supplies is diverse both in terms of primary energy source (hydroelectric, nuclear, coal, oil, natural gas, and demand-side management [DSM], although downstate areas still rely heavily on oil-fired generation—primarily for environmental reasons) and in terms of institutional structure. Of the 35,000 MW of available capacity in NYS, 73 percent is provided by investor-owned utilities, 7 percent is provided by non-utility generators (NUGs) and the remaining 20 percent is provided by the NY Power Authority (NYPA). Because the statewide transmission grid interconnects most regions in the state and there are few transmission bottlenecks, and because existing generating sources are dispatched economically through a statewide "tight" power pool, the current total generating costs using existing facilities are approaching their minimum.

The biggest problem with electricity supply in most areas of the state is its high price, due in part to the distance from NYS to low-cost fuel supplies.[1] The cost of building and operating large-scale non-hydroelectric generating facilities by utilities over the past fifteen years has been extremely high. Although implementation of the 1978 Public Utility Regulatory Policy Act (PURPA) in NYS has induced waves of independent power producers (IPPs) to build additional capacity so that this non-utility source of supply now accounts for 7 percent of the state's total, NYS law has guaranteed a six-cent-per kilowatt-hour minimum price for qualifying IPPs that signed contracts before 1992. The continued high cost of generation in NYS makes NYS electricity customers a likely target for future out-of-state competitive supply by other utilities in the near term. In the twenty-first century, transmission lines may provide the solution as power produced in the Midwest races east through New York to capture markets here and in New England. Can adequate highways for these interstate power flows be developed, given ever-increasing public reluctance to accept aesthetic and environmental losses, no matter how great the benefit might be for others? Will adverse environmental impacts in New York be magnified by these power flows since most large, existing utility-owned generating units in Pennsylvania and in the Midwest are coal-fired? Will New York continue to be a recipient of the air emissions from generation in those states as well as a conduit for their sales? How can New York resolve these questions by itself when so many of the causes and effects lie outside the state? These are the important regulatory and institutional issues to be resolved.

Electricity is also expensive in NYS, particularly downstate, because the cost of other expenses, including distribution, customer services, general administration and taxes, on a per-kilowatt-hour basis is also extremely high in comparison to similar costs for utilities in other urban areas outside of NYS. These costs associated with getting electricity to end-use customers range between two and four cents per kilowatt hour more in downstate New York as compared to other urban areas in the Northeast.[2] These are costs that are not easily forced down by competitive pressures because all competitive suppliers would have to use this same distribution system to reach end-use customers in most instances.[3]

FUTURE COMPETITIVE PRESSURES

There are two major sources of competitive pressure for bulk power supplies in NYS: One is the conviction of many NUGs that they can generate power at lower costs than either the utilities or NYPA, and the other is the efforts by customers to avoid paying prices that are greater than marginal cost.[4] Federal government policies, including the recent changes in the 1992 Energy Policy Act, merely facilitate the fruition of these fundamental pressures for competition; they are not the primary cause. It is this grass-roots movement seeking and offering competitive supplies that will precipitate further institutional and regulatory change.

The generation-cost-difference basis for competition is rooted in a variety of economic forces that arose ten to twenty years ago. Middle East petroleum disruptions of the 1970s magnified regional fuel price differentials substantially, leading to strengthened transmission ties to facilitate economic exchanges. Today that strengthened and lower-cost wheeling capability facilitates competition from more distant generation sources. In addition, the oil embargoes of the 1970s led to the deregulation of the well-head price of natural gas and mandatory wheeling requirements for gas pipeline companies. These federal regulatory changes (a substitution of market for regulatory pressures) with respect to natural gas have had a profound effect on the competitiveness of small independent power producers by opening up and securing for them substantial, reliable supplies of natural gas at competitive prices.

Another economic force that allowed NUGs to produce electricity at a competitive price was the leveling out of additional scale economies in the generation of electricity that first became apparent in the late 1970s.[5] Ever greater savings with larger sizes are no longer being achieved.[6] The net result is that NYS, with a current peak demand of 27,000 MW, would require thirty-three of the largest, most-efficient 1,000-MW utility-built units to serve the state's electricity needs. If each unit were operated by a different firm, there would be thirty-three different competitive suppliers in NYS—far more than are available in most unregulated competitive markets.

And, in fact, what the past decade has shown us is that units of much smaller size than 1,000 MW can compete effectively both because of smaller unit capital costs and much shorter construction times. In fact, mass-produced combustion turbines frequently compete effectively in terms of combined running and capital costs with much larger central station units, in part because of the low construction costs of mass-produced units, and in part because of the consistent gas supplies that have emerged as a result of competitive natural gas markets. The added advantage of these decentralized sources of supply is that the required planning lead time is shortened significantly (we do not have to start designing now for facilities needed in a decade)[7]; what is required is to be certain that the proper price signals are given to independent suppliers, over time, so that the desired amount of generating capacity is forthcoming.

A MARKET-BASED STRUCTURE FOR THE ELECTRIC SUPPLY INDUSTRY

Given the evolution in electricity supply technology and its associated costs, how might we organize the electricity supply industry if we were starting over from scratch? Distribution is certainly a localized decreasing cost industry, and in most instances it would be inefficient to have several distribution companies competing to serve the same

customer. However, it is not clear how large in geographic area a distribution company needs to be in order to take advantage of all scale
benefits. Several statistical studies suggest that all efficiencies are
achieved once a served population of from 250,000 to 1 million is
reached.[8] Therefore, there is plenty of room for many distribution
companies in NYS located side-by-side, each a natural monopoly
within its own service territory. Generation, on the other hand, can be
highly competitive, so long as an adequate transmission system exists,
because generating facilities would not have to be located adjacent to
loads they serve.

   The key then to competitive generation markets is adequate
transmission facilities and managing the transmission system to serve
the dual functions of maintaining a fair market and providing back-up
reliability. Both functions can be served through adequate, properly
located transmission facilities and market-based prices for wheeling.
If a substantial subset of generators or buyers of electricity control the
transmission function, however, they will control the market. That
may not lead to economically efficient outcomes. Perhaps some autonomous cooperative venture, similar to an entity like a stock exchange,
or a public body like the New York Power Authority could manage the
transmission system (and construct needed new facilities) with a view
toward ensuring a fair, competitive marketplace.

MAKING THE TRANSITION TO COMPETITIVE
MARKETS FOR GENERATION

   With or without a substantial effort on the part of utilities, NYPA,
and NYS regulatory agencies, the markets for power will become more
competitive in NYS as a result of cost differentials and the wheeling
provisions of the 1992 Energy Policy Act. As demonstrated in a recent
analysis,[9] many utilities to the south and west of New York have average operating costs for their generation that are one to two cents per
kilowatt hour less than those of some NYS utilities, and their total
average generating costs including sunk capital costs are from two to
three cents per kilowatt hour lower.[10] Similarly, several New England
utilities have average generating costs that range from one to two
cents per kilowatt hour higher than in NYS. With the opening of
transmission to greater wheeling, some of those utilities in Pennsylvania, West Virginia, and Ohio that have excess capacity might attempt
to displace the sales of NYS utilities to their large customers and
municipalities. In turn, NYS utilities might market their generation
in New England. However, without a formal market-clearing entity,

many of these bilateral contracts are likely to be idiosyncratic, relying on the bargaining skills of the parties and the happenstance of the location of adequate transmission capability.[11] Furthermore, in many instances no entity has the geographic breadth or motivation to construct additional transmission lines merely to facilitate economic exchanges of electricity and capacity.

What NYS regulatory agencies can accomplish is to hasten and smooth out the transition to a competitive market; the eventual outcome is inevitable. The steps required to facilitate this transition are as follows:

1. Establish both spot and long-term markets for generating capacity as well as for energy transactions between all generators, utilities, and their customers.

2. Ensure the centralized management and autonomy of the transmission network. Wheeling fees should be assessed in an economically efficient manner. The transmission agency should have the authorization to construct new transmission-related facilities, as required, by market forces.[12]

3. Prohibit existing utilities that provide distribution services from buying electricity from their own generating facilities unless that is the lowest price available source.

4. Assess environmental costs, and/or subsidies to cover DSM programs, on electricity transactions in a consistent manner statewide, based on estimated incremental damages or benefits associated with each type of generation or conservation activity.

The key to establishing broad and deep markets for power is the establishment of a spot market for all electricity. This market would differ from the New York Power Pool's (NYPP's) current economy exchanges that are based solely on running costs. The spot market would not restrict the prices to running costs. That way, in periods of short capacity, the exchange price might rise considerably above running costs. When, however, capacity was plentiful, the exchange prices might drop down near to the running costs. Although there has been an increased number of bilateral contracts arranged between and among generators and utilities in NYS, the existence of a spot market for both energy and capacity would facilitate longer-term bilateral contracts, since if a buyer subsequently discovered they did not need all of the contracted capacity, they could recover some expenses by reselling on the spot market. Note that the current bidding process for utilities to acquire additional capacity that has been established by the New York State Public Service Commission (PSC) is no substitute for a spot market. In fact, the existence of a spot market should make the bidding process more robust.

A question remains regarding the optimal geographic extent of the spot market. As a beginning, since NYPP already exists as a tight pool, the state's borders could define the initial market, although NYPP should continue to attempt to make purchases and sales outside the state. If and as other states and regions also establish spot markets (New England and Pennsylvania, New Jersey and Maryland [PJM], as examples), specialists will arise naturally to facilitate transactions between pools.[13] Once again, beginning the process of a competitive market is more important than being able to predict how every nuance will work out in the years ahead, provided that structural impediments are eliminated.

The second and third steps are more difficult because they imply ceding jurisdiction of existing utility transmission facilities to other entities and the rapid write-off and retirement of uneconomic utility generating facilities. There are many legal impediments to accomplishing these asset transfers in a non-voluntary manner, including the primacy of contract associated with mortgage bond covenants that are tied to particular groups of utility assets. Government cannot easily abrogate those contractual rights, even indirectly, without a drawn-out constitutional test. Prolonged legal wrangling, like that surrounding the state's attempts to implement PURPA a decade ago, will only drag out the inevitable transition to a competitive market. Furthermore, there is no Judge Greene holding the threat of an anti-trust conviction over the heads of the utilities to force a compromise. A mutually agreeable solution has to be found.

As a first step, the utilities must be encouraged by the PSC to write down their uneconomic generating facilities rapidly. The PSC may be reluctant to do this, of course, because in the short run it will mean higher electricity rates; although, in the long run the benefits of competition should more than compensate the customers with lower future prices. Current efforts by some utilities in providing industrial promotion rates are an effort to recover these costs by increasing kilowatt hour sales, as opposed to higher rates that attempt to recover more per unit sale. The promotional approach, although potentially beneficial to the state's economy, also bears the risk that if it is too successful, it may encourage the construction of even more generation facilities requiring even larger capital cost recovery. To the extent that those future needs are met through an open competitive market, however, future customers should not be misled by "subsidized" prices so long as the promotional rates approach the market prices as excess capacity dwindles.

Another way of sharing and spreading the expense would be if the

NYPA provided some of the cash to write down high-cost utility generation facilities by acquiring each utility's transmission lines, valued at depreciated *replacement* cost. The utility could then use the difference between the *replacement* and *book costs* of the transmission lines to offset, in part, the generating plant write-offs.[14] Having acquired all of NYS's transmission facilities, NYPA could be assigned the responsibility for maintaining and extending the system. Meanwhile, its purchase expenses could be recovered in part by a broker's fee associated with spot market transactions. Furthermore, a wise investment of a portion of the difference between the marginal value of electricity, as determined in the spot market, and the cost of NYPA's hydroelectric production would be in facilitating the transition to a statewide competitive market.

An additional important step is to establish a mechanism to review and set the prices for wheeling services. These prices need to be worked out carefully and applied consistently to all buyers and sellers. Furthermore, if NYPA is the manager and coordinator of wheeling services, so long as it also manages generation facilities (particularly renewable-resource-based generation like its hydroelectric facilities), then pricing review should not be the exclusive prerogative of NYPA.

Finally, a combination of relevant state agencies could be empowered to establish and assess externality-based fees and/or subsidies to motivate conservation on all bulk power exchanges between generators and distribution companies and/or retail customers. Somewhat similar to access fees in telephone service that are assessed equally on all long-distance providers, these externality fees should be applied consistently to each type of generation, regardless of institutional arrangement. Similarly, the cost of other social initiatives (e.g., DSM) might be assigned equitably through an add-on to all bulk power exchanges. Thus, regulatory-induced "bypass" might be lessened.

A structural problem facing the smooth transition to more competitive markets for bulk power supply is that the optimal scale for planning and coordinating the transmission grid may in most cases be on a multi-state, regional level,[15] but uniform nationwide action may not be warranted. Unfortunately, no regional-level government exists to coordinate the optimally sized geographic markets. Similar problems arise with respect to environmental regulation. Again, uniform national regulation may be unnecessarily restrictive in dealing with a public "bad" whose scope is interstate but does not extend to national boundaries (except for greenhouse gases). With the exception of the interstate definition of some urban air sheds, most environmental regulation is also developed within the context of traditional national, state, and local government jurisdictions. In fact, the appropriate scale may be quite different.

PLANNING AND NEW YORK STATE'S FUTURE ELECTRICITY SUPPLY

If the wave of the future is for competitive electricity supply in NYS, what is the future need for regulators and planners? First, the skill and foresight of these agencies can either facilitate or hamper the inevitable transition, resulting in a great benefit or cost to NYS. Second, for reasons detailed here, there are important rules and government oversight that are essential to make a market work efficiently. The rules of the game must be laid out clearly and applied fairly, and transactions (transmission) costs should be minimized. Furthermore, government intervention is necessary to deal with externalities (environmental impacts) and to be sure that all parties receive similar information on market conditions. There will be a large government role to play, furthermore, in facilitating the siting of new electricity supply facilities.

Because NYS is involved in many aspects of the state's economy through regulatory practice and the provision of goods and services, a primary function of the continued NYS energy planning process is to identify, rectify, or reinforce areas where the independent actions of various agencies may conflict with or complement each other. As an example, enhanced fiber-optic networks may imply fewer work-related commuting trips (or at least less peak hour travel) and therefore have profound effects on the nature of and need for the state's transportation network. These developments, in turn, may influence the acceptability of electric vehicles and their battery charging patterns, which of course implies varying electricity needs and costs. A primary purpose of integrated energy planning, then, is to lay out these scenarios and to anticipate needed regulatory changes.

The one problem that remains in New York is the high cost of distribution of electricity. Reducing these costs are important for the state's future well-being because they influence residential rates, and the residential rates in NYS are among the highest in the nation. If the future of a high-tech economy hinges on the location of skilled, professional employees—particularly if many work out of their homes— then lower residential rates will be a contributing factor to the desirability of working in NYS and therefore a key to future business expansion. And since the electricity distribution function is still a natural monopoly,[16] innovative NYS regulatory mechanisms are required to encourage utilities to hold these costs down.[17]

NOTES

1.   The exceptions are the substantial hydroelectric resources along the Niagara Frontier and the St. Lawrence River. However, the amount of this capacity that can be developed economically is limited at a fraction of the total state's needs, and hydroelectric power currently accounts for 14 percent of NYS's generation.

2.   Distribution, customer service and general administrative expenses and taxes per kWh in 1992 were 5.07 cents/kilowatt hour for Long Island Lighting, 6.73 cents/kWh for Consolidated Edison, 4.23 cents/kWh for Orange and Rockland Utilities, 2.66 cents/kWh for Atlantic City Electric, 2.46 cents/kWh for Boston Edison, 1.95 cents/kWh for Detroit Edison, 2.27 cents/kWh for Philadelphia Electric, and 2.31 cents/kWh for United Illuminating. (Hyman and Kelley, 1993.)

3.   The exception would be if customers made massive moves toward self-generation.

4.   Either through DSM, by self-generation, or, in the future, by purchasing power directly from IPPs or from distant, low-cost utilities.

5.   Previously, the combined functions of electricity generation and transmission represented a decreasing cost industry for most market areas in the United States. In fact, the history of the industry over the previous 100 years was one of a complementary leap-frogging of generation and transmission improvements resulting in lower unit costs. This hand-in-hand evolution of the two functions was essential since improved efficiencies in ever larger generation facilities would have been of little value without the development of lower-cost transmission to reach the larger geographic market necessary to consume the output of ever bigger generating units.

6.   Distinguish between theoretical efficiency improvements that are predicated on higher pressures and temperatures for larger generating units that can lead to improved thermal efficiency and actual cost experience that factors in escalating construction costs and unit downtime.

7.   Changing perspectives about future sources have altered the capacity planning process dramatically. Ten years ago, if there were only a decade's worth of adequate capacity to spare, the utilities and NYPA would be gearing up to begin work on a new large generating station, given the six to ten year lead time required. However, with the success of independent power producer (IPP) generation under PURPA and the relative speed of IPP planning and construction, strong NYS Public Service Commission initiatives to encourage utilities to promote DSM, and the commission's intention to arrange for all future utility generation through competitive bidding processes, any future generating units are likely to be smaller than typical new utility-built units, and therefore they may be planned and completed within two to four years. In fact, current NYS efforts are focused on forestalling the addition of new IPP generation, as evidenced by the repeal of the law guaranteeing a minimum price of 6 cents/kWh for electricity from new IPP facilities.

8.   See Neuberg (1977) and Weiss (1975) as examples.

9.   See Hyman and Kelley (1993).

10.   With lower average costs, this means that those out-of-state utilities have some generating units with lower marginal costs than many in NYS.

11.   In fact, many low-cost Ohio utilities do not have large amounts of spare generating capacity, and transmission routes from Ohio through Pennsylvania to New York are limited.

12.   Ideally the transmission agency should generally be multi-state in nature to capture available scale economies for reliable transmission services and to span the feasible market for bulk power transactions.

13.   Again, there is a substantial need to develop a multi-state, quasi-public agency to eliminate transmission bottlenecks to economical transfers of power. This transmission agency, in addition to serving the market-clearing function, would also need to serve the other public purpose of siting new transmission facilities in a safe, aesthetically acceptable and environmentally sound manner. See Linke and Schuler (1988) for a detailed discussion of the technical, economic, and policy issues.

14.   This idea is attributable to Leonard Hyman.

15.   The existing regional Electricity Reliability Councils were established to coordinate interstate cooperation to improve system reliability and avoid major blackouts, but these voluntary collaborations do not emphasize economic matters like insuring competitive supplies.

16.   See Hobbs and Schuler (1986) for a discussion of the limited competitive forces that might arise with deregulated distribution systems.

17.   Early similar and still relevant analyses of revised structures for the electricity supply industry were performed a decade ago in collaboration with Benjamin Hobbs and were supported in part by National Science Foundation Grant PRA 7913072. A recent analysis of needed regulatory changes in New York State to accommodate and respond to evolving market structures for electricity was supported by the NYS Energy Office.

REFERENCES

Hobbs, B., and Schuler, R. "Deregulating the Distribution of Electricity" *Journal of Regional Science* 26 no. 2 (1986): 235-265.

Hyman, L., and Kelley, D. "U.S. Utility Industry: Measuring Competitive Risk." Report. New York: Merrill Lynch & Co., August 23, 1993.

Linke, S., and Schuler, R.E. "Electric-Energy-Transmission Technology: The Key to Bulk-Power-Supply Policies." *Annual Review of Energy.* 13 (1988): 23-45.

Neuberg, L.G. "Two Issues in the Municipal Ownership of Electric Power Distribution Systems" *The Bell Journal of Economics.* 8 (1977): 303-323.

Weiss, L.W. "Anti-Trust in the Electric Power Industry." in A. Phillips, ed. *Promoting Competition in Regulated Markets.* Washington DC: Brookings, 1975.

21

Pacific Gas & Electric Company Case Study

Jackalyne Pfannenstiel, Steven Kline, and
Kathleen Treleven

On the surface, the regulation of Pacific Gas and Electric's (PG&E)
electric business would seem to raise few, if any, federalist issues.
Indeed, jurisdictional questions have been less pressing for the California utilities than for those in many other states, where multi-state
and federal/state matters affect virtually every rate proceeding. Our
utility electric business is wholly conducted within the borders of California and we have a single state regulator (for ratemaking), the California Public Utilities Commission. Yet, for PG&E the questions of
regulatory jurisdiction and regional coordination are becoming
increasingly thorny as the traditional "regulatory rules of the game"
have not adapted to the significant changes occurring in this industry.

PG&E is the nation's largest combined gas and electric utility,
serving 4.4 million electric customers in a 94,000 square mile service
area that stretches from the middle of California to the Oregon border
and from the Pacific Ocean almost to Nevada. In 1993, we sold 75.7
billion kilowatt hours of electricity and met a peak demand of 14,607
MW. Our electric business brought in $7.9 billion of revenue in 1993.
Gas sales and deliveries produced another $2.7 billion in revenue.
PG&E Enterprises, a wholly owned unregulated subsidiary, includes
U.S. Generating Co. (a joint venture with the Bechtel Power Corporation), which is presently the largest constructor of independent power
plants in the nation.[1]

In 1993, to provide electricity to our utility customers, we generated 65 percent of our energy from our own power plants (and of that,
34 percent was natural-gas fired, 30 percent was nuclear, and the rest
was divided between 26 percent of hydro and 10 percent of geothermal), purchased 25 percent from "qualifying facilities," and purchased

10 percent from other utility sources. Of the purchases from other utilities, about 35 percent came from out-of-state sources, primarily from the Pacific Northwest.

EVOLUTION OF THE REGIONAL SYSTEM

PG&E was incorporated in 1905, but predecessor companies provided utility service to Californians as early as 1852. PG&E's immediate forerunners were the San Francisco Gas and Electric Company and the California Gas and Electric Company, which merged in 1905 to create PG&E. PG&E continued to merge with many other small- and medium-sized utilities companies until reaching its present boundaries in the early 1940s. In 1911, amidst this merger activity, PG&E's chief regulator, the California Public Utilities Commission (then the State Railroad Commission) was voted into existence.

Several older municipal utilities in PG&E's control area maintained their independence as PG&E consolidated companies around them. Other municipal utilities in the area were formed via municipalization, chiefly in the 1910s and early 1920s.

In its early years, a substantial part of PG&E's power came from hydroelectric plants in the Sierra, which had been converted from hydraulic gold mining facilities. Supporting power was supplied by steam electric plants located in the load centers in the Central Valley and along the coast.

From the end of the Depression through the 1960s, PG&E's loads and resources grew tremendously, in step with California's own growth from the wartime economy and the post-war boom. New fossil resources were built rapidly, with fuel supplied by California's gas fields and, eventually, out-of-state gas fields (a Southwest pipeline opened in 1950 and a Canadian pipeline in 1961). In the 1960s, PG&E began to add more diverse sources of generation, starting with nuclear plants in 1957 and 1963, geothermal plants in 1960, and a 500-kV line to purchase excess power from the Northwest in 1968. This trend continued in the 1970s and 1980s, as PG&E built pumped storage, two large nuclear units, and more geothermal plants and began to integrate qualifying facility (QF) power purchases.

The regional scope of PG&E's business has been shaped by the available resources, the steady growth in demand in the state, and PG&E's success in completing mergers with other systems. The borders between PG&E and its neighboring utilities have also been influenced by natural geographic patterns, such as transportation corridors and mountain ranges. PG&E's system is interconnected, physically and contractually, with the other West Coast utilities, with most purchases and exchanges flowing north and south rather than east and west.

CURRENT REGULATORY STRUCTURE

The California Public Utility Commission (CPUC) is our primary regulator, setting the retail prices for electricity and natural gas according to conventional marginal cost-of-service ratemaking principles. In addition, the CPUC directs the process through which we will procure new generating resources in the future.

There is a second regulatory body in California, the California Energy Commission (CEC), which has a myriad of responsibilities related to energy use and the siting of electric generation facilities. The CEC was set up by legislative mandate in 1974, in part prompted by concern that the CPUC was unable to comprehensively control electric resource development.[2] The CEC's responsibility most relevant to the current discussion is its jurisdiction over the siting of thermal power plants of more than 50 MW. In order to determine the need for plants that it might be asked to site, the CEC prepares and adopts an "official" biennial forecast of the demand for electricity in California and the amount of utility-specific resources that are needed to meet that demand. It has been a number of years since the CEC has been called on by a utility to site a plant; however, the CEC has allowed a number of non-utility plants to be sited in the interim.

In practice, the CPUC uses the CEC's adopted demand forecasts as a "starting point" for its own process through which it decides whether the California investor-owned utilities will need additional generating capacity within the subsequent eight years. The need assessment is highly analytical and heavily litigated. If need is found, the CPUC administers a bid for that capacity. Under current rules, only QFs are able to bid.

This relatively new bidding process has finally completed one cycle, with bids totalling 1,500 MW awarded in mid-1994. Moreover, widespread dissatisfaction with the process is expected to lead to significant changes in the bidding process. Although some parties want to modify the basic structure by changes such as eliminating the CEC's and the CPUC's dual review of need, others, including PG&E, would like to move away from a regulatory process and rely instead on negotiating for the best source from a broad range of resource alternatives. CPUC oversight would continue but the utilities would be freed from substantial micro-management.

PG&E is also regulated by the Federal Energy Regulatory Commission (FERC) in several very important ways. First, it is FERC that has jurisdiction over sales of power for resale and over transmission in interstate commerce. PG&E owns over 18,000 miles of transmission facilities and last year wheeled about 16,000 GWh of power for other entities. Second, FERC-regulated wholesale transactions, although small relative to the retail business, brought in about $242 million in revenue in 1992. Also, it is FERC that has the responsibility, under Part I of the Federal Power Act (originally the Federal Water Power Act of 1920), for licensing and re-licensing hydroelectric facilities. Currently, PG&E's 3,900-MW of hydroelectric power plants represent the least cost resource on our system, but the cost of relicensing requirements may narrow that advantage.

PG&E's nuclear power plant, Diablo Canyon, is also federally regulated both for licensing and safety by the Nuclear Regulatory Commission (NRC).

The Changing Federal-State Relationship

The federal-state relationships that characterize the current regulatory situation evolved over time to meet the needs of the industry and the public of a different era. Until recent years, for PG&E, the impact of tensions between federal and state regulation has not been substantial. Where tensions have occurred, the focus has tended to be on PG&E's natural gas business, especially relative to the importation and purchase of Canadian gas through Pacific Gas Transmission, a PG&E affiliate.

By the end of the 1980s, however, the industry, and the public's demands on it, were fundamentally different from the world that the state and federal regulatory agencies were designed to address. The changes were largely brought about not by direct regulatory or legislative mandate, but through the emergence of powerful market forces. These market forces arose through two important pieces of broad energy-related legislation developed in 1978: the Public Utility Regulatory Policies Act (PURPA) and the Natural Gas Policy Act (NGPA).

The implementation of PURPA in California involved the adoption of an aggressive methodology for deriving what came to be called "avoided costs," the cost to the utility of energy that, *but for* the purchase from a new resource, the utility would generate or purchase from another source. Based on very high forecasts of fossil fuel prices and the use of standard offer contracts, PURPA created a substantial non-utility generation sector of QFs, which today comprises approximately 25 percent of PG&E's energy supplies (see Table 21.1). On the gas side, extension by the FERC throughout the 1980s of the deregulation principles embodied in the NGPA have created a competitive

Table 21.1
Qualifying Facilities (QFs), 1993 Statistics

Capacity under contract	6,000 MW
Operational capacity	4,600 MW
Power delivered	21,303 GWh
Payment to QFs	
Energy	$1,094 million
Capacity	$503 million
Average price paid per kWh (Energy plus capacity)	7.5 ¢/kWh
By technology	
Cogeneration	60%
Wind	18%
Solid waste/biomass	13%
Hydro	5%
Geothermal	3%
Solar	Less than 1%
By contract type	
Standard Offer 1 and 3 (short run)	15%
Standard Offer 2 (fixed capacity)	21%
Standard Offer 4 (fixed capacity, some fixed energy)	64%

Source: Pacific Gas & Electric (1993).

natural gas industry structure today that has been vertically disintegrated.

CURRENT ISSUES—REGULATORY DECISION-MAKING EXAMPLES

The regulatory world that resulted from the energy legislation of 1978 was significantly different from the world proceeding it. These changes and their impacts can be clearly seen by reference to three areas of considerable urgency to PG&E: natural gas pipeline issues, wholesale transmission access, and retail transmission access.

The Mojave Natural Gas Pipeline

One possible model for the regulatory issues the electric business may be facing in the future is playing out now in PG&E's natural gas business.

The Mojave Pipeline Company (a subsidiary of El Paso Natural Gas, an interstate pipeline company) is planning to extend its existing pipeline up the Central Valley into Northern California, specifically to compete with PG&E to serve a few large industrial customers. There is a fundamental question about the regulatory jurisdiction over the pipeline, because this extension is built to function effectively as an *intrastate* distributor, but does include a small section of non-California pipeline extending into Arizona and connecting to El Paso. The CPUC and FERC have both asserted jurisdiction.

This jurisdictional claim becomes a significant issue because some customers have indicated that their interest in Mojave stems largely from their desire to avoid CPUC regulation and to attempt to secure lower, and more stable, gas rates. The loss of these customers would result in significant stranded investment for PG&E. We have estimated that the remaining gas customers would have to carry about an extra $200 to $300 million in higher rates over the next fifteen years should the pipeline be built.

It takes little imagination to apply this situation to the market for electricity where customers seek to use their market power to gain price concessions from the serving utility and its regulators or, failing that, secure other sources of electricity. In the electric market, the more worrisome concern is not a competing transmission line being built (a direct analogy to the Mojave experience), but rather the loss of some of the market for which we now procure or generate electricity, even if we continue to provide those customers with transmission service. The key future jurisdictional question arising out of the growing competition in the electric supply industry is the control of access to utilities' transmission systems.

Wholesale Transmission Access

Although the Natural Gas Act of 1938 distinguishes between the *inter-* and *intrastate* transportation of natural gas, and limits the jurisdiction of the FERC to interstate transmission, the jurisdictional break on the electric side is not so clear. The Federal Power Act of 1935 (FPA) gives the FERC jurisdiction over "the transmission of electric energy in interstate commerce" and the sale of electric energy at wholesale in interstate commerce. Because electricity flows according to the laws of physics, and it is impossible to determine whether electricity flowing on an interstate grid (or an intrastate grid interconnected with an interstate grid) originated inside or outside the state, FERC has exclusive jurisdiction over all wholesale sales by investor-owned utilities and over the rates, terms, and conditions for virtually all transmission services, whether or not the points of receipt and delivery under the contract are in the same state.

Thus, as to *electricity sales*, the FPA's distinction between retail and wholesale means that any sales of electricity by PG&E to its retail customers in our franchised service territory are regulated by the CPUC and not by FERC, whereas sales to other utilities, whether investor-owned utilities (such as Southern California Edison), publicly owned utilities (such as municipal utilities like the Sacramento Municipal Utility District), or federal power marketing agencies (like the Western Area Power Administration), are regulated by the FERC.

Transmission service, however, is a different matter—transmission service is federally regulated if it is in interstate commerce (i.e., if electricity flows at any time on an interstate grid) without regard to whether the service is to another utility or a retail customer. Of course, when transmission service is bundled for a utility's native retail load with other services such as the generation and procurement of power, distribution, energy efficiency, and other customer services, the revenue required to support that transmission function is a component of the rates regulated by the state.

Until the enactment of the Energy Policy Act of 1992, FERC had only very limited authority to order a utility to provide transmission service, and had never exercised it. But Title 7 of the Energy Policy Act changed all that. The act empowers FERC to require transmission-owning utilities to provide transmission services, including adding more transmission capacity, if needed, to other *wholesale* market participants (utilities, munis, and the newly created "exempt whole-sale generators") at rates that are "just and reasonable" and will recover all of the transmitting utility's costs. The intent of this "whole-sale access" provision is to facilitate development of a competitive generation market, in conjunction with the act's reform of the Public Utility Holding Company Act (PUHCA).

In the near term, although the impact of this wholesale access provision on PG&E will result in continued growth in PG&E's whole-sale transmission service, it will probably not result in significant increases, because PG&E has opened up its transmission system to wholesale customers to a large extent already. Starting in the late 1970s, after extensive discussions with municipal entities, PG&E agreed to provide significantly expanded transmission access to the munis. As the desire of transmission-dependent utilities (generally publicly owned) to access power supply market opportunities has grown, so too has the transmission service PG&E provides. PG&E's transmission system currently delivers about 4,600 MW to wholesale loads and 14,000 MW to native loads.

Another factor in the continued moderate growth of transmission volume in our area is the Western Systems Power Pool (WSPP) agreement, a once experimental, now permanent arrangement among nearly fifty utilities in the fourteen western states, British Columbia, and Baja California, which allows its members to voluntarily buy and sell surplus power and transmission capacity. Prices are negotiable under a ceiling approved by FERC. The advantage of the WSPP arrangement is that it creates a multi-lateral enabling agreement for purchases and sales and allows for flexibility in pricing for transmission services, and sales of energy and capacity, of up to one year in duration. The WSPP has been well received by regulators; however, one jurisdictional issue has not been totally satisfactory. FERC's review of the prices charged by the investor-owned utility members of the WSPP, but not the publicly owned members, does create what some parties feel is not a level playing field.

Although a significant expansion of transmission capacity access in northern California is not an expected outcome of the Energy Policy Act, many expect that a long-run effect may be to ease or simplify the contractual issues that currently impede the ability of entities to obtain access. It is possible that FERC's new mandatory transmission access authority may induce utilities to develop open access transmission tariffs to simplify wholesale transmission contracting and avoid case-by-case negotiations or FERC adjudications. In addition, two other important *non-federal* forums may lead to mechanisms that will enhance and streamline transmission access for various parties in the state while protecting the interest of the transmission-owning utilities and their native load customers.

In 1990, the CPUC launched a proceeding intending to develop rules for its jurisdictional utilities (PG&E, Southern California Edison, and San Diego Gas & Electric) to provide transmission access for non-utility power, in order to ensure the development of a competitive electricity generation sector in California. The proceeding considers both the access needs and the costs that may be borne by a utility buying non-utility power; and the service required by a non-utility generator that needs transmission service to access a utility purchaser. A 1993 decision in the first phase of the case approved a joint agreement among the proceeding participants (utilities and QFs) to provide transmission access for the initial round of bidding in the subsequent resource procurement auction. The second phase will consider broader long-term transmission access and cost issues.[3]

PG&E has also been exploring regional transmission groups and voluntary transmission associations. As a result of those efforts, on May 20, 1994, the nation's first RTG, the Western Regional Transmission Association (WRTA) was filed with the FERC. The more than thirty WRTA Charter Members, which include PG&E, the California Municipal Utilities Association, and the Independent Energy Producers Association, represent a broad spectrum of industry participants from across the western states. We believe groups like WRTA will play a significant role in providing coordinated planning of transmission capacity in the future.

Retail Transmission Access

The same title of the Energy Policy Act of 1992 that provides for *wholesale* access also prohibits the FERC from ordering a utility to provide access on its transmission lines to another entity wishing to sell power to a retail customer. There is considerable uncertainty about whether there is state authority to order *retail* access. The act's provision allowing for the ordering of wholesale, but not retail, access, was a political compromise among many parties, ranging from advocates of wide-open access wishing to maximize the numbers of buyers and sellers, to those who believed no enhancement of access was needed at all.

Regardless of the states' ability to order retail wheeling, because FERC's jurisdiction over the rates, terms, and conditions of transmission service is not limited by the Federal Power Act to wholesale service, and because most retail transmission service will be on a path interconnected with an interstate transmission system, FERC probably would have exclusive jurisdiction on the rates, terms, and conditions of retail transmission services as well as wholesale. Although this apparent discrepancy is of rather academic interest as long as retail access is a distant concept, it takes on more immediate interest as some states begin to contemplate "experimenting" with retail access. In early 1994, the Michigan Public Service Commission proposed just such an experiment, followed in April of that year by a California Public Utilities Commission Order with potentially even more profound implications. After a year-long process of hearings and comments, the CPUC released a proposal to dramatically restructure California's electric services industry. The centerpiece of that proposal is the availability of "direct access" (retail wheeling) commencing in 1996 for the largest retail customers. Under the CPUC's proposed schedule, the smallest residential consumer could choose an electric power supplier by the year 2002.

One question is whether FERC will enter this battlefield at all. If FERC has jurisdiction, it must exercise it. Perhaps FERC will take the non-interventionist approach of approving all terms and conditions proposed by the state regulatory agency, since the latter historically has had purview over the transmission investments related to serving the utility's native load. Countering this supposition is the FERC's apparent willingness to reject many voluntarily agreed-on transmission rates, on economic grounds.

FERC's fundamental interest is that the investor-owned seller's transmission rate and the terms and conditions for the services it offers be economically just and reasonable. FERC has much less reason to be concerned about the end-user, or about the financial health of the utility, than do state regulatory agencies, both by their differing charters and by the political realities of the state regulators' proximity to their constituents. The stranded investment that FERC policy decisions may create, whether on the gas or on the electric side, and whether the financial impacts flow to the shareholders or remaining customers of the utility, are of much more concern to state regulators.

THE FEDERALIST QUESTION

With the fundamental restructuring of the industry, it is an appropriate time to consider when *should* the states and when *should* the federal government regulate public utilities, or more specifically, electric utilities. To explore this question we need to examine the basic purposes served by regulation in the present era. To us, there are two reasons to regulate utilities: to ensure adequacy of supply and to secure the necessary supply at the least cost. To our way of thinking, the two other reasons for regulation that parties might raise—

preventing utilities from extracting monopoly rents and protecting the environment—are appropriately considered "folded in" to the concept of providing supply at "least cost." Our emphasis on low-cost supply is admittedly different from the FERC's objective as mandated by the FPA—to ensure that the service provider recovers only its costs plus a *reasonable* return on investment—but transmission rates set by this objective will facilitate obtaining least-cost supplies.

How can adequate electric supply be assured? We believe that this is predominantly a state concern, helped, in part, by the FERC's encouragement of increased wholesale transmission access and by regional transmission groups that should streamline capacity expansion decisions. Similar to the gas world, vertical integration continues to become a less necessary component of our business, and our supplies are likely to be procured from a wider range of suppliers than a decade or two ago.[4] Moreover, our customers, neighbors, and competitors need to use the same integrated system to ensure reliable supply, and methods need to be in place so that the transaction costs associated with moving electricity are not insurmountable. As the rules for coordinated transmission planning and wholesale transmission access become more streamlined, whether through state actions, regional transmission groups, FERC rulings and actions on open access transmission tariffs and applications for transmission service, or a combination of these, the ability of many wholesale buyers and sellers to meet and compete should, if done well, improve the breadth and reliability of supply. Although what we buy and how much reliability we seek remains properly the concern of our state regulators, we do look to FERC as the principal entity to *facilitate* the transmission of electric supply.

How can we be certain that supplies and their transport are least cost? This same enhanced wholesale access that provides us and our neighbors with increased sources of supply, can, when radically out of balance, provide "too much" supply and cause stranded investment, which, if large enough, harms the utility, its customers, and society at large. Finding the balance is a difficult economic task that can be easily politicized by "forum shopping," as the Mojave experience illustrates. Were electric retail wheeling to be immediately available to all customers, the migration of large customers to cheaper sources of supply might lead to uneconomic bypass and results that are not societally optimal, when the concerns of all customers and stockholders, environmental quality, and other factors are taken into account. Although we need a transmission system that is open and fair (and FERC can provide that), we do not wish to see access opened up so quickly and so broadly that we lose the customers for whom we have procured resources under a long-standing *obligation to serve.*

CONCLUSIONS

The electric industry is entering a new era, one in which the market plays a far larger part. Both our state and federal regulators recognize that change and are cognizant of the balance that is required. We hope that as the new electric utility paradigm is shaped, the state will be the dominant force helping us to obtain adequate supply for our customers and to ensure that the supply and its transport are least cost. The state regulators, after all, are closest to the customers and to the affected businesses. That proximity ensures close attention to important allocational questions of benefits and costs. We look to the federal regulators to help us and others obtain a wide variety of supplies by facilitating the smooth operation of an integrated transmission system, and ensuring that electric transmission rates are just, reasonable, and not unduly discriminatory.[5]

NOTES

1. To avoid affiliate transaction complications, U.S. Generating Co. does not build any projects to serve load in our northern and central California service territory.

2. For example, the CPUC has no authority over municipal generation resources.

3. California Energy Commission, Order Instituting Investigation, I.90-09-050.

4. In fact, PG&E has even offered to remove itself from the new generation business in our own service territory, as part of a *quid pro quo* for a more market-based procurement process than the current complicated and costly system.

5. The views expressed in this case study are those of the authors and do not represent the policies of PG&E.

REFERENCES

California Energy Commission (CEC). *1993 Electricity Report*. Sacramento, CA: CEC, January 1994.

California Public Utility Commission (CPUC), Division of Strategic Planning. "California's Electric Services Industry: Perspectives on the Past, Strategic for the Future." White paper. San Francisco, CA: CPUC, February 1993.

Pacific Gas and Electric (PG&E). *Financial and Statistical Report*. San Francisco, CA: PG&E, 1993.

22

Comment on the Pacific Gas & Electric Company Case

Lyna L. Wiggins

When should public utilities be regulated by the state and federal governments? In the Pacific Gas and Electric (PG&E) case study the authors provide two rationales: to ensure adequacy of supply and to secure the necessary supply at the least cost. The authors "fold in" two additional reasons—prevention of the extraction of monopoly rents and protection of the environment. Both of these rationales for regulation seem valid and reasonable. Here I wish to consider them as goals toward which we might agree to aspire.

Over the past twenty years, topics directly and indirectly related to these two goals have generated an exceedingly large number of hours of analysis and discussion by utility staff and management, regulatory staff and decision makers, and public interveners in the state of California. Have these sometimes painful hours in hearing rooms been well spent? Do we now have a better understanding of the complexity of integrated resource planning? Can planning and regulation be expected to do a better job meeting these two goals than the market? Here I will argue that all three of these questions can be answered affirmatively. To construct this argument I will take a historical perspective.

HISTORICAL PERSPECTIVE: DEMAND

Going back twenty years, we find PG&E staff and the California Energy Commission (CEC) staff spending many hours engaged in discussions about methods of demand forecasting. This was the beginning of the process of adopting an "official" biennial forecast of the demand for electricity in California. Long-range forecasting is never an easy exercise, and this was no exception.

The initial models were primitive by today's standards. The utilities were using econometric models, and the CEC was developing more disaggregated end-use models. These end-use models estimated final consumption by appliance type, multiplied the consumption estimates by the number of each appliance, and then summed over all appliances. The initial data sets for the more disaggregated end-use models were incomplete. Discussion focused on the "too aggregate" approach of the utilities' econometric models, and the lack of price elasticities and the weak data of the CEC's end-use model.

Hindsight is a great advantage, and looking back we find that all of the parties' forecasts from this period were much too high. Later discussions would focus on who was least wrong. Yet over the intervening years, we can see that both the data and the models improved. I believe we can also say that the sharing of information and learning about others' views and modeling approaches created a higher level of consensus and respect between the parties.

HISTORICAL PERSPECTIVE: SUPPLY

In that now seemingly distant past, the supply side hearings focused on evaluating alternative technologies and coming up with conclusions about those that were "preferred." Much of the environmental activism of the period was reflected in the regulatory bias against particular technologies (i.e., nuclear and coal) and against large facilities. The influence of those advocating the "soft energy path" was reflected in favorable rankings of wind, geothermal, and solar technologies. During this period, a systems planner for one California utility described his supply plan to me: "We're throwing lots and lots of balls in the air and keeping them up there. We hope the regulators will let some of them start to fall, and when they do fall we hope we can actually land them somewhere on the ground."

It was the actual landing on the ground—the prolonged siting processes and "not in my backyard" (NIMBY) opposition—that solved the problem of oversupply that might have resulted from the regulatory approval of those too-high demand forecasts. Regulators and utilities alike discovered that this new environmentally sensitive era created siting constraints which gave the supply side as large a range of uncertainty as the demand-side forecasts. As time passed, opposition arose not just to proposed large-scale base-load plants, but also to additions to geothermal facilities, wind farms, and other renewable energy technologies.

HISTORICAL PERSPECTIVE: INCREASED COMPETITION

The next regulatory forecasting error of major importance to our story comes in the 1980s. Under Public Utility Regulatory Policies Act (PURPA) regulations, standard offers were developed by the California Public Utilities Commission (CPUC) to simplify and standardize a process for the qualifying facility (QF) community. The response to these offers was, to say the least, a surprise to all concerned. At one point there was approximately 16,000 MW of potential QF supply on the books—mostly gas-fired cogeneration. The regulatory correction in this case was the institution of bidding procedures to control supply, yet the siting uncertainties may still dominate the equation.

Again we were saved from the onerous appearance of oversupply by the effective NIMBYism of Californians. You thought that a large coal plant was difficult to site in California? Try a municipal solid waste (MSW) facility or a large gas-fired cogeneration plant in a gentrifying neighborhood! The size factor became less of an issue as it became clear that it was often almost as hard to site small decentralized facilities—being hung for lots of little lambs was not all that different than being hung for a sheep. Small facilities often took just as long to site as large ones. The new model seemed to be: "Lots of actors throwing competitive balls in the air, but only a few with real places on the ground. If they do find the ground, they mostly bounce."

THE SPATIAL COMPONENT OF THE UTILITY SYSTEMS PLANNING PROBLEM

Can we assume that market forces alone can land us a "least-cost" supply of electricity in the future? I believe that this spatial component of supply is worth another look. I have noticed that most economists do not think spatially, and the reality of the siting process is often absent from their analyses. Yet I believe the reality of finding places on the ground is central to utility systems planning. We have seen that there is tremendous uncertainty in forecasting demand. There is also tremendous uncertainty in forecasting what is likely to be least-cost supply in the future. Remember oil shale and the Synfuels Corporation and the Energy Mobilization Board of the 1970s? In a period of supply crisis, all stops came out to expedite the siting process for large facilities.

Can we imagine something similar happening in the future? There is a tendency for all parties to believe that the near future will be similar to the recent past. It is this belief that underlies our forecasting models. When this assumption fails we are often in a crisis situation. We are fairly able to plan and take action during a crisis. We seem less able to adequately plan ahead for emergency management and uncertain contingencies. Although our models and analyses are often based on a foundation assumption of rational planning, our actions are more often based on incremental planning ("muddling through").

In a similar crisis to the oil disruptions of the 1970s, we would undoubtedly respond differently today. Yet how confident are we that this crisis management would be successful? How about a DSM Mobilization Board? Or a new organization called "Friends of Small Cogeneration Units"?

Let's face it, our track record in forecasting and contingency planning has not been great. Are we as confident today of our estimates of QF supply and of our demand-side management (DSM) and conservation program numbers as we were of oil prices and the demand for oil shale in the 1970s? Actually, I do believe that we have learned a lot from these lessons of the past two decades, that we are now much more able to analyze alternatives, and that we are more cognizant of the importance of our ability to respond quickly and flexibly to changing economics and political structures.

CONCLUSIONS

At this point you may be thinking, "Hum, you certainly haven't made much of a case for continuing in the current mode of planning and regulation. If we've made such a mess of forecasting and planning, why not let the market take over?" About some products I would agree. About electricity generation and transmission I am not so sure. The market can indeed respond quickly to changes in demand for some products. But in the case of electricity generation, the participants in the market would need to put capital-intensive facilities on the ground. Shipping production to Asia is not in the cards here.

Let us suppose for a minute that the market will work here and that generation and transmission facilities are placed quickly where it is easiest to find places on the ground. What kind of siting patterns are likely to emerge? We are likely to be in for:

- remote sites that need additional transmission capability (And if there's anything more difficult to site than a power plant, it's transmission lines!);
- areas where there is little public opposition because of economic pressure (leading to some significant environmental equity issues);

- existing sites (assuming they are available and that the scrap-and-build economies work); or

- many quite small facilities of the "easiest-to-site" technology (but which cumulatively may have significant regional impacts and may not add to supply diversity).

To meet the two goals of ensuring adequacy of supply and securing necessary supply at least cost, I do have more faith in planning than in the market. I believe that we have learned from our modeling and planning experiences of the past twenty years. I think we are better able to discuss together the possible ranges of uncertainty in demand and supply, and to evaluate alternative "what-if" scenarios. We have learned a significant amount about integrated resource planning. We now have data on DSM and conservation programs, and on the success rates of QF generation. We have worked together to construct "environmental adders" and on designing bidding processes for supply from competitive parties.

I advocate that we consider continued planning and regulation of the supply mix to hedge against all these uncertainties and to ensure diversity in:

- location (that we use some "fair share" basis and revisit the "site banking" proposals from the 1970s);

- size (that we preserve large base-load facilities as well as small facilities);

- technology (that we don't put all of our eggs into any one basket); and

- innovation (that we refocus on and fund well technological R&D).

Suppose that we can agree to a goal of a rich supply mix to help us hedge against uncertainties, and that we also choose to agree that this should be implemented through planning and regulation. Where should the boundary fall between state and federal regulation? Different parties draw different lines. As a planner, I would suggest that the logical regulatory unit is neither the federal nor the state government. For demand forecasting, supply planning, integrated resource planning, and particularly for transmission planning, the logical spatial unit is the region. Consider the diversity goals stated in the last paragraph. With respect to flexibility of site selection and fair share allocations, a multiple state region is clearly the appropriate scale. When we consider the need for a mix of large and small facilities, the region again gives us enough space to look for good sites. To obtain a rich resource mix across many technologies, we again need a large region to cover all of our bases. Finally, groups of utilities sharing resources are more able to invest in risky new technology.

The reliability councils are already in place and have the right scale to do the planning and modeling required. Member utilities might cooperate in staffing the technical modeling areas needed to support planning. A federal role might still be required to provide policy, oversight, and some uniformity between regions. The states might continue in their historic ratesetting roles and as participants in the planning process at the regional level. This picture is admittedly idealistic, as we seem to be singularly unable to agree to plan regionally in the United States. However, we might want to take this opportunity, within an environment of increased deregulation, to ask what really might be the appropriate geographic scale for utility systems planning. In a complex world, considering what it may take to provide adequate supply while meeting multiple and conflicting public goals, this may lead us to attempt cooperation across state boundaries.

As a planner, I have always admired the electric utility industry for taking a longer-term view of the world. Partly, the necessity for this longer view came from working with capital-intensive facilities with long lead times. On the other hand, taking the short-term view of the market may lead us down paths we cannot currently foresee—and paths that may leave us no alternative for action but that of crisis management.

23

Tennessee Valley Authority Case Study

Mary Sharpe Hayes

The Tennessee Valley Authority (TVA) serves portions of seven states, yet it does not report to state utility regulators. Neither does it answer to shareholders as investor-owned utilities must, because it is a public enterprise. It is a multi-purpose organization that does much more than simply provide electricity to the Tennessee River Valley. At its inception, it was charged with the planning for the proper use, conservation, and development of the natural resources of the Tennessee River drainage basin and its adjoining territory.

This chapter examines the evolution of the TVA system, the nature of its decision-making processes, and the current set of issues facing the organization. The TVA occupies a unique position in the spectrum of case studies; as a unitary public agency it differs dramatically from decentralized and privately owned systems. As a self-regulated federal enterprise it enjoys substantial autonomy in its decision making, while living within important legislative and political constraints.

EVOLUTION OF THE TVA SYSTEM

TVA was created in 1933 following a nine-year battle led by Senator George Norris from Nebraska, who was especially concerned about improving the quality of rural life. At the time of TVA's creation, the Tennessee Valley was one of the poorest regions of the United States, with per capita income only 45 percent of the national average (Mills, 1987, p. 205). As a result of the work that has been performed, TVA has often been viewed as the catalyst for improving the quality of life in the Tennessee Valley region.

The agency's mandate was to serve the people of the valley by supplying electricity, stimulating economic growth, protecting the environment, and providing recreation. It developed in the crucible of the Great Depression amid widespread disillusionment with the performance of private enterprise as an engine of economic development. This opened the door to public power projects like those of the TVA (Callahan, 1980, pp. 24–30).

The same issues that affect energy policy today were manifest in the debate over the TVA: Should government be in the power business? Should planners play a role in economic decision making? How should equity and efficiency goals be balanced? In a message given to Congress in 1933, President Roosevelt synthesized a bold vision, stating that the TVA was to be formed as a "corporation clothed with the power of government but possessed of the flexibility and initiative of private enterprise."[1]

A three-member board was appointed by the president to run the corporation, with one of the board members serving as chairman. Unlike other agencies of the federal government, the board was given full power to direct the exercise of all the powers of the corporation. The TVA was charged with the "broadest duty of planning for the proper use, conservation, and development of the natural resources of the Tennessee River drainage basin and its adjoining territory for the general social and economic welfare of the Nation."[2]

Physical System

The service area of the TVA encompasses Tennessee and parts of Alabama, Georgia, Kentucky, Mississippi, North Carolina, and Virginia. Combined, the Tennessee River watershed area and the TVA power service area comprise a region of 201 counties with an area of 91,000 square miles and a population of approximately 8 million.

The Tennessee River is 652 miles long and is the nation's fifth-largest river system. This river is a source of transportation for more than 40 million tons of cargo shipped each year.

In terms of capacity and energy production, the TVA power system is one of the largest in the nation and is the tenth-largest electric utility in the world.

The TVA developed its physical system in three main phases, with each phase being driven by a particular need. The first phase was driven by the need to bring the river under control and prevent the annual floods which devastated the valley. In addition, hydro power was needed to generate electricity for homes and businesses throughout the region. The TVA began construction of its first dam five months after the agency was created. These dams were multi-purpose (navigation, flood control, recreation, economic development, and power), which allowed for significantly lower costs than if the dams had been built for a single purpose. There was organizational congruence during this period; building dams served the multiple goals of the TVA. The agency chose to undertake rural electrification after some hydro facilities had been completed.[3]

The second phase of construction resulted from an increased demand for power, which could not be fully supplied from hydro sources. The TVA built its first fossil fuel plant in 1941 to provide an additional source of generation. Defense activities including the top-secret Manhattan Project burgeoned during World War II, and construction to satisfy national security needs proceeded rapidly. Projects of the Atomic Energy Commission (AEC) and other federal agencies were key drivers of load growth during the 1950s, 1960s, and 1970s, and still play a role today. Eventually, twelve coal-fired plants were constructed. These fossil plants currently provide over half of TVA's total generating capacity.

Although decisions to construct fossil plants allowed demand to be met, they also created a new series of problems that would have to be addressed in the future. The rising cost of coal in the 1960s spurred the need to raise electric rates. In addition, environmental issues, such as clean air and surface mining, came to the forefront.

The third phase of construction was spurred by rapidly rising coal costs in the 1960s. As a result the TVA began an ambitious nuclear construction program in 1966 to meet projected system load growth. At the height of the construction program, the TVA had seventeen nuclear units either under construction or in commercial operation at seven plant sites.

By the 1980s, the previously expected load growth had not occurred. TVA canceled construction of four nuclear units in 1982, and canceled four more units in 1984. By 1985, the TVA elected to shut down its three-unit Browns Ferry Nuclear Plant and its two-unit Sequoyah Nuclear Plant because of an increasing number of safety, technical, operational, and management problems. After correcting these problems through extensive review and reorganization of the nuclear program, both units at Sequoyah were restarted in 1988 and one unit at Browns Ferry was restarted in 1991.

Currently, the TVA's power generating facilities include twenty-nine hydroelectric plants, twelve coal-fired plants, two licensed nuclear plants, one pumped storage hydroelectric plant, and four gas turbine facilities. The estimated dependable capacity for the system is as follows: hydroelectric capacity of approximately 5,224 MW; coal-fired capacity of approximately 16,057 MW; nuclear power capacity of approximately 5,491 MW; and gas turbine capacity of approximately 2,066 MW. Total generating capacity is approximately 28,838 MW.

Power is delivered to TVA customers over a transmission system of approximately 16,800 miles of lines, including 2,400 miles of extra-high-voltage (500,000 V) transmission lines.

The TVA system interconnects with fourteen neighboring utilities at numerous points, with various types of interchange arrangements with each system. The extent and types of interchange transactions depend on the characteristics of the systems' loads, the management policies of the systems, and other factors. TVA seeks to maximize efficiency through the use of these interchange agreements, and in doing so, these arrangements help minimize investments in facilities and increase reliability of services.

As part of the 1959 self-financing amendment to the TVA Act, a "fence" was placed around the TVA at the request of neighboring private utilities. The result is that the TVA and its distributors cannot directly or indirectly be a source of power supply outside the area supplied with TVA power on July 1, 1957. In addition, the TVA is only permitted to enter into exchange power arrangements in the fourteen generating organizations having such arrangements with the TVA on that date.

Customer Relationships

As set forth in its enabling legislation, the TVA is charged with providing a reliable, adequate supply of power at the lowest feasible rates.

TVA's customers are generally divided into three groups: distributors, directly served industries, and federal agencies. The agency sells approximately 85 percent of its power to local municipal and cooperative distributors, and the other 15 percent is sold to large directly served and federal customers. Five of the municipalities that purchase power from the TVA account for approximately 30 percent of total revenues each year. Because so many valley residents heat their homes with electricity, the TVA for many years had its highest peaks in winter. However, the widespread use of air-conditioning in summer has turned the TVA into a dual-peaking system. TVA's all-time winter peak exceeded 24,600 MW in December 1989, its all-time summer peak was 22,081 MW in July 1991, and its net generation totaled 121.7 billion kWh in fiscal year 1992.

TVA has entered into long-term wholesale power contracts with the 160 municipal and cooperative distributors.[4] TVA serves approximately fifty large industrial customers directly, rather than through a distributor.[5] Power is also sold to federal agencies under the same contract terms and rates as directly served industries. The TVA serves seven federal customers, accounting for approximately 5 percent of total revenue.

TVA is organized into customer service areas to focus attention on customer relationships with its 160 distributors. It also has a team of industrial representatives who work directly with the large industrial customers and federal agencies. In addition to its daily customer service activities, it has also undertaken new service and quality initiatives with all of its customers over the past few years.[6]

Conservation and load management have proven to be valuable as customer relations tools, as well as relatively flexible, inexpensive resources compared to other alternatives.[7] TVA's earliest efforts at demand-side management (DSM) were with its directly served industries. From the early years, the TVA encouraged such customers to contract for interruptible power. Industries doing so received a credit against the charges for firm power in exchange for agreeing to curtail use of the interruptible load, on the TVA's request, within five minutes of being notified. Over the years the TVA has added a number of interruptible power options from which industries can choose. Demand-side management will continue to play an important role in TVA's overall planning, with new programs under development to meet anticipated needs.

Non-Power Activities

Some of TVA's most well-known non-power programs include the Demonstration Farms, the tree seedling program, and various forestry and wildlife programs. In addition, the agency has created a number of recreational opportunities in the Tennessee Valley region. These efforts have resulted in a vast recreational area, which includes 11,000 miles of shoreline, thirty-six dam reservations, and 199 recreation sites. Campgrounds, picnic areas, boat launching ramps, and trails are available at many of these recreational sites.[8]

Another key program in the resource area is the National Fertilizer and Environmental Research Center (NFERC), located in Muscle Shoals, Alabama. This center is known throughout the world for its fertilizer research. It is estimated that the research and developments from NFERC are used in producing up to three-fourths of the fertilizers in this country. Today, the center is placing greater emphasis on environmental research and less on fertilizer development since most of the fertilizer objectives have already been achieved.

Sources of Revenue and Financing

From a financial standpoint, TVA programs fall into two categories. One category is the power program, which is self-supporting and self-liquidating. The other category consists of all non-power programs, including navigation, flood control, fertilizer development, and regional resources development.

Originally, most of the money needed for the construction of dams and steam plants was provided by congressional appropriations. However, a 1959 amendment to the TVA Act changed this provision. The 1959 amendment, along with subsequent amendments, authorizes the TVA to borrow up to $30 billion to finance the construction of power facilities. The TVA power borrowings consist of bonds, notes, and other evidences of indebtedness issued by the TVA as a federal agency, and are authorized by Section 15d of the TVA Act.

Principal and interest on the borrowings are payable solely from the TVA's net power proceeds. Power operating revenues continue to pay for all operating expenses. Remaining power revenues supplemented by the proceeds from borrowing provide most of the capital needed for additions to power plant and equipment. The 1959 amendment also provides for the TVA to make payments to the United States Treasury to repay $1 billion of the appropriations that were invested in the TVA power system, plus an annual return on the outstanding investment computed on the Treasury's average cost of borrowed money.

Federal appropriations to support TVA's non-power activities are made by Congress after the Office of Management and Budget and the Congressional Appropriations Committees have made a detailed examination of TVA's annual budget request. The appropriated funds can vary from year to year, but recent funding has been in the range of $135 million annually. Although the fertilizer development program is not operated for the purpose of producing income, substantial revenues are realized from the sale of fertilizers and are used to finance part of the operating expenses of the program. The remainder of the operating expenses of the program are financed from appropriations and proceeds derived from the sale of other property items. The other non-power programs depend almost entirely on appropriations for both operations and construction.

DECISION MAKING AT THE TVA

TVA is self-regulated by its Board of Directors, which has the ultimate power in making all decisions at the agency regarding both power and non-power programs. Because TVA is a not-for-profit entity, it can be customer focused, rather than focusing on a return to stockholders. Instead of having stockholders, the TVA views its power distributors, end-use customers, and other interested groups as its stakeholders. The Board of Directors can focus on balancing the needs of these stakeholders rather than providing a return to investors.

The TVA board's decisions and goals are in some ways similar to those of a regulatory commission—to maximize the benefits to ratepayers by minimizing the cost of producing electricity and other services.

Internal Decision Making

The TVA's Board of Directors is composed of three persons appointed for nine-year staggered terms, with one term expiring at each three-year interval. Ultimately, all decisions are voted on and confirmed by the board at monthly board meetings.

As explained by the congressmen who managed the TVA legislation on behalf of the House of Representatives in 1933, "We are fully persuaded that the full success of the Tennessee Valley development project will depend more upon the ability, vision, and executive capacity of the members of the board than upon legislative provisions. We have sought to set up a legislative framework, but not to encase it in a legislative straitjacket."[9]

With this power, the board carries out four major responsibilities:

- It establishes and reviews the results of TVA's general policies and programs.

- It approves the agency's annual budget and spending plan.

- It approves appointment of key managers and maintains an organization for carrying out TVA policies and programs.

- It approves activities of major importance to TVA or the public. In support of the board, there is a management structure that changes with the evolving needs of the agency.[10]

The total number of TVA employees is currently about 19,000, down from a high of 53,248 in 1980.[11]

In 1988 the agency made a dramatic change in its direction. Due to spiraling costs, the TVA's customers had been experiencing rate increases averaging 10 percent per year since 1965. By the late 1980s, some customers—including the city of Memphis, TVA's largest customer—were beginning to look elsewhere for their power supply.

Under new leadership, TVA took swift action to make fundamental changes. The Board of Directors set goals to hold rates constant, reduce overhead costs, and become more businesslike in day-to-day operations. To meet these goals, TVA reduced its total work force, trimming management layers and TVA programs.

Financial decisions have also been important. From 1960 to 1974, the TVA issued Evidences of Indebtedness in the public markets. In 1974, with the exception of its borrowings from the Treasury, the TVA borrowed solely from the Federal Financing Bank (FFB). Based on discussions with the Treasury, the TVA decided to break away from the FFB in 1989. Instead, the agency would access the public markets to effect refinancing of its high-coupon debt through an in-substance defeasance. This decision has allowed the TVA to save more than $200 million in annual interest expense since 1989 and has helped to hold electric rates stable from 1988 to 1993 with plans for stable rates through the year 2000.

External Influences

Analytical historians of the agency have noted that "the autonomy of the TVA has limits," and that the key to understanding the agency's evolution is "the tension between a strong autonomous bureaucracy and the shifting tides of public opinion."[12]

The stakeholders which the TVA today seeks to satisfy are many and varied. It maintains especially strong ties with its distributors through the Tennessee Valley Public Power Association (TVPPA), which represents the 160 local power distributors. TVA also works with other distributor organizations such as the Tennessee Electric Cooperative Association, the Tennessee Municipal Electric Power Association, and the Alabama Rural Electric Association. Another key partner is the Tennessee Valley Industrial Committee, representing large industries that receive electricity directly from TVA. Similarly, the Association of Valley Industries provides TVA with the views of industries served by the local power distributors.

To obtain the perspective of state and local governments, TVA maintains ties with state legislators and governors' staffs in the states served by the agency. In addition, managers of TVA programs work with their counterparts in state governments on such issues as energy, the environment, and economic development.

Since 1975, TVA has allowed for direct public input by conducting business in a public forum (Mills, 1987, p. 255). Its monthly board meetings are open to the public; anyone can comment on any agenda item before the board takes a vote; and a public listening session and news conference are held at every meeting.

Because TVA is a federal agency, all significant environmental decisions must be made using the National Environmental Policy Act (NEPA) guidelines. That translates into preparing Environmental Impact Statements (EISs) on many proposed actions. NEPA requires public input, but TVA generally goes beyond the letter of the law. For example, the agency has sponsored public open houses in order to discuss public concerns with electro-magnetic field (EMF) risks.

Nature of Governmental Oversight

From a government decision-making standpoint, the most important factor is not what Congress did in creating the TVA, but what it did not do. Two characteristics of the TVA set it apart from other federal departments and agencies, and even most other federal corporations.

First, the enabling legislation created an entity with powers and authorities—and a vision—but no specific programs. The few programs specified in the act were described in only the most general terms. For the TVA's entire existence, spanning six decades of change in the United States, the act has never been amended to specify new programs, a testament to its breadth and original grant of authorities. New programs, projects, and facilities were initiated by the TVA without the need of individual or annual special congressional approvals.[13]

Second, in creating the TVA, Congress also did not follow the traditional pattern of making each federal entity dependent on the decisions and actions of other federal entities in carrying out many basic aspects of day-to-day operations. In contrast, TVA operates quite independently.[14]

For example, the marketing arrangements for TVA power were developed by TVA. Many details of both the wholesale and retail aspects of this arrangement, which in most areas would be handled through public service commissions by tariffs, are handled by contracts between TVA and its distributors. Indeed, in recognition of the nature of this relationship, both the National Energy Conservation Policy Act and the Public Utility Regulatory Policies Act defined the TVA as a "state regulatory authority" (and, at one place, a "governor") and its distributors as "regulated utilities." Even the most critical decisions related to electric power service—the setting of rates—reside exclusively with the TVA board, not with the state public service commission or FERC.

Presidential and Congressional Influence

Although the TVA board has the ultimate authority to make decisions regarding the agency, the president and Congress have the power to influence the decision-making process at the TVA. The president decides who will make decisions at the TVA by appointing board members, designating the chairman of the board, and removing a board member from the board, if necessary.[15] The Senate is involved in decision making through approval and confirmation of board members.

Congress determines how much money TVA will receive and if the money is being used appropriately. In addition, Congress has reserved the right to alter, amend, or repeal the TVA Act, but has provided that no amendment or repeal shall operate to impair the obligation of any contract made by the TVA in the exercise of any power conferred by the act. Although Congress does not have direct power over the specific programs the TVA implements, Congress approves the appropriated funds for the agency's non-power programs on an annual basis. In some cases, the TVA can lose funding, particularly if Congress and its committees do not feel that the agency is implementing the right programs or managing existing programs in the proper manner. The amount of public and political support TVA receives for its non-power programs often determines how much the agency will receive in the form of tax money.

TVA must report on its programs and financial condition directly to the president and Congress each year. The House Public Works Committee is TVA's oversight committee in the House of Representatives. TVA maintains an office in Washington, D.C., to work with this committee and others.

CURRENT ISSUES

Environmental protection and competition, forces that affect the rest of the electric power industry, also dominate the TVA's management agenda. Privatization is another issue that periodically takes center stage.

Integrated resource planning (IRP) is currently the mechanism by which stakeholders (power distributors, end-use customers, and other interested groups) are expected to influence the long-term energy strategy of TVA. Stakeholders will comment on a wide range of supply-side, demand-side, and customer service options through public participation techniques such as opinion leader interviews, surveys, public meetings, informative publications, and a review group.

The IRP provides a vehicle for analyzing the tradeoffs the TVA board must make among its various objectives. Balancing cost, quality, environmental, and financial goals is an ongoing managerial and political challenge.

The Environment

TVA is regulated like all other utilities with respect to environmental issues, and most of its recent boards have placed environmental protection and enrichment among the top three objectives of the agency. Current top environmental issues include acid rain compliance, toxic air emissions, global climate change, cooling water use, and electro-magnetic fields.

Many of the agency's coal-fired plants were built during the postwar years when minimal environmental standards existed, and nearby high-sulfur coal was the resource of choice for both cost and political reasons. Thus TVA must now make major efforts to comply with the 1990 Clean Air Act Amendments.[16] TVA's compliance strategy will result in overcompliance during Phase I, which will allow building of an allowance bank. Phase II of the acid rain requirements of the Clean Air Act Amendments starts in the year 2000 and will require additional controls at the remaining TVA plants.[17]

Another environmental issue is the need for regulation of utility industry toxic air emissions, which is currently being studied by the Environmental Protection Agency (EPA). Global warming is currently receiving considerable national and international attention and could be a costly proposition to utilities that have substantial emissions of CO_2.[18] Bills to reauthorize the Clean Water Act have included proposals to eliminate the option to obtain a variance from stream standards for temperature. Growing concerns about health effects from electric and magnetic fields are also potentially a tremendous challenge for electric utilities over the next decade.

Competition

One of the dominant forces in the utility industry is increased competition in the wholesale market, the retail market, and the industrial market. As changes within the industry drive increased competition, the TVA must consider a number of issues, including price, quality of service, other utilities, foreign competition, and legislation.

The Energy Policy Act of 1992 and related policies being explored by the Federal Energy Regulatory Commission (FERC) are increasingly pointing to stiffer competition in the wholesale market. This places TVA in a vulnerable position since TVA sales are approximately 85 percent wholesale, as compared to other utilities with 6 percent to 10 percent wholesale sales. However, there is a TVA anti-cherry-picking amendment to the Energy Policy Act, which prevents other wholesalers from selling inside the TVA area to distributors. In essence, this exemption makes the TVA "fence" a two-way fence, so that any energy sold within the fence must be sold to TVA for the beneficial use of all customers, not a select few. This reduces the significant disadvantage TVA would face due to the wholesale customer mix and also helps eliminate the potential for stranded investment. However, future legislative changes or judicial decisions could alter the "two-way" fence and create increased competitive pressure.[19]

Competition in the bulk power market is expected to become a more important force in decision-making under the Energy Policy Act of 1992. Price will be the most critical factor, but TVA management expects that choices will also be influenced by reliability, degree of firmness, and flexibility to meet other utilities' requirements. Retail open access may eventually provide suppliers of electricity with transmission access to retail customers.

International competition in the industrial market is becoming an important threat. TVA has always competed with other utilities on a regional and a national basis for large industrial loads, but now TVA finds itself competing in a global marketplace to keep industrial loads in the valley and to attract investment from overseas. Industry provides economic stability in the form of jobs and stimulates investment. Historically, industry has been the backbone of the Tennessee Valley. Overseas investment flows to the communities that offer the most favorable environments for business, and that includes communities with low power rates.

The TVA has held rates constant since 1988 in a valley-wide effort to maintain cost-competitiveness. The TVA and the Tennessee Valley Industrial Development Association (TVIDA) also have opened economic development offices in Japan, Canada, and Europe. The purpose of these international offices is to encourage investment, joint ventures, and the exchange of technology between these regions and the Tennessee Valley.

Privatization

Another issue specific to the TVA is the threat of privatization. Private utilities have challenged the governmental role in power production since the first year of the TVA's existence,[20] and they continue to do so. Several times in the past, governmental actors have tried to sell the assets of the TVA to public or private groups. For example, in 1955 former President Herbert Hoover was involved with such an effort. The group wanted to limit TVA operations by encouraging private companies to assume responsibility for power plant construction, and by transferring many of the TVA's non-power activities to other agencies. Congress did not approve the plan.

Other proposals made in the past have also been denied. Most administrations have been supportive of TVA and have recommended full funding in the annual budgets for the TVA's appropriated programs.

CONCLUSIONS

This overview suggests that even insulated enterprises like TVA are feeling the effects of competition and environmental regulation. Historically, TVA has enjoyed a broad mandate to improve the quality of life for valley residents by improving the economic conditions of the valley. Today, as TVA continues in this mission, the focus is on providing services at lower cost and with higher value than the agency's competitors.

As both retail and wholesale markets become increasingly competitive, TVA will need to respond quickly to improve the agency's competitiveness in meeting customer needs and to balance its roles as a utility and as a protector of natural resources. The sheer size of the agency and the trappings of bureaucracy will have to be counteracted if it is to be an important force in shaping the dynamics of the new electricity marketplace.

In the future, the agency expects to make decisions based on customer needs, the environment, economic growth, and the quality of life for generations to come. In a 1963 speech, President John F. Kennedy remarked that "the work of the TVA will never be over. There will always be new frontiers for it to conquer. For in the minds of men the world over, the initials TVA stand for progress, and the people of this area are not afraid of progress." However, for the TVA's ongoing mission, progress increasingly will be measured by its response to the competitive marketplace.

NOTES

1. Franklin D. Roosevelt, message accompanying proposed legislation (TVA Act of 1933), May 1933, quoted in Callahan (1980, p. 28).

2. See Callahan (1980, p. 28). Other responsibilities included

improving the navigability and providing for flood control of the Tennessee River, reforestation and proper use of marginal lands in the valley, agricultural and industrial development, and the production of low-cost electricity for distribution to farms, homes, and industries within the valley.

3.   Although rural residents and local power companies were resistant to the idea at first, eventually rural electrification was put in place, and access to electricity increased comfort and annual incomes for many rural residents.

4.   Such contracts are for terms of twenty years and require distributors to purchase substantially all of their electric power and energy requirements from the TVA. The power contracts with distributors require ten years' notice before termination. One additional year is automatically added to the term on each anniversary of the contract, beginning with the tenth anniversary. The contracts contain standard provisions specifying the wholesale rates, resale rates, and terms and conditions under which the power is to be distributed. Under the contracts, the TVA, on a quarterly basis, may adjust the rate schedules to meet all requirements of the act and the provisions of bond resolutions. The resale rates under which the distributors serve ultimate consumers are stipulated in the power contracts between the distributors and the TVA. These rates are revised from time to time to reflect changes in costs, including changes in the wholesale cost of power. The rates are designed to promote the act's objective of providing an adequate supply of power at the lowest feasible rates.

5.   TVA implemented an Industrial Service Policy as a result of Section 11 of the TVA Act, which stipulates that TVA is to spread the benefits of large loads to all electricity consumers throughout the entire region. If these loads were to be served through the distributor, a small fraction of the 160 distributors would receive major increases in net revenue, resulting in substantially lower rates for their customers. However, the system as a whole would require electric rate increases by the remaining distributors, and the majority of customers would suffer higher rates. TVA and the distributors jointly developed provisions for the standard wholesale power contract that set a ceiling on the size of industrial customer that may be served by a distributor. Contracts with industries served directly by the TVA are normally for terms of ten years, but are subject to termination by the TVA or the customer. Termination requires a minimum notice period that varies according to the customer's contract demand and the period of time that service has been provided at that location. The power sold directly to industries is delivered under contracts at rates established by the TVA. These rates are the same as those charged by distributors to large industries whose demand is greater than 5 MW.

6.   It has initiated an Account Planning Program that enables TVA and each distributor to work together to prepare a joint plan for future, addressing marketing needs, system needs, competition, and day-to-day business needs. In addition, as a recent partnership effort, TVA and its distributors have formed the Quality Alliance, allowing TVA and its distributors to share resource information and individual strengths in a joint effort to enhance the overall quality of service.

7. The TVA's best-known demand-side management program was the Home Insulation Program, which began in 1977. This program provided free energy conservation surveys for residential customers, coupled with low- or no-interest financing of recommended weatherization measures (chiefly attic insulation and storm windows) and free post-installation inspections. In total, more than 1 million homes were surveyed, and recommended measures were financed in about 600,000 of them.

8. One of the most popular recreational areas is Land Between the Lakes, which is located on 170,000 acres between Kentucky Lake, built by the TVA, and Lake Barkley, a U.S. Army Corps of Engineers project. Land Between the Lakes receives 2.3 million visitors a year and boosts the local economy by attracting $350 million a year from tourists. The area is managed by TVA and serves as a center for outdoor recreation, environmental education, and resource stewardship.

9. See H.R. Report No. 130, 73rd Congress, 1st Session, 19 (1933).

10. A half-dozen senior managers typically form the executive core of a larger management group that coordinates the agency's many functions. In addition to administrative functions such a finance, communications, and human resources, there are major operating divisions within the TVA. For many years the non-power operations (fertilizer, recreation, navigation, wildlife) have been separated from the electric power operations. On the electric power side, a customer group performs planning, billing, dispatching, transmission, customer service, and demand-side management functions. A generating group builds and operates the power plants. Recently, nuclear generation has spun off administratively from the rest of TVA operations.

11. According to Mills (1987, p. 2) and recent TVA internal records.

12. See Hargrove (1983, p. xvii).

13. The 1933 conference report on the TVA Act explained Congress's decision to entrust decision making to the TVA's Board of Directors, in lieu of subjecting TVA to the type of controls exercised by Congress over most federal agencies, including many federal corporations: "The board is charged with the duty of constantly studying the whole situation presented by the Tennessee River Valley, and the adjoining territory, with the view of encouraging and guiding in the orderly and balanced development of the diverse and rich resources of that section."

14. Every organization needs certain "tools" to meet its objectives. It needs to operate a personnel system and otherwise conduct its internal affairs. It needs to buy and sell goods and services. It needs to buy, sell, or lease office space and other real property. And, when necessary, it needs to participate in litigation. The possession of these "tools" is taken for granted in the private sector. For example, it might not ever occur to a private businessman that he could not retain any attorney he wished, or bring or defend any court action he found necessary to the conduct of his business. In contrast, federal departments and agencies take for granted the absence of such tools. The Justice Department handles, or chooses not to handle, their litigation. The General Services Administration handles their real property and often much

of their personal property needs. The Office of Personnel Management operates their personnel system. Consequently, in the federal sector, generally there are often other agencies whose own policies, priorities, and budgets determine whether or how well another agency can achieve its objectives. In the energy field, TVA has invested in a broad range of technologies over time, building power houses at dams, combustion turbines, coal-fired power plants, and nuclear plants to meet the growing demand for electricity. The kind, size, location, and nature of these energy facilities have been largely determined by the TVA board. Similarly, from 1977 through the mid-1980s, TVA operated the nation's largest utility-run residential energy conservation program. Since 1959, all of the capital investment has been paid for from retained earnings or proceeds from the sale of bonds, which are backed only by future revenues. They are not obligations of or guaranteed by the United States.

15. Only once in the past has the president exercised his power to remove a board member before the board member's term expired. The first Board of Directors at the TVA, appointed by President Roosevelt in 1933, included Chairman Arthur E. Morgan, David Lilienthal, and Harcourt Morgan, no relation to the chairman. Chairman Morgan wanted to distribute TVA power through privately owned utilities, but directors Lilienthal and Morgan strongly opposed this idea. Chairman Morgan publicly attacked his colleagues, questioning their motives and integrity. As a result, Lilienthal and Morgan passed a resolution that condemned the chairman for his behavior. Chairman Morgan failed to substantiate his claims against his fellow board members, and President Roosevelt removed Chairman Morgan from office.

16. TVA will spend up to $700 million through 1999 to satisfy Phase I acid rain requirements, which require major reductions in SO_2 and NO_x. This money will be spent on new emissions-control equipment such as the scrubbers at Cumberland Fossil Plant and low NO_x-burners at most of TVA's other Phase I sources. In all, twenty-six of TVA's fifty-nine coal-fired, power-producing boilers are affected by Phase I acid rain provisions. TVA control activities will result in approximately a 30 percent reduction in the amount of SO_2 that would have otherwise been emitted between 1995 and 1999.

17. These controls will result in an overall reduction in SO_2 for a total systemwide reduction of over 60 percent from levels expected without the acid rain legislation. Air quality impacts to the Great Smokey Mountain National Park could lead to additional emission controls at many of the TVA's fossil plants.

18. At a minimum, offsets might be required. Efficiency improvements, major fuel switches, or even CO_2 scrubbers could eventually be required. Control of CO_2 emissions could radically change the future fuel mix for many utilities and might revive interest in nuclear power.

19. For example, in 1990 the TVA faced the loss of its largest single customer—Memphis Light, Gas, and Water. The TVA's power contract came up for renewal, and Memphis looked to other utilities for a better offer. The loss of Memphis would have meant higher power rates to all customers in the valley. When Memphis officials evaluated all aspects of service and the changes that

had been made, they decided to stick with TVA, but they drove the point home that TVA does have competitors. For those distributors on the periphery of the TVA service area, competition for these customers continues.

20. See *George Ashwander et al v. TVA*, 297 U.S. 288, filed in 1934, decided in U.S. Supreme Court in 1936.

REFERENCES

Callahan, North. *TVA: Bridge Over Troubled Waters*. Cranbury, NJ: A.S. Barnes and Company, 1980.

Hargrove, Erwin C. "Introduction." In Erwin C. Hargrove and Paul K. Conkin, eds. *TVA: Fifty Years of Grassroots Bureaucracy*. Urbana, IL: University of Illinois Press, 1983.

Mills, Debra D., ed. *TVA Handbook*. TVA/OCS/PS-87/8. Knoxville, TN: TVA Technical Library, 1987.

U.S. Congress, H.R. Report No. 130, 73rd Congress, 1st Session, 19 (1933).

U.S. Supreme Court. *George Ashwander et al v. TVA*. 297 U.S. 288. filed in 1934, decided in U.S. Supreme Court in 1936.

24

Comment on the Tennessee Valley Authority Case

Allan G. Pulsipher

TVA is a unique power system; however the attributes that make it unique are not very fully discussed in the TVA case study. TVA's uniqueness has three major facets. The first is structural: It is managed by a three-member board that has complete authority to set its rates as well as its policies and strategies. The other two facets are strategic: (1) TVA's singular and resilient commitment to a nuclear-based power supply plan, and (2) TVA's determination to remain a vertically integrated utility, functionally isolated from the evermore competitive electric utility industry.

TVA'S AUTONOMOUS, DUAL-PURPOSE BOARD

TVA is both "regulated" and managed by a presidentially selected, three-member board. It functions without any independent, external review or control save that of the general powers of oversight and appropriation of the United States Congress. Although TVA's federally funded natural resource and development programs are reviewed annually during the federal budget cycle, TVA's legally and financially separate power program receives only ad hoc oversight at the irregular initiative of interested members of the Congress. Until 1974, both the public and the press were barred from all TVA board meetings, including those at which rates were set. It was not until 1993 that the TVA board's agenda was circulated in advance of its meetings. TVA does not document for the public its load forecast or power supply plan as other utilities routinely do.

When it was created sixty years ago, at the bottom of the Great

Depression, TVA was structured in this uniquely autonomous way because it was to be an explicit federal intervention in the economy of a region presumed to be either too poor or too exploited to trust to the existing institutions in either the public or private sectors of the regional economy. The goal was to keep politics from sapping TVA's efficiency and to preclude hostile, regional economic or political interests from frustrating the TVA experiment.

At the time, such "structural insurance" made sense, and it worked. TVA built a system of dams and reservoirs that, if evaluated purely as a business investment, yield a rate-of-return approximately twice as high as the average return to private capital (TVA, 1987). TVA also built an efficient system of coal-fired power plants. No major scandal or episode of corruption mars TVA's nearly sixty-year history.

However, in contemporary circumstances there is neither theoretical nor empirical support for such an arrangement in the public utilities, administration or regulation literature, and none is provided in the TVA case study. Further, every independent study of TVA's organization and performance in the past two decades (ranging in origin and political inclination from the report of President Reagan's 1980 TVA transition team to a study by Alex Radin, an establishment Democrat and former executive director of the American Public Power Association) has concluded that the time has come to replace TVA's unique, autonomous, dual-purpose board with an expanded part-time board, clearly separated from managerial responsibility and decision making, representative of those served by TVA-generated power, and responsible for the debts of the TVA power system.[1]

TVA'S NUCLEAR COMMITMENT

From a strategic perspective, clearly, today what distinguishes TVA from other power systems is that TVA is the only U.S. utility still in the nuclear construction business—and in it in a big way. According to its own estimates, TVA plans to invest an additional $6.6 billion in nuclear construction over the next ten years.[2] Adjusting for past performance could bring that estimate to $10 billion.

Although many utilities started nuclear plants in the 1960s and early 1970s, they were either completed or canceled after investors lost confidence in the commercial profitability of nuclear power during the late 1970s. TVA canceled eight of its planned seventeen nuclear units in the 1980s at a cost of $4.6 billion, but its customers still paid for much more canceled nuclear plant than any other power system[3] —without any credit being given for its 5,200 MW "investment" in currently incomplete and unlicensed units, or the 2,134 MW of licensed capacity that has been cold since 1986.[4]

The singularity of TVA's nuclear supply strategy raises the simple, central question that should have been a major focus of the TVA case study. To wit: Why does a multi-billion dollar "investment" in nuclear construction make sense for TVA but not for any of the nation's other 500 or so electric utilities?

An equally relevant question, at least for students of the electric utility industry, is: Why is TVA determined to remain a traditional, vertically integrated utility, operationally isolated from the evermore interdependent, market-organized, and competitive electric utility industry?

Although neither of these questions is either answered or asked in the TVA case study, my thesis is that the answer to the second is derivative of the answer to the first and that both can be traced to TVA's uniquely autonomous, dual-purpose board.

THE RUNYON REFORMATION

TVA's routine response to questions about its nuclear-based power planning strategy has been that TVA was reformed by Marvin Runyon, who was chairman of the TVA board from 1987 to 1992 before becoming postmaster general of the United States.[5] As a consequence of Runyon's reforms, the argument goes, TVA has not increased its rates for five years, and, the implication is, TVA has put its nuclear troubles behind it.

Marvin Runyon was a very popular TVA chairman. When President Reagan appointed him Chairman of the TVA board, many feared his charge was to privatize the agency. Five years later, as he left, he was widely regarded as the right man in the nick of time who saved it. His popularity rivaled Senator Al Gore and eclipsed figures such as Senator Jim Sasser or former Governor (and Bush cabinet member) Lamar Alexander.

But, more to our point, during his tenure, Runyon became a champion of nuclear power. He resurrected at least three and possibly six nuclear reactors, which, according to the conventional wisdom prevailing when he came to TVA, were slated for cancellation or early retirement.[6]

Nuclear Power and the Runyon Reforms

With no intent either to document or to demean his successes, the relevance of Chairman Runyon's reforms to TVA's nuclear problems needs to be better understood.

First, the stable rates that TVA has experienced since 1989 have been the rule rather than the exception in the U.S. electric utility. Industrial rates for the U.S. peaked on 1985 at 5.2 cents per kWh and had declined to 4.9 cents per kWh by 1993 (USDOE, 1993). Indeed, a symbolic irony is that the Sacramento Municipal Utility District headed during this period by S. David Freeman, the ex-chairman of TVA who became the resident devil for Runyon's new management team, also has avoided rate increases since 1989, *and* has retired, prematurely, its only nuclear plant. Moreover, when Runyon took over, the customers of the large, modern, contiguous utilities that form TVA's competition, such as Duke Power, Kentucky Utilities, and Alabama Power, enjoyed substantially lower industrial rates than TVA's customers—and they still enjoy that advantage today.[7]

Second, although most TVA watchers would agree that the post-Runyon TVA is a more efficient entity than the pre-Runyon TVA, most of the post-Runyon cost reductions are attributable to favorable but *external* forces beyond TVA's control.[8]

TVA's Recent Nuclear Record

However, the most persuasive evidence of Runyon's inability to solve TVA's nuclear problems is provided by direct observation of TVA's nuclear program itself.

To illustrate, in March of 1993, after an accident forced TVA to shut down both operating reactors at its Sequoyah plant near Chattanooga, Ivan Selin, chairman of the Nuclear Regulatory Commission (NRC), paid TVA a rare, surprise site visit. Afterwards, Selin said his previous perception that TVA's two Sequoyah units were well managed (a perception widely shared in the nuclear industry) simply was wrong. The units, he said, "had never been on firm ground." He also questioned the advisability and realism of TVA's plans to bring its Watts Bar 1 unit on-line in 1994.[9] Thus TVA's nuclear record appears to remain lodged somewhere between "spotty" and "clearly sub-par," despite the Runyon reforms.[10]

Reorganization and Nuclear Revival

When Runyon came aboard in late 1987, TVA's nuclear czar was Admiral Steven White, a recently retired submariner who had marketed his services to TVA as a "nuclear recovery expert," although he had never worked a day for an electric utility before he assumed command of TVA's stone-cold nuclear program (both its construction and operations components) in January 1986.

In addition to Admiral White and its well-publicized nuclear woes, TVA's power system also was silently suffering from advanced managerial sclerosis. Although many of its top managers were loyal and able, almost all had spent their entire careers not only at TVA but entirely within the divisions for which they were now responsible.

With admirable insight and dispatch, Chairman Runyon attacked both problems by:

- gracefully re-retiring Admiral White and replacing him with Oliver Kingsley, a young, aggressive veteran of (then) Mid-South Utilities' nuclear program, and

- initiating an iterative process of reorganization, which replaced veteran TVA managers with younger but experienced managers from "the outside."

Eventually, by 1991, Runyon had created a managerial structure with five operating "groups":

- generation,

- customer,

- administration and finance,

- information and personnel, and

- resources (essentially, TVA's non-power programs financed by congressional appropriations).

This organizational structure not only looked much more like other utilities and reduced the age of TVA's top management by at least a decade, but also repaired operating and decision-making imbalances that had hindered TVA since the 1960s.

In the reshuffling, however, the entire power generation responsibility was given to Oliver Kingsley—the first time in TVA's history that a manager from the nuclear side had been given control over its coal-fired and hydro as well as nuclear facilities.[11]

Nuclear Revival and Revisions in Key Planning Parameters

Like potted plants will turn toward a sun-lit window, after Kingsley's purview had been expanded to include conventional as well as nuclear facilities, internal analysis began to find that nuclear facilities were easier to build, cheaper to operate, and that the need for them had grown.

As these internal reevaluations began to surface in public documents, they showed that not only had TVA's load forecast grown, but, in sharp contrast to previous history, TVA's estimate of the cost of

Table 24.1
Revisions in TVA Planning Assumptions during the
Runyon Reformation and Nuclear Revival

	Pre-Revival value	Post-Revival value
Load Forecast (BkWh in 2000)	141[a]	158[b]
Cost to Complete Bellefonte Nuclear Plant ($B)	3.25[c]	2.75[d]
Generating Capacity (Dependable Summer kW)	29,288[c]	24,791[d]

Sources: a. TVA Load Forecast, 1987.
       b. NERC, S&D for Electricity, 1991.
       c. TVA Bond Circular, 4/9/92
       d. TVA Bond Circular, 2/25/93

completing its nuclear units had fallen, and even its reported total generating capacity appeared to decline. Table 24.1 contrasts the pre-nuclear-revival values for load, cost to complete its Bellefonte nuclear plant, and capacity with the latest available estimates. Estimated load grew about 12 percent, the cost to complete fell by about 16 percent and the capacity of TVA's system to generate electricity shrank by about 20 percent.

Although there was no discussion of these revisions in TVA's financial reports or bond circulars, they all appear to go against trends in the industry and TVA's own experience. For example, according to the North American Electric Reliability Council (NERC) (1991), TVA expects its peak load to grow faster over the next ten years than any other NERC sub-region in the country—3.1 percent per year as opposed to the (next fastest) 2.5 percent per year forecast by Florida utilities. The U.S. Census Bureau (1990), in contrast, expects Florida's population to grow about twice as fast as that of the population within the TVA service area over the period.

Intimidation of Internal Checks and Balances

In theory, one might have expected countervailing analysis from TVA's newly formed customer and financial groups; however, little was forthcoming.[12] Most important, however, was Marvin Runyon's own enthusiasm for nuclear power. Runyon's nuclear predilections were so far outside the range of informed opinion that they became a matter of ridicule within the electric utility industry. In 1990, the *Energy Daily*'s

April Fool's Day edition, *Not the Energy Daily,* gave its front-page-above-the-fold place of place of honor to a story poking fun at Runyon's nuclear enthusiasm. The force of his own personality and leadership style meant that once his nuclear inclination was perceived within TVA, it would take an unusually confident and committed, or fool-hardy, manager to question its wisdom.[13]

TVA'S ISOLATIONIST STRATEGY

In support of its nuclear revival, an important parallel strategy for TVA has been to try to isolate itself from the increasingly competitive national electricity market. This is illustrated most clearly by the tongue-twistingly-titled provision "Equitability Within Territory Restricted Electric Systems," added to the Energy Policy Act of 1992 (Sec. 722:j) at TVA's initiative. This provision attempts, in effect, to make the "TVA fence" (which many assert prevents the agency from selling power outside its service area) "work both ways"— by keeping cheaper power out of TVA's service area. Similarly, TVA has unilaterally prohibited the legally independent wholesale distributors of the power it generates from purchasing power from independent power distributors or industrial cogenerators located in their service areas.[14]

I will not belabor how out-of-sync with the rest of the industry TVA's isolationist strategy appears to be; two representative quotes suffice. Walter M. Higgins, President of Louisville Gas and Electric Company, observes that "The marketplace and evolving technology already portend the demise of the vertically integrated utility. Customers will not tolerate being artificially blocked from access to competitively priced energy options" (PUF, June 1, 1993). Karl Rabago, Commissioner, Texas' Public Utility Commission is more direct: "Our mission is to exterminate the old regulated monopoly and to replace it with competition" (PUF, October 1, 1993).

Would the Separation of Regulation from Management Have Helped?

Perhaps the best answer to this question was given, with customary directness, by Marvin Runyon to a newspaper reporter (Gregory, 1993) who asked him why TVA was the only power system willing to put all its eggs in the nuclear basket. Runyon replied: "[I]nvestors in other utilities worry about whether public service commissions will approve rate hikes to cover unexpected nuclear power costs. TVA doesn't have that problem. If in fact a nuclear plant cost more money than anticipated, TVA wouldn't need anybody's permission to raise the rates to cover the increased cost."

TVA's autonomous, dual-purpose board is a paternalistic, strong-man, theory of governance and management, resting on the ahistorical expectation that the presidential porkbarrel will produce the required strongman. Although history shows the porkbarrel has provided five faithfully partisan Rotarians in need of a job for every David Lilienthal, Gordon Clapp, or David Freeman, the saga of the Runyon reformation-and-nuclear-revival demonstrates that the system can expose the TVA ratepayer to real risks even when a capable, creative, well-motivated strongman like Marvin Runyon does turn up.

Structuring TVA's system of governance in this way may have been prudent in the 1930s to protect TVA from hostile regional, economic, and political forces. Today, however, no competent student of regulation or public administration would recommend it as a sensible way to govern a large regional power system.

TVA is currently preparing to undertake a two-year, congressionally mandated integrated resource plan (IRP), which is intended to be a comprehensive and objective analysis of the cost and risks of alternative ways of meeting the demand for electricity in future. But TVA's IRP is not likely to answer to the concerns about TVA's nuclear revival summarized here.[15]

OPENING UP "THE" ACT

For over sixty years, both because of TVA's unique status, nationally, as the concrete symbol of the New Deal's accomplishments and TVA's own political popularity in the region, any suggestion that the TVA Act be amended ("opened-up" is the insider's preferred lingo) to improve TVA's system of governance and control was regarded as a naive or duplicitous invitation to expose TVA to its enemies who were waiting in the halls of the Congress to strike fatal blows at this grand institutionalization of New Deal imagination and initiative.

President Clinton recently was able to put two seasoned Tennessee politicians on the TVA board, one of whom, Craven Crowell—who headed TVA's public information office during the 1980s, until he left to become head of Senator Jim Sasser's staff—is its new chairman. Traditionally, like presidents, new TVA chairmen get a honeymoon, which precludes any tinkering with the TVA Act. But a honeymoon should not supersede the right of TVA's ratepayers for a modern and responsive system of regulation and governance. Moreover, with a Democratic president and a native Tennessean, TVA-supporter as vice president, this is an auspicious time to do so. Neither the prospect of an IRP two years hence nor a new Democratic board should reassure TVA ratepayers that they will not bear excessive and unnecessary costs as a consequence of TVA's singular attempt at nuclear revival.

To relapse into popular jargon, Marvin Runyon did a lot to "reinvent" TVA. Unfortunately the force of his leadership, unchecked by external accountability or review, has resulted in cost and load forecasts that might be described as attempts to "reinvent" the buoyant energy and economic expectations of the 1960s and 1970s, which pushed the nation into its initial nuclear adventure.

It is now time for Craven Crowell (and Al Gore) to finish the job of reinventing TVA by giving it a 1990s, rather than a 1930s, kind of board.

NOTES

1. See Sansome (1981). The Radin report was done for the Tennessee Valley Public Power Association and also formed the basis for the organization and management recommendations of the report of the Southern States Energy Board (1987).

2. Calculated from TVA bond circular dated December 8, 1993. As elsewhere in this chapter, midpoints were used when estimates were given in ranges. The estimate excludes capitalized interest on the $3.25 billion cost to complete the Bellefont Units.

3. The top ten utilities in cancelled nuclear capacity are, in order, TVA, Public Service of Indiana, Consumers Power (MI), Cincinnati Gas and Electric, Washington Public Power Supply System, Mississippi Power and Light, Duke Power (NC, SC), Public Service Electric and Gas (NJ), Virginia Power, and Jersey Central Power and Light (NJ).

4. The unlicensed units are Watts Bar 1, which has been reported as "substantially complete" since 1985; Watts Bar 2, which is reported as 60 percent complete; and Bellefont Units 1 and 2, which are also about 60 percent complete according to TVA's cost estimates. Browns Ferry Units 1 and 3 are the units that were shut down in 1986 and have not been restarted. See TVA (1993).

5. President Clinton appointed two veteran Democratic Tennessee politicians to the TVA board, and the rhetorical reliance on the Runyon reforms recently seems to have weakened. TVA's current response to such questions is that all supply options will be evaluated as a part of the congressionally mandated integrated resource plan (IRP) that TVA has been trying to get underway since it was mandated in the 1992 Energy Policy Act. But, as argued later, with its current dual-purpose board, the IRP process is predicated on an unrealistic willingness by TVA's managers to engage in self-criticism. The coincidence of the switch in the political control of the TVA board with the implementation of TVA's IRP may increase the willingness to consider non-

nuclear strategies, but the staff work and analysis that forms the meat of the IRP will be formulated and reviewed by the same managers responsible for the strategies and decisions under review.

6. At the time Runyon came to TVA, the units that almost every observer thought would be canceled were the two units at Bellefont in Alabama and the second unit at Watts Bar in Tennessee. In addition many believed that the three reactors at Brown's Ferry in Alabama, which were licensed but shut-down, would never be re-started.

7. See Pulsipher (1991) for a discussion of the evidence on this point.

8. Clearly the dominant cost- and rate-stabilizing factor for TVA has been the decline in interest rates in national credit markets. As interest rates fell, TVA was able to refinance its multi-billion dollar nuclear debt, much of which was borrowed at double-digit interest rates in the late 1970s and early 1980s.

9. See Lane (1993). TVA said the two Sequoyah units would be on-line in time to help TVA meet its summer (1993) peak and that it still planned to move ahead with its nuclear program according to its original schedule. TVA was unable to bring Sequoyah 2 on line until October 30, 1993. Then valve and voltage regulator problems developed that kept the unit off line during most of November and December. TVA has no firm date for returning Sequoyah 1 to service—saying only they hope to do so during the "winter." The unit was cold when TVA had to meet a record-high peak demand in January of 1994 (*Southeast Power Report*, December 17, 1993). Further, TVA continues to postpone the scheduled fuel loading for Watts Bar 1 (a unit which has been "physically complete" since the 1985 and, if successfully licensed, will be TVA's first "new" nuclear unit since the two Sequoyah units in the early 1980s). In October 1993, fuel loading for Watts Bar 1 was postponed until October 1994, which meant that commercial operation could not begin until the spring of 1995 if the start-up proceeds as currently envisioned (*Southeast Power Report*, November 5, 1993). TVA has also had to ask NRC for a one-year extension of its (twenty-year) construction license as a consequence of the slip.

10. NRC's latest SALP (Strategic Assessment of Licensee Performance) for Sequoyah was completed in October 1993. In two of the four areas evaluated, Plant Operations and Plant Management, NRC gave its lowest mark, a "3," which NRC says means "performance does not significantly exceed that needed to meet minimal regulatory requirements; NRC attention should be increased above normal levels." See the TVA bond circular dated December 8, 1993, p. 10.

11. It is a significant, if little known, fact that the effective questioning of TVA's original plans to build seventeen nuclear units in the late 1970s and early 1980s, which eventually led to the belated cancellation of eight of them, came not from TVA's board, TVA's corporate staff, TVA's customers, or nuclear critics, but from managers in TVA's Office of Power who were immersed operationally in the detailed comparison of the economics of conventional coal-fired as opposed to nuclear generation.

12. The financial group was occupied full time with TVA's transition

from the friendly Federal Financing Bank to the private capital market and the task of refinancing the agency's high-interest debt as interest rates fell. Its challenge was to explain to potential bondholders why TVA's unique nuclear strategy made sense, not to question the strategy internally.

13. Runyon was an exceptionally strong manager who eventually did away with even the pretense of a chief operating officer at the corporate level, but well before that time he had imposed corporate-level direction, coordination, and control through the considerable force of his own personality. In doing so, he was guided largely by his own experience and generalized managerial intuition rather than utility experience, TVA's institutional history, or formal-MBA-esque decision or financial analysis.

14. In contrast, its competitor to the northeast, Virginia Power, recently asked its public utility commission to let it work with ten large industrial firms to develop cogeneration facilities in order to help these firms minimize their energy costs and, thereby, help Virginia Power retain their load (*Southeast Power Report*, June 18, 1993). The North American Reliability Council's annual supply and demand for electricity volumes (1991) show how different TVA's isolationist strategy is from its competitors. The utilities in Florida, for example, predict non-utility generation within their subregion to increase by ten times between 1990 and 2000. To TVA's north, utilities operating in Virginia and the Carolinas expect a 213 percent increase. TVA's plan, as reported to NERC, shows zero non-utility capacity in 1990 with none expected by the end of the decade. Similarly, load management and interruptible demand forecasts—the only demand-side data that NERC reports—show that the utilities in the least bullish of the sub-regions that compete with TVA predict a 77 percent increase between 1991 and 2000, while TVA anticipates a *decline* of 12 percent.

15. First, it is twenty years late. Second, by the time it is complete, TVA will have "invested" at least another $1 billion to $2 billion in nuclear facilities. Third, and more fundamentally, an IRP is normally prepared by a utility but reviewed by an independent public utility commission staff. Under the current "dual-purpose" TVA board system, the IRP process will have to rely on an unrealistic willingness by TVA to engage in massive self-criticism. Without an independent regulatory authority in charge of the IRP or; at least, a larger, regionally based, part-time board for TVA that is clearly separated from management and has independent analytical capability, TVA's IRP will merely summarize and defend TVA's current power planning strategy.

REFERENCES

Gregory, E. *Nashville Tennessean* (May 16, 1993).

Lane, E. "In Debt and Off Line: Uncertain Future Faces Nuclear-Driven TVA." *Energy Daily* (May 4, 1993).

North American Electric Reliability Council (NERC). *Electricity Supply and Demand for 1990–2000: Annual Summary of Electric Utility Supply and Demand Projections*. Princeton, NJ: NERC, July 1991.

Public Utilities Fortnightly (PUF) (June 1, 1993): 28.

Public Utilities Fortnightly (PUF). Quoted in "Remarkable Remarks," (October 1, 1993): 6.

Pulsipher, Allan. "TVA and Restructuring: Will More Competitive Markets Put TVA on the Ropes?" *The Electricity Journal* 4 (June 1991): 46–59.

Sansome, Robert. *TVA Transition Report*. Washington, DC. 1981.

Southeast Power Report (December 17, 1993): 9.

Southeast Power Report (June 18, 1993).

Southeast Power Report. "TVA Restarts 1,221-MW Sequoyah 2 Plant but Watts Bar Start-up Pushed to 1995."(November 5, 1993): 2–3.

Southern States Energy Board. *TVA: A Path to Recovery*, 1987.

Tennessee Valley Authority (TVA), Chief Economists Staff. *Measuring the Rate-of-Return of TVA's Reservoir System*. Knoxville, TN: TVA, 1987.

Tennessee Valley Authority (TVA). *TVA Bond Offering Circular*. Knoxville, TN: TVA, December 8, 1993.

U.S. Department of Commerce, Bureau of the Census. *Current Population Reports, P-25*. No. 1017, Washington, DC: U.S. Department of Commerce, 1990.

U.S. Department of Energy (USDOE), Energy Information Administration. *Monthly Energy Review*. Washington, DC: USDOE, December 1993.

25

European Community Case Study

Francis McGowan

The issue of federalism in the electricity supply industry (ESI) is not unique to the United States. In countries such as Australia and Canada, the extent to which electricity operation, planning, and regulation should be centralized is currently under debate, while progress in integrating electricity systems across borders continues in such regions as Southern Africa, South East Asia, the Southern Cone of Latin America, and, the topic of this paper, the countries of the European Community (EC). Federalism is a highly charged political topic, particularly so in regions where it entails a pooling of sovereignty among ostensibly independent nation-states (in contrast to the more widely understood idea of devolution within a single nation-state). Thus in Europe, the F-word is rarely uttered; instead, such issues are discussed in code, with "subsidiarity" the key. Unfortunately, as we will see, the concept of subsidiarity is also open to more than one interpretation.

The issue of federalism or subsidiarity is further confused in the EC context by two related and largely economic phenomena: integration and liberalization. The key to federalism in the Community has been the opening of markets and the breaking down of trade barriers between nations. For supporters of the Community, liberalization has been an important prerequisite for the integration of national economies, and in the process has created the basis for closer political ties, possibly even a federal Europe. However, is the relationship between these three factors so straightforward? Integration of Community markets need not necessarily be achieved by liberalization and does not necessarily require federal political structures.

The development of the electricity industry in Europe has been based on national, even local autonomy—and the tradition of self-sufficiency dies hard. Now the European Commission is seeking to introduce measures to draw the ESI into the process of integration and liberalization characteristic of the Community as a whole. The effort is not appreciated by the governments and industries of most member states, which seek to maintain their autonomy. Yet, although the final shape of Community reforms is not yet clear, it is unlikely that the old model of national and natural monopolies can survive; the industry is becoming much more European, and probably more open.

This chapter examines how this development has taken place and what the consequences of subsidiarity and reform in the industry might be for the Community and other regions. After a brief review of the concept of subsidiarity and an examination of how the industry has developed, the paper will examine how the Community came to be involved and what the impact might be, particularly with regard to the division of regulatory responsibilities (the subsidiarity question) and the possible restructuring of the industry. The chapter considers the scope for the EC and U.S. electricity systems to learn from each other's federal experiments.

DEFINING SUBSIDIARITY

Subsidiarity is both a means of defining how competences are to be divided between different levels of political authority and of delineating the boundaries between the activities of the state and of individuals.[1] It is interesting to note that this latter aspect has been largely ignored in current political debates, as, to a large extent, has the sub-state aspect, in so far as, in most debates, it is up to national governments to determine how far subsidiarity percolates down the political system. In contrast to the United States, therefore, subsidiarity or federalism is concerned primarily with the balance between national and supra-national, not sub-national, authorities.

In the Community, subsidiarity is invoked both by those who favor greater Community integration (who regard it as a way of accelerating integration) and those who oppose it (for whom it is equivalent to decentralization and a constraint upon Community-level decision making) (McCrone, 1992). Thus it is possible for the concept of subsidiarity to be invoked by both supporters and opponents of a greater European dimension in policymaking: What matters is who exercises it.

The malleability of the concept is well illustrated in the case of the electricity industry: Both those in favor of integration and those against it make much of subsidiarity, the former seeking to interpret it as the application of rules agreed at an EC level, the latter viewing it as grounds for leaving as much room for maneuver as possible in implementing rules decided at an EC level. To understand why the balance of opinion is so strongly weighted toward this latter minimalist interpretation of subsidiarity, it is necessary to examine how the European power industry has developed.

THE EUROPEAN INDUSTRY: PATCHWORK OR SHARED MODEL?

The European ESI evolution has followed the same path of technological improvement on the supply side and increased requirements on the demand side as that experienced in the United States.[2] A move to more capital-intensive technologies and the growing complexity of financing and planning led to institutional adjustments. In order to reap the benefits, utilities consolidated horizontally and vertically; the number of utilities has decreased in almost all countries over the last century. The growing concentration of the industry has for most of its history been accompanied by higher public participation, whether at a national or a local level. In all cases, moreover, the industry has developed (for at least the last fifty years) on a national basis.[3]

The Community ESI in the 1980s comprised three types of industrial structure. There was a cluster of publicly owned, centralized monopolies created between the 1920s, when the Irish Electricity Supply Board was founded, and the 1970s, when the post-revolution government in Portugal nationalized its industry. Included in this group were countries such as Britain and France where, although separate entities existed for some activities (principally distribution), there was de facto integration with the powerful transmission and production firms. Other countries had an apparently more decentralized structure with local or cooperative public ownership dominant in the system. The Danish and Dutch systems were the exemplars of this structure. In both countries, the industry comprised transmission companies owned by production companies, which in turn were owned by distribution companies: In Denmark the distributors are a mix of local authorities and cooperatives, and in Netherlands the industry is purely municipally based. In a few cases, private companies made up the bulk of the industry, though even in these cases there was a significant public element. In Belgium and Spain, state-owned utilities increased their role in the industry's operations in the 1980s. In Germany, local and Laender governments have been closely involved in the industry, either operating utilities themselves or owning significant shareholdings in other utilities organized as private firms.

There has also been an apparent diversity in the technical characteristics of the industry. This diversity stems from organizational factors (e.g., the prevalence of municipal cogeneration systems in some countries), natural resource endowments, political decisions (for and against nuclear power), and the configuration of relationships between government, industry, and suppliers.

This last factor reflects an important aspect of the conduct of utilities within the EC. In most countries, utilities, whether private or public, have tended to buy capital equipment and fuel nationally. The reasons for this lie in a mixture of factors including the possibility of supplier cartels agreeing not to compete in home markets, government pressures on utilities, and the utilities' own preferences for technical and security of supply reasons. Above all, however, there was little incentive to do otherwise.[4] Although in many respects utilities carried out strategies that reflected the industrial policy objectives of governments, those objectives were largely shared, and to some extent shaped, by the utilities themselves (nuclear power policy is a good example).

Thus, although the specific differences of institutional and technical structures are important, we should also be aware of some fundamental and important similarities. It is perhaps because of these shared characteristics that European utilities have generally enjoyed good relations with one another, often sharing more in common with each other than with their governments, suppliers, and consumers, drawing perhaps on a shared set of values and perceptions of what is the optimal way to develop electricity supply. The relative harmony between them may also reflect the limited contacts, particularly any involving rivalry. Until the last few years, there was no semblance of competition for supply, internally or internationally (beyond occasional skirmishes to encourage large customers to locate in their territory). Cooperation has been relatively limited and has concentrated on joint ventures (in areas such as advanced nuclear technologies, perhaps the quintessential precompetitive research ventures), joint representation (in international technical and promotional bodies such as Unipede), and mutual trading arrangements.

Trade in electricity has been a feature of the industry for much of this century, with utilities willingly cooperating to exploit joint resources (such as rivers for hydroelectric development), to take advantage of different patterns of demand and profiles of power plant capacity (thereby optimizing their national systems through cooperation), and to assist each other in the event of an emergency.[5] Loose cooperative organizations such as the Union for the Coordination of Production and Transmission of Electricity (UCPTE) in Western Europe and NORDEL in Scandinavia have been formed by utilities to facilitate trade, but they fall well short of centralized dispatch and planning.[6]

Such trade has always been carried out by utilities alone, however, and scarcely challenges their autonomy (for example, in the area of investment). Utilities have retained their national autonomy, arguing that the need to ensure security of supply and the technical stability of the system requires that trade be conducted on this basis. Pooling sovereignty in long-term decisions would, it has been felt, undermine the benefits of the nationally integrated ESI.

PRESSURES FOR CHANGE AND REFORMS

The European electricity industry has evolved over nearly one hundred years according to a single model. Despite institutional and technical differences, all systems have moved in the direction of a more centralized and integrated system, operating on the basis of long-term planning.[7]

In the last twenty years, however, the conditions that underpinned the successful development of the industry have changed, and the international harmony among utilities has come to be tested. Energy crises and economic recessions played havoc with input prices and demand. The technical economies that had delivered ever lower costs of production began to be exhausted, as the technical limits of larger plant were reached and their operational limitations emerged. Not only did the benefits of larger plant diminish, but the costs of that plant, either through longer construction times or poor load factors, were greater than anticipated. Yet utilities continued to plan for future capacity on the basis of the historic trend of large increases in demand at a time when the rate of growth was slowing dramatically. As a result, in a number of countries, there was substantial oversupply. Moreover, the decisions taken by utilities were often unpopular, and they encountered increasing opposition, particularly when nuclear power plants were planned. Such controversies inevitably undermined the image of the ESI as acting in the public interest. Environmental concerns played a major role in criticisms of utilities' bias toward large supply-side technologies, rather than toward renewable forms of energy and/or energy efficiency.[8]

The idea of the utility acting for the public interest was also undermined by government's use of the industry. Throughout the 1970s and early 1980s governments intervened in the ESI's decision-making far more than in previous decades. In many countries, the utility was used as a part of the public sector to control inflation (through price controls) and public expenditure (through financial controls), while the utility's traditional role as a purchaser of local fuel and plant was exploited more by government. The extent and nature of government intervention varied from country to country, but in many countries, government policy compromised the utilities' task of providing cheap and relatively efficient electricity supply.

In a sense, therefore, the implicit contract between the ESI and government broke down in many countries. There was growing criticism of the utility's conduct and its relationship with government. As the traditional models of control and influence were seen as having failed, the legitimacy of the existing system of organization came into question. It would be wrong to suggest that the overall record of the ESI dramatically deteriorated in this period; in most countries, a high standard of service and relatively low electricity prices prevailed. Nonetheless, where there were shortcomings (whether technically, organizationally, or politically rooted), these were often ascribed to a more general malaise in the regime that underpinned the industry.

In some countries, the collapse in energy prices in the mid-1980s exacerbated the utilities' problems. Although the price of certain internationally traded fuels fell dramatically, utilities were not always able to take advantage of them (because of obligations to local suppliers or government fiscal requirements). The collapse in prices, rooted in apparent oversupply of most fuels, had a number of effects. It exposed the utilities' role in protecting national fuel industries, in some cases leading to trade tensions with potential exporters. On the demand side, large consumers in particular began to place more importance on price than security of supply, and a number questioned the value of their existing supplier's monopoly. The fall in energy prices weakened the scarcity culture that had dominated energy policy in the 1970s, fostering the perception that energy was just another commodity and that the energy industries were not "special cases."

Nor should the role of technology in permitting new solutions be ignored. Earlier, the difficulties with existing systems of technology, particularly those associated with the pursuit of scale economies, were noted as contributing to the problems faced by utilities. The advent of combined cycle gas turbine (CCGT) technology and developments in information technology (IT) have undoubtedly transformed both short-term and long-term planning decisions within the industry, in both Europe and the rest of the world. Without these developments, many of the institutional reforms currently under debate would not be possible. Whereas the construction of new plant (conventional and nuclear) had increasingly hindered the industry's flexibility and locked it into thirty- to forty-year planning horizons and highly capital-intensive investment strategies, the option of CCGTs has reduced the need for such long-term-ism and increased the industry's responsiveness. At the same time, IT developments have transformed the day-to-day operations of the industry, allowing for much more sophisticated "market" arrangements in both the dispatch and the supply of power.[9]

Just as the nature of criticisms has varied from country to country, so have the types of reforms proposed to address the problems of the industry. Claims that the publicly owned ESI has failed have been strongest in those countries with neo- liberal governments (principally the UK and, to a lesser extent, Portugal); although they are not unique to them, as the debate on privatization in countries such as Ireland and Italy demonstrates. In the context of neo-liberalism, it is hardly surprising that the industry came to be considered as part of the privatization/deregulation agenda. Ideas of market liberalization and structural change that were applied to other regulated industries were considered for the energy sectors, including the ESI. The reforms have involved internal reorganization, the introduction of competitive mechanisms into the industry, and privatization. In the case of the UK, the industry has undergone a more or less complete transformation from a vertically integrated and publicly owned utility to a more decentralized and largely privately owned industry, where competition extends to sales to final consumers and regulation largely consists of price-cap controls and anti-trust provisions. Although many question the extent and the benefits of competition, there is little doubt that the British industry is now driven by a dynamic based on short-term profit maximization and competition rather than on long-term planning and cooperation.[10]

Elsewhere, the reasons for reform are focused on factors such as the need to secure operational efficiency (France and the Netherlands) by rationalizing the structure of the industry or to contain environmental problems (Denmark and Germany) by fostering energy efficiency or renewable energies, although in each of these cases the changes have not challenged the basic structure of the sector. There are those countries where the debate on reform is a matter of struggle between government and industry, whether privately or locally owned (Spain and the Netherlands). Finally, there are those where the reforms are at least partially motivated by the prospect of a more European electricity industry (Belgium and Spain), which seem designed to preempt the efforts of the European Commission, to devise a policy for the industry.[11]

THE COMMUNITY ROLE

To understand how policies toward the ESI are developing within Europe, it is necessary to review how decisions are made within the

Community. The Community comprises four main institutions: the Council of Ministers, where all member states are represented and where decisions are agreed upon; the Court of Justice, where legal questions relating to the interpretation of Community law are adjudicated; the Parliament, where elected representatives from member states debate Community policies; and the Commission where policies are initiated and, following Council approval, monitored. The Commission is therefore much more than a simple administrative bureaucracy, particularly given its exclusive power of initiating policy. Although proposals can be and are altered by the Council, the Commission is closely involved in the decision-making process. The balance of power is shifting within the Community, following changes made in the Treaty on European Union, which came into force in 1993. However, the Commission remains a central actor within the Community.

What is the orientation of Community policies, in place or under consideration, toward the ESI? Community rules on procurement, on environmental protection, taxation, research and, most controversially, competition all impact on the industry. Why should this be? The Treaty of Rome, which is the basis of European Community law, applies, by implication, to the ESI. It is true that the electricity industry has often been regarded as a special case both in economic theory and in national policy practice. The near monopolistic characteristics and the close links with public authorities were (and often still are) reflected in exemptions from national monopoly laws or in direct public ownership. Nonetheless, there are key principles enshrined in articles of the treaty that could be applied, particularly the articles on freedom of movement and competition. Possibly the most important of these are the rules concerning competition, which effectively constitute European anti-trust provisions. Thus, although many states have exempted the electricity industry from their national anti-trust laws, no exemption from Community law has ever been granted (or sought) for the ESI.[12]

Given the potential of the treaty to address the industry, what has been the impact of Community law and policy on the sector? Until recently, very little. Other issues took precedence in Community deliberations. Moreover, the energy sector as a whole was one in which member states sought to maintain their autonomy, while public utilities were even more closely protected than other industries. Since the ESI straddled both areas; the sector's organization and conduct were not up for debate. The Commission was largely happy to leave member states to determine the pace and nature of change in the industry as they thought fit.[13]

It was only in the mid-1980s that the Commission demonstrated both the willingness and the competence to challenge the national utilities, which had previously been effectively protected from Community purview by member states. The new initiatives occurred in the context of developments on environmental policy and more relevantly to this chapter the broader debate on the single-market initiative.[14] An increased activism on anti-trust affected public enterprises and public utilities in particular. In cases concerning the telecommunications and transport industries, the Commission effectively established precedents for action in the energy industry.[15]

The new activism followed the success of the single-market initiative. The original proposals on the internal market did not touch on energy directly, aside from its proposals on harmonizing taxes and standards and liberalizing equipment procurement.[16] In 1988, however, the Commission published its proposals for an internal energy market. It was clear that the most significant changes were planned for the ESI. The Commission noted that, although the level of trade was increasing in the sector, it only constituted 7 percent of total requirements. The relatively low level of trade was ascribed to the structure and conduct of the industry, which, it argued, acted as a barrier to greater trade and competition. According to the Commission, "a change in the operational (as distinct from the ownership) system would be conducive to further opening of the internal market."[17]

The analysis and Commission's initial proposals for greater trade and transparency were fiercely debated within the industry, with the trade issue being the major area of concern. Many utilities expressed doubts both on the technical feasibility of some options and whether they would improve upon existing arrangements for trade (although inevitably, such arguments also reflected their own concerns at loss of autonomy).[18] Nonetheless, the Commission began a gradual process of reform, helped in part by pressures from large, energy-intensive consumers and by the example and support of the British.

The Commission's first practical step came at the beginning of 1989 in its proposed package of directives covering the transparency of electricity prices, investment coordination, and trade among utilities.[19] The proposed directives met with mixed success. In debating these measures, member states and the industries were anxious to ensure that the changes did not include any commitments to further radical reforms to the sector. After much debate the directives on transit (setting out terms of wheeling between production-transmission utilities) and transparency were passed, confirming the EC Commission role in this area. However, a number of amendments to the transit directive restricted the scope for using it as the basis for more open trade arrangements. Moreover, the proposal for greater coordination of national investment programs was effectively rejected.

Given the slow progress of the initial proposals and the degree of controversy they provoked, the second stage of the program—moving towards greater competition on a Community basis—was handled very carefully. The Commission established two working groups (one government based and one industry based) to investigate the pros and cons of competition in the industry. Within those groups, the balance of opinion was against change, although the presence of the governments of Britain and some other states (principally Ireland and Portugal) on the government inquiry, and that of their utilities and some consumers on the industrial committee, meant that these bodies were unable to present a unanimous rejection of further liberalization.[20] Even so, as a result of lobbying by opponents of the policy and the uncertain balance of opinion within the Commission, proposals for further liberalization were steadily watered down throughout 1991.[21]

The Commission's proposals set out to introduce competition and greater industry transparency within a framework of safeguards regarding system operation and consumer protection. Competition was to be put into operation at the levels of generation, transmission, and, within limits, final consumers.[22]

The policies met with vigorous opposition from the moment of their publication, and at the time of this writing, it was unclear whether the proposals would be pursued further, diluted substantially, or allowed to lapse.[23] In November 1992, the Council requested the Commission to reconsider its proposals and passed them to the Parliament, which proposed in 1993 that the program of reforms be slowed down, and the emphasis be placed on harmonization of market conditions (e.g., over planning law, fiscal treatment, etc.) rather than liberalization.

The final shape of the policy will depend on competing pressures within the Commission. On the one hand, the political climate within the Community is such that any radical reforms imposed by the Commission may lead to serious political crises. Sensitivity over member states' attitudes toward the power of the Commission has led it to adopt a generally cautious approach to controversial policies. On the other hand, some in the Commission have indicated that they will push ahead in order to maintain the momentum of Community integration and the credibility of the Commission in that process. This determination is demonstrated by a decision to take a number of states to the European Court to strike down trade monopolies in the power sector.[24] In these respects, it could be argued that at least the Commission's Competition Directorate is maintaining the pressure.[25]

As if to complicate the political calculus still further, two new policy initiatives appear to reinforce the arguments of those opposed to radical restructuring of the Community ESI. The first is that of trans-

European networks. The defining characteristic of the Commission's initiative was to facilitate convergence in member states' policies and utilities strategies, with the emphasis being placed on questions of standardization and "interoperability."[26] The utilities, which have in the past been hostile to initiatives aimed at encouraging greater integration, have welcomed the provision, seeing it as a counter to the deregulatory thrust of much of Community policy, emphasizing cooperation over competition.[27]

A more recent development, which builds on the idea of trans-European networks, is the initiative of the French government to develop a "European Public Service Charter." This aims to develop a code of conduct that would embody a number of duties that utilities would be expected to carry out, in terms of universal service provision and other social obligations.[28]

Taken together, these initiatives could be seen as rear-guard actions by the opponents of the Commission to reestablish their credentials in a European context. By broadening the issues which the Community should address, these policies seek to dilute the pro-competition bias of the Commission, or at least provide some ammunition to the industry and its supporters to resist further liberalization. Yet resorting to these measures may also imply a recognition that change in the organization and conduct of the ESI is unavoidable, with a corresponding need to distinguish between the different aspects of the industry, and that a European role in that process is inevitable whether the orientation of policy is toward greater competition or greater cooperation.

SYSTEM IMPLICATIONS

The impact of reforms is potentially greatest in terms of the operation of the system itself and the way in which planning is undertaken. The Commission's proposals sketch an outline of how the regional operators would manage each system, but they do not provide a detailed picture of how, for example, future investment would be undertaken or regulated. At one level it might be possible to leave this process to "the market," but if UK experience is anything to go by, the incentives will remain imperfect enough to threaten not a shortage of investment but a substantial overcapacity.[29]

The impact on day-to-day operations is presumably manageable, although designing the pooling system will be complex: The existing, largely cooperatively organized arrangements within UCPTE and NORDEL will not be sufficient. Moreover, many system management costs that were previously internalized (reactive power, transmission pricing) will have to be externalized. Calculating such costs has proved difficult within countries; it will be even more difficult where the proposed operating regions breach national borders. From a European perspective, such a development might be a laudable step toward integration, but it might look very differently at a national level, being perceived as a serious loss of sovereignty.[30] Much will depend on to what extent the member states and utilities are prepared to relinquish autonomy in this area, and the degree to which market-based decision making will be tolerated.

If the system moves toward greater competition, how will the utilities themselves be affected? If a highly competitive system is developed, then it may be worth noting how the U.K. industry has changed.

Since privatization and reorganization in the UK, there has undoubtedly been a shift in perception vis-à-vis the business of electricity supply. Whereas this has traditionally been viewed as a long-term business (involving the use of long- term forecasting techniques and a range of strategic research options), in a competitive regime, where electricity becomes less a public infrastructure and more of a competitive commodity, the commitment of utilities to the "long run" has weakened, and the focus of planning and the time scales involved have correspondingly altered. There is greater interest in short-term profitability as well as an interest in diversification away from the core business of electricity supply.

Of course, many of these changes in Britain result as much from the fact that the industry has been moved into the private sector as they do from the shift to competition, but the effect of competition in reducing the cost-plus nature of the business cannot be ignored. It will be interesting to see how a shift to competition can be sustained if the bulk of the industry within the Community remains in public hands. Even if it does, it is likely that a tougher competition policy would probably oblige the utility to behave more like a short-term-profit-maximizing private company, and that some of the changes seen in the UK might be replicated.

If a less competitive structure is adopted, the changes in utility operation are likely to be less radical. Nonetheless, the need to move toward greater coordination of investment and operations would probably put pressure on costs and prompt at least some reorientation of utility priorities.

REGULATORY IMPLICATIONS

The most obvious solution to this and to other problems is for some form of regulatory scrutiny in the system. There is a need for regulatory intervention for consumer protection and the promotion of competition. However, where should that process take place and how should it be managed?

The Commission has understandably been very hesitant on these issues. The directives make clear that, as far as possible, the principle of subsidiarity will be respected in both the operation of the directive and in the conduct of any regulation that may be necessary. However, to the extent that the final proposals involve greater competition, then there must be a question mark over how far it is possible to leave the regulatory task with national authorities. There is a real risk of regulatory capture within such systems, particularly where the regulator is also the industry owner.

Of course, where a matter of dispute arose involving another country as a supplier or a consumer, a Community role is probably inevitable. It may be that such a role should also be available for "internal matters" (i.e., a dispute between two parties within a country), should the outcome from national regulatory procedures prove unsatisfactory to one party. The problem then becomes one of resources (How can such a Community regulatory facility be developed?) and accountability (Who regulates the regulators?).

In these matters, the UK experience—where regulation and ownership have been separated—is again instructive. Over the last ten years, a system of regulation has developed in Britain for the privatized utilities. This model, which is rooted in the anti-trust system, has proved relatively successful, although increasingly it is coming under criticism for a variety of (not always consistent) reasons: The regulator has been criticized for allowing too much and not enough competition, for exercising too much and not enough discretion, and for being populist and unaccountable. Although the origins of this model are obviously unique to British circumstances, the model may be worth replicating at a Community level. The linkage to competition law would of course be a point of similarity, whereas the UK model's relatively low resource requirements might also render it attractive.

Even so, there are likely to be issues where such a regulatory authority would find it extremely difficult to provide a solution. To what extent, for example, are the goals of protecting the captive consumer and promoting competition compatible? There are already visible strains in this balancing act in a UK context. How much harder will they be to sustain in other Community countries? Moreover, how would the duties of a regulatory authority be reconciled with those of other national or Community policies?

Whatever regulatory solution is chosen and wherever the balance of regulatory power lies, it is likely to be more transparent than the prevailing utility-government relationships in most member states.

The extent to which governments would be able to use utilities for the pursuit of other policies may be limited, even in the area of energy policy. Both as a result of the changes in policy and the mechanisms of regulation put in place, the old patterns of influence may be harder to sustain. As governments find themselves unable to use the industry as an industrial policy instrument, they may be less defensive of the existing structure. Yet, as the UK experience demonstrates, the consequences of reforming the sector may be far reaching: Suppliers such as the local coal industry, consumers who have enjoyed low tariffs, and activities such as long-term research have all been "losers" in the more competitive electricity market. How should such public policy issues be addressed?

One solution would be to address many of the issues arising from a Europeanized ESI at a European policy level. Thus, where there are conflicts between different policies (e.g., between competition and environmental protection) or between priorities in different member states, it would be possible to resolve these at a Community level, or even better, to anticipate them through Community policies. The only snag with this solution is that a coherent and "enforceable" Community energy policy has already been rejected by member states over many years, most recently in the Treaty of European Union. Energy policy has been an area where national states have not been prepared to pool sovereignty, and it has been easier for the Commission to intervene on the basis of pursuing competition policy or single market objectives. The development of "federal" regulation of the electricity (and other parts of the energy) industry might prompt member states to reconsider that opposition.

STRUCTURAL IMPLICATIONS

The emergence of a Community dimension to the regulation of the electricity industry may also prompt changes in the structure and conduct of the industry itself. There are a number of developments that suggest that the shape of the industry itself is becoming more European. Although the spate of national reorganization plans clearly owes a lot to the interest of the Community, perhaps more interesting are the cases that involve cross-border alliances or even mergers. The most active in this regard are the British and French industries: Both are buying into projects inside and outside the Community. There are also instances of privately owned utilities in Germany, Spain, and Belgium purchasing stakes in each other.

These structural developments are marginal at the moment; the industry continues to be organized and operated at a national level.

Yet, along with the growing levels of trade in electricity, they indicate that we may be moving toward a more European electricity industry, prompted, at least in part, by the prospect of greater regulatory intervention by the institutions of the European Community. They appear to be designed in large part to respond to the development of Community policies, although whether they constitute a preemptive move or an adjustment to new rules is less clear.

Similarly, the interventions of the Commission seem to demonstrate that the Community dimension of the electricity industry cannot be ignored, even if its final shape is not defined.[31]

CONCLUSIONS: FEDERALISM AND ELECTRICITY IN THE EC AND THE UNITED STATES

This chapter has examined the progress toward a European electricity regime and the part played by the European Community. Whatever the outcome of current debates, it does appear that after a century of development along the lines of nationally based natural monopolies, the industry in Europe (or at least within the Community) is facing a new institutional setting, one that emphasizes a greater degree of cross-border interaction (cooperative or competitive) than exists at present, and at least an element of supra-national regulation.

Whether these changes constitute a move to a federal regime is open to debate. As we noted at the beginning, the invocation of subsidiarity ostensibly leaves the focus of control at a national level. Yet, if the rules governing the system incorporate such factors as investment coordination, transborder regional operation, and competition in power production, then some form of Community regulation will be necessary. It may be possible to leave the implementation of that regulation to national authorities, but there will almost inevitably be disputes that straddle national borders and require some arbitration. Moreover, although the Commission claims to be ready to leave the bulk of the regulatory task to member states, if the overall policy is to be credible (i.e., if we are to see a European electricity system develop according to the rules agreed upon at the Community level), the Commission will almost certainly have to intervene; the relationship between national industries and national regulators is too close in many member states for one to be confident that a form of regulatory preference, let alone capture, will not prevail.[32] If effective reform of the industry is to take place, then we have to adopt a maximalist interpretation of subsidiarity, not leaving everything to the member states, but allowing some scope for regulation at the Community level.

Given that regulation is required at the Community level, how can it best be organized? Are there grounds for a permanent and sectoral-specific European regulatory agency (a EuroFERC), or should the task be left to the European competition authorities in the Commission operating in tandem with the European Court of Justice? Perhaps the U.S. experience of a federal energy regulator is relevant here. As relevant, if not more so, is the relationship between the federal government and state regulators, particularly in relation to such initiatives as independent power production and competitive bidding.

What is less clear is whether there are lessons from the Community for the United States as opposed to those to be drawn from experiments within particular member states; in that respect, for better or worse, the UK is probably the main exemplar. The apparent lack of applicable experience is due both to the relatively early stage that the debate in the Community has reached and the different nature of the federal problem in Europe. In the United States, federalism concerns the allocation of responsibilities between different levels of government within a single nation state. In the Community, federalism (if we can call it that) involves independent nation-states pooling sovereignty, agreeing to be bound by common rules in order to promote economic (and, for some, political) integration. At the moment, the limits on the dimensions and the scope for that federalism are still set by national governments. We may now be at a stage where the extent of economic integration is such that the momentum behind greater political integration (i.e., a federal system) is irresistible (notwithstanding the very real sensitivities regarding national sovereignty). In its own way, how reforms in the electricity industry progress and how far regulatory tasks are granted to Community institutions may indicate whether we have reached that stage.

NOTES

1. See Emiliou (1992) and Adonis and Tyrie (1991). The origins of the subsidiarity concept lie in the canon law of the Catholic Church, where it was invoked against the encroachment of state power on individuals. It subsequently reemerged in 1950s German legal thinking in the process of defining the balance of powers in the new Federal Republic. Indeed, more generally, federalist thinkers have been talking about subsidiarity without knowing it for centuries. For the background to this debate, see Wilke and Wallace (1990) and Commission of the European Communities (1992).

2. The best accounts of the development of the ESI deals primarily with the United States; see, for example, Joskow and Schmalansee (1983).

3. No general histories of the European industry exist; most are

confined in terms of geography and/or the time examined, of which the most notable is Hughes (1983). A useful conceptual treatment of the industry is provided in Bouttes and Lederer (1990).

4.   The monopoly structure of the industry was not generally subject to tough regulation; public ownership and the generally weak controls on nationalized industries were seen as sufficient to protect the public interest, whereas in private systems, the level of regulation was minimal, certainly nothing equivalent to the legalistic structures developed in the United States, reflecting both the closeness of the utility to national interests and, in a sense, the capture of those interests by the utilities (whose shareholders often included the major industrial and financial players in the economy). On the pattern of regulation, see Helm and McGowan (1989).

5.   In 1992, electricity production in the EC was just over 1900 TWh; aggregated exports were 110 TWh.

6.   The UCPTE was founded in 1951 to achieve a more efficient utilization of power production and transmission in Western Europe. In the course of the reconstruction of the Europe, the Organization for European Economic Cooperation (OEEC) brought together European and American utility experts with a view to Europe emulating the system of pooling and coordination established in the United States. See, for example, OEEC (1950). See Bruppacher (1988) on the operation of the UCPTE. On the development of NORDEL and its antecedents, see Kaijser (1991). However, the national industries in Europe preferred to maintain their autonomy and created the looser framework of the Union. There has, therefore, been no central organ to coordinate national systems (instead, they inform each other bilaterally of supply and demand conditions), let alone plan future development. Nordel was founded in 1963 and brings together the Scandinavian utilities to pool their different production resources. The cooperation within this group is arguably closer than that in the UCPTE (there are committees for planning, operations, and generation as well as a secretariat), but, as in UCPTE, dispatch is not centralized and bilateral arrangements dominate. Some details of the workings of European electricity trade are provided in International Energy Agency (1985). For more information, see Remondeulaz (1991).

7.   In most countries, the government has played a significant ownership role and has obliged the industry to operate in the "national interest." Moreover, even in private systems, they have tended to conduct themselves as "public service" companies. Whether public or private, the industry has been managed on a "cost-plus" basis, with very little scope for competition. It has also developed within national boundaries, with cooperation across borders only a limited part of most systems' activity.

8.   On the flagging performance of the industry as a whole, see Thomas (1988).

9.   On the role of new technology in the electricity industry, see Walker (1986). A thoughtful perspective on the past and future of the industry is given by Lonnroth (1989).

10.   See Vickers and Yarrow (1992) for details of the UK privatization.

11. See McGowan and Thomas (1992).

12. On the possible application of Community law to the sector, see Hancher and Trepte (1992).

13. In the 1970s, the Commission sought to influence decisions in the industry, but its efforts were made in the context of the prevailing debate on supply security, which aimed to diversify sources of supply and reduce dependence on imported oil in power generation. For the most part, these efforts came to very little; national autonomy prevailed (McGowan, 1990).

14. The Commission launched an Internal Energy Market initiative on the back of the revival of its authority following the signing of the Single European Act (a major revision of the Rome Treaty that increased the potential for decision making), the renewed commitment to a single market and, arguably most importantly, the Commission's increased readiness to apply competition law to the Community economy. See Commission of the European Communities (1988).

15. See de Cockborne (1990).

16. See McGowan and Thomas (1989) on procurement changes and Haigh (1989) on environmental issues.

17. See Commission of the European Communities (1988, COM (88)238).

18. See, for example, the report prepared by the German electricity industry association, VDEW, defending the status quo (1988).

19. See three items from the Commission of the European Communities in 1989 (COM (89) 332; COM (89) 336 SYN; COM(89) 335).

20. However, both the industry pressure group Eurelectric (speaking, incidentally only, for its "continental members" and not for the British industry) and the public enterprise pressure group, the Center for European Public Enterprises (CEEP), were vigorous in challenging the Commission's proposals; see Agence Europe (10 and 13 April 1991).

21. In particular, plans to use special powers under the Rome Treaty to break the utilities' exclusive rights (effectively by-passing member states' approval) were put on the shelf, and the Commission proposed its liberalization under provisions that required member state agreement. Instead of forcing the issue (and risking a conflict in the courts and pressures on the Commission), it sought instead to secure agreement by majority vote. The content was also weakened, restricting access to the largest consumers (at least until 1996) and emphasizing the extent to which implementation of the proposals would be left in national hands. See Commission of the European Communities (1991, COM (91)548). See also Financial Times (16 October 1991), and on the continued opposition of the public enterprise, see Agence Europe (21 February 1992).

22. Competition in generation would require harmonizing access conditions and a licensing procedure. The exclusive right to produce electricity would be abolished and the terms for building plant were to be made clear to all and applied without discrimination. The proposal makes provision for

ensuring that production capacity is adequate to meet demand (through a regional review of future trends in supply requirements). Competition in transmission would also be allowed, subject to a licensing system. The key element, however, is that of third-party access. This would allow generators to sell their power to a range of potential customers, not just the local utilit,y and permits consumers to purchase from a wider range of suppliers. For this to work, the legislation requires that producers and consumers have access to the networks of distribution and transmission companies on fair terms. As noted, this access would, in the first instance, be limited to large consumers (i.e., those with annual consumption of over 100 GWh/year) and distribution companies. To ensure that existing utilities do not abuse their position in the system, particularly in competitive situations, the directive also proposes that the utilities separate out different functions of the industry. Production, transmission, and distribution would each be carried out in separate divisions with separate accounts. On this basis it was hoped that it would be possible to ensure that there would be no discrimination. In order to coordinate this new competitive market and to ensure stability of the system in the long run and on a day-to-day basis, the proposal also calls for a management system. In each of a set of regions (some countries, some parts of countries, etc.), there will be a system operator responsible for secure and reliable supply. They will define conditions for connection in their system, cooperate with each other, review future requests, and so forth.

23. See *Financial Times* (1 December 1992).

24. See, for example, the treatment of this issue by the commission's Competition authorities (1992).

25. See *Financial Times* (5 February 1993).

26. This initiative is the culmination of a long effort by the Commission to encourage member states to coordinate more closely national infrastructure investment programs and to view them in the context of a European economy. To a large extent, therefore, the emphasis was on completing the European infrastructure; the means by which this was to be achieved were largely cooperative rather than competitive. The concept's importance was reinforced by its inclusion in the Treaty on European Union, a further set of amendments to the Rome Treaty, signed in 1991 and entering into force in 1993. See Commission of the European Communities (1989, COM(89)643).

27. See Commission of the European Communities (1992, COM(92)231 and SEC(92)553).

28. The initiative, which is aimed at sectors beyond but including the electricity industry, appears to be aimed at protecting the core activities of the utilities and countering the pro-competition initiatives of the late 1980s, by emphasizing monopoly tasks and social obligations. It has been welcomed by the Commission president, although the substantive impact of it, relative to the more legalistic basis of the deregulatory policies of the Commission, remains to be seen. See *Financial Times* (5 February 1993).

29. Of course, some aspects of the British system, such as the subsidies given to the state-owned nuclear industry and the close links between many of

the new "independent" power projects and the distribution companies, may be encouraging the over-investment. Perhaps a proposal that focused competition on the production of power would be better able to manage this problem, perhaps by a system of competitive bidding for new capacity, as in the U.S.

30. This concern may reflect the persistence of "supply security" as an issue for industry and government in Europe: most countries need to import more than 50 percent of their energy needs, and it could be that they perceive the electricity industry as the only element in their energy balances over which they maintain control. Equally, however, such arguments may obscure the extent to which they perceive their national industries as vulnerable in a more integrated and competitive electricity market.

31. At times, the Commission has seemed more interested in the Europeanness of the industry than the degree of competition within it. One of the key estimates of the benefits of integration is premised on increased cooperation among utilities rather than increased competition, see Coherence (1990).

32. Although it does not address the added complexities of regulation in an international setting, a good account of the idea of regulatory capture is given in Stigler (1972).

REFERENCES

Adonis, A., and A. Tyrie, "What Kind of European Union? Some Community Reforms for the 1990s." *National Westminster Quarterly Review* (May, 1991: 47-54).

Agence Europe 10 April 1991, p.14 and 13 April 1991, p.14.

Agence Europe 21 February 1992, p.14.

Bouttes, J. P., and P. Lederer. "The Organization of Electricity Systems and the Behavior of Players in Europe and the US." Paper presented at the Conference, "Organizing and Regulating Electric Utilities in the Nineties." Paris: CEPRIM, 1990.

Bruppacher, F. "How European Electricity Trade is Conducted—the Balance between Market Forces and Regulation." Paper presented at the Financial Times' World Electricity Conference. London, November 1988.

Coherence. "The Benefits of Integration in the European Electricity System." Working Document 9. Brussels: Directorate General for Energy, 1990.

Commission of the European Communities. *Draft Council Directive Concerning a Community Procedure to Improve the Transparency of Gas and Electricity Prices Charged to Industry End Users.* Brussels: Commission of the European Communities, 1989 (COM (89) 332).

Commission of the European Communities. *Draft Council Regulation Amending Regulation no 1056/72 on Notifying the Commission of Investment Projects of Interest to the Community in the Petroleum, Natural Gas and Electricity Sectors.* Brussels: Commission of the European Communities, 1989 (COM(89) 335).

Commission of the European Communities. *Electricity and Natural Gas Transmission Infrastructures in the Community.* Brussels: Commission of the European Communities, 1992 (SEC(92)553).

Commission of the European Communities. *Increased Intra-Community Electricity Exchanges, a Fundamental Step towards Completing the Internal Energy Market and Proposed Council Directive on the Transit of Electricity through Transmission Grids.* Brussels: Commission of the European Communities, 1989 (COM (89) 336 SYN).

Commission of the European Communities. *Proposal for a Council Directive Concerning Common Rules for the Internal Market in Electricity.* Brussels: Commission of the European Communities, 1991 (Com(91)548).

Commission of the European Communities. *The Internal Energy Market.* Brussels: Commission of the European Communities, 1988 (COM (88) 238).

Commission of the European Communities. *The Principle of Subsidiarity.* Brussels: Commission of the European Communities, 1992.

Commission of the European Communities. *Towards Europe Wide Networks.* Brussels: Commission of the European Communities, 1989 (COM(89)643).

Commission of the European Communities. *Transport Infrastructure.* Brussels: Commission of the European Communities, 1992 (COM(92)231).

Commission of the European Communities. *Twenty-First Report on Competition Policy 1991.* Luxembourg: Office for Official Publications of the European Communities, 1992.

de Cockborne, J. "Liberalizing the Community's Electricity Market—Should Telecom Show the Way?" *International Business Law Journal* no. 7. (1990): 851-878.

Emiliou, N. "Subsidiarity: An Effective Barrier against the Enterprises of Ambition." *European Law Review* 17 (1992): 383-407.

Financial Times. "EC Energy Break-up Plan Tabled in Brussels." 16 October 1991, p. 2.

Financial Times. "EC Energy Utilities Warned." 5 February 1993, p. 3.

Financial Times. "Energy Plans Survive Row." 1 December 1992, p. 3.

Haigh, N. *EEC Environmental Policy and Britain.* Harlow: Longmans, 1989.

Hancher, L., and Trepte, P. "Competition and the Internal Energy Market." *European Competition Law Review* 13, no.4 (1992): 149-160.

Helm, D. R., and F. McGowan. "Electricity Supply in Europe: Lessons for the UK." In D. R. Helm, J. A. Kay, and D. Thompson (eds.), *The Market for Energy.* Oxford: Clarendon Press, 1989.

Hughes, T. P. *Networks of Power.* Baltimore: Johns Hopkins, 1983.

International Energy Agency. *Electricity in IEA Countries.* Paris: OECD, 1985.

Joskow, P., and R. Schmalansee. *Markets for Power.* Cambridge, MA: MIT Press, 1983.

Kaijser, A. "Trans-Border Integration of Electricity and Gas: the Case of the Nordic Countries." Paper presented at the Third Meeting of the Large Scale Technical Systems Conference, Sydney, 1991.

Lonnroth, M. "The Coming Reformation of the Electric Utility Industry." In T. B. Johansson et al. (eds). *Electricity*. Lund: Lund University, 1989.

McCrone, G. "Subsidiarity: its Implications for Economic Policy." National *Westminster Quarterly Review* (November 1992): 46–56.

McGowan, F. "Conflicting Objectives in EC Energy Policy." Political Quarterly. Special Edition, *The Politics of 1992* (December 1990): 121–137.

McGowan, F., and S. Thomas. *Electricity in Europe: Inside the Utilities*. London: FTBI, 1992.

McGowan, F., and S. Thomas. "Restructuring in the Power Plant Equipment Industry and 1992." *World Economy* 12, No 4. (December 1989): 539–555.

OEEC. *Interconnected Power Systems in the USA and W Europe*. Paris: OEEC, 1950.

Remondeulaz, J. "Interconnection of Electric Systems in Europe." Paper presented at Unipede Congress, Copenhagen, 1991.

Stigler, G. "The Theory of Economic Regulation." *Bell Journal of Economics* 2 (1972): 3–21.

Thomas, S. "Power Plant Life Extension." *Energy* 13, no. 10. (1988): 767–785.

VDEW. *Der Europaische Strommarkt*. Frankfurt: VDEW, 1988.

Vickers, J., and Yarrow, G. "The British Electricity Experiment." *Economic Policy* no. 12. (1992).

Walker, W. "Information Technology and Energy Supply." *Energy Policy* 14, no. 6. (1986): 450–470.

Wilke, M., and H. Wallace. *Subsidiarity: Approaches to Power Sharing in the European Community*. London: RIIA, 1990.

26

Comment on the European Community Case

Richard D. Tabors

Although the European Community's Treaty of Rome provides the framework for economic integration, it does not specify the manner in which utility structures should be integrated within a cooperative economic framework and may, in fact, have been a long way from the minds of both the drafters and the signers of the agreement. Nonetheless, the utility structure, particularly the electricity sector, is a critical component of integration, specifically because the reality of having an interconnected electrical network—even if only for "security"—is that there will be power flows across boundaries as load flows change. These flows are both intentional in terms of power transfers for economic efficiency and inadvertent as part of loop flow conditions within the network.

The effort to further integrate the European utilities into a coordinated, more or less unified system has run squarely into objections based on national sovereignty, objective economic differences, and arguments of electrical engineering feasibility. Of the arguments, McGowan has shown clearly in his chapter that it is the question of subsidiarity that is the most critical. This question of subsidiarity can, I would suggest, be seen to be directly analogous to state (and frequently utility company) level questions being discussed within the U.S. electric utility industry; thus, there are significant lessons to be learned by players on both sides of the pond about issues in increased integration of physical systems and the implicit conflicts (or points of cooperation) that emerge between the political (and electrical) subunits and the super-unit.

It is particularly interesting to review McGowan's piece from each of four perspectives: structure, culture, technology, and economics.

Each, I would suggest, provide to the United States an added perspective on the federal/state relationships as we attempt to reform both operations and regulation of the electric sector.

STRUCTURE

In large part because of the sovereignty of individual states in Europe, the electric utilities have established organizational structures which range from totally government-owned to privately owned and government regulated. In an effort to realign their competitive positions vis-à-vis likely European Community (EC) requirements and to achieve specific national objectives, the individual utilities have taken different routes.

The most dramatic of these has been the complete restructuring of the British power industry. The vertical disintegration of the system, the explicit introduction of competition on generation and supply, the establishment of an entity that controls the grid system, and the use of complex integrated engineering models in conjunction with the bookkeeping function of the system are all innovations that bear careful observation from both the continent and from the United States. The latest proposal from Brussels aims toward using the British model for the whole of the Community, but the Community objects. The model (referred to incorrectly as an "experiment") is oft quoted but seldom accurately within the U.S. debate on restructuring. It provides an excellent source of experience in market-based operations. What is clear from the British case is that the lights stayed on even when the basic unit of transaction became a half-hourly generator bidding system. Further, the system reliability has not suffered and, although the jury is still out, it appears to this observer that the conditions of increased equity to consumers have been met as have the desired reduction in average costs.[1]

The second example that can be carefully watched is that of Electricité de France (EdF). EdF has developed in a tightly French style, both in terms of the structure of the grid system (radial with Paris at the heart) and in terms of the economic attitude of *knowing* how to run the system correctly. EdF, and more specifically France, has objected to the British system and publicly denounced it as infeasible in the long run, a foolish experiment, and so on. EdF has been firm in not wanting independent power production, and certainly not wanting other national competitors entering to supply EdF native customers. On the other hand, EdF, because of its high concentration of low-marginal-cost nuclear energy, has been very interested and willing to sell off-system to other national utilities. It will be interesting for us in the

United States to see how long the economic incentive can maintain this one-way flow of power and reverse flow of currency. The low marginal cost areas of the Midwest have, in the past, exported power for economic gain. This question of market power and how it affects sectoral decisions in a more integrated political system will be worth watching carefully.

CULTURE

Culture takes on a number of aspects in the EC case that bear watching on the U.S. side. The most interesting one is, "Whose culture?" Although, at the national level in Europe it is easy to argue that the French are tolerant of the British—but only just—it is also clear that the French and British are, at best, cautious of their relations with the now much larger integrated Germany. The cultures are different, the national identities (and even the currencies) have Balkanized, and "I am . . .," "Je suis . . .," and "Ich bin . . .," have probably not been stronger since the 1940s. This has overflowed into the technical structure of the power industry. Electricity (and energy) has become a battleground for national identity and sovereignty. At the political and the management level, this posturing is important in the EC—as it appears to be in the United States. The battles in the EC over subsidization of employment in coal mining in the UK (broken by privatization) and in Germany have striking similarities to actions taken in Ohio and other midwestern states after the Clean Air Amendments were passed. National culture is playing out a role in the EC, a role that is worth watching and learning from as the United States tries to unscramble the national/federal versus state/regional objective function.

Within the electric power industry—and possibly more strongly than in any other industry—there is a similarity of culture and objective that has exceeded that between industrial operators and their national governments. Operators will cooperate to *keep the system* up at nearly any cost. Helping an adjoining system's operator maintain reliability and or integrity of supply guarantees the same code of conduct in reverse the next time "my system" needs help. This culture of cooperative operations neither mirrors well the competitive position proposed for utility operations nor does it mirror well the posturing of management and politicians who would have us believe that the national (or utility) supply systems are somehow different. The EC and the United States will step—hopefully gently—through the process of redefining the operational rules by which utilities interact on the cycle-by-cycle time scale of the power system operation.

TECHNOLOGY

Both Europe and the United States have a common force at play that will provide a tremendous impetus for change in the next decade. Technological change is occurring on the transmission/control side of the system at points where we have seen little but incremental change for decades. In transmission operations, we are seeing the introduction of Flexible AC Transmission Systems (FACTS)—generally solid state—being developed and introduced into the system. Although not violating Kirchhoff's laws, these devices certainly move in the direction of bending them. Their impact on the system is little understood but will continue to provide additional capabilities for directing the flow of power to correspond to transactional paths as opposed to resistive paths.

At the same time, we are seeing the development of smarter traditional transmission system devices, and with them, better control systems that manage the transmission closer to the margin. These devices and systems will revolutionize the manner in which utilities operate their grids and will make competition for both generation *and transmission services* a reality. The issue on both sides of the Atlantic is how well, how quickly, and where these will be introduced and tested first. Wherever that occurs will come a basic change in the management and operation of the system.

The final point to consider in technology is one of competitive ownership. The industry has been actively involved in technological research, much of which has been cooperative in the U.S. *but not*, generally, in Europe. As the U.S. moves toward competitive positioning, we have seen research become far more "nationalistic" or at least "ethnocentric" in its focus. U.S. industry may have much to learn about the effect of Balkanized research activities. As utilities like Pacific Gas and Electric, American Electric Power, Southern Company, and even the Tennessee Valley Authority enter into proprietary research developments, the value of these developments in an extremely rapidly developing technological environment needs to be measured. Watching or measuring the development of, for instance, the old Central Electricity Generating Board research experiences, EdF, and the like can provide additional insights into the long-term economic and development benefits of non-cooperative research efforts.

ECONOMICS

As a final point, it is important to note the role that raw economics, or more accurately, the gradient in relative costs or prices between adjoining utilities may have in determining the long-run structure of the utility system. This discussant would argue that the steeper the gradient, the less likely are nationalistic objectives to hold sway within Europe or the United States. Whether because the operators force the exchange in the short run, or industries "vote with their feet" in the openly competitive markets, the results are the same: increasingly smaller differentiation in cost!

CONCLUSIONS

What seems clear from McGowan's chapter and from this one is that there is much to be learned by treating both the United States and the EC as case studies of mutual interest for the other party in terms, specifically, of the impacts of "subsidiarity" or federalism on the operation, planning, and overall economic viability of individual members of the industry.

NOTE

1. See Nigel Burton, "UK System Post-Deregulation," *IEEE Power Engineering Review* (June 1993): 19–22.

27

Regional Diversity: Circumstance or Choice?

Clinton J. Andrews

Regional power system regulation offers both challenge and controversy. Topical chapters of this volume have outlined general arguments for regulatory reform, and the case studies have sketched the evolution of specific regional systems. To focus the evolving policy debate, this closing chapter examines the gaps and overlaps in our prescriptions and shares my personal conclusions regarding regulatory reform. It provides empirical evidence regarding a particularly contentious aspect of the debate: Is regional diversity a function of circumstance or choice?

OVERLAPS: SOME WIDELY ACCEPTED PREMISES

I perceive several areas of agreement emerging from the preceding chapters. They represent possible common ground among the diverse regional, ideological, and professional perspectives held by the authors. They are now outlined as premises.

Premise 1: The Economic Benefits of Large-Scale Interconnected Electric Power Systems Are Significant

Samuel Insull's business strategy of growing, building, and interconnecting was a clear winner (Hirsh, 1989, p. 19). Whether achieved through regional markets, power pools, or interstate holding companies, there have been economic and reliability advantages to

Figure 27.1
Diminishing Electricity Price Gradient within the United States
(based on revenues/sales by state [EEI, various years], in 1990 dollars calculated using
implicit GNP price deflators [USDOE, 1991, p. 307])

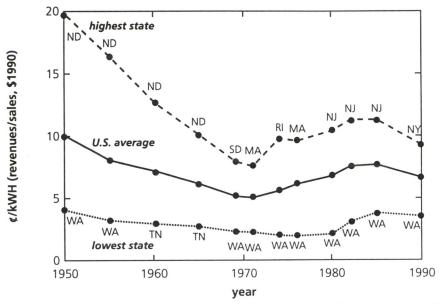

increasing system size. There is still scope for diversity-related
economies between areas with different seasonal or other temporal
variance in peak loads and generating capability. Yet as long ago as
1981, studies were concluding that most parts of the country had
already achieved many of these benefits, using a range of coordination
mechanisms (e.g., FERC, 1981, pp. 165–169). Additional efficiency
gains, therefore, must come from reducing transactions costs, x-
inefficiency, and redundant capacity.

Figure 27.1 shows the diminishing electricity price gradient over
time within the continental United States, crudely measured using
the range among states of electric utility revenues normalized by sales
(the state average electric rate).[1] It can be seen that a substantial nar-
rowing of the range occurred through 1970, in part because of interconnections and in part because of technical improvements. Yet since
1970, the range has remained relatively fixed, with about a 6¢/kWh
difference between the cheapest and most expensive states. During
this period, the industry has become increasingly interconnected, as
shown in Figure 27.2, which reports the growth in circuit miles of
transmission line over time. Differences in available generating
resources thus may explain most of the current price gradient.

Figure 27.2
Increasing Connectedness of the Electric Power Industry
(circuit miles of overhead electric lines ≥ 22,000 volts for the total continental U.S. electric utility industry [EEI, various years])

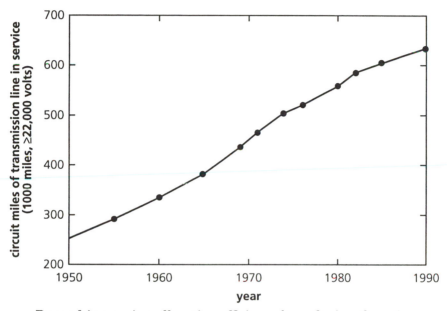

Beyond increasing allocative efficiency by reducing the price gradient between neighboring utilities, there may be scope for exploiting inter-regional complementarities. For example, one can readily identify benefits to consumers in the resource-poor northeastern states with easier access to cheap midwestern coal-based electricity, or in operating underutilized capacity in one region to serve consumers elsewhere. But this means creating inter-regional as well as regional markets. Finally, future dispersed generation technologies will benefit systems independently of size.

Premise 2: Competition at the Generation Level Offers Potentially Significant Economic Benefits

Both short- and long-term factors support arguments in favor of a competitive generating sector. Allocative efficiency will improve if price signals are available to equilibrate supply and demand levels. In the longer term, competition will ensure a market test for new technology choices and replace litigated, forecast-based decisions with the broader-based information revealed by the marketplace. A well-developed marketplace could also provide risk management options beyond what traditional monopoly regulation typically offers, for example, allowing flexible pricing to recover fixed costs at variable rates, or permitting the creation of secondary markets to absorb excess capacity or hedge against future shortfalls.

A few caveats are in order. First, if the U.S. experience parallels that of Great Britain, then nuclear generation may not successfully spin off from the regulated enterprises because the technology will fail to attract investors. Since existing players generally have an advantage in competitive markets, transition rules and entry/exit rules will have to be carefully thought out to prevent dysfunction. An already contentious question is whether wholesale competition will fully exploit the efficiency gains of market-based decision making. Authors such as Stalon argue that the next step, retail competition, is inevitable, whereas others such as Wooley and Cavallo see no benefit and much harm from extension of the market to the retail level.

Premise 3: Regulatory Responsibilities Will Be Reallocated on a Function-by-Function Basis; Solutions Will Not Be Monolithic

Regulatory objectives and regional characteristics are too diverse for simplistic solutions such as complete federal preemption. Instead, specific economic and social regulatory responsibilities will be allocated between state and federal actors. Arguably, the federal government can most effectively set the rules which govern regional power markets, including setting transmission tariffs and ensuring that distortions are minimized in the markets that establish wholesale electricity prices. The federal government also may be best equipped to set ground rules for the environmental regulation of utilities in regional power markets, but much policy implementation should be assigned to the states. The experience of existing regional clubs suggests that a federal forum for resolving intra-regional disputes is indispensable.

Retail ratesetting for distribution companies will be performed by states, because federal regulators are poorly equipped to evaluate local social and economic tradeoffs beyond minimizing monopoly rents. Generation siting decisions may be best taken at the state level to ensure fairness, although information about proposed new facilities also should be reported at the system-wide level. States could continue to govern transmission siting decisions in coordination with regional neighbors and the Federal Energy Regulatory Commission (FERC), but if states behave parochially, then they should expect federal preemption.

Integrated resource planning (IRP, i.e., balancing demand-side investments and the acquisition of new electricity supplies) must change in many ways as vertical de-integration of the industry takes place. Demand-side information would best be exploited at the distribution company level because it is closest to the end-users whose equipment and behavior would be modified. Yet, to provide a clear picture of the integrated resource balance, a system-wide or regional perspective would be valuable. Thus, planning as "communication" to improve market operations is appropriate for regions, while IRP to create service bundles should be more localized.

Premise 4:   The Need for Cooperation Will Continue

Under competition, the relationships among actors in regional power systems are likely to become more formal, and contracts or mergers may replace some types of voluntary cooperation. Yet because they share the network, players still must cooperate in the areas of operations and planning. State regulators must strive to improve the coordination of activities at the regional level, not necessarily by forming regional regulatory bodies, but by sharing information, resolving conflicts, and developing common visions of regional needs.

This suggests a new role for planning that emphasizes joint fact finding and consensus building. Master planning, or technical optimization, will contribute only minimally in a competitive regional marketplace; strategic planning, or the development of steering capacity, only makes sense for individual actors in this multi-party context. Communicative planning, or the development of mutual understanding among actors, will be a crucial element of successful cooperation in the electricity marketplace. The effectiveness of this type of planning depends on developing standardized information, more accessible integrated modeling tools, and better connections among efforts at the local, regional, and national levels.

Cooperative research on generating technology is likely to suffer under competition. Perhaps this will be mitigated by equipment suppliers undertaking competitive research, as that which occurred during the early years of the industry. There is a danger that needed transmission, distribution, and demand-side research activity will fall by the wayside as a by-product of diminished cooperation on generation-related research. Explicit efforts are needed to ensure that this does not happen.

GAPS: TWO SPECULATIVE HYPOTHESES

The show-stopping dichotomies mentioned in the introduction permeate the policy debate as it unfolds in this book. The issues include:

- public versus private ownership of utilities,
- planning versus market-based decision making,
- state versus federal jurisdiction,
- economic versus social regulatory emphasis, and
- commodity energy versus end-use service provision.

Dramatic differences in the contributors' core beliefs about the nature of government and industry have been revealed, and each region has a different story to tell.

These differences in opinion lead me to suggest two hypotheses about the regulation of regional systems. I offer them here in a provocative spirit and to help frame the policy debate; there was no consensus regarding them among the participants in this project.

Hypothesis 1:   Regulatory Reform Must Credibly Resolve Conflicting Economic and Social Objectives

Social objectives include environmental protection and access to basic service. Since spillovers from the sector are significant, society wants at least a national regulatory "floor" to guarantee minimally acceptable environmental choices everywhere. Above that floor, state-level or cooperative regional planning could be effective for resolving other issues, such as meeting ambient air quality standards or siting generation and transmission facilities. Nationally mandated incentives, such as tradable emissions permits, could help to internalize many social costs if the market size is appropriate (e.g., regional for NO_x emissions).

Equity issues also do not get resolved by markets; solutions must be imposed on markets by society. Electricity is considered a necessity, so lifeline rates or other means of providing basic service will be maintained. Marginal cost pricing, and eventually market-based pricing, also can serve equity by reducing inadvertent cross subsidization among customer classes. Likewise, freer entry and increased choice can improve fairness. Regulated utilities have been used as instruments of social policy since the dawn of the industry. Balancing economic and social tradeoffs has been a traditional domain of the states, which have the best information about local needs.

The state role in making policy tradeoffs will diminish, but not disappear. What remains contentious is the appropriate height of the regulatory "floor" and whether an inexorable market discipline will sweep aside local social and environmental concerns.

Hypothesis 2:   Regional Diversity Will Persist

We see much sub-national regulatory experimentation and many situation-specific regulatory regimes. Different regions have very different resource bases, demand characteristics, and environmental problems. Siting and integrated resource planning responsibilities have been reserved largely for the states. Varied patterns of ownership are evident, and the problems of market distortion by publicly financed enterprises are being managed, to a large extent, with legislation or regulation. What remains contentious is whether this diversity has intrinsic value, and whether it should continue.

REGIONAL DIVERSITY: CIRCUMSTANCE OR CHOICE?

The speculative hypotheses just outlined beg to be tested. The historical determinants of regional diversity provide one test. If regions have become different by choice, then arguments favoring local resolution of policy tradeoffs gain credibility, and preserving this diversity may have value in the future. Yet if circumstance has dictated most regional differences, then arguments favoring a larger federal role become salient. This section offers some preliminary evidence.

A Small-Sample Analysis (N = 50 States + DC)

State-level data indicate the great diversity of the U.S. electric power sector. Figure 27.3 shows large differences in cost and environmental performance among states, measured by average rates (revenues normalized by sales) versus unit sulfur dioxide emissions (normalized by generation). For example, northwestern states enjoying federally constructed hydro-electric generation show a strong cluster in the low-cost, low-emissions corner, while coal-producing midwestern states cluster on the far right, and resource-poor northeastern states cluster near the top of the figure.

Diversity exists, but is it more a function of different resource endowments or different preferences? To explore these alternatives, I constructed a set of multi-variate linear regression models using state-

Figure 27.3
Electric Power Sector Sulfur Dioxide and Cost Performance by State in 1990
(based on Andrews [1994], using data in USDOE Electric Power Annual 1990 [1992])

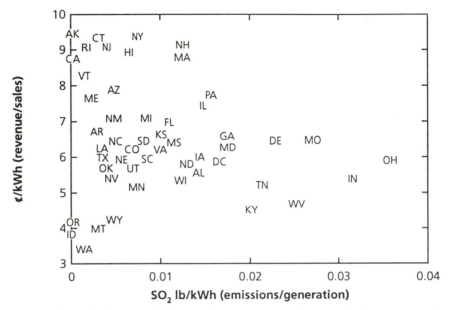

aggregate data to provide a small but systematic sample. I tested models predicting fundamental, average performance indicators: electricity costs (¢/kWh) and emissions rates (SO_2 lb/kWh). In addition, I tested models predicting the level of demand-side management effort (percent DSM), a more responsive indicator of preferences at the investment margin. See Andrews (1994) for the details of this analysis.[2] The results are summarized as follows:

- In predicting electricity cost, variables with significant explanatory power included the available resources (percentage hydro, fossil fuel costs), the physical structure of demand (percentage residential), and the level of environmentalism (with more environmentalists correlating with higher costs, independent of income effects). None of the other "preference" variables examined (regulatory choices and those proxied by per capita income) showed significance.

- In predicting emissions rates, different resource endowments played the primary role. The only significant variables were percentage hydro; and indigenous oil, gas, and high-sulfur coal production. None of the preference variables, including environmentalism, showed significance.

- In predicting DSM effort, a marginal indicator, preferences and circumstances seemed to share the limelight. The only significant variables were environmentalism and fossil fuel costs.

Different circumstances seemed to explain much of the variation in electricity costs (¢/kWh) and emissions rates (SO_2 lb/kWh) among states. Ironically, environmentalism correlated with increasing electricity costs but not decreasing emissions levels. Institutional structures also seemed to matter less than resource endowments.[3]

Perhaps historical decisions did not reflect societal preferences. These results could be an indictment of a flawed regulatory process, suggesting a need to open up decision making in the utility sector to better incorporate societal preferences. The raw data do show an order-of-magnitude variation in environmentalists/1,000 population across states, and an inverse correlation between environmentalism and the importance of mining to the state economy, beyond what can be attributed to income differences. As analysts such as Elazar (1984) suggest, different preferences exist. Perhaps environmental preferences are being inefficiently fought instead of efficiently incorporated into regulatory and business decisions.

Decision makers responding to environmental concern may have backed the wrong technological horse. System-level engineering analyses of emissions reduction opportunities show that, while reducing electric bills, 1990-era (low capacity factor) DSM programs were unlikely to affect SO_2 and NO_x emissions because they did not displace the dirtiest of the existing power plants (e.g., Andrews, 1992).

An equally disturbing interpretation of the results would be that some of the so-called "circumstance" variables (indigenous oil, gas, and high-sulfur coal production) really serve as "choice" variables. State governments could be forcing utilities to use indigenous resources, regardless of whether they are least-cost, in order to protect local jobs. Strong evidence of this phenomenon is seen in state responses to the Clean Air Act Amendments of 1990.[4]

A related argument is that environmental preferences may vary among states, but not significantly so. The raw data provide this clue: Dues-paying environmentalists are a tiny minority in any state (varying from less than 4 environmentalists/1000 population in Mississippi to a high of 40/1000 in the District of Columbia, with a national average of 17/1000 in this data set).[5] Environmentalists may not have enough of a presence to change resource choices, in part because resource extraction interests simply may carry more weight in the policy making arena. Yet the mobility argument of fiscal federalism should serve as a constraint on both parties: States cannot express social preferences that strongly diverge from national norms or economic logic because price-conscious consumers will flee.

Our marginal (rather than average) indicator reinforces the impression that there have been different regional choices. Environmental preference plays a major role in explaining the level of DSM effort in each state (see Figure 27.4). In the next section of this chapter, data drawn from the regional case studies will confirm that choices have been diverse.

In sum, there is historical evidence that state actors have expressed divergent preferences regarding economy-environment tradeoffs in the past. Arguably, their option to do so should not be foreclosed. But more effective methods for resolving these tradeoffs may need to be invented.

Comparing Regions: The Dimensions of Diversity

Here I provide a brief comparative analysis of the regions discussed in the case studies; see those chapters for a wealth of additional detail. These systems differ in their mix of generating resources, demand structures, load growth, capacity utilization, public/private ownership split, cost and environmental performance, and decision processes. They provide further evidence on the relative importance of circumstance versus choice in creating diversity. They also become points of reference for imagining the endpoints of regulatory reform.

Figures 27.5 through 27.12 contain comparative data which was largely provided by the case study authors. Figure 27.5 shows the mix of generating resources in each of the six U.S. regional cases, and it suggests that resource endowments have not been the sole determinant of technology choice. For example, although both the American Electric Power Company (AEP) and the Tennessee Valley Authority (TVA) are adjacent to coal fields, TVA has chosen to rely more heavily on nuclear resources than has AEP.

Figure 27.6 shows the powerful effects that policy decisions have had on industry structure: The AEP and New England systems are dominated by private enterprise, whereas the TVA and Northwest systems are dominated by federal agencies. Twenty years ago, the Pacific Gas and Electric Company (PG&E) system looked like that of AEP, but state policies aggressively promoting non-utility generation have significantly diminished PG&E's role.[6]

Figure 27.7 illustrates the great regional differentials in load

Figure 27.4
Environmentalism, Fossil Fuel Costs, and Demand-Side Management by State
(based on Andrews [1994], using DSM data from Hirst [1992], fuel cost data from USDOE [EIA-0191(90), 1992], and environmentalism data from a survey by the author.)

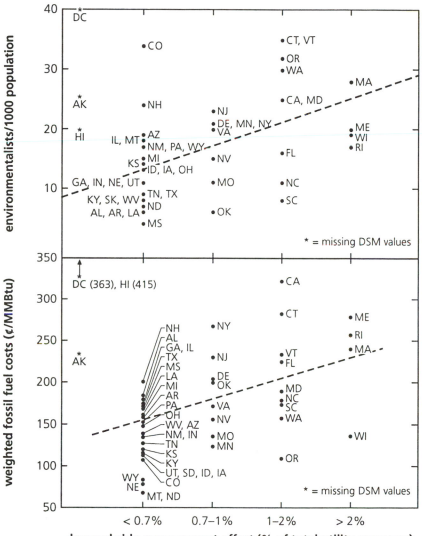

Figure 27.5
Regional Supply Mixes, 1990
(based on survey of regions and USDOE [EIA-0348(90)], 1992)

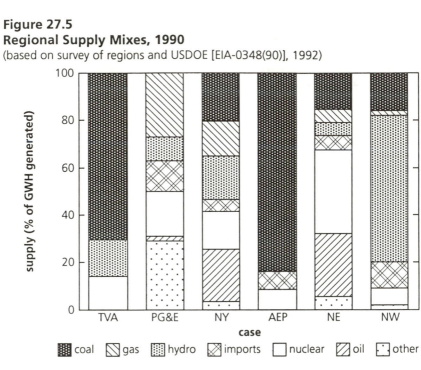

Figure 27.6
Mix of Regional Ownership, 1990
(based on survey of regions and EEI [1991])

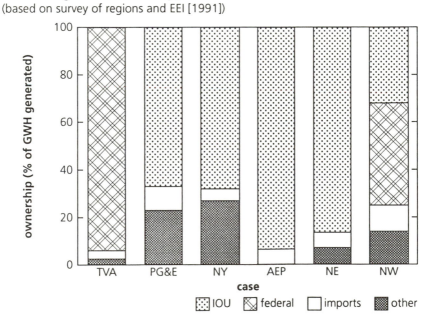

Figure 27.7
Regional Load Growth Rates
(based on survey of regions and NPPC [1991])

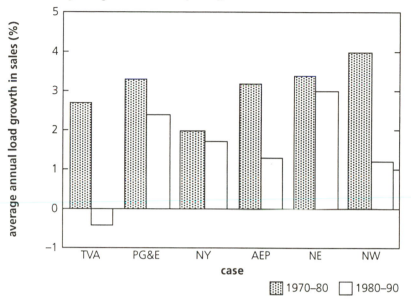

Figure 27.8
Jurisdictional Oversight within Regions, 1990
(based on survey of regions and USDOE [EIA-0437(90), 1992])

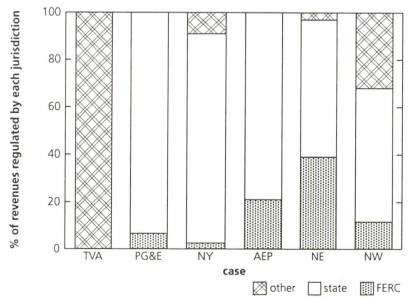

growth over the past twenty years. All regions experienced higher load growth during the 1970 to 1980 period than in subsequent years. The 1980 to 1990 period shows especially great diversity, from negative load growth in the TVA territory[7] to 3 percent average annual growth in New England.

Figure 27.8 confirms that the FERC is already making jurisdictional inroads, following an expected pattern. Systems crossing state boundaries tend to see more FERC involvement than those lying wholly within one state. Yet a strong element of choice exists, in the form of forum-shopping. Among the registered multi-state holding companies in New England, for example, Eastern Utilities Associates and the New England Electric System have both chosen to organize generating subsidiaries that place over 70 percent of electric revenues under FERC jurisdiction, while Northeast Utilities has maintained vertical integration and has about 15 percent of revenues under FERC jurisdiction.[4]

There are clearly divergent strategic views of the industry—some enterprises emphasize commodity kilowatthours and others emphasize end-use service as their primary product. Although megawatts and negawatts are technically complements, the relative emphasis given to each is a strategic, usually policy-motivated choice. Figure 27.9 shows that the AEP system, for example, is making only a minimal commitment to DSM in comparison with utilities elsewhere. Figure 27.10 confirms this strategic difference: AEP has by far the most efficient supply-side operation, in terms of systemwide fossil heat rate. AEP is good at providing commodity kilowatthours and is not interested in adding demand-side services to the bundle. PG&E, by contrast, has instead followed a non-generation, DSM-oriented strategy.

Existing regional decision processes are quite diverse. As Figure 27.11 shows, TVA has contained planning, coordination, approvals, and implementation within a single governmental entity. As the comment to the case study suggests, this closed system offers few opportunities for stakeholder intervention. PG&E, although monolithic in terms of its planning, coordination, and implementation functions, has powerful regulators who ensure responsiveness. The multi-state holding company AEP instead faces a more fractionated group of regulators (e.g., only four out the seven states require integrated resource planning) and may feel less need to be responsive to outside concerns.

In New York, the state is powerful relative to the utilities it regulates, allowing it to conduct policy experiments (for example, New York was one of the first states to employ environmental externality adders during resource planning). The Northwest Power Planning Council, because of the regional dominance of the Bonneville Power Authority with which it is associated, has, at least until recently, been able to

Figure 27.9
Regional Demand-Side Management Efforts, 1990-95
(based on survey of regions, NEPOOL [1991], NPPC [1991], and TVA [1993])

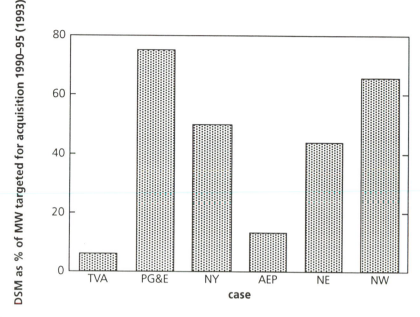

Figure 27.10
System-Average Regional Fossil Heat Rates, 1990
(based on survey of regions and USDOE [EIA-0348(90) and -0191(90), 1992])

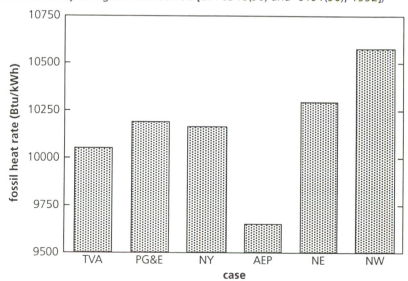

Figure 27.11
Existing Regional Decision Processes

1. Tennessee Valley Authority

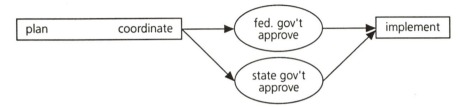

2. Pacific Gas & Electric Company

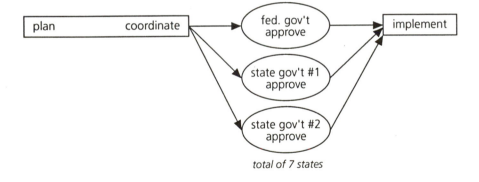

3. American Electric Power Company

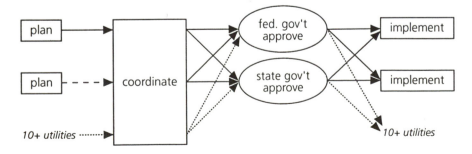

4. New York Power Pool

Figure 27.11 (cont.)

5. New England Power Pool

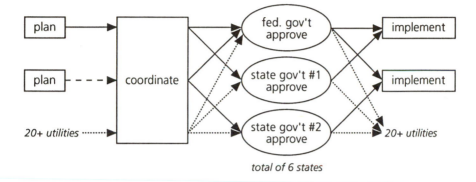

total of 6 states

6. Northwest Power Planning Council

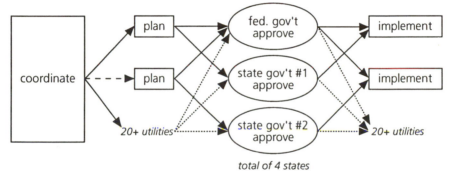

total of 4 states

play a pivotal coordinating role and ensure that all points of view are heard during the decision making process. New England's small utilities and six state jurisdictions ensure many opportunities for stakeholder intervention. On the one hand, this encourages policy experiments, but on the other, it forces realistic compromise among the many relatively weak actors.

Given such a diversity of decision processes, one would expect dramatic differences in the ultimate performance of these regional systems. Figure 27.12 bears this out, but as we saw in the fifty-state sample, circumstance and choice both probably play important explanatory roles. Although there is some scope for focusing on the decision process (the relatively closed TVA and AEP enterprises certainly have higher sulfur dioxide emissions rates and lower DSM efforts), the locations of the dots in the scatter plot echo those in Figure 27.3, and so, presumably, do the determinants of their locations.

Figure 27.12
Regional Cost and Emissions Tradeoffs in 1990
(based on survey of regions and USDOE [EIA-0348(90), 1992])

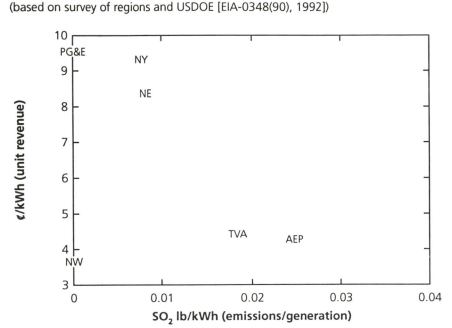

Yet there are worthwhile lessons on the efficacy of regional "clubs" which may be extracted from this comparison of decision processes. Most obviously, it appears that responsiveness to social preferences is in part a function of the relative concentrations of regulatory and industry decision making authority. Monolithic regulators (or fractionated regulators overseeing fractionated producers) seem to conduct more policy experiments designed explicitly to address tradeoffs between economic and social objectives. By default, the raised federal regulatory "floor" is likely to dominate decision making elsewhere, in the large subset of regions with powerful industry actors and fractionated state regulators. The experience to date also reinforces the importance of a federal role in resolving regional disputes and highlights the crucial importance of improved coordination among state regulators.

My evidence suggests that clubs created to foster system reliability have been relatively successful; reliability council members work together to optimize a single, non-controversial objective. Clubs intended to improve system economics seem to have had a harder time; power pool members work together to optimize two well-defined objectives of efficiency with equitably distributed benefits, but sometimes take each other to court. I suspect that clubs developed to satisfy social preferences will encounter even greater difficulties; for example, a regional IRP involves individuals with diverse perceptions and preferences who attempt to optimize across multiple, ill-defined objectives such as job security and environmental quality. Indeed, simple club theory predicts that no such clubs would form, because the basis of a club is collective consumption of specific, homogeneously valued (quasi-public) goods (Buchanan, 1965). Negotiation theorists would view this regional activity quite differently, however, describing the diversity of perceptions and preferences as an opportunity to engage in positive sum trades (Raiffa, 1982). An implication of this integrative bargaining perspective is that regional forums should be equipped to facilitate, mediate, arbitrate, provide joint fact-finding, or otherwise serve as a court of first resort in resolving intra-regional disputes. The FERC can hear on appeal any disputes not resolved "out of court." In short, dispute resolution should be a central function of future regional clubs.

The conclusions sketched earlier can now be refined. The case studies confirm a diversity in regional preferences, reflected in items such as DSM effort and levels of non-utility generation. They also show a substantial amount of sub-national policy experimentation (sometimes by the federal government), in terms of institutional arrangements and specific regulatory policies. Yet they ultimately confirm the relevance of at least a local economic logic in governing decisions; regions seek to preserve their comparative advantage. This weakens my speculative hypotheses, which are revised as follows:

- Regulatory reform must preserve a means of aligning economic objectives and social priorities.

- Regional diversity will persist because both circumstances and preferences differ, and sub-national experimentation is useful during restructuring.

CONCLUSIONS

Structural change in the electric power sector requires reforms in the regulatory apparatus. The regional nature of these systems makes the job of regulatory reform particularly complex, because it raises federalism issues. Some increased federal preemption of responsibilities can be expected, but any reallocation must occur at the level of specific regulatory tasks. Competitive pressures will make traditional cooperation among actors problematic and will exacerbate conflicts between social objectives and economic imperatives. It is important to develop effective means of continued cooperation and an improved analytical basis for making policies that carefully weigh tradeoffs.

Existing regional systems provide very different starting points—and models—for the evolution of the electric power sector. It is likely that much of this heterogeneity will be preserved as the industry restructures. Given controversy surrounding issues such as retail wheeling, the efficacy of demand-side management, and the role of public power, continued decentralized policy experimentation holds great value.

NOTES

1.   The range of prices on a utility-by-utility basis is greater than what these aggregated state-level data suggest. There are significant intra-regional as well as inter-regional disparities in price.

2.   Dependent variables were ¢/kWh (annual revenues/sales), SO_2/kWh (annual sulfur dioxide emissions/generation), and percent DSM (percentage of annual total utility revenues devoted to demand-side management programs). Explanatory variables were percent Hydro (percentage of total generation), percent Nuclear, Fossil Fuel Cost (weighted average delivered cost of fossil fuel receipts at electric utilities), High Sulfur Coal Production (annual quantity of coal with greater than 1 percent sulfur content by weight that is mined for utility consumption, normalized by state population, tons/capita), Oil and Gas Production (annual quantity of oil and natural gas extracted, normalized by state population, million Btu/capita), percent Residential (percentage of annual sales), Population Density (people/square mile), percent Investor-owned (percentage of annual generation), Income/capita (gross state product/state population), IRP (rating of state's progress in developing an integrated resource planning process, 0 = none through 4 = good, based on Mitchell (1992)), Externalities (dummy variable for state environmental externality policy, 0 = No regulations, 1 = Yes, based on Mitchell (1992) and NARUC (1992)), Lifeline Rates (dummy variable for state rate design policy, 0 = No, 1 = Yes, based on NARUC (1992)), Aggressive Regulation (rating of aggressiveness in implementing regulatory reforms including pre-hearing public participation requirement in certification proceedings, a power plant siting law, required use of bidding to procure new resources, and rates designed on a marginal cost basis, scored from 0 = none through 4 = all reforms implemented), Environmentalism (number of members of national environmental organizations/state population, based on a survey by the author that included responses from Adirondack Council, American Forest/ Global ReLeaf, Earth Island Institute/Friends of the Earth, Greenpeace USA, Hawk Mountain Society, Izak Walton League, Livestock Breeds Conservancy, National Audubon Society, Natural Resources Defense Council, Rainforest Action Network, Save the Redwoods League, Sierra Club, Trout Unlimited, Waterfowl USA, Wilderness Society, and World Wildlife Fund). Data sources not specifically cited were standard USDOE publications. Natural log

transformations were performed on many of the variables prior to the regression analysis. The models had substantial predictive power, explaining at least one half and sometimes as much as two thirds of the variation in electricity costs and sulfur dioxide emissions across states (based on adjusted R^2 statistics), and they confidently rejected the null hypothesis of no relationship among variables (based on F-ratios significant at the 1 percent level or better). They were also relatively robust, maintaining their performance across alternative specifications and transformations of underlying variables. Models predicting percent DSM had less explanatory power (adjusted R^2 statistics in the 40 percent range) but otherwise performed well. See Andrews (1994) for detailed results.

3. The public/private ownership split seems to affect performance (along ¢/kWh and SO_2 lb/kWh attributes) primarily as a proxy for hydropower availability. Independent of hydro it seems to have little explanatory power. Other analysts support this finding, e.g., Denning and Mead (1990).

4. Legislatures and regulators in states producing high-sulfur coal have offered pre-approval provisions for scrubbers, tax credits for in-state coal, or automatic pass-through of costs, or have mandated specific Clean Air Act compliance actions (Rose et al., 1993, p. 42–43).

5. While the survey this result is based on does not pretend to capture all active environmentalists, it is adequate for order-of-magnitude comparisons.

6. The Public Utilities Regulatory Practices Act (PURPA) of 1978 was federal legislation that depended to a great extent on state implementation. Hence, efforts across states were uneven.

7. This was primarily due to the loss of a few large U. S. Department of Energy defense-related enterprises; other components of load grew at normal rates.

8. Based on USDOE *Financial Statistics 1990*. (1992, Table 39), and confirmed through the companies' annual reports and personal communication with a representative of each company. The market's vote of confidence in each utility's choice of structure, based on its 1990-era Standard & Poor's bond rating, was A+ for the New England Electric System and BBB+ for Northeast Utilities and Eastern Utilities Associates.

REFERENCES

Andrews, C.J. "Electricity and Federalism: Understanding Regional Diversity." *Energy Policy* 22 (July 1994): 629–638.

Andrews, C.J. "The Marginality of Regulating Marginal Investments." *Energy Policy* 20 (May 1992): 450-463.

Buchanan, J. M. "An Economic Theory of Clubs." *Economica*. (February 1965): 1–14.

Denning, Michael A., and Walter J. Mead. "New Evidence on Benefits and Costs of Public Utility Rate Regulation." In James Plummer and Susan Troppman, eds. *Competition in Electricity: New Markets and New Structures.* Arlington, VA: Public Utilities Reports/QED Research, 1990.

Edison Electric Institute (EEI). *Statistical Yearbook of the Electric Utility Industry 1990.* Washington, DC: EEI, 1991, plus various years from 1950-1990.

Elazar, D. *American Federalism: A View from the States.* 3rd ed. New York: Harper and Row, 1984.

Federal Energy Regulatory Commission (FERC), Office of Electric Power Regulation. *Power Pooling in the United States.* FERC-0049. Washington, DC: FERC, December 1981.

Hirsh, Richard. *Technology and Transformation in the American Electric Utility Industry.* Cambridge: Cambridge University Press, 1989.

Hirst, E. *Electric-Utility DSM Programs: 1990 Data and Forecasts to 2000,* ORNL/CON-347, Oak Ridge, TN: Oak Ridge National Laboratories, 1992.

Mitchell, C. "Integrated Resource Planning Survey: Where the States Stand." *Electricity Journal* (May 1992): 10-15.

National Association of Regulatory Utility Commissioners (NARUC). *Utility Regulatory Policy in the United States and Canada: Compilation 1991-1992.* Washington, DC: NARUC, 1992, Table 181.

New England Power Pool (NEPOOL). *Capacity, Energy, Loads, and Transmission Report.* Holyoke, MA: NEPOOL, April 1991.

Northwest Power Planning Council (NPPC). *1991 Northwest Conservation and Electric Power Plan.* Portland, OR: NPPC, 1991.

Raiffa, H. *The Art and Science of Negotiation.* Cambridge, MA: Belknap Press, 1982, p. 131.

Rose, K., A. Taylor, and M. Harunuzzaman. *Regulatory Treatment of Electric Utility Clean Air Act Compliance Strategies, Costs, and Emission Allowances.* Columbus, OH: National Regulatory Research Institute, December 1993.

Tennessee Valley Authority (TVA). *Economic Impacts of Climate Change Policies on TVA.* Report prepared by ICF Resources Inc. Chattanooga, TN: TVA, June 1993.

U.S. Dept of Energy, Energy Information Administration (USDOE). *Annual Energy Review 1990.* DOE/EIA-0384(90). Washington, DC: USDOE, 1991.

U.S. Dept of Energy, Energy Information Administration (USDOE). *Cost and Quality of Fuels for Electric Utility Plants 1990.* DOE/EIA-0191(90). Washington, DC: USDOE, 1992.

U.S. Dept of Energy, Energy Information Administration (USDOE). *Electric Power Annual 1990.* DOE/EIA-0348(90). Washington, DC: USDOE, 1992.

U.S. Dept of Energy, Energy Information Administration (USDOE). *Financial Statistics of Selected [Investor- and Publicly-Owned] Electric Utilities 1990*. DOE/EIA-0437(90)/1&2. Washington, DC: USDOE, 1992.

Index

About the Editor and Contributors

Praveen K. Amar is a senior program manager at the Northeast States for Coordinated Air Use Management (NESCAUM), where he is involved in programs relating to the control of NO_x emissions from major utility and industrial sources, photochemical modeling requirements for non-attainment areas as part of the state implementation planning process, market-based emissions-reduction approaches, and energy-environment issues. Prior to this position, he served with the California Air Resources Board, where he managed programs on air pollution research, strategic planning, and industrial source pollution control. Dr. Amar is a member of the EPA's New Source Review panel (Reform Subcommittee) and has also been a member of the Peer Review Panel which evaluated research efforts under the National Acid Precipitation Assessment Program.

Clinton J. Andrews is assistant professor of public and international affairs in the Woodrow Wilson School, Princeton University, where he recently helped launch a program in science, technology, and public policy. His current research focuses on the "joint" aspects of regulatory problems: comparative policy choices, planning methods for regulated firms, and the nature of multi-party decision-making. He publishes in a variety of scholarly journals, and recently co-edited the book, *Industrial Ecology and Global Change* (with R. Socolow, F. Berkhout, and V. Thomas). A planner and a licensed mechanical engineer, his nonacademic experience includes project management in the private sector and technology assessments for government.

William J. Balet is the executive director of the New York Power Pool, an association of the seven investor-owned utilities in New York State and the New York Power Authority. After graduating from Cornell University with a degree in electrical engineering, Mr. Balet was employed by Consolidated Edison for twelve years. In 1971, he became assistant chief of the Bureau of Power, Federal Power Commission. Prior to assuming the executive directorship in 1979, Mr. Balet had also served the New York Power Pool as planning manager.

Donna M. Boysen is a policy analyst at Northeast States for Coordinated Air Use Management (NESCAUM), where she focuses on evaluating the economic impacts of the air quality options available to NESCAUM and its participating states. Her current work emphasizes the potential adoption of the California Low-Emission Vehicle Program in the Northeast as well as the implementation of emissions trading programs and the development of state- and region-wide market incentives for stationary and mobile-source emissions reductions.

Michael J. Bradley is executive director of the Northeast States for Coordinated Air Use Management (NESCAUM). NESCAUM is an association of the state air pollution control divisions in the six New England states (Connecticut, Maine, Massachusetts, New Hampshire, Rhode Island, and Vermont), New Jersey, and New York. NESCAUM's purpose is to promote cooperation and coordination among the member states on technical and policy issues relating to air pollution. He has also served 1989–1990 as a policy advisor to the British Department of Environment (on a sabbatical leave). Prior to this position, he served as an air quality program specialist and as an air permitting engineer at the Alaska Department of Environmental Conservation. He is a member of numerous regional, national, and international committees in the field.

Alfred J. Cavallo is currently a research physicist at the Department of Energy's Environmental Research Laboratory in New York City. His recent work at the Center for Energy and Environmental Studies at Princeton University includes the examination of the technical and economic issues involved in tying transmission lines to intermittent energy sources, in addition to experimental work on indoor air pollution. He previously worked at the Princeton Plasma Physics Laboratory, as well as at the Commissariat de l'Energie Atomique in France and at the Max Planck Institute for Plasma Physics in Germany.

Stephen R. Connors is director, Analysis Group for Regional Electricity Alternatives (AGREA), of the Energy Laboratory at the Massachusetts Institute of Technology, where he has worked with New England's electric utilities, regulatory agencies, and various business, consumer, and environmental concerns to identify long-range strategies that concurrently address the issues of cost, pollutant emissions, and reliability. Over his career—which includes service in the Peace Corps in West Africa, where he focused on the development of appropriate energy technologies—Mr. Connors has worked on a broad range of energy and environmental issues, including electricity planning and regulation, and the identification of cost-effective emissions reductions on both the international and domestic levels.

Kenneth W. Costello is associate director of electric and gas research at the National Regulatory Research Institute (NRRI). Prior to this position, he worked for the Illinois Commerce Commission, the Argonne National Laboratory, Commonwealth Edison Company, and as an independent consultant. He is a frequent speaker to industry and other groups on regulatory matters. He has also conducted research and written widely on topics relating to energy industries and public utility regulation.

Michael N. Danielson is director of the Center of Domestic and Comparative Policy Studies and B.C. Forbes professor of public affairs at the Woodrow Wilson School at Princeton University, where he teaches courses in urban politics and political analysis. He is the author of many books and articles on issues relating to urban development and American politics, including *One Nation, So Many Governments* (with Alan Hershey and John Bayne) and *American Democracy* (with Walter Murphy). He serves on the Technical Review Panel; New Jersey Office of State Planning; and has consulted for the Commission on Population and the American Future; the Ford Foundation; the Institute of Public Administration, the Charles F. Kettering Foundation, a wide range of New Jersey state agencies, departments, and commissions; the U.S. Department of Housing and Urban Development, and the U.S. Task Force on the Cities.

Michehl R. Gent is president, North American Electric Reliability Council, a position to which he was promoted from executive vice president in 1982. Prior to joining NERC, he served for seven years as the general manager of the Florida Electric Power Coordinating Group—a voluntary power pool for all of Florida's electric utilities. He has also served with the Los Angeles Department of Water and Power, working primarily in the areas of operations and planning. Mr. Gent has also taught in the graduate programs at the University of Southern California and Loyola University.

Kenneth Gordon is chairman of the Massachusetts Department of Public Utilities, a post he has held since the beginning of 1993. Prior to this position, he served as chairman of the Maine Public Utilities Commission, as an industry economist at the Federal Communications Commission's Office of Plans and Policies, and as a faculty member at several colleges, including Smith College. He is a member and past president of the National Association of Regulatory Utility Commissioners (NARUC). He is also a member of the Executive Committee and the Committee on Communications of NARUC. He has served as chair of the New England Conference of Public Utilities Commissioners Telecommunications Committee and is a former chair of the Power Planning Committee of the New England Governor's Conference. He currently serves as Chair of the Bellcore Advisory Committee, as well as several other boards and committees. He has authored a number of publications and lectures widely on topics related to utility regulation.

Charles R. Guinn is deputy commissioner for policy and planning of the New York State Energy Office, a post he has held since 1980. He supervises the Office's Division of Policy and Planning, which provides energy policy analysis to the legislature and governor, and chairs the energy planning coordinating committee which develops and updates the New York State Energy Plan. Prior to this position, he served in a variety of administrative capacities with the New York State Energy Office and with the New York State Economic Development Board, the New York State Office of Planning Services, the New York State Office of Planning Coordination, and the New York State Department of Public Works. He was the initial chair of the National Association of State Energy Officials, where he remains a board member.

Benjamin F. Hobbs is professor of systems engineering and civil engineering at Case Western Reserve University, where he teaches and conducts research in the application of systems analysis and economics to energy and environmental problems. Prior to this position, he served on the staff of the National Center for the Analysis of Energy Systems at Brookhaven National Laboratory and as a Wigner Fellow with the Energy Division of Oak Ridge National Laboratory.

He is an Institute Associate of the National Regulatory Research Institute and a former National Science Foundation Presidential Young Investigator. In addition to numerous prior scholarly publications, he is currently working on a textbook entitled *Analysis for Integrated Resource Planning*.

Mary J. Hutzler is the director of the Office of Integrated Analysis and Forecasting at the Energy Information Administration (EIA) in the Department of Energy, where she is responsible for EIA's mid-term and long-term forecasting and analysis projects and the National Energy Modeling System. Prior to this position, she was the director of the Electric Power Division of EIA; chief of the Data Analysis and Forecasting Branch, Coal Division, EIA; and director of the Long-Term Energy Analysis Division. Prior to joining DOE, Ms. Hutzler worked for the Logistics Management Institute and the Institute for Defense Analysis.

Kevin A. Kelly is vice president of the Keystone Center and director of the Keystone Energy Program. Prior to this position, he served as director of the Office of Electricity, Coal, Nuclear, and Renewable Policy in the U.S. Department of Energy, where he analyzed electricity issues in the National Energy Strategy. He has also served as associate director of the National Regulatory Research Institute, and as an adjunct member of the nuclear engineering faculty at Ohio State University. He has authored many publications, including *Using Game Theory to Analyze Electric Transmission Pricing Policy in the United States* (with B. Hobbs) and "Analytical Tools for Economic Regulation of Energy Utilities" *Interfaces* 16 (July/August 1986).

Steven Kline is manager, Strategic Planning, at Pacific Gas and Electric Company, responsible for corporate and strategic business planning, budgeting, and review and analysis of major capital investments. He is the former acting manager, Stockton Division, PG&E. Mr. Kline is a member of the National Association of Regulatory Utility Commissioners (NARUC) Technical Advisory Group, and a past participant in the California Collaborative, which produced *Energy Efficiency Blueprint for California* (1990).

Christopher Mackie-Lewis is a graduate student at Princeton University in the Woodrow Wilson School of Public and International Affairs, Center of Domestic and Comparative Policy Studies. Prior to his return to graduate study, he spent several years in management and policy-related positions in healthcare firms. His principal research interests concern questions of representation and accountability in American politics; his current research involves an exploration of how the news media in the United States mediate political learning and issue evaluation. He has published a series of articles on aspects of U.S. higher education policy, most recently, "Persistence to the Baccalaureate Degree for Students Who Transfer from Community College," with Valerie Lee and Helen Marks, in the November, 1993 issue of the *American Journal of Education.*

Raymond M. Maliszewski is senior vice president—system planning for the American Electric Power Service Corporation, where he has worked for thirty-eight years in the area of transmission system planning and interconnection, reliability, and coordination. In this capacity, he has worked with several of the reliability organizations, including ECAR and NERC. He serves on various Edison Electric Institute task forces and working groups dealing with industry regulatory issues. He is a member of the International Conference on Large High-Voltage Electric Systems (CIGRE) and serves as the U.S. Representative on CIGRE's Study Committee on Power System Planning and Development. He is also a fellow of the Institute of Electrical and Electronic Engineers.

Francis McGowan is lecturer in politics, School of European Studies, University of Sussex, England. He is the author of numerous books and articles on energy policy, including "The World Market for Heavy Electrical Equipment" (with S. Thomas) and "The Struggle for Power in Europe: Competition and Regulation in the EC Electricity Industry."

Richard P. O'Neill is chief economist and director of the Office of Economic Policy at the Federal Energy Regulatory Commission, where he is responsible for economic analysis and policy in the areas of natural gas, electric power, and oil pipeline regulation. Prior to this position, he served within FERC as director of the Office of Pipeline and Producer Regulation. He has also held faculty positions at the University of Maryland and Louisiana State University in the fields of operations research and statistics and has consulted for states and private firms in the areas of energy modeling and forecasting.

Jackalyne Pfannenstiel is vice president, Corporate Planning, Pacific Gas and Electric Company. Prior to her current position with

PG&E, she was manager, Revenue Requirements Department; director of Rate Analysis; and director of Rate Design for PG&E. She has also served as senior economist for the California State Public Utilities Commission, economist for the Connecticut Public Utilities Control Authority and as a statistician for the Connecticut Welfare Department. She is a member of the Board of Directors, Pacific Institute; Executive Advisory Committee, Strategic Planning, Edison Electric Institute; and the Senior Advisory Panel, Energy Modeling Forum.

Allan G. Pulsipher is the director of the Policy Analysis Program at the Center for Energy Studies and a professor in the Institute of Environmental Studies at Louisiana State University. From 1980 to 1988 he was the chief economist for the Tennessee Valley Authority. He also has been the chief economist for the Congressional Monitored Retrieval Storage Review Commission, a program officer with the Ford Foundation's Division of Resources and the Environment, a senior staff economist with the President's Council of Economic Advisors, and a member of the faculties of Texas A&M and Southern Illinois Universities.

Kenneth Rose is a senior institute economist in the Electric and Gas Division of the National Regulatory Research Institute. He works primarily in the area of electric utility regulation and was project leader and principal investigator of the Institute's Clean Air Act and environmental externalities research projects. Currently, he is working on a study of public utility commission implementation of the Energy Policy Act of 1992. Prior to his current position, Dr. Rose was employed by Argonne National Laboratory.

Richard E. Schuler is professor of economics and professor of civil and environmental engineering at Cornell University, where he is also senior fellow, Cornell Center for the Environment. His teaching and research have emphasized the location, management, pricing, and environmental and regional economic consequences of public infrastructure and utilities. In the past six years he organized and directed both the Cornell Waste Management Institute and the (affiliated) New York State Solid Waste Combustion Institute. He has also served as commissioner and deputy chairman of the New York State Public Service Commission, where he previously directed the Research Office. He has published extensively, including the book, *The Future of Electrical Energy: A Regional Perspective of an Industry in Transition* (with Sid Saltzman). His ongoing research includes analyses of alternative organizations of the electric utility industry in the United States under evolving technologies (originally funded by the National Science Foundation).

Mary Sharpe Hayes is president, Customer Group, Tennessee Valley Authority, where she is responsible for the transmission system that supplies power to 160 local distributors and approximately fifty large industrial customers. She also oversees TVA's rate design and energy service programs and facilitates long- and short-range power planning. She has also served as vice president, marketing and strategic planning for TVA. Prior to joining TVA, Ms. Sharpe Hayes was a senior consultant with the Energy Group of Temple, Barker, and Sloane in Atlanta and a consultant with Bower, Rohr, and Associates of Hanover, New Hampshire.

Barry D. Solomon is the senior economist in the Acid Rain Division of the U. S. Environmental Protection Agency. His previous positions include the staff of EPA's Climate Change Division, the Energy Information Administration's Office of Energy Markets, and the Federal Energy Regulatory Commission's Office of Electric Power Regulation. He was also a visiting assistant professor of energy economics and geography at West Virginia University from 1982 to 1984. Major co-authored publications include "International Reductions of Greenhouse Gas Emissions: An Equitable and Efficient Approach," *Global Environmental Change*, December 1991; "A Least-Cost Energy Analysis of U.S. CO_2 Reduction Options," in J.W. Tester et al., eds., *Energy and the Environment in the 21st Century*, 1991; *The International Politics of Nuclear Waste*, 1991; and "Nuclear Waste Repository Siting: An Alternative Approach," *Energy Policy*, December 1985. Dr. Solomon's major awards include the EPA's Bronze Medal for Commendable Service in 1993 for his work on the Conservation Verification Protocols, and the 1988 *Journal of Geography* award.

Charles G. Stalon is recently retired as director of the Institute of Public Utilities and professor of economics at Michigan State University (MSU). Prior to joining MSU, he served for five years as a commissioner of the Federal Energy Regulatory Commission (FERC); as a director of Putnam, Hayes, and Bartlett, Inc.; and as a commissioner on the Illinois Commerce Commission. He is currently a member of the Board of Directors of the National Regulatory Research Institute, the Advisory Council of the Gas Research Institute, and the Advisory Council of Bellcore. Previously, he was active in the National Association of Regulatory Utility Commissioners, serving on the Administration, Natural Gas, and Executive Committees.

Richard D. Tabors is senior research engineer and assistant director of the Laboratory for Electromagnetic and Electronic Systems and a member of the faculty of the Program in Technology Management and Policy at the Massachusetts Institute of Technology. He is also founding partner and chairman of Tabors, Caramanis & Associates of Cambridge, MA, which has recently developed the commercial pricing and reliability options being implemented in the National Grid Company, Ltd., in the United Kingdom. Prior to joining the MIT research staff, he was a member of the faculty at Harvard University. He has authored or coauthored more than fifty articles and five books on environmental and energy issues, including *Spot Pricing of Electricity* (with Fred C. Schweppe, Michael C. Caramanis, and Roger E. Bohn) and *Energy Aftermath* (with Ben C. Ball and Thomas H. Lee).

Kathleen Treleven is coordinator in the Corporate Planning Department of the Pacific Gas and Electric Company, where she also serves on the Strategic Planning Team reviewing the restructuring of the electric utility industry. Her prior experience includes an earlier position within PG&E as an engineer in the Generation Planning Department, with a focus on power plant planning issues. She has also worked extensively with the firm of Morse, Richard, and Weisenmiller, where she was a technical researcher and regulatory witness in areas of electric resource planning, environmental externalities, and gas deregulation.

Richard H. Watson is director, Power Planning Division, Northwest Power Planning Council (NPPC), where he is responsible for the technical analyses underpinning the council's regional plan and for facilitating implementation of the plan. Mr. Watson is the author of several articles on energy policy and a former chair of the Western Interstate Energy Board and the National Association of State Energy Officials. Before joining NPPC in 1992, he was director of the Washington State Energy Office. He has also been a senior research analyst with the Washington State Senate Committee on Energy and Utilities and a research assistant professor at the University of Washington, where he carried out research and teaching in the field of technology and public policy.

Charles S. Whitmore is the assistant director of the Office of Economic Policy at the Federal Energy Regulatory Commission. The office analyzes economic issues for regulated energy industries, including electric power, and recommends policy options to the commission. Dr. Whitmore is particularly charged to coordinate gas and electric analyses and to improve internal management. Prior to joining FERC, he worked as a consultant for the Energy Information Administration and held faculty positions at the State University of New York, Stony Brook, and at the University of Dar es Salaam, Tanzania. He is also the author of a novel, *Winter's Daughter* (1984).

Lyna L. Wiggins is professor and associate director of the Center for Urban Policy Research at Rutgers University. She specializes in computer applications in urban and regional planning, with a focus on geographic information systems (GISs) and spatial decision support systems. Professor Wiggins has co-edited three books and has authored many articles on subjects relating to planning, GIS, and spatial decision support systems. Prior to her tenure at Rutgers, she held faculty positions at Stanford University and the Massachusetts Institute of Technology. She is a member of the editorial boards of *InfoText*, *Geo Info Systems*, and *Computers, Environment, and Urban Systems*, as well as several specialist groups for the National Center for Geographic Information and Analysis; she is also an active member of the Urban and Regional Information Systems Association.

Jerry L. Wissman is the director of the Utilities Department, Public Utilities Commission of Ohio (PUCO). He has served with PUCO for over fifteen years, beginning as an economic analyst and advancing through the positions of chief economist, division chief, and assistant director. Prior to his affiliation with PUCO, he taught economics at The Ohio State University, Kenyon College, and Ohio Wesleyan University.

David R. Wooley is the executive director and professor of law at the Center for Environmental Legal Studies, Pace University Law School in White Plains, NY. In addition to his scholarly activities, he serves as lead counsel for a coalition of environmental and consumer groups in rulemaking and ratemaking proceedings before the New York Public Service Commission regarding energy conservation programs, integrated resource planning, incentive regulation, and renewable energy development, as well as vice-chairman of the American Bar Association Subcommittee on Air Quality. Prior to his current position, he served as assistant attorney general for the State of New York, specializing in litigation and lobbying on air pollution issues. He has led coalitions in litigation campaigns against the U.S. Environmental Protection Agency on issues of acid rain and incinerator regulation. He has been recognized by the Canadian Coalition on Acid Rain as one of twenty-nine leading contributors to the passage of the 1990 Clean Air Act. He is a member of the Bar of New York, three other states, and the United States Supreme Court.

ISBN 0-89930-943-7